Praise for Marc Morano

"*Green Fraud: Why the Green New Deal Is Even Worse Than You Think* is the ultimate guidebook to exposing and fighting this Marxist plan masquerading as environmental policy. The Green New Deal is simply the old Red movement dressed up as the green movement. Don't be conned, this is nothing more than a Red New Deal. Everything in your home, your home itself, your automobile, the clothing you wear, the job you have, all of it will be affected. All of it will be monitored. All of it will be regulated. To make you poorer, to make you less independent, to make you less free. Morano's book reveals it as an enormous power grab by the federal government, politicians, and bureaucrats. If you care about America's future, read this book."
  —**Mark R. Levin,** author and nationally syndicated TV and
    radio broadcaster

"*Green Fraud* reveals the radical, extreme agenda behind the Green New Deal. Morano takes you into a history of the environmental movement, the UN agenda, and the socialist vision for America of Ocasio-Cortez. The book reveals that the Green New Deal is not about controlling the climate, it is about controlling us, our economy, our energy, and destroying America. This is a must-read book that shows how the Green New Deal is dangerous, impractical, misguided, and guaranteed to fail with disastrous results for the American people."
  —**Sean Hannity,** host of *Hannity* on Fox News and of the
    nationally syndicated radio program *The Sean Hannity Show*

"Marc Morano is continuing the fight against the global warming hoax with a sharp and focused look at the 'Green New Deal.' In *Green Fraud*, Morano shows that the growing movement from the Left isn't about the climate at all—it's about controlling every aspect of American lives and implementing broad, socialist policies. The

Left's green activist movement isn't going away—making books like Marc's that tell the truth even more important."
—**Senator James Inhofe**, Republican of Oklahoma, chairman of the Senate Armed Services Committee, and member of the Environment and Public Works Committee

"*Green Fraud* exposes the Green New Deal's false premises and so-called 'solutions.' Morano's timely book reveals how the Green New Deal is being backed by a crew of radicals bent on using the global warming scare as a cover to impose socialism on the U.S.A. The book unmasks what the media won't tell you—the Green New Deal has nothing to do with 'climate change.' The Green New Deal is one of the gravest threats facing America. This indispensable book is the most comprehensive takedown of the plan you will ever read."
—**Brent Bozell**, founder of the Media Research Center

"Tired of hearing only one side of the climate debate from the mainstream media? Tired of Hollywood preaching to you about 'global warming' while they ignore their own blatant hypocrisy? Tired of failed climate doomsday predictions? If so, then Marc Morano's new book *Green Fraud* is your ticket to understanding and fighting back against the climate agenda. Morano's book exposes the Green New Deal from A to Z. Don't be climate hustled, read this book."
—**Kevin Sorbo**, actor and narrator of the film *Climate Hustle 2*

"Marc Morano's book *Green Fraud* provides a factual scientific and political account of the Green New Deal and other misanthropic and self-serving schemes of the global elite and their opportunistic or deluded acolytes. For many important issues, the contemporary mainstream media closely resembles the 'Ministry of Truth,' of Orwell's prophetic book *1984*. Scientifically unsophisticated but well-meaning adults and impressionable children have been misled and terrified about global warming and other 'existential threats.' Supposedly, these impending catastrophes can only be remedied by surrendering our inalienable rights to liberty and the pursuit of happiness. Some fanatics even deny the inalienable right to life. They maintain that the Earth can only provide sustainable support for less than 1 billion of its current human inhabitants."

—**Will Happer,** Cyrus Fogg Brackett Professor of Physics emeritus, Princeton University, and former Deputy Assistant to the President and Senior Director of Emerging Technologies on the National Security Council

"Marc Morano is number one. Morano is truly the Pete Rose and Hank Aaron of climate contrarians."

—**Steven Hayward of Powerline**

"Morano's probably single-handedly, in a civilian sense, the guy (other than me, of course) doing a better job of ringing the bells alarming people of what's going on here."

—**Rush Limbaugh,** nationally syndicated radio host and bestselling author

Rage at Marc Morano

"Marc Morano makes for a jocular—and weirdly unapologetic—advocate for what can only be called ignorance."

—**Michael O'Sullivan, the** *Washington Post*

Morano is a "professional climate smearmonger."

—**Penn State University professor Michael Mann**

"Marc Morano, a prominent denier of established climate change science."
—*New York Times*

Morano is "clearly someone who's just a straight climate denier."
—former UN IPCC chair Robert Watson

"Marc Morano—perhaps the most notorious climate denier in the U.S."
—Media Matters

"Just a troll with a love for conspiracy, a hatred for science and reality."
—Seth Borenstein, Associated Press

"Morano is one of a relative handful of self-described climate 'skeptics' who have wrestled thousands of the world's leading scientists to a standstill of their own.... They are the ones who have convinced millions that there is no scientific consensus that climate change is real and human-caused."
—environmental columnist Rick Holmes

"Morano is the real-world fossil fuel industry version of Nick Naylor."
—*The Guardian*

"Ringleader" of the "climate deniers."
—*The Guardian* columnist Dana Nuccitelli

"Morano left the Senate staff in 2009 for a private-sector career as the P. T. Barnum of climate denial."
—former CNN producer Peter Dykstra

"One of the most active pushers of climate science denialism in the country."
  —DeSmogBlog

"One of the most powerful climate skeptics."
  —the German magazine *Süddeutsche*

"Morano.... pretty much chewed up Bill Nye the Science Guy on CNN with Piers Morgan a couple of years ago."
  —Randy Olson in a Dot Earth column at the *New York Times*

"An evil person...a badass person."
  —Canadian environmentalist David Suzuki

GREEN FRAUD

GREEN

FRAUD

Why the Green New Deal Is Even Worse Than You Think

MARC MORANO

Bestselling author of *The Politically Incorrect Guide to Climate Change*

REGNERY
PUBLISHING

A Division of Salem Media Group
Washington, D.C.

Regnery® is a registered trademark of Salem Communications Holding Corporation

ISBN: 978-1-68451-085-6
eISBN: 978-1-68451-114-3

Library of Congress Catalog Number: 2020945137

Published in the United States by
Regnery Publishing,
A Division of Salem Media Group,
Washington, D.C.
www.Regnery.com

Manufactured in the United States of America

10 9 8 7 6 5 4 3 2 1

Books are available in quantity for promotional or premium use. For information on discounts and terms, please visit our website: www.Regnery.com.

CONTENTS

Foreword

On the day the "New Green Deal" was announced, I was en route to a TV appearance with Tucker Carlson and did a bit of perfunctory Googling in case it came up. The FAQ sheet declared the Deal's commitment to, in its words, "fully get rid of farting cows and airplanes." Which would be bad news for me, as I always travel with a flatulent Holstein as my emotional support animal. Go on, try it—twenty minutes out of LAX, you'll have the first-class cabin all to yourself.

And then I forgot about it, assuming that it would be just a bit of (if you'll forgive the expression) red meat for the hardcore loons that fellows like John Kerry, the flatulent bovine of the climate-conference jet set, would toss out at Davos black-tie galas of the Committee for Transnational Gasbaggery.

Six months later I turned the page of my newspaper and was confronted by a photograph of German cattle attempting to graze while wearing what appeared to be metal lederhosen. They had been fitted with these awkward contraptions by scientists anxious both to measure and to contain the poor beasts' flatulence. And you guffaw and pass on to the sports news—forgetting that, in today's world, no one who matters is laughing: not Joe Biden, not Justin Trudeau, not Leonardo di Caprio, not the sainted Greta. They're deadly serious. No pilot program is intended to remain such: if they can put flatulence lederhosen on a cow, they can put them on you. I regret to say that my old chum Boris Johnson, a man who once breezily waved away the subject of global warming with the words "it's all bollocks," seems exactly the sort of chap to mandate flatulence lederhosen for residents of designated Tier Three COVID-lockdown zones.

Unlike most of us, Marc Morano doesn't laugh and move on. We face a malign alliance of politicians who "follow the science" and scientists who follow the politics—and he takes them as seriously as they take themselves, and possibly more so. I have had the pleasure of interviewing Marc a few times on TV, and he is every booker's must-get guest on this topic—trenchant, forensic, effective. His enemies grasp that: in 2019 a peer-reviewed study in a prestigious scientific journal found that Marc ranks as the Number One "climate contrarian" on the globe. If the oceans really do rise to swallow Barack Obama's and Barbra Streisand's waterfront property and the planet fries and the lone-surviving homo sapiens on earth are floating on an ice floe with a couple of emaciated polar bears circa 2031 (as Representative Ocasio-Cortez predicts), one of them will surely use the last bars of his dying cellphone to pull up that prestigious, peer-reviewed hit parade and curse Morano's name to the heavens as they melt into the inferno of the broiling waters.

What an honor! Marc should put it on his business card.

Take a look around: politicians and activists who can't save their state or county, town or school district instead claim to be able to save the planet. The Green New Deal is their ultimate omnibus spending bill: it asserts jurisdiction over every aspect of life—which is to say every aspect of *you*. At their Monday night poker game in Hell, Hitler, Stalin, Mao, and Pol Pot must be laughing their socks off: "'Oh, we're only doing this to save the planet'? Why didn't we think of that?"

Marc Morano is the perfect guide to pierce through the fog of bovine flatulence and delineate the Green New World they're planning for us.

—**Mark Steyn**

CHAPTER 1

The Green Raw Deal

What should people know about the Green New Deal?

The Green New Deal is the ultimate wish list of the progressive environmental agenda. And it has almost nothing to do with science or "saving the planet." The Green New Deal would impact literally every aspect of your life, from your lightbulbs to your appliances, to your home heating and air conditioning, to your SUV, to the food you eat and the clothes you wear, to land use and the size of your home, to your job and the prices you pay, and finally to America's national sovereignty.

The Green New Deal is the culmination of a half century of wish lists from the environmental Left.

The deal barged on the American scene in 2018. The face of the GND was newly elected twenty-nine-year-old New York congresswoman Alexandria Ocasio-Cortez, or AOC. AOC was a former Bernie Sanders volunteer organizer and a self-described "democratic socialist."

Ocasio-Cortez teamed up with Democrat senator Ed Markey of Massachusetts to introduce a fourteen-page, nonbinding Green New Deal resolution in Congress in February 2019. The resolution attracted over one hundred cosponsors in Congress and was embraced by many of the

Democratic presidential candidates. The Green New Deal is an all-encompassing transformation of society that includes energy, economics, social justice, agriculture, transportation, construction, wealth redistribution, massive expansion of centrally planned government control, and a host of new restrictions on Americans in order to—ostensibly—battle man-made climate change.

It may have appeared that the Green New Deal just sprang up out of nowhere, but as chapter 2 will reveal, it bears striking resemblance to the United Nations' Agenda 21 sustainable development plan put forth at the 1992 Rio Earth Summit.

"We're like, the world is going to end in 12 years if we don't address climate change," AOC explained.[1] Ocasio-Cortez became an overnight media sensation.

Packed with terms like "farting cows," "tipping points," "free college," "healthy food," "net zero," "adequate housing," and incomes for those "unable or unwilling" to work—and much, much more[2]—the Green New Deal was billed as "a 10-year plan to mobilize every aspect of American society at a scale not seen since World War 2 to achieve net-zero greenhouse gas emissions."[3]

And it won't be cheap. Some estimates ranged between $51 trillion and $93 trillion over ten years.[4] Many other versions of the Green New Deal appeared as well, with each Democratic presidential candidate coming up with his or her own variation, including former vice president and now president Joe Biden.

The alleged "climate emergency" is merely a premise for achieving the political goals that the Left has sought for decades. The Green New Deal will mean a complete takeover of a massive swath of the U.S. economy, disrupting and destroying lives as formerly free decisions are turned over to the bureaucratic state. The Green New Deal would bestow upon the bureaucratic state a massive increase in power to manage the economy and redistribute wealth, taking choices out of the hands of individual consumers and businesses and putting them into the hands of those who are allegedly more enlightened. The GND will also lead to another massive round of government "investment" in solar and wind power, picking winners and losers with taxpayer money.

And meanwhile, the Green New Deal would do absolutely nothing to ward off a "climate catastrophe"—even if we were in fact facing one. (We're not.)

The Green New Deal era is upon us. The COVID lockdowns and resulting massive increase in government powers have made the Green New Deal an even bigger threat to liberty and freedom. As I reveal in chapter 11, COVID and climate are a marriage made in authoritarianism. Many of the COVID solutions are nearly the same as the Green New Deal's claimed "solutions." The morphing of the public health bureaucracy and the climate establishment is at hand, and a technocracy or rule by unelected government "experts" is now upon us.

> **Architects of Green New Deal Admit: It Is Not about the Climate**
>
> AOC's chief of staff Saikat Chakrabarti revealed that the Green New Deal was not about climate change.[6] The *Washington Post* reported Chakrabarti's unexpected disclosure in 2019. "The interesting thing about the Green New Deal," he said, "is it wasn't originally a climate thing at all." He added, "Do you guys think of it as a climate thing? Because we really think of it as a how-do-you-change-the-entire-economy thing."[7]
>
> Former Ocasio-Cortez campaign aide Waleed Shahid admitted that Ocasio-Cortez's GND was a "proposal to redistribute wealth and power from the people on top to the people on the bottom."[8]

In 2020, the chairman and founder of the World Economic Forum in Switzerland called for "a Great Reset of capitalism" to fight COVID and climate change. Klaus Schwab said the virus has given us an "opportunity" to pursue "equality & sustainability." The Green New Deal is the road map for the "Great Reset."[5]

There is a very real danger that the GND will be imposed on America one way or another—enacted by politicians that we're persuaded to vote for by the relentless scaremongering, or even mandated through the court system. To understand what is driving the Green New Deal, it is important to understand the history of the U.S. progressive move-ment, the modern environmental movement, and specifically the cli-mate movement.

The Green New Deal is not about the climate or "saving the planet." Repeat that over and over. The GND is about much more than the cli-mate or the environment. It is about transforming modern America into a centrally planned and managed society and imposing an ideology that will reign in the freedoms of individual Americans.

The premise of the Green New Deal is very simple: if you pay more taxes, regulate industry, drive up the cost of energy, micromanage every aspect of your life—we can then control the climate in order to avoid a climate emergency.

Left out of the equation is when we will finish paying and doing our World War II–style sacrifice of our freedoms (already severely depleted under COVID lockdowns) so the government can allegedly control the climate. What criteria will the overlords of the Green New Deal use to say, "Okay, that's enough taxes spending and regulations; the climate has been fixed"? Or is this just an endless parade of money, regulations, bureaucracy, loss of freedom, redistribution of wealth, and enforced mandates on people? At what point do we say we've achieved the Green New Deal goals?

This book will explain that there are no criteria for a climate end game; the GND is an endless con game.

The underlying reality, which is lost on many today, is that fossil fuels—coal, oil, and natural gas—have been one of the greatest liberators of mankind in the history of our planet. Is it greedy to want heat, air conditioning, lower infant mortality, and longer life expectancy?

The GND would affect the poor by forcing them to pay a higher share of their income for energy that will cost much, much more and be less reliable, with regular blackouts like the ones they're already experiencing in "green" California. Fossil fuels have been and are the moral choice for energy. The power behind the greatest advances in modern civilization is not something anyone should be apologizing for. Limiting energy choices to "address" hyped climate concerns will not improve life in America.

The Green New Deal is camouflage for a progressive agenda that would be a very difficult sell to the American public if it were not repackaged as a "solution" to a "climate emergency."

A Refreshingly Rational Energy Policy

Under President Trump, the U.S. has pursued and achieved an "energy dominance" policy that involves cutting regulations, modernizing infrastructure, supporting innovation, and boosting exports.[9] In a huge victory for sound science, the Trump administration removed "climate change" from our stated national security concerns, overturned former president Obama's executive order climate "legacy," and started the process of pulling the U.S. out of the UN Paris Pact.

Meanwhile, the United States has continued its success in reducing traditional air pollution and is beating most of the European signatories of the UN Paris Pact in reducing carbon dioxide emissions, despite signaling its intent to withdraw from the Paris Pact in 2017.

Of course, the planet will not care one way or the other about the fate of the UN Paris Pact; even if it were fully enacted, it would have no measurable impact on global temperatures.

Instead of "climate regulations," the Trump administration was focused on innovation, technology, and improving energy efficiency as the path forward. President Donald Trump's entire energy policy consisted of boosting U.S. energy to achieve energy dominance in the world by not only ignoring man-made climate change, but also working to undo the Obama administration's "climate legacy," achieved mostly through bypassing democracy with executive orders. By 2018, Trump had won bragging rights on energy: the United States had become the world's largest global crude oil producer, surpassing Russia and Saudi Arabia, according to the Energy Information Administration's (EIA) Energy Outlook.[10]

Trump energy achievements were so off the charts that the last time the U.S. saw this kind of energy dominance was when Harry S. Truman was president in 1952! In 2019, "U.S. energy exports exceeded imports for the first time since 1952," the EIA reported. The EIA also reported, "In 2019, U.S. energy production exceeded energy consumption for the first time since 1957," when Dwight D. Eisenhower was president.[11]

In 2019, BP reported that the U.S. now led the world in both oil and natural gas production growth as the shale natural gas fracking boom continued unabated.[12] Of course the COVID-19-inspired lockdowns of 2020 put a huge damper on energy production: economic growth and thus the demand for energy dipped and may take a while to recover.

The editors of the *Los Angeles Times* were incensed that under Trump, American energy was booming. "As global warming continues, Trump wants to burn fossil fuels with an arsonist's glee," the paper's editorial board declared.[13]

Former vice president Joe Biden joined in, calling Trump a "climate arsonist" during the 2020 presidential campaign.[14]

For his energy plan, Biden seemed hesitant to even say publicly that he supported the Green New Deal. When asked in a debate with President Trump, Biden denied he even supported the plan. "No, I don't support the Green New Deal," Biden pleaded. But Biden's campaign website clearly stated, "Biden believes the Green New Deal is a crucial framework for meeting the climate challenges we face."[15]

Biden further explained that the Green New Deal "is not a bad deal, but it's not the plan I have—that's the 'Biden Green Deal.'"[16]

There was no hesitation about the GND from Biden's vice presidential pick, Kamala Harris. In 2019, Harris praised the Green New Deal as a way "we can change human behaviors." She said, "It is a fact that we can change human behaviors without much change to our lifestyle and we can save the future generations of our country and this world."[17]

Biden was trying to make a nuanced distinction between his slightly less ambitious version of the GND and the one presented by Rep. Alexandria Ocasio-Cortez of New York. Of course AOC is pretty confident Biden will be persuaded to follow her lead. "I think, overall, we can likely push Vice President Biden in a more progressive direction across policy issues," AOC said.[18]

"Foolish Fortune-Tellers"

Trump gave perhaps his best summation on climate in his 2020 Davos address, when he compared climate activists to "prophets of doom" and "heirs of yesterday's foolish fortune-tellers....

"To embrace the possibilities of tomorrow we must reject the perennial prophets of doom and their predictions of the Apocalypse. They are the heirs of yesterday's foolish fortune-tellers, and they want to see us do badly but we won't let that happen. They predicted an overpopulation crisis in the 1960s, mass starvation in the 70s, and an end of oil in the 1990s. These alarmists always demand the same thing: absolute power to dominate, transform and control every aspect of our lives."[20]

The speech underlined why progressives, particularly the climate Left, despised Trump and his presidency. He did what no other recent GOP president or recent nominee would ever have done: he stood up to the campaign to push the Green New Deal and the UN Paris Pact. Could you imagine a President McCain or President Romney having the political courage to stare down the climate lobby and withdraw from the UN Paris Pact? In fact, both of them were big supporters of the agreement.[21]

"Simply Turning a CO2 Button"

In 2019, Dutch scientist and professor Guus Berkhout of the new international climate institute in the Netherlands declared, "You can't stop climate change by simply turning a CO2 button." Berkhout noted how "doomsday scenarios became a kind of religion."

Professor Berkhout ripped the UN climate panel for its "extreme message." As he explained, "As a geophysicist, I warn that it is highly unlikely that the natural [climate] movements would have stopped abruptly after 1850. And that since then only mankind would be responsible for this warming."[19]

Recent Appearances

My bestselling 2018 book, *The Politically Incorrect Guide to Climate Change*, went into its seventh printing and continued to be ranked by

Donald J. Trump ✔
@realDonaldTrump

Marc Morano, ClimateHustle2.Com "Perhaps President Trump's greatest accomplishment is United States Energy Dominance."

RISE OF THE CLIMATE MONARCHY
CLIMATE HUSTLE 2
ARE THEY TRYING TO CONTROL THE CLIMATE...OR YOU?

CLIMATE HUSTLE 2
Buy now on DVD or Blu Ray. #climatehustle2
🔗 climatehustle2.com

10:33 AM · Nov 25, 2020   ⓘ

♡ 54.9K   ♡ 17.4K people are Tweeting about this

Trump's tweet featuring my film *Climate Hustle 2*.

Amazon as number one in the categories of Climatology and Environmental Science, Nature, and Earth Sciences. The book even outsold Rachel Carson's venerable environmental book, *Silent Spring,* during the week of Earth Day in 2018.[22] It has been translated into several languages, and in 2019 a new edition with a bonus chapter on the Green New Deal was published.

My film *Climate Hustle* was released to over four hundred theatres in the U.S. and Canada in 2016. I traveled to Brussels in 2016 for a presentation of *Climate Hustle* to the EU. I also traveled to Canada in 2016 for a movie tour, followed by a trek to Australia in 2017 for another film tour.[23] In 2020, I released the sequel, *Climate Hustle 2*, hosted by actor Kevin Sorbo. It was originally scheduled to show in nearly eight hundred theaters in the U.S. and Canada—until the COVID lockdowns. *Climate Hustle 2* received a huge boost when President Trump tweeted it out to his eighty-eight million followers.[24]

Since publishing *The Politically Incorrect Guide to Climate Change* in 2018, I have been very busy, testifying at several congressional climate and Green New Deal hearings, and in the Pennsylvania legislature and other venues, plus television and speaking engagements. In 2018 I debated the pros and cons of a carbon dioxide tax (hint, all cons) at the University of Minnesota. In 2019, I was invited to speak at Georgetown University by the College Republicans group. My talk was titled: "'Climate Emergency' CANCELLED! Politicians Cannot Legislate Weather, Storms, and the Climate."

Comment of a Climate Denier
"This was a wild climate hearing. Invited witnesses comparing climate skeptics to Holocaust deniers, racists and there were tin foil hat protestors, legislators speaking out of turn, a warmist legislator walking out, and my testimony being interrupted by my fellow testifiers at the hearing! This is the first time I have been heckled at a hearing by a fellow invited witness!" I commented after the hearing at the Pennsylvania House Environmental Resources & Energy Committee, hosted by Chairman Daryl Metcalfe.[25]

A climate skeptic speaking at Georgetown in the age of Greta Thunberg and woke campuses? As it turned out—well, this was my headline at Climate Depot: "No Dissent Allowed: Chaos as Protesters Disrupt Climate Skeptic Morano's Speech at Georgetown University—Campus Police Shut Down Event—Activists 'Would Not Accept the Hosting of' Skeptics."

The *Georgetown Voice*, the campus newspaper, reported:

> The protestors played music and alarms, held up signs in the windows from outside, and chanted throughout the event. One of these protestors, sporting a clown costume, interrupted Morano's presentation by blowing an air horn....
>
> As tensions rose, GUPD (Georgetown University Police Dept) arrived at the event. Two officers came inside and asked

those who had been disrupting the event, including Ferguson and the protester dressed as a clown, to step outside. They refused to leave the room, prompting the GUPD officer to say he would only ask so many times. When asked to present their GoCards, the students did not comply....

Torbert, who appeared to be one of the leaders of the protests, said the group would not accept the hosting of these speakers on campus.

I shouted back and engaged the protesters as I continued my presentation for a while, and then, eventually, campus police removed the protesters and I got my chance to restart after nearly an hour's delay. Campus police told me that they had never before seen such a massive disruption of a speaking event at Georgetown University.

I have attended nearly every UN climate and Earth summit since 2002, including the climate summits in Argentina in 2004; Canada in 2005; Kenya in 2006; Bali in 2007; Poland in 2008; Copenhagen in 2009; Durban, South Africa in 2011; Warsaw, Poland in 2013; Lima, Peru in 2014; Paris in 2015; Morocco in 2016; Germany in 2018; Poland in 2018; and Madrid in 2019.

In May 2019, I got to go head-to-head with former UN IPCC (United Nations Intergovernmental Panel on Climate Change) chief Robert Watson as an invited witness at a congressional hearing.[26] I appeared with former Greenpeace co-founder

"An Evil Person," or "a Badass"?

Famed Canadian environmentalist David Suzuki—who had just declared that "capitalism is at the heart of what is driving" climate and "we've got to throw the system out"—refused a copy of my new skeptical Climate Talking Points report on December 10, 2019, shouting at me:

"You are an evil person."

I responded: "An evil person?"

Suzuki: "Yes, you are. You are an evil person."

Suzuki later added, "You are a badass person. And I am sure you are proud of that."[27]

Dr. Patrick Moore, who long ago turned against the group he founded and is now a climate skeptic.

The House Natural Resources Committee held the hearing on the subject of the UN's massive new 2019 Intergovernmental Science-Policy Platform on Biodiversity and Ecosystem Services (IPBES) climate and species report, which had just been issued. Congressman Jared Huffman, the California Democrat who chaired the subcommittee holding the hearing, claimed on the basis of the report that the Earth was "currently in what they call the sixth mass extinction."

But Moore countered, during his testimony, "As with the manufactured 'climate crisis,' they are using the specter of mass extinction as a fear tactic to scare the public into compliance....The [UN report] itself is an existential threat to sensible policy on biodiversity conservation."

Moore added, "The so-called Sixth Great Extinction has been predicted for decades. It has not come to pass, similar to virtually every doomsday prediction made in human history."

How the Sausage Is Made

During my testimony, I was able to explain what was actually going on at the United Nations. This excerpt of my testimony is key to understanding how the "scientific basis" for the claims of a "climate emergency" and solutions like the Green New Deal is manufactured by a political process at the UN.

> **Morano:** I want to thank the House Natural Resources Committee for hosting this hearing on the UN species report. My background is in political science, which happens to be an ideal background for examining the latest round of UN environmental claims. I have been following the UN species reports since 2010 when the UN first announced they were going to be elevating species to near the level of climate as a concern.

Testifying at the 2019 congressional hearing on climate and species extinction, with Greenpeace co-founder Patrick Moore on the left and former UN IPCC chief Robert Watson on the right.

I have been passionate about environmental issues since I began my career in 1991 as a journalist. I produced a documentary on the myths surrounding the Amazon rainforest in 2000, titled *Clear-Cutting the Myths*, which dealt extensively with claimed species extinctions and how such claims are used to instill fear for political lobbying....

During my investigative journalism career, I have reported on the heavy hand of the U.S. government when it conducted armed raids into private homes of animal breeders all in the name of protecting endangered species. It turns out, the government's "good intentions" on species resulted in the animals' deaths on numerous occasions when the animals were seized and left to die in government care....

As an investigative journalist studying the United Nations for decades, there is only one conclusion to be made of this new report: The UN's Intergovernmental Science-Policy Platform on Biodiversity and Ecosystem Services (IPBES), hypes

Watson is clearly not enjoying my testimony.

and distorts biodiversity issues for lobbying purposes. This report is the latest UN appeal to give it more power, more scientific authority, more money, and more regulatory control....

I have been anticipating this expansion of the UN mandate into biodiversity and species with this report for many years. My 2000 Amazon rainforest documentary revealed the hopeful news on species and the natural world's biodiversity.

My testimony focused on the way the sausage is made with these big UN "science" reports which are the basis for much of the underlying scientific claims used by Green New Deal supporters.

> **Morano:** According to media reports, the UN species report requires that "a huge transformation is needed across the economy and society to protect and restore nature...."
>
> And just how does the UN justify this "huge transformation" of economics and society which it will lead? By invoking

what the UN describes as "authoritative science" produced by—the UN itself of course.

UN IPBES executive secretary, Dr. Anne Larigauderie, declared: The "IPBES presents the authoritative science, knowledge and the policy options to decision makers for their consideration."

The UN boasts it is producing "authoritative science" on biodiversity! The UN's biodiversity panel claims it is representing "authoritative science." But these unsupportable boasts will no longer be tolerated.

At best, the UN science panels represent nothing more than "authoritative bureaucracy," claiming they hype the problem and then come up with the solution that puts them in charge of "solving" the issue in perpetuity. A more accurate term for the UN than "authoritative science" may be "authoritative propaganda." ... I have conducted interviews with UN IPCC scientists and documented how the UN twists and hypes and distorts science in order to push a political agenda.

We know that the past UN IPCC chair, Rajendra Pachauri, declared "global warming is my religion." Ottmar Edenhofer, former co-chair of the IPCC's Working Group III and a lead author of the IPCC's Fourth Assessment Report in 2007, explains the UN agenda.

"One must say clearly that we redistribute de facto the world's wealth by climate policy. Obviously, the owners of coal and oil will not be enthusiastic about this. One has to free oneself from the illusion that international climate policy is environmental policy. This has almost nothing to do with environmental policy anymore, with problems such as deforestation or the ozone hole."[28]

We know that the former UN climate chief called for a "centralized transformation" led by the UN. Christiana Figueres explained, "This is a centralized transformation that is taking place because governments have decided that they need to listen to science." Listen to science? The UN claims to be the "authority" on the science and the UN gets to put itself in charge of the "solutions." How convenient....

Former UN IPCC chief Rajendra Pachauri admitted the IPCC is an arm of world governments and serves at their "beck and call." Remember, the UN's IPBES Global Assessment Report on Biodiversity and Ecosystem Services is modeled after the UN IPCC climate panel and their reports.

Pachauri admitted the purpose of the UN IPCC report was to make the case that "action is needed on climate change." Pachauri: "There will be enough information provided so that rational people across the globe will see that action is needed on climate change."

Pachauri conceded that the UN IPCC science reports are tailored to meet the political needs of governments: "We are an intergovernmental body and we do what the governments of the world want us to do. If the governments decide we should do things differently and come up with a vastly different set of products we would be at their beck and call," Pachauri told the UK *Guardian* in 2013.[29]

Let me clear: I am not talking about the UN and its science reports in some abstract or vague way. I am here to say that the three lead witnesses representing the United Nations today on this new biodiversity report are explicitly part of these UN scientific manipulations.

Make no mistake about it, Sir Robert Watson, Dr. Eduardo S. Brondizio, and Dr. Yunne Shin are the leaders of the UN's bastardization of species endangerment science and are fully engaged in using what they claim to be "science" to lobby for more power and expanding bureaucracy of the United Nations.[30]

I repeat: I am not speaking vaguely about the UN. But specifically of the organization represented by these three witnesses today. They are playing the role of science bureaucrats doing the bidding for their political- and lobbying-prone mother UN organization.

As I publicly stated hours after the release of the report: "The UN has juiced up the issue and put themselves in charge of solving it. That's called a self-interested lobbying organization."[31]

The head honcho, Robert Watson, (who formerly chaired the UN Intergovernmental Panel on Climate Change) the man responsible for the UN IPCC sausage making, is here in person today.

I say to you Mr. Watson: The U.S. will not be duped by the UN's "torquing up" (Gore's own words) of science for your own organization's self-interest. You personally have helped sculpt and craft science into the predetermined narrative that enriches your organization—the UN....

I will be presenting and submitting for the record, the voices of current and past scientists that reveal the UN's pre-determined narrative process and expose how the UN's panels are not rooted in honest science.

Actor Harrison Ford urged the UN to hype the species fears for political purposes. "One of our missions is to create a sense of urgency.... The urgency can't be overemphasized.... We are at a tipping point...a global agreement is essential," Ford said in 2010 at the UN summit.

Concern over species can be used to justify massive government intrusion into business, private lives, and property rights, therefore, it is extremely important that we get the science right.[32]

My dissenting voice and Moore's at this hearing caused quite a commotion in the media and climate activist world. The media demanded to know how two climate "deniers" had hijacked a Democrat congressional hearing.

The climate activist group Media Matters lamented that Dr. Moore and I "got more time at the hearing than the four scientists invited by the Democrats, according to Public Citizen." A report at the Media Matters website complained, "Morano and Moore made a mockery of the House hearing, and that's exactly what Republicans wanted.... Fox News has helped to put Morano and Moore in the public eye by giving them a platform to sow doubt about climate change and other serious environmental issues, and now the two men's latest Fox-worthy rants are part of the congressional record. So far in 2019, Morano has appeared on Fox News shows at least 10 times." A commenter on the Media Matters story wanted to know, "How did these two dominate a hearing run by Democrats?"[34]

What really galled the climate campaigners was my blunt face-to-face confrontation of former UN IPCC chair Watson during my opening statement. Eos, a media division of the American Geophysical Union, reported, "Marc Morano, editor of ClimateDepot.com and a prominent climate change denier criticized Watson, whom he sat next to at the witness table: 'Watson says it's our last chance to save the planet. These are the words of a salesman, a science bureaucrat, not a disinterested...' Morano never finished that sentence because subcommittee chair Rep. Jared Huffman (D-Calif.) interrupted and told Morano to direct testimony to him." Huffman told the media that Morano "brought a provocative, almost like a World Wrestling type of ethos to his testimony."[35]

The *Guardian* described Moore's and my testimony at the hearing as "appalling...bullying...strident and personal" and said, "At the hearing, Morano characterized the IPBES report as a piece of

> ## "Leave Science to Smart People"
>
> "You don't pay attention to reality, science or anything with common sense You're just a troll with a love for conspiracy, a hatred for science and reality. Leave science to smart people. Bye."
> —AP activist climate reporter Seth Borenstein to Marc Morano in 2020, in what can only be described as a classic Twitter debate[33]

A Sociopath, or Just a Terrible Person?

Dr. Gavin Schmidt, NASA's lead climate change scientist and the director of its Goddard Institute for Space Studies (GISS), smeared scientific dissenters from man-made climate change claims on September 12, 2020. "A reminder (if one was needed) that most climate deniers are sociopaths," wrote Schmidt, referring to me. "There is no 'mode of discourse' that will make Morano suddenly stop being an awful person who is (well) paid to try to prevent any efforts to reduce fossil fuel use by fair means or foul. So, might as well call it as one sees it."[37]

Dictionary.com defines "sociopath" as "a person with a psychopathic personality whose behavior is antisocial, often criminal, and who lacks a sense of moral responsibility or social conscience."

'propaganda' meant to give the United Nations 'more money, more power, more scientific authority, more money and more regulatory control of the economy and people's lives.' He then went on to smear the recent chair of the IPBES, Sir Robert Watson, who was sitting beside him, alleging that Watson and his fellow IPBES officials 'are part of this con' and 'the leaders of this UN politicization of species endangerment science,' calling the well-pedigreed Watson 'not a scientist, but a science bureaucrat.'"[36]

Climate skeptic Steve Milloy cheered the hearing: "Thanks for having a hearing that allowed climate skeptics Patrick Moore @EcoSenseNow and Marc Morano @ClimateDepot to totally outclass your climate bedwetters. Now you know what bedwetters generally avoid sharing a stage with skeptics."[38]

In 2018, a Facebook video I made about my *Politically Incorrect Guide to Climate Change* book with the Heritage Foundation's Daily Signal went viral with over 10.2 million views. The video prompted efforts to ban "climate deniers" from social media, and the video's popularity was used to attack Facebook founder Mark Zuckerberg for allowing it on the social media platform.[39]

My testimony to the Pennsylvania House in 2019. *Courtesy of The Harry Read Me File*

"A climate denial video has 6 million views. Facebook doesn't care," blared the headline at the magazine Grist. The climate activists at Grist lamented that the "two-minute video attacking the scientific consensus on climate change—made by infamous denier Marc Morano—is going viral." As this book will detail later on, traditional media and social media censorship is in full swing and poses a major threat to battling the Green New Deal.[40]

Top Billing

But the greatest honor bestowed upon me was being ranked the world's number one "climate contrarian"—number 1 out of 386 skeptics—by a peer-reviewed study in the journal *Nature Communications* in 2019.[41]

The *Nature Communications* study looked at "prominent climate change contrarians (CCCs) and scientists (CCSs) in the media...386

prominent climate deniers and 386 climate scientists. They looked at 200,000 scientific journals and 100,000 media articles—from both traditional and new formats." They found that yours truly was ranked the most cited climate "contrarian" in the world.

"Marc Morano is number one, with 4,171 media references, nearly double Senator James Inhofe's 2,628 and Secretary Rick Perry's 1,903," explained Craig Rucker at CFACT (the Committee for a Constructive Tomorrow).[42] My fellow climate skeptic Steven Hayward of the Power Line Blog wrote, "Marc Morano is number one" and added, "Morano is truly the Pete Rose and Hank Aaron of climate contrarians."[43]

Warmist Randy Olson commented on the study, asking, "Does the climate community realize Marc Morano is the most prolific voice of skepticism by a looooong way? He has 35% more articles than any others. There should be an Institute for the Study of Morano."[44] As Olson pointed out, he has been warning the world about me for a long time. "In 2007, I had climate 'contrarian' Marc Morano in my movie 'Sizzle.' In 2010, I warned of his media savvy, today he is a Fox News regular and the most prolific skeptic in this new article."[45]

A Preview

In this book, I lay out an overview of the "science," history, ideology, and costs of the Green New Deal.

Chapter 2 demonstrates how Franklin Delano Roosevelt's original New Deal in the 1930s both it is and is not the model for the shiny new "green" version. FDR's original New Deal expanded the size and scope of government; the Green New Deal will go much further. Find out how the Green New Deal may be guilty of plagiarizing the UN's Agenda 21 sustainable development proposal.

Chapter 3 shows why there is no real threat from man-made climate change. The latest climate science claims will be presented along with the alleged "solutions" in a simplified talking points format. Not only does Earth not face a "climate emergency," but even if we did, symbolic climate "solutions" would only make us poorer and have no impact on the climate system.

Chapter 4 is a detailed analysis of what the Green New Deal means, the specifics, and the goals of the various versions. Prepare for some truly wacky and off-the-wall proposals that just may become law one day.

In chapter 5, the reader will see how Europe is already "enjoying" their version of a Green New Deal—and it's not going well. Europeans are paying much more for their energy even though the U.S. is beating them on CO_2 emission reductions.

In chapter 6, which is perhaps my favorite chapter, readers will learn how the Green New Deal plagiarizes the same "solutions" from previous environmental scares. I reveal how the real driving force behind the GND is the ideological agenda against free enterprise. Find out how the pushers of the 1970s ice age scare also proposed the same "solutions" as the progressives are offering for global warming today. Yes, global cooling and global warming amazingly both have the same symptoms and "solutions"!

In chapter 7, the real motives of the movement for "de-growth" and "planned recessions" to fight "global warming" are exposed. The Green New Deal is literally borrowing from the same anti-capitalist and anti-freedom progressive playbook that has been around for decades.

In chapter 8, the reader will find out how support for the Green New Deal is fracturing, with even presumed allies of the Green New Deal, including the big Democrat Party–endorsing labor unions, bailing on the GND.

Chapter 9 will explore the crippling worldwide economic costs of the Green New Deal and the dire impact it will have on Americans in particular. The GND will harm the poorest Americans first, as its mandates raise energy costs and depress economic activity—and all of this for no impact on the climate.

Chapter 10 will burst renewable energy claims and explain why banning reliable fossil fuel–based energy in favor of mandating solar and wind power—known as "renewables" but more accurately called "unre-liables"—is not the way forward. Banning energy that is powering America while mandating energy that is not ready to take over is not the moral or rational option. Even progressives like Michael Shellenberger and Michael Moore reveal how they can no longer tolerate the folly of solar and wind energy claims.

In chapter 11, the reader will be shown the toxic politics, funding, and "science" behind the push for the Green New Deal and the UN Paris Pact. "Science" has now morphed into a lobbying arm of the U.S. government and the UN. Ever wonder how and why every "scientific" climate prediction is so dire? This chapter will take you through the process by which the extreme scenarios of climate "models" became mainstream in the climate science community.

I Really Don't Care, Do You?

As *Fortune* reported in 2020, "Amid COVID-19, Americans Don't Care About Climate Change Anymore."[46]

Harris Poll CEO Will Johnson fretted, "In a survey we at the Harris Poll conducted last December [2019], American adults said climate change was the number one issue facing society. Today, it comes in second to last on a list of a dozen options, ahead of only overpopulation....

"Coronavirus didn't elbow aside other issues as muscularly as it did climate change," Johnson added.[47]

No doubt the environmental Left is now striving to figure out how to piggyback the climate issues onto COVID in order to stay relevant.

Then, in chapter 12, comes my exposé of how the climate movement is using kids as human shields to push the Green New Deal. School indoctrination, children's lawsuits against the government to force "climate action," and the origins and funding of the international school-skipping movement led by Greta Thunberg will be revealed.

Next, in chapter 13, I report on how identity politics has invaded the climate debate, with NASA climate scientists going woke and linking "white supremacy" to "climate change." The reader will learn how what used to just be called science is now the allegedly racist "white man's own science."

Perhaps the most shocking part of the book is chapter 14, "The COVID–Climate Connection." This chapter shows how envious the climate activists are of the COVID lockdowns, which they see as a dress rehearsal for their "climate emergency." You'll read in chilling detail how the COVID pandemic has accelerated the march toward rule by unelected bureaucratic "experts." In the vein of never letting a crisis go to waste, the climate community is seeking a green "great reset" of the economy. The COVID–Climate Technocracy has arrived. If you enjoyed the COVID lockdowns, you will *love* the coming climate lockdowns.

In the final chapter, I will show how the Green New Deal may become the ultimate achievement of the progressive movement, dwarfing past advances in state power and government control of people's lives. I will look ahead on what to expect from a Joe Biden–Kamala Harris administration. By tackling all aspects of human endeavor in one grand Green New Deal, the Left may be able to achieve what they have sought for so long—to centrally plan and regulate all human beings—in one single leap.

There is nothing new about the Green New Deal. "Global warming" is merely the latest alleged environmental scare that is being used to push the same "solutions." Instead of arguing the merits of the economic and political changes of the Green New Deal, they are using—to quote Al Gore—a "torqued up" climate change scare to urge quick imposition of the policies they claim will protect us from a climate emergency.

As we shall see, the environmental Left has used the same rhetoric and proposed the same purported "solutions" for very different environmental scares in the 1960s and 70s—whether it was overpopulation, the disappearing rainforest, resource scarcity, or the hole in the ozone layer.

There is no shortage of activists and bureaucrats willing to appoint themselves in charge in order to oversee the "solution."

The climate activists are openly using climate scare tactics to achieve their ends. In order to reach those ends, they *have* to hype and scare. And it has been a very effective strategy; they have bullied even Republican

"The Issue Is Power"

MIT climate scientist Richard S. Lindzen summed up the climate debate perfectly. "For a lot of people including the bureaucracy in government and the environmental movement, the issue is power," Lindzen explained.

"It's hard to imagine a better leverage point than carbon dioxide to assume control over a society. It's essential to the production of energy, it's essential to breathing. If you demonise it and gain control over it, you so-to-speak, control everything. That's attractive to people," Lindzen said.

"If you ever wanted a leverage point to control everything from exhalation to driving, this would be a dream. So it has a kind of fundamental attractiveness to bureaucratic mentality."[48]

politicians, who should know better, into submissiveness and silence over climate change.

"A Semi-Religious Campaign"

Geologist Robert Giegengack, former chair of the Department of Earth and Environmental Science at the University of Pennsylvania, explained, "None of the strategies that have been offered by the U.S. government or by the EPA or by anybody else has the remotest chance of altering climate if in fact climate is controlled by carbon dioxide."

Giegengack lamented the "enormity of the hubris that leads us to believe that we can 'control' climate by controlling anthropogenic emission of CO_2." Global warming, he pointed out, has evolved into "a semi-religious campaign advanced by well-intended people who feel, deep in their hearts, that they are 'saving the planet.'"[49]

UK scientist Philip Stott, professor emeritus of Biogeography at the University of London, noted that climate change "has become the grand political narrative of the age, replacing Marxism as a dominant force for controlling liberty and human choices."[50]

Green Fraud will detail how this "grand political narrative" is being deployed as the Green New Deal.

This book will serve as your guide to understanding the Green New Deal, its goals, its distortions of science, and the tactics that are being used to get it enacted. Get ready, because the battle over the Green New Deal is a battle over the future of America. I wrote *Green Fraud: Why the Green New Deal Is Even Worse Than You Think* to show you why it must be stopped cold in its tracks—and how it can be defeated.

CHAPTER 2

A History:
Every New Crisis Has the Same
"Solution": Expanding the Size
and Power of Government

The Green New Deal is the ultimate culmination of decades of environmental activism seeking societal change through "solutions" to environmental problems. A long history of eco-scares—overpopulation, deforestation, the hole in the ozone layer, the depletion of natural resources, and so forth finally led to "global warming," or "climate change." And the environmental activists are all in on climate change. As we will see in chapter 6, the same "solutions" have been proposed for every green problem ever: immense central planning, sovereignty-limiting treaties, wealth redistribution, and "sustainable development"—in other words, crippling the economy and impoverishing the world's population. The Green New Deal has even added identity politics to the mix as well. (More on that in chapter 13.) To address all environmental problems, the greens have always sought increase in government control through more central planning.

The Green New Deal was introduced to much fanfare in 2019 as the successor to the legacy of the original New Deal of Franklin Delano Roosevelt (FDR). The original New Deal, in the Great Depression in the 1930s, brought into being a massive network of

27

federal programs designed to alleviate the bad economic times and stimulate an economic resurrection. It greatly expanded the size and scope of the federal government and forever changed the American political landscape.

The New Deal's origins can be traced back to Democratic-Populist Party presidential candidate William Jennings Bryan's anti-capitalism speech in 1896, when he declared, "You shall not crucify mankind on a cross of gold."

In 1933, FDR was sworn in and immediately moved to enact his New Deal, which ended up spanning eight years and creating an "alphabet soup" of new government agencies. During the Great Depression, unemployment levels exceeded 80 percent in some American cities, including Toledo—approaching 90 percent in Lowell, Massachusetts—as fifteen million Americans were out of work.[1]

Doubling Down on Failure

"Despite the best efforts of President Roosevelt and his cabinet, however, the Great Depression continued. Unemployment persisted, the economy remained unstable, farmers continued to struggle in the Dust Bowl and people grew angrier and more desperate," explains History. com. FDR even came out with a second New Deal in 1935 but "still, the Great Depression dragged on."

Many historians credit the U.S. entering World War II as the reason the Great Depression finally ended. But many others dispute that claim. "Unemployment did virtually disappear, it is true. But it disappeared primarily because eleven million people were added to the armed forces, mostly by conscription," Thomas E. Woods Jr. wrote in *The Politically Incorrect Guide to American History*. "What finally brought the Depression to an end was neither economic legislation nor World War II. Instead, it was the return to normal conditions following the war and the removal of the uncertainty that had haunted business during the FDR years. Prosperity would have returned much sooner had it not been for the destructive and foolish policies of [President Herbert] Hoover and [Franklin] Roosevelt," Woods explained.

In a 2019 analysis in *The Nation* entitled "The Greening of the New Deal," progressive author Steve Fraser claimed, "Republicans and conservatives of every stripe defamed Democratic President Roosevelt's New Deal from its inception, as has

> ### Isn't That a River in Egypt?
> Steven Fraser in *The Nation*, making use of the "denial" smear that is meant to equate skepticism about catastrophic man-made climate change with Holocaust denial:
> "There were no Great Depression deniers. Clearly, the same cannot be said about the climate crisis."
> —**Steven Fraser in *The Nation***

been true of the very idea of a Green New Deal in the age of Trump....For those opposed to it, the Green New Deal, like the original one, is already considered little but camouflage for a program to introduce socialism to America." Fraser believes "climate change" represents a "much larger catastrophe" than the Great Depression. "In 1932, the Great Depression was essentially the only issue. Nobody was foolish enough to pretend it wasn't happening."

As Fraser accurately pointed out, the New Deal changed American politics over the past century. "President Harry Truman's 'Fair Deal' (including proposals for universal health insurance and federal aid to education) and Lyndon Johnson's 'Great Society' were conceived as elaborations and extensions of what the New Deal had wrought in the 1930s," said Fraser.[2]

But FDR's New Deal was not the economic and societal panacea that many claim it was. "Today, many economists and historians agree that these policies backfired," David Ridenour of the free-market group National Center for Public Policy Research explained in 2019. "Harold L. Cole and Lee E. Ohanian of UCLA have shown that the wage and price inflation [from FDR's wage and price controls] actually made things worse for working-class Americans" by increasing wages which "made it much more difficult to find work."

Did Karl Marx Inspire the Green New Deal?

The Green New Deal may have been ultimately inspired by something sixty-six years before FDR's New Deal: Karl Marx's *Das Kapital*.

"Karl Marx perceived the environment as an effective tool to push his anti-capitalist, anti-God, agenda," notes meteorologist Brian Sussman, the author of *Eco-Tyranny: How the Left's Green Agenda Will Dismantle America*. "Reading from one of his most popular screeds, *Das Kapital*, Marx sounds like Bernie Sanders or Alexandria Ocasio-Cortez.... Like Marx, the new breed of socialists in the U.S. sees capitalism as unjust, the use of natural resources for profit immoral, and the human population something that must be controlled."[3]

According to Ridenour, "All told, the New Deal might have prolonged the Great Depression by seven years. This not only left many Americans homeless and hungry but also stifled economic productivity. Cole and Ohanian estimate the gross national product at the time would have been 27 percent higher without New Deal policies. The GND would similarly crush poor Americans today. Low-income Americans already spend a higher than average percentage of their income on energy. These costs will only increase as fossil fuels aravie heavily taxed. Electricity costs would skyrocket."

Ridenour also pointed out, "The Roosevelt administration's tax increases and labor regulations forced the closure of many businesses. And the GND is similarly shortsighted in its regulatory approach. To reach zero net-carbon emissions in 10 years, the government would regulate and ultimately prohibit the use of affordable energy sources. This would trigger a massive decline in industrial productivity and result in mass layoffs."[4]

And the original 1930s New Deal was nowhere near as ambitious as today's Green New Deal.

"It's important to add that the Green New Deal, despite the bow to the old one in its name, is anything but pure imitation," Fraser pointed out in his article for *The Nation*.[5]

Fraser details how the Green New Deal is truly all-encompassing: "To begin with, the scale of its public investments would dwarf those of the original, which allotted an estimated 13 percent of the country's gross domestic product to its public works spending. Green New Deal projects, as now imagined, would probably at least double that. Furthermore, at least as a proposal, the Green New Deal is even more socially capacious than the old one, embracing as it does the need for universal health care, a guaranteed annual income, a program of affordable housing, commitments to truly clean water and air, and a revolution in the production of healthy food. In the way it forefronts the struggle for social, racial, and environmental justice, it also goes beyond anything the original New Dealers contemplated."[6]

And other climate activists want the Green New Deal to go even further.

"The Green New Deal Can't Be Anything Like the New Deal," blared a 2019 *New Republic* headline. Samuel Miller McDonald, who studies climate and energy politics at Oxford University, argued, "Climate change demands a much more ambitious plan than the Great Depression did. It even requires reversing some of FDR's successes.... The objection to the Green New Deal from mainstream Republicans and Democrats alike is that it's too ambitious. They must realize—quickly—that it's not nearly ambitious enough.... The climate crisis is much bigger than the Great Depression, for the very fate of humanity is at stake. Worse, the crisis is being accelerated by the very thing that the New Deal helped save: fossil fuel capitalism. Thus, rather than emulating its predecessor, the Green New Deal must undo many of its accomplishments instead."[7]

As McDonald claimed, "FDR's programs not only made industrial capitalism financially and socially stable; they sent it into overdrive by leaving monopolistic corporations intact, building the foundation of the interstate highway system, expanding car-dependent suburban housing, incentivizing consumption, expanding air travel, accelerating mechanized extraction, and ramping up resource-intensive manufacturing.... The Green New Deal needs to look less like the New Deal and

Abolish the Suburbs!

Olivia B. Waxman claimed in *Time* magazine that FDR's New Deal had many negative environmental and climate aspects. "Scientists now know that the mass construction of dams, such as the Grand Coulee dam on the Columbia River in Washington state, has disrupted ecosystems. And the Federal Housing Administration, started in 1934, became known for subsidizing the construction of suburbs; the farther out of cities Americans moved, the more it fueled a way of life dependent on fossil fuels."[8]

"This whole suburban boom has been at the center of our really unsustainable lifestyle, automobile dependence [and] sprawl," says Peter F. Cannavò, a professor of government at Hamilton College and an expert on environmental politics.

more like the industrial revolution itself—fundamentally shifting the way we produce and distribute virtually all material goods, and building entirely new sectors while dismantling long standing ones. With climate emergencies set to displace hundreds of millions, we'll also have to rebuild cities and change settlement patterns."

Pat Buchanan, advisor to Presidents Nixon and Reagan, pointed to the failure of FDR's original New Deal, and called the Green New Deal "a Democratic suicide note."

According to Buchanan, "The Green New Deal is designed to recall the halcyon days of the 1930s, when, so the story goes, FDR came to Washington to enact the historic reforms that rescued America from the Great Depression. Only that story is more than a small myth. The unemployment rate when FDR took the oath in 1933 was 25 percent. It never fell below 14 percent through the 1930s. In June 1938, despite huge Democratic majorities in Congress, FDR was presiding over a nation where unemployment was back up to 19 percent.... World War II and the conscription of 16 million young men gave us 'full employment.' And the war's end and demobilization saw the return of real prosperity in 1946, after FDR was dead."[9]

Ridenour believes that "the best environmental outcomes result not from government fiat, but from national prosperity and free-market innovation. The United States has slashed carbon emissions by 13 percent since 2005, thanks to its increased reliance on natural gas, which produces fewer greenhouse gas emissions than coal. The New Deal prolonged the Great Depression it was meant to end. Almost a century later, the GND would prove just as counterproductive. This crusade for environmental and economic justice would actually lead to more pollution and poverty."

Economist Walter Williams of George Mason University noted how the myths about the 1930s New Deal live on today. "Americans have been miseducated into thinking that Roosevelt's New Deal saved our economy. That miseducation extends to most academics, including economists, at our universities, who are arrogant enough to believe that it's possible for a few people in Washington to have the information and knowledge necessary to manage the economic lives of 313 million people," Williams wrote.[11]

> ### Green New Deal, or Green in Your Pocket?
> "While rhetorically mimicking one of the most successful government initiatives in our country's history, there is a significant difference between the real New Deal and the 'Green New Deal.' The real New Deal put green in working people's pockets, won massive public support and lifted our nation out of despair. The latter threatens to destroy workers' livelihoods, increase divisions and inequality, and undermine the very goals it seeks to reach. In short, it is a bad deal."
> —labor leader Terry O'Sullivan, head of the Laborers' International Union, which endorsed Obama twice and Joe Biden in 2020[10]

Where the Green New Deal Really Came From

"Did Hugo Chavez Write the Green New Deal?" asked Steve Milloy of JunkScience.com, comparing the Green New Deal with the Venezuelan Constitution. He concluded that both are "siren call[s] for the naïve, beckoning them to a socialist utopia." According to Milloy, "The reason the Green New Deal and the Venezuelan Constitution are so similar is

Cheap Energy, Rich Lives

"Access to clean water, food, education, abundant and inexpensive energy, fertilizer, advanced agriculture, vaccination and modern health care, science, technology, the internet, and democracy—all made easier through the wealth that the free-market generates—improved global standards of living at an unprecedented speed. Freedom, in other words, has done more to improve humanity's quality of life in the last 200 years than have any other systems or tools over the last 15,000 years."

—Tony Morley, "The Great Decline in Poverty over Time"[14]

that their common source is likely a United Nations document called the 'International Covenant on Economic, Social and Cultural Rights,' which was passed by the UN General Assembly in 1966 at the behest of the Soviet Union. The UN Covenant itself can be traced back to the Stalin-written Soviet Constitution of 1936."[12]

A very likely source for the Green New Deal is the UN Agenda 21 (later updated by the UN in 2015 to Agenda 2030).[13]

"The origins and the purpose of the Green New Deal couldn't be more transparent," wrote Tom DeWeese of the American Policy Center. "From its inception in 1992 at the United Nation's Earth Summit, 50,000 delegates, heads of state, diplomats and non-governmental organizations (NGOs) hailed Agenda 21 as the 'comprehensive blueprint for the reorganization of human society.'" DeWeese added, "The 350-page, 40 chapter Agenda 21 document was quite detailed and explicit in its purpose and goals."

The UN documents explained, "Effective execution of Agenda 21 will require a profound reorientation of all human society, unlike anything the world has ever experienced. It requires a major shift in the priorities of both governments and individuals, and an unprecedented redeployment of human and financial resources. This shift will demand that a concern for the environmental consequences of every human action be integrated into individual and collective decision-making at every level."

Sound familiar?

Earth Summit chairman Maurice Strong announced at the 1992 UN Summit, "Current lifestyles and consumption patterns of the affluent middle class—involving meat intake, use of fossil fuels, appliances, air-conditioning, and suburban housing—are not sustainable."[15]

Sound even more familiar?

That same year, Nancy Pelosi introduced an Agenda 21 resolution in Congress to support "a comprehensive national strategy for sustainable development in accordance with the principles of Agenda 21."[16]

According to DeWeese, "In 1993, President Bill Clinton ordered the establishment of the President's Council for Sustainable Development, with the express purpose of enforcing the Agenda 21 blueprint into nearly every agency of the federal government to assure it became the law of the land....

"Though the label 'Green New Deal' has been passing around globalist circles for a while, it's interesting that its leaders have now handed it to a naïve, inexperienced" freshman New York Congresswoman. AOC "suddenly found herself rise from bartending to a national media sensation, almost over night," DeWeese explained.[18]

> **"Every Aspect of Our Lives"**
> Democratic House Speaker Nancy Pelosi told audiences in China in 2009 that "every aspect of our lives must be subjected to an inventory" in order to combat climate change.[17]

Maurice Newman, who was an advisor to then-Prime Minister Tony Abbott of Australia, noted that the UN has been behind all of these green schemes for decades. "After 50 years of failed predictions, people are reasoning that something other than science is behind this alarmism. And that something is the UN. What else?" Newman asked. "Its global reach, back corridors and duplicity have allowed it to build an unchallenged, mutually-reinforcing $1.5 trillion industry of captive politicians, scientists, journalists, crony capitalists and non-governmental organisation activists bent on globalism through anti-Western sentiment and wealth transfer."

> ### "Doomsday Scenarios"
> "The modern pattern of environmental scares started with Rachel Carson's *Silent Spring* claiming chemicals are killing birds, only today it is windmills doing the carnage. That was followed by ever expanding doomsday scenarios, from DDT, to SST (supersonic transport), to CFC (chlorofluorocarbons), and now the most glorious of them all, CO2."
> —Ron Clutz at Science Matters[19]

There are other competing stories about who came up with the Green New Deal. Many would like to claim the mantle.

According to Grist magazine, *New York Times* columnist Thomas Friedman "started calling for a 'Green New Deal' to end fossil fuel subsidies, tax carbon dioxide emissions, and create lasting incentives for wind and solar energy" in 2007.

But, as the same Grist article reported, there is a UK tax scholar named Richard Murphy "who also claims to have coined the phrase 'Green New Deal' around the same time as Friedman." Murphy has claimed, "I don't even know who Tom Friedman is. If he used the term, it's complete coincidence."[20]

Liyu Woldemichael of the Kenan Institute for Ethics at Duke University posits a different origin for the Green New Deal: "It was in fact first proposed in 2006 by the European Greens, an incredibly progressive European party, during the global market crash." As Woldemichael explained, "The European Greens fought to address climate change and embraced an economic bill of rights. Moving from European politics to American politics, the Green New Deal became central to the Green Party with Jill Stein 2012 run for President."[21]

If at First You Don't Succeed . . .

Michael Shellenberger, who was named a "Hero of the Environment" by *Time* magazine, has detailed how he co-founded an earlier version of the Green New Deal back in 2003. "I was one of the founders of sort of the original Green New Deal between 2003 and 2007," Shellenberger

Of the People—or of the Elites?

"In a stunning revelation from a 2009 UN document titled 'Rethinking the Economic Recovery: A Global Green New Deal,' it is discovered that Alexandria Ocasio-Cortez' (AOC) Green New Deal is not a new movement of the people, but rather a crafty (and plagiarized) creation of a small group of global elite working through the United Nations," author Patrick Wood reported at Canada Free Press in 2019. "The 144-page report was headed by Edward B. Barbier, a professor of Economics and Finance at the University of Wyoming at the time, but specifically prepared for the United Nations Environment Programme (UNEP)."

The acknowledgements from the UNEP report reveals a who's who of the environmental Left involved. The report states that a "consultation meeting was held at the UN Foundation, Washington DC, February 4, 2009 with experts, amongst others, from the Center for American Progress, Pew Center on Global Climate Change, Union of Concerned Scientists, UN Foundation, World Resources Institute and the Worldwatch Institute."

Wood added: "The modern 'creators' of the Green New Deal claim that they developed it over a weekend. If true, it was only because they had a copy of 'Rethinking the Economic Recovery: A Global Green New Deal' sitting in front of them to copy text and then localizing it for the United States."[22]

revealed in 2019.[23] "In the early 2000s, my colleagues and I dusted off the Green New Deal created by [New Yorker writer Barry] Commoner and called it a 'New Apollo Project,'" Shellenberger wrote. "All of the basic elements were the same: massive taxpayer investments in renewables, organics, efficiency, mass transit, and much else in the progressive agenda that can be justified as somehow reducing emissions."[24]

The principles of climate "action" embedded in the Green New Deal came to life with the election of President Barack Obama in 2008.

As Grist magazine explained, "Presidential candidate Barack Obama added a Green New Deal to his platform. In 2009, the United Nations drafted a report calling for a Global Green New Deal to focus

Deja Vu All Over Again

"In 1930s, President Franklin Roosevelt, progressive Republicans, and Democratic socialists similarly understood the necessity of cheap energy and food for lifting people out of poverty. That essentially materialist and progressive vision continued through President Lyndon Johnson's 'Great Society' programs of the sixties. That all changed in the 1970s. It was then that Malthusian conservationists and socialists in the US and Europe argued against helping poor nations develop as they had done, with dams, fossil fuels, industrialized farming, and factories."

—environmentalist Michael Shellenberger[26]

government stimulus on renewable energy projects."[25]

Cap-and-trade climate legislation, which had gone down to defeat in Congress in 2003, 2005, and 2008, did pass the House in 2009. But the members of Congress who had voted for the cap-and-trade bill got an earful from their constituents when they went back to their home districts.

And the UN's 2009 Copenhagen Climate Summit ended up fizzling out due to the growing lack of trust in the UN climate claims after the leaked "Climategate" emails showed top UN officials colluding to keep the climate narrative alive by suppressing dissent, deleting evidence, threatening science journal editors, and avoiding Freedom of Information Act requests.

The Climategate scandal and the cost of the cap-and-trade legislation prompted many Democrat senators to pull their support, and as a result Majority Leader Harry Reid never allowed a vote on cap-and-trade in the upper house.

The Obama administration had been poised to enforce a climate-regulation scheme that would have huge costs to America's economy, liberty, and sovereignty—and that was scientifically meaningless. In fact, it was based not on science but on a superstition: that government regulations and UN treaties could regulate the climate and storminess of the Earth.

So when Climategate made it impossible to get cap-and-trade legislation passed, President Obama went the way of executive orders and green stimulus instead. And then, as Grist magazine lamented, "Big-ticket policies like a carbon tax or a cap-and-trade system and sunsetting the $20 billion in subsidies to oil, gas, and coal each year never came to fruition. Even the regulations the administration did achieve—like tightening fuel economy standards and incentivizing utilities to produce more renewable energy—disintegrated as soon as the Trump administration took over."[27]

"Is a Green New Deal likely to work? Ours didn't," Shellenberger wrote of the early attempts with his version of the plan. "People

> **"Fraud, Pure and Simple"**
> The Climategate emails showed that UN IPCC scientists were holding together the global warming narrative and the supposed scientific "consensus" that supported it by subterfuge and intimidation. The Climategate scandal opened a lot of eyes to the fact that the UN's Intergovernmental Panel on Climate Change was more political than scientific.
> "I view Climategate as science fraud, pure and simple." —Princeton physicist Robert Austin's take on the scandal that exposed the very unscientific conduct of UN IPCC scientists[28]

don't remember, President Obama—we spent about $150 billion dollars on renewables between 2009 and 2015. And we just kept encountering the same kind of problems everywhere that were related both to the essential unreliability of solar and wind. They just depend on when the sun is shining and the wind is blowing, which is 10% to 40% of the year....

"Twenty-five billion was wasted on biofuels. Tens of billions more were wasted on energy efficiency programs that cost more than they were worth. Well-connected venture capitalists got rich. Wealth was distributed upwards. And the renewables it subsidized contributed to rising electricity costs," Shellenberger said.

Solar energy has a long track record. "I traced the history back as far as it goes until I finally discovered the first call for the U.S. to invest 'hundreds of millions' for solar energy due to its 'tremendous potential.' It was made by the U.S. secretary of the interior—in 1949," Shellenberger disclosed.

Headlines from the long history of unrequited solar energy hopes is revealing, as a list put together by Shellenberger demonstrates:

> "Solar Energy: What the Sun's Rays Can Do and May Yet Be Able to Do"— The author notes that while solar is not yet economical "the day is not unlikely to arrive before long" [*Washington Star*—July 20, 1891]
>
> "Use of Solar Energy Near a Solution." "Improved Device Held to Rival Hydroelectric Production" [*New York Times*—April 4, 1931]
>
> "MIT Will 'Store' Heat of the Sun" [*New York Times*—November 5, 1939]

The history of solar power optimism goes back to at least 1833, according to Shellenberger. "In 1833, a utopian socialist German immigrant to the U.S. proposed to build massive solar power plants that used mirrors to concentrate sunlight on boilers, mile-long wind farms, and new dams to store power. 'It is just possible the world is standing at a turning point,' a *New York Times* reporter gushed in 1931, 'in the evolution of civilization....'" Shellenberger wrote. "All that was needed was a Green New Deal." [29]

CHAPTER 3

Man-Made Climate Change Is Not a Threat

Global warming hype and hysteria dominate the news media, academia, schools, the United Nations, and the U.S. government. The Green New Deal is being pushed on Capitol Hill and in the 2020 presidential race as the "solution" for an alleged "climate crisis."

School-skipping teen climate activists testify before the U.S. Congress and the United Nations, and young children are recruited for lawsuits against the U.S. government for its alleged climate "inaction."[1] The phrase "climate emergency" has emerged as the favorite for climate campaigners.[2]

But the arguments put forth by the global warming advocates grossly distort the true facts on a host of issues, ranging from rising sea levels and record temperatures to melting polar caps and disappearing polar bears.

In fact, there is no "climate crisis" or "climate emergency."

The UN, climate activists, the media, and academia are using the climate scare as an opportunity to lobby for their alleged "solutions," which require massive government expansion and central planning.

This chapter will take the reader through the facts on the claims about climate, energy, and the environment from the media, UN, and Green New Deal advocates.

Princeton professor emeritus of physics Will Happer explained why climate activists are wrong. "Aside from the human brain, the climate is the most complex thing on the planet. The number of factors that influence climate—the sun, the earth's orbital properties, oceans, clouds, and, yes, industrial man—is huge and enormously variable," Happer said.[3]

The global warming coalition can accurately be called climate change cause deniers. They deny the hundreds of causes and variables that influence climate change and instead try to pretend that carbon dioxide is the climate control knob overriding all the others factors and that every bad weather event is somehow "proof" of "global warming" and an impending climate "emergency."

The Consensus "Pulled from Thin Air"

Despite former vice president Al Gore's 2019 claim that the threat from anthropogenic climate change is "beyond consensus of 99 percent of the scientists," the facts say otherwise.[4] There is absolutely no scientific "consensus" about catastrophic man-made climate change. Claims that 97 or 99 percent of scientists agree are not backed up by any credible study or poll.

UN IPCC lead author Dr. Richard Tol has admitted, "The 97% is essentially pulled from thin air, it is not based on any credible research whatsoever."[5]

The claim that 97 percent of scientists agree is based in part on a survey of seventy-seven anonymous scientists. Not thousands of scientists or even hundreds of scientists—but seventy-seven.[6]

Scientists were quick to debunk another study, authored by blogger John Cook and claiming a 97 percent consensus of climate studies. Climatologist David Legates of the University of Delaware and three co-authors reviewed the same studies as Cook did, and their research revealed that "only 41 papers—0.3 percent of all 11,944 abstracts or 1.0 percent of the 4,014 expressing an opinion, and not 97.1 percent—had been found to endorse" the claim that human beings are to blame for a majority of the current warming.[7]

MIT climate scientist Richard Lindzen called the purported 97 percent consensus "propaganda."

Dr. Lindzen: "They never really tell you what they agree on. It is propaganda. So all scientists agree it's probably warmer now than it was at the end of the Little Ice Age. Almost all scientists agree that if you add CO2 you will have some warming. Maybe very little warming. But it is propaganda to translate that into it is dangerous and we must reduce CO2, etc."[8]

In 2017 Princeton professor emeritus of physics William Happer pointed to the parallels with the seventeenth-century "consensus" on witches. "I don't see a whole lot of difference between the consensus on climate change and the consensus on witches. At the witch trials in Salem the judges were educated at Harvard. This was supposedly 100 percent science. The one or two people who said there were no witches were immediately hung. Not much has changed," Happer quipped.

Carbon Dioxide Is Not the "Control Knob" of the Climate

There is a lack of connection between higher levels of CO2 and warming. During the Ice Age, CO2 levels were ten times higher than they are today.[9]

There are many, many factors that impact climate—including volcanoes, wind oscillations, solar activity, ocean cycles, volcanoes, the tilt of the Earth's axis, and land use. CO2 is just one factor, not the control knob of the climate.

University of Pennsylvania geologist Dr. Robert Giegengack has declared, "CO2 is not the villain that it has been portrayed."

Today's levels of roughly four hundred parts per million (PPM) of CO2 are not alarming. In geologic terms, today's CO2 levels are among the lowest in earth's history.[10]

"Climate change is governed by hundreds of factors, or variables, and the very idea that we can manage climate change predictably by understanding and manipulating at the margins one politically selected factor (CO_2), is as misguided as it gets. It's scientific nonsense," University of London professor emeritus Philip Stott has noted.

Atmospheric scientist Hendrik Tennekes, a pioneer in the development of numerical weather prediction and former director of research at the Netherlands' Royal National Meteorological Institute, declared: "I protest vigorously the idea that the climate reacts like a home heating system to a changed setting of the thermostat: just turn the dial, and the desired temperature will soon be reached."[11]

According to Greenpeace co-founder Dr. Patrick Moore: "We had both higher temperatures and an ice age at a time when CO2 emissions were 10 times higher than they are today."

MIT climate scientist Lindzen's 2020 study debunked the "implausible claim that a change in one variable—CO2—is predominantly responsible for altering global temperatures."[12] The study, which was published in the *European Physical Journal*, found that a "doubled- CO2 effect has less than 1/5th of the impact that the net cloud effect has. And yet we are asked to accept the 'implausible' claim that change in one variable, CO2, is predominantly responsible for altering global temperatures."

There Is No "Climate Emergency"

Princeton physicist Will Happer, a former science advisor in the Trump administration, ripped the claims of a "climate emergency" in 2019. "We are here [at the UN climate summit in Madrid] under false pretenses, wasting our time talking about a non-existent 'climate emergency,'" Happer explained. "It's hard to understand how much further the shrillness can go as this started out as 'global warming' then it was 'climate change' or 'global weirding', 'climate crisis', 'climate emergency'. What next? But stick around it will happen. I hope sooner or later enough people recognize the holiness of this bizarre environmental cult and bring it to an end."[13]

University of Colorado's Roger Pielke Jr. explained how the UN has helped shape the hysterical nonsense of a "climate emergency." The UN IPCC switched to "extreme scenarios" in their most recent report and thus "helped to create the climate apocalypse, a scary but imaginary future," Pielke explained in 2019. "The decision by the IPCC to center its fifth assessment report on its most extreme scenario has been incredibly consequential. Thousands of academic studies of the future impacts of climate change followed the lead of the IPCC, and have emphasized the most extreme scenario as 'business as usual' which is often interpreted and promoted as where the world is heading."

Pielke added, "The bottom line for today is to understand that a fateful decision by the UN IPCC to selectively anoint an extreme scenario from among a huge range of possible futures has helped to create the climate apocalypse, a scary but imaginary future."[14]

Actress Barbra Streisand helped pioneer the phrase "climate emergency" back in 2005. "Al Gore passionately stressed that our world no longer has a climate problem, we are in a climate emergency," said Streisand. She told ABC's Diane Sawyer that we were "in a global warming emergency state."[15]

The 2018 federal National Climate Assessment warned of dire consequences from man-made global warming. But even a cursory reading of the National Climate Assessment reveals that it was written by environmental activists and overseen by President Obama's former UN Paris climate pact negotiator, Andrew Light. The National Climate Assessment is a political report masquerading as science. The media hyped a rehash of frightening climate change claims by Obama administration holdover activist government scientists. The National Climate Assessment report reads like a press release from environmental pressure groups—because it is. Two key authors are longtime Union of Concerned Scientist activists, Donald Wuebbles and Katharine Hayhoe. The government is paying our National Academy of

Sciences (NAS) to come up with alarming report with a bunch of scary climate computer models. (NAS is almost entirely dependent on federal funding.)[16]

The End Is Nigh!

Green New Deal–pusher Alexandria Ocasio-Cortez (AOC) famously predicted in 2019, "We're Like the World Is Going to End in 12 Years if We Don't Address Climate Change."[17]

But relax. AOC is wrong.

Dire predictions about climate tipping points date back to at least 1864. "As early as 1864 George Perkins Marsh, sometimes said to be the father of American ecology, warned that the earth was 'fast becoming an unfit home for its "noblest inhabitant,"' and he warned of 'climatic excess, as to threaten the depravation, barbarism, and perhaps even extinction of the species.'"[18]

In 1989, the United Nations was already trying to sell their "tipping point" rhetoric to the public. According to a 1989 AP article, "A senior U.N. environmental official says entire nations could be wiped off the face of the Earth by rising sea levels if the global warming trend is not reversed by the year 2000. Coastal flooding and crop failures would create an exodus of 'eco-refugees,' threatening political chaos."

It's difficult to keep up with whether it is hours, days, months, or years until the climate apocalypse arrives. Here are a few recent examples of alarmists predicting "tipping points" of various durations.

> Hours—Flashback March 2009: "'We Have Hours' to Prevent Climate Disaster," declared Elizabeth May of the Canadian Green Party.[19]
>
> Days—Flashback October 2009: UK's Gordon Brown warns of global warming "catastrophe"; only "50 days to save world."[20]
>
> Months—Flashback July 2009: Prince Charles claimed a ninety-six-month tipping point in July 2009.[21]

Years—Flashback 2009: NASA's James Hansen declared Obama only "has four years to save Earth."[22]

Decades—Flashback 1982: UN official Mostafa Tolba, executive director of the UN Environment Program (UNEP), warned on May 11, 1982, that the "world faces an ecological disaster as final as nuclear war within a couple of decades unless governments act now."[23]

A Millennium—Flashback June 2010: a thousand years' delay: Green Guru James Lovelock: "Climate change may not happen as fast as we thought, and we may have 1,000 years to sort it out."[24]

Perhaps the best summary of the tipping-point phenomenon comes from UK scientist Philip Stott: "In essence, the Earth has been given a 10-year survival warning regularly for the last fifty or so years. We have been serially doomed."[25]

Mass Extinction!

And despite the claims of a 2019 UN report, climate change is not driving a mass extinction event.

Climate analyst Kenneth Richard rebutted the report: "During the last few hundred years, species extinctions primarily occurred due to habitat loss and predator introduction on islands. Extinctions have not been linked to a warming climate or higher CO_2 levels. In fact, since the 1870s, species extinction rates have been plummeting." He added that there is "no clear link between mass extinctions and CO_2-induced or sudden-onset warming events."[26]

Der Spiegel's Axel Bojanowski reported, "The IPCC admits that there is no evidence climate change has led to even a single species becoming extinct thus far. At most, the draft report says, climate change may have played a role in the disappearance of a few amphibians, freshwater fish and mollusks. Yet even the icons of catastrophic global warming, the polar bears, are doing surprisingly well."

"If You Believe in Magic..."

MIT climate scientist Richard Lindzen said that believing CO_2 controls the climate "is pretty close to believing in magic." As Lindzen explained, "Doubling CO_2 involves a 2% perturbation to this budget. So do minor changes in clouds and other features, and such changes are common. In this complex multifactor system, what is the likelihood of the climate (which, itself, consists in many variables and not just globally averaged temperature anomaly) is controlled by this 2% perturbation in a single variable? Believing this is pretty close to believing in magic."[27]

CO_2 is not "pollution." The term "carbon pollution" is unscientific and misleading. Carbon dioxide—CO_2—is a harmless trace essential gas in the atmosphere that humans exhale (after inhaling oxygen).

Princeton professor William Happer testified to the U.S. Congress: "Warming and increased CO_2 will be good for mankind....CO_2 is not a pollutant and it is not a poison and we should not corrupt the English language by depriving 'pollutant' and 'poison' of their original meaning."[28]

As Happer also pointed out, "To call carbon dioxide a pollutant is really Orwellian. You are calling something a pollutant that we all produce. Where does that lead us eventually?"[29]

A 2016 study published in the journal *Nature Climate Change* found that "Carbon Dioxide Fertilization" was in fact "Greening Earth." The research revealed, "From a quarter to half of Earth's vegetated lands has shown significant greening over the last 35 years largely due to rising levels of atmospheric carbon dioxide."

The Hottest Year EVAH!

Global temperatures have been holding nearly steady for almost two decades, according to satellites from the Remote Sensing Systems (RSS) and the University of Alabama at Huntsville (UAH).[30]

Many peer-reviewed studies have found the Medieval Warm Period and the Roman Warming Period were as warm as or warmer than current temperatures.[31]

Climatologist Pat Michaels explained that the world's current temperature "should be near the top of the record given the record only begins in the late 19th century when the surface temperature was still reverberating from the Little Ice Age."[32]

So-called "hottest year" claims—based on surface data dating only back to the nineteenth century—are political statements designed to persuade the public that the government needs to take action on man-made climate change.[33] In addition, temperature revisions made by NASA and NOAA have enhanced the "warming" trend by retroactively cooling the past.[34]

"While NOAA/NASA claims 2019 as the 'second warmest year ever,' other data shows 2019 cooler than 2005 for the USA," noted meteorologist Anthony Watts, who analyzes temperature surface station data.[35]

In his 2018 *State of the Climate Report*, Norwegian professor Ole Humlum explained, "After the warm year of 2016, temperatures last year (in 2018) continued to fall back to levels of the so-called warming 'pause' of 2000–2015. There is no sign of any acceleration in global temperature, hurricanes or sea-level rise. These empirical observations show no sign of acceleration whatsoever."[36]

Professor Humlum's 2020 report found that the global temperature in 2019 was "cooler than 2016....In 2019, the average global air temperature was affected by a moderate El Niño episode, interrupting a gradual global air temperature decrease following the strong 2015–16 El Niño."[37]

While global warming proponents declared 2005, 2010, 2015, and 2016 all to be "hottest years" or "near-hottest," based on heavily altered surface data, a closer examination revealed that the claims were "based on year-to-year temperature data that differs by only a few HUN-DREDTHS of a degree to tenths of a degree Fahrenheit—differences that were within the margin of error in the data."[38]

MIT climate scientist Richard Lindzen ridiculed "hottest year" claims. "The uncertainty here is tenths of a degree. It's just nonsense. This is a very tiny change period," Lindzen said. "If you can adjust temperatures to 2/10ths of a degree, it means it wasn't certain to 2/10ths of a degree."

Award-winning climate scientist Lennart Bengtsson has stated, "We are creating great anxiety without it being justified.... There are no indications that the warming is so severe that we need to panic.... The warming we have had the last 100 years is so small that if we didn't have meteorologists and climatologists to measure it we wouldn't have noticed it at all."[39]

Prominent Scientists Bail Out

Nobel Prize–winning scientist Ivar Giaever, who endorsed Barack Obama, called the president "ridiculous" and "dead wrong" on global warming: "Global warming is a non-problem.... I say this to Obama: Excuse me, Mr. President, but you're wrong. Dead wrong." Dr. Giaever also said, "Global warming really has become a new religion."[40]

Climate scientist Anastasios Tsonis retired, and then declared, "I am a skeptic" in 2019. Tsonis, a distinguished professor emeritus at the University of Wisconsin-Milwaukee who has authored more than 130 peer-reviewed papers and nine books, said, "I am a skeptic not just about global warming but also about many other aspects of science.... Climate is too complicated to attribute its variability to one cause.... The fact that scientists who show results not aligned with the mainstream are labeled deniers is the backward mentality. We don't live in medieval times."[41]

Prominent climate activist Michael Shellenberger officially recanted in 2020: "On Behalf of Environmentalists, I Apologize for the Climate Scare."

The former *Time* magazine "Hero of the Environment" explained, "On behalf of environmentalists everywhere, I would like to formally apologize for the climate scare we created over the last 30 years. Climate change is happening. It's just not the end of the world. It's not even our most serious environmental problem.... I feel an obligation to apologize for how badly we environmentalists have misled the public."[42]

UN IPCC Japanese scientist Dr. Kiminori Itoh, an award-winning environmental physical chemist, said that global warming fears are the "worst scientific scandal in history.... When people come to know what the truth is, they will feel deceived by science and scientists."[43]

UN IPCC lead author Richard Tol ripped the warmist narrative: "It disturbs me hearing people like Al Gore say that he is worried about the future of his grandchildren. Complete madness."[44]

"Rivers and Seas Are Boiling!"

Ocean levels have been rising since the last Ice Age. Global sea levels have been naturally rising for ~20,000 years. There is no evidence of an acceleration of ocean-level rise, and therefore no evidence of any effect of mankind on sea levels. According to tide gauges, ocean levels are rising less than the thickness of one nickel (1.95 mm thick) per year or about the thickness of one penny (1.52 mm thick) a year.[45]

The 2018 "State of the Climate Report" by Norwegian professor Ole Humlum explained, "Data from tide gauges all over the world suggest an average global sea-level rise of 1–1.5 mm/year, while the satellite record suggests a rise of about 3.2 mm/year. The large difference between the two data sets still has no broadly accepted explanation."[46]

As former NASA climatologist Dr. Roy Spencer's research has shown, "Sea level rise, which was occurring long before humans could be blamed, has not accelerated and still amounts to only 1 inch every 10 years."[47]

University of Pennsylvania geologist Robert Giegengack has said, "At the present rate of sea-level rise it's going to take 3,500 years to get up there [to Al Gore's predicted rise of 20 feet]. So if for some reason this warming process that melts ice is cutting loose and accelerating, sea level doesn't know it. And sea level, we think, is the best indicator of global warming."[48]

Spencer's research on Miami flooding and sea-level rise found "that flooding is mostly a combination of 1) natural sea level rise (I show there has been no acceleration of sea level rise beyond what was already happening since the 1800s), and 2) satellite-measured sinking of the reclaimed swamps that have been built upon for over 100 years in Miami Beach."

Polar Bears *Are* Disappearing...from Al Gore Films

A 2019 study found that polar bears are "thriving" and their numbers may have "quadrupled." In *The Polar Bear Catastrophe That Never Happened*, a book published by the Global Warming Policy Foundation (GWPF), evolutionary biologist and paleozoologist Susan Crockford of the University of Victoria reported, "My scientific estimates make perfect sense and they tally with what the Inuit and other Arctic residents are seeing on the ground. Almost everywhere polar bears come into contact with people, they are much more common than they used to be. It's a wonderful conservation success story."[49]

Crockford found in her study that despite a 2007 prediction of "a 67% decline in global polar bear numbers," bear populations have increased to the highest levels in recent decades.[50]

The report revealed, "The US Geological Survey estimated the global population of polar bears at 24,500 in 2005. In 2015, the IUCN Polar Bear Specialist Group estimated the population at 26,000 (range 22,000–31,000) but additional surveys published 2015–2017 brought the total to near 28,500. However, data published in 2018 brought that number to almost 29,5009 with a relatively wide margin of error. This is the highest global estimate since the bears were protected by international treaty in 1973."[51]

She pointed out, "Polar bears have survived several episodes of much warmer climate over the last 10,000 years than exists today....There is no evidence to suggest that the polar bear or its food supply is in danger of disappearing entirely with increased Arctic warming, regardless of the dire fairy-tale scenarios predicted by computer models."[52]

The International Union for the Conservation of Nature 2017 estimate of the current polar bear population is "the highest estimate in 50 years."[53]

The polar bear catastrophe that never happened has been so embarrassing that Al Gore, after helping make the bears the poster child of his cause in his first film, failed to mention them once in his 2017 sequel.

Not-So-Extreme Weather Events

In 2017 Roger Pielke Jr. of the University of Colorado testified to Congress there was simply "'no evidence' that hurricanes, floods, droughts, tornadoes are increasing."[54]

A 2020 study by Pielke published in the journal *Environmental Hazards* found that the "evidence signal of human-caused climate change in the form of increased global economic losses from more frequent or more intense weather extremes has not yet been detected."[55]

On nearly every metric, extreme weather is on either no trend or a declining trend on climate timescales. Even the UN IPCC admitted in a 2018 special report that extreme weather events have not increased. The IPCC's special report found that "there is only low confidence regarding changes in global tropical cyclone numbers under global warming over the last four decades."[56] The IPCC report also concluded "low confidence in the sign of drought trends since 1950 at global scale."

Pielke testified to Congress on the current state of weather extremes, "It is misleading, and just plain incorrect, to claim that disasters associated with hurricanes, tornadoes, floods, or droughts have increased on climate timescales either in the United States or globally."[57]

Floods

A 2017 study on floods found "approximately the number expected due to chance alone."[58]

Another 2017 study in the *Journal of Hydrology* found no increase in global floods: "Compelling evidence for increased flooding at a global scale is lacking."[59]

A 2019 study found that the world is the safest from climate-related disasters that it has ever been: "A decreasing trend in both human and economic vulnerability is evident. Global average mortality and loss rates have dropped by 6.5 and nearly 5 times, respectively, from 1980 to 1989 to 2007–2016. Results also show a clear negative relation between vulnerability and wealth."[60]

Climatologist John Christy has explained why the extreme weather claims are unscientific: "The non-falsifiable hypotheses can be stated this way, 'whatever happens is consistent with my hypothesis.' In other words, there is no event that would 'falsify' the hypothesis. As such, these assertions cannot be considered science or in any way informative since the hypothesis' fundamental prediction is 'anything may happen.' In the example above if winters become milder or they become snowier, the non-falsifiable hypothesis stands. This is not science."[61]

Tornadoes

Big tornadoes have dropped in frequency since the 1950s. The years 2012–2018 all saw at- or near-record low tornado counts in the U.S.[62] Twenty nineteen, on the other hand, was a more active tornado year, with the most tornadoes since 2011 and the deadliest tornado season of the previous five.[63] And 2020 saw below average activity in the U.S. Meteorologist Paul Dorian reported, "In terms of tornado activity in the U.S. during 2020, the year will end up below-normal and, fortunately, this year has featured no EF-5 tornadoes which are the most powerful of all."[64] "The annual incidence of all U.S. tornadoes from 1954 to 2017 is shown in the figure below. It's obvious that no trend exists over a period that included both cooling and warming spells," wrote physicist Ralph B. Alexander in a 2020 analysis entitled "No Evidence That Climate Change Causes Weather Extremes."

Hurricanes

An August 2019 NOAA statement concluded, "It is premature to conclude…that global warming has already had a detectable impact on hurricane activity." The NOAA statement added that U.S. landfalling hurricanes "'show a slight negative trend' since 'late 1800s.'"[65]

Norwegian professor Ole Humlum explained in his 2020 *State of the Climate Report*: "Tropical storms and hurricanes have displayed large

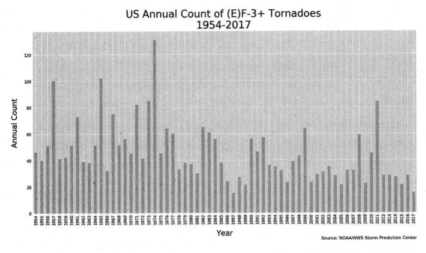

"The figure depicts the number of strong (EF3 or greater) tornadoes observed in the U.S. each year during the same period from 1954 to 2017. Clearly, the trend is downward instead of upward; the average number of strong tornadoes annually from 1986 to 2017 was 40% less than from 1954 to 1985. Once more, global warming cannot have played a role. The most ferocious tornado outbreak ever recorded, spawning a total of 30 EF4 or EF5 tornadoes, was in 1974."[66]

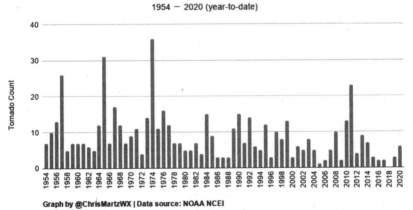

The data from 1954 to 2020 shows that the most violent tornadoes are declining.
Courtesy of Chris Martz

annual variations in accumulated cyclone energy (ACE) since 1970, but there has been no overall trend towards either lower or higher activity. The same applies for the number of continental hurricane landfalls in the USA, in a record going back to 1851."[67]

In 2019, extreme-weather expert Roger Pielke Jr. noted that the federal National Climate Assessment released in 2018 ignored one of its own expert reviewers, who wrote: "National Hurricane Center going back to the 1800s data clearly indicate a drop in the decadal rate of US landfalling hurricanes since the 1960s...instead you spin the topic to make it sound like the trends are all towards more cyclones."[68]

The WMO (World Meteorological Organization) said, "No observational studies have provided convincing evidence of a detectable anthropogenic influence specifically on hurricane-related precipitation." The WMO assessment concluded that "anthropogenic signals are not yet clearly detectable in observations for most TC (tropical cyclones) metrics."[69]

A study by NOAA hurricane researcher Chris Landsea found that "only 2 of these [recent] 10 Category 5s would have been recorded as Cat 5 if they had occurred during the late-1940s period."[70]

Hurricane Maria, which hit Puerto Rico in 2017, with the eighth-lowest landfall pressure (917 MB) on record in the Atlantic Basin, was not an unprecedented storm. Meteorologist Anthony Watts noted, "With Irma ranked 7th, and Harvey ranked 18th, it's going to be tough for climate alarmists to try connecting these two storms to being driven by CO_2/global warming. But they'll do it anyway."

Pielke noted in 2019 that the "13 yrs ending 2018 had fewest Cat 3+ USA landfalls since 1900 with 3....3 periods had 12, most recently 1915–1927. 13 yrs ending in 2018 saw a 14 total Cat 1+ (tied 2nd fewest). The most? 33: 1938–1950."[71]

Meteorologist Paul Dorian noted that despite a very active Atlantic hurricane season in 2020, the "Pacific hurricane season was well below normal" and overall global hurricane activity was "below normal."[72]

Climate analyst Kenneth Richard's 2018 survey of scientific literature found, "The peer-reviewed scientific literature robustly affirms that land-falling hurricane frequencies and intensities have remained steady or declined in recent decades. So have droughts, floods, and other extreme weather events."

Atmospheric research scientist Philip Klotzbach's research also found no trend in global accumulated cyclone energy (ACE) in the past thirty years.[73]

Droughts Aren't Getting Worse, Either— and Neither Are Wildfires

"Droughts have, for the most part, become shorter, less frequent, and cover a smaller portion of the U.S. over the last century," Professor Roger Pielke Jr. observed.[74]

NOAA (National Oceanic and Atmospheric Administration) has concluded there is "no trend in global droughts since 1950." Other studies found "a decline in drought levels in recent decades," noted the Global Warming Policy Forum in 2020. "The IPCC says it is hard to say ('low confidence') whether global drought has become better or worse since 1950," said the GWPF.[75]

A 2015 study found that megadroughts in the past two thousand years were worse and lasted longer than current droughts.[76]

There is "less fire today than centuries ago," as scientists and multiple studies counter the claim that wildfires are due to "climate change."

As I lay out in *The Politically Incorrect Guide to Climate Change,*

> A 2016 study published by the Royal Society reported, "Indeed there is increasing evidence that there is overall less fire in the landscape today than there has been centuries ago, although the magnitude of this reduction still needs to be examined in more detail.... The 'wildfire problem' is essentially more a social than a natural one."[77]

In the United States, wildfires are also due in part to a failure to thin forests or remove dead and diseased trees. In 2014, forestry professor David B. South of Auburn University testified to the U.S. Senate Environment and Public Works Committee that "data suggest that extremely large megafires were four-times more common before 1940," adding that "we cannot reasonably say that anthropogenic global warming causes extremely large wildfires." As he explained, "To attribute this human-caused increase in fire risk to carbon dioxide emissions is simply unscientific."[78]

"It's Like a Heat Wave!"

Multiple studies find that long-term data show extreme heat waves in the United States have decreased since the 1930s.[79] A study published in the *Journal of Applied Meteorology and Climatology* found that extreme heat waves in the United States decreased from 1930 to 2010. According to the authors, "Several daily maximum [extreme heat events]

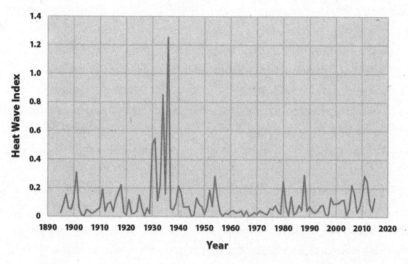

EPA: "This figure shows the annual values of the U.S. Heat Wave Index from 1895 to 2015."

near the 1930's led to 1930-2010 trends of daily maximum [extreme heat events] decreasing." The overall trend of U.S. heat waves saw a decline from the 1930s until the 1970s global cooling and the coming–ice age scare, followed by a warming with temperatures still not up to levels seen in the 1930s in the U.S.[80]

University of Alabama climate scientist John Christy's research has found that "about 75% of the states recorded their hottest temperature prior to 1955, and over 50 percent of the states experienced their record cold temperatures after 1940."[81]

Data from the Environmental Protection Agency agree. The EPA website features a 2016 chart labeled "the U.S. Heat Wave Index from 1895 to 2015," and it reveals that the worst U.S. heat waves by far happened in the 1930s.[82]

"Melting, Melting—Oh What a World!"

A 2015 NASA study found that Antarctica was not losing ice mass and "not currently contributing to sea level rise."[83] NASA glaciologist Jay Zwally is working on a paper that will show the eastern ice sheet is expanding at a rate that's enough to at least offset increased losses in the west. The ice sheets are "very close to balance right now," Zwally has said.[84]

A 2017 NASA study found volcanic activity is heating up the western portion of the continent's ice sheet.[85]

Other Antarctica ice studies receive lots of media hype, but miss the key scientific significance.

A 2019 hyped study that alleged a six-times increase in Antarctic ice melt was found to be "statistically insignificant" by climate analysts. "Such a tiny loss in comparison to the total mass of the ice sheet, it's microscopic.... insignificant," writes Anthony Watts.[86]

A 2019 study in the *Journal of Geophysical Research: Atmospheres* found that the West Antarctic ice sheet was growing. The ice saw a "significantly positive trend" in the twentieth century.

The Associated Press has a long history of hyping alleged catastrophic Antarctic melt fears. The AP recycled the same scary Antarctic melt claims from 2014, 1990, 1979, 1922, and 1901.[87] Meanwhile, at the other pole of the planet, a 2019 study revealed that the Arctic region was 4.6°C warmer during the decade of the 1930s than today.[88]

Recent Arctic ice changes are not proof of man-made global warming, nor are they unprecedented, unusual, or cause for alarm, according to experts and multiple peer-reviewed studies.[89]

A study published in 2017 in the *Hydrological Sciences Journal* found that Arctic sea ice extent grew during the 1940s to about 1980 before declining. "The recent period of Arctic sea ice retreat since the 1970s followed a period of sea ice growth after the mid-1940s, which in turn followed a period of sea ice retreat after the 1910s." The study found that the start of the satellite era monitoring of Arctic ice in the late 1970s "coincided with the end of several decades during which Arctic sea ice extent was generally increasing."[90]

Norwegian professor Ole Humlum explained in his 2020 *State of the Climate Report*: "Since 1979, Arctic and Antarctic sea-ice extents have had opposite trends, decreasing and increasing, respectively."[91]

Dr. Jochem Marotzke, who has been director of the German Max Planck Institute for Meteorology in Hamburg since 2003, dismissed Greenland melt fears in 2020. "It's gonna take so long—a couple thousand years. I don't see any risk with Greenland," Marotzke said.[92]

A 2019 study of sea surface temperatures in Greenland between 1796 and 2013 found warmer temperatures from the 1920s to the 1940s: "Temperatures were warmer than today in the 1920s and 1940s and even briefly during the 1800s," Kenneth Richard wrote of the study, which was published in the American Geophysical Union's journal *Paleoceanography and Paleoclimatology*.[93]

As climatologist Pat Michals said in 2016, "Humans just can't make it warm enough up there to melt all that much ice."[94]

In 2019, NBC News reported, "A Major Greenland Glacier That Was One of the Fastest Shrinking Ice and Snow Masses on Earth Is Growing Again, a New NASA Study Finds."[95]

A 2006 peer-reviewed study published in the *Journal of Geophysical Research* concluded, "The warmest year in the extended Greenland temperature record is 1941, while the 1930s and 1940s are the warmest decades."[96]

Another study the same year, by Danish researchers from Aarhus University, found that "Greenland's glaciers have been shrinking for the past century, suggesting that the ice melt is not a recent phenomenon caused by global warming." Glaciologist Jacob Clement Yde pointed out, "Seventy percent of the glaciers have been shrinking regularly since the end of the 1880s."[97]

Projections Are Not Evidence

The scientific fact is that heralded "state-of-the-art" climate models can "show" any outcome their creator wants them to. Even Penn State climate activist professor Michael Mann admitted in 2017: "Predictions can never be 'falsifiable' in the present: We must ultimately wait to see whether they come true."[98]

Prominent scientists have exposed the climate model con. In 2007, top UN IPCC scientist Jim Renwick admitted that climate models do not account for half the variability in nature and thus are not reliable. "Half of the variability in the climate system is not predictable, so we don't expect to do terrifically well," Renwick conceded.[99]

Former UN IPCC reviewer and climate researcher Vincent Gray of New Zealand, the author of more than one hundred scientific publications and an expert reviewer on every single draft of the IPCC reports going back to 1990, had declared that IPCC claims are "dangerous unscientific nonsense," because "all the [UN IPCC does] is make 'projections' and 'estimates.' No climate model has ever been properly tested, which is what 'validation' means, and their 'projections' are nothing more than the opinions of 'experts' with a conflict of interest, because they are paid to produce the models."

Atmospheric scientist Hendrik Tennekes, former director of research at the Netherlands' Royal National Meteorological Institute and a pioneer in the development of numerical weather prediction, rejected the overemphasis on climate models. "I am of the opinion that most scientists engaged in the design, development, and tuning of climate models are in fact software engineers. They are unlicensed, hence unqualified to sell their products to society," Tennekes wrote.

No, Global Warming Is Not a National Security Threat

The data reveal that warm periods coincide with less conflict—which helps explain why, in 1974, the CIA claimed that "global cooling" would cause conflict and terrorism.[100]

The Center for Strategic and International Studies report pointed out that the truth is the opposite of recent claims regarding "global warming" and war: "Since the dawn of civilization, warmer eras have meant fewer wars."[101]

The proposed climate "solution" of the Green New Deal is a threat to U.S. national security as the plan would only serve to shrink U.S. energy production and increase our dependence on Middle Eastern oil and force us to rely on energy from other potentially hostile nations, which could increase the odds of future wars.

Climate activist Robert F. Kennedy Jr. (RFK Jr.) has explained in 2020 that "American wars have been, to a greater or lesser extent, strategic struggles over control of coal ports, shipping routes and oil fields." Kennedy added, "Protecting American oil and coal resources and ports became a raison d'être for an endless parade of new American wars and interventions."[102]

But what climate activists like RFK Jr. fail to comprehend, is that a policy that promotes a massive expansion of U.S. domestic energy production is one of the best safeguards against going to war over energy supplies. The Trump administration actually achieved energy independence and dominance as the U.S. exceeded energy imports in 2019 for the first time since 1952 and U.S. energy production exceeded energy consumption in 2019 for the first time since 1957.[103]

The Green New Deal is bad for America's national security because its goal is to either place more restrictions or eliminate altogether American drilling, mining, fracking, pipelines and energy extraction. The GND will result in more reliance on conflict energy from such places as the Middle East, Venezuela, and China, where human rights and environmental protection may be less than desirable.

"Shutting down U.S. energy supplies means dependence on Middle East oil, which means a permanent state of war for the Military Industrial Complex," climate skeptic Tony Heller wrote in 2020.[104]

The GND with its restrictions on fossil fuels and mandates on solar, wind, and electric vehicles will result in the U.S. losing both energy independence and dominance, and the GND will further increase U.S. dependence on rare earth mining operated by China and Russia.

"China, for example, supplies about 90% of rare-earths for the world. On the cobalt front, China has also quietly gained control over more than 90% of the battery industry's cobalt refining, without which the raw ore is useless. Russia is a massive nickel producer," explained energy analyst Mark P. Mills of the Manhattan Institute.[105]

If We Had a Problem, This "Solution" Wouldn't Solve It

A 2019 study by the American Enterprise Institute found that the Green New Deal would have "no effect" on climate change: "In total, completely enacted, funded, and efficiently meeting goals—things AEI does not anticipate the GND would ever do—the full plan would cut the global increase in temperature by a whopping "0.083 to 0.173 degrees"— a number that is "barely distinguishable from zero."[106]

In 2019, climatologist Patrick Michaels ran the Green New Deal through the National Center for Atmospheric Research's so-called "MAGICC" climate model simulator, developed with funding from the Environmental Protection Agency. The result? "I seriously think the effect would at best—be barely detectable in the climate record," Patrick Michaels explained. "The year-to-year variation is very close to the total amount of warming that would be 'saved' by 2100, according to EPA's own model."[107]

Would anyone purchase fire insurance on their home that had a huge upfront premium for virtually no payout if your home burned down? If you answered yes to such an "insurance" policy, then the Green new Deal is the deal for you. If we actually did face a man-made climate crisis and we had to rely on the U.S. Congress or the United Nations to save us, we would all be doomed.

University of Pennsylvania geologist Robert Giegengack noted, "None of the strategies that have been offered by the U.S. government or by the EPA or by anybody else has the remotest chance of altering climate if in fact climate is controlled by carbon dioxide."[108]

In 2017 Danish statistician Bjørn Lomborg, the president of the Copenhagen Consensus Center, noted of the UN Paris Agreement: "We will spend at least one hundred trillion dollars in order to reduce the temperature by the end of the century by a grand total of three tenths of one degree...the equivalent of postponing warming by less than four years.... Again, that is using the UN's own climate prediction model." Lomborg added, "If the U.S. delivers for the whole century on President Obama's very ambitious rhetoric, it would postpone global warming by about eight months at the end of the century."

In 2015 President Obama's EPA chief admitted the regulations have no measurable climate impact—but still defended them as "enormously beneficial" for their symbolic effect.[109]

Former Obama Department of Energy assistant secretary Charles McConnell slammed EPA climate regulations as "falsely sold as impactful." He pointed out, "All U.S. annual emissions will be offset by 3 weeks of Chinese emissions."[110]

"Go to Jail, Go Directly to Jail"

Given the facts, it's no wonder alarmists don't want to debate skeptics. Instead, prominent climate activists now call for jailing their critics. In

2014, Robert F. Kennedy Jr. declared climate skeptics "ought to be serving time for it."

Bill Nye "the Science Guy" also entertained the idea of jailing climate skeptics for "affecting my quality of life" in 2016, while U.S. senators and top UN scientists called for RICO-style charges against skeptics.[111]

A Danish academic even suggested that the UN might use military force to enforce the climate agenda.[112] In a 2019 interview Professor Ole Wæver, an international relations professor at the University of Copenhagen, warned, "If there was something that was decided internationally by some more centralized procedure and every country was told 'this is your emission target, it's not negotiable, we can actually take military measures if you don't fulfil it', then you would basically have to get that down the throat of your population, whether they like it or not."[113]

The UN and EPA regulations are pure climate symbolism designed to promote a more centrally planned energy economy. The Green New Deal is simply a vehicle to put politicians and bureaucrats in charge of our economy on the pretense of saving us from bad weather.

Letting the Cat out of the Bag

UN official Ottmar Edenhofer, co-chair of the IPCC Working Group III, admitted what's behind the climate issue: "One must say clearly that we redistribute de facto the world's wealth by climate policy.... One has to free oneself from the illusion that international climate policy is environmental policy. This has almost nothing to do with environmental policy anymore."[114]

In 2009, former vice president Al Gore touted U.S. cap-and-trade legislation as a method to help bring about "global governance."[115]

UN climate chief Christiana Figueres declared in 2012 that she is seeking a "centralized transformation" that is "going to make the life of everyone on the planet very different."[116]

Greta Thunberg explained in 2019, "The climate crisis is not just about the environment. It is a crisis of human rights, of justice, and of political will. Colonial, racist, and patriarchal systems of oppression have created and fueled it. We need to dismantle them all. Our political leaders can no longer shirk their responsibilities."[117]

Environmentalist George Monbiot, an advisor to Thunberg, said in 2019 that in order to prevent "climate breakdown," a complete change to our way of life has to occur: "We've got to go straight to the heart of capitalism and overthrow it."[118]

Climatologist Judith Curry warned in 2019 of the UN-led "drive to manufacture a scientific consensus" and the "tremendous political pressure on scientists" to support policy-making goals.

Curry explained,

> For the past three decades, the climate policy "cart" has been way out in front of the scientific 'horse'. The 1992 Climate Change treaty was signed by 190 countries before the balance of scientific evidence suggested even a discernible observed human influence on global climate. The 1997 Kyoto Protocol was implemented before we had any confidence that most of the recent warming was caused by humans. There has been tremendous political pressure on the scientists to present findings that would support these treaties, which has resulted in a drive to manufacture a scientific consensus on the dangers of man-made climate change. Fossil fuel emissions as the climate "control knob" is a simple and seductive idea. However this is a misleading oversimplification, since climate can shift naturally in unexpected ways.... We have no idea how natural climate variability (solar, volcanoes, ocean circulations) will play out in the 21st century, and whether or not natural variability will dominate over man-made warming.[119]

Climatologist Roy Spencer wrote, "Global warming and climate change, even if it is 100 percent caused by humans, is so slow that it cannot be observed by anyone in their lifetime. Hurricanes, tornadoes, floods, droughts, and other natural disasters have yet to show any obvious long-term change. This means that in order for politicians to advance policy goals (such as forcing expensive solar energy on the masses or creating a carbon tax), they have to turn normal weather disasters into 'evidence' of climate change."[120]

CHAPTER 4

The Details of the Deal

There is nothing essentially new about the Green New Deal. "Global warming" is merely the latest alleged environmental scare that is pushed to promote the same tired "solutions." The climate alarmists are using what Al Gore called "torqued up" language to urge quick imposition of their desired policies, purportedly to protect us from a "climate emergency."

The Green New Deal is "going to require a lot of rapid change that we don't even conceive of as possible right now," declared Democrat congresswoman Alexandria Ocasio-Cortez (AOC) of New York on *60 Minutes* in 2019.

AOC has acknowledged that her "deal" will require "massive government intervention." NPR's Steve Inskeep in February 2019 asked Ocasio-Cortez whether her critics were correct about the size of the Green New Deal. "Are you prepared to put on the table that, 'Yes actually they're right, what this requires is massive government intervention'?"

"It does, it does, yeah, I have no problem saying that," Ocasio-Cortez answered.[1]

The current Green New Deal debuted on the national stage in 2018 after the election of AOC and the other members of "the squad" to the

116th Congress. Democrat representatives Ilhan Omar of Minnesota, Ayanna Pressley of Massachusetts, and Rashida Tlaib of Michigan are the other three "squad" members representing the progressive wing of the Democratic Party that often clashes with the party leadership.

AOC achieved a huge upset victory during the 2018 midterm elections, knocking off a ten-term incumbent, the establishment Democrat Joe Crowley, in the primary for the 14th Congressional District in New York City. AOC, at age twenty-nine, is also the youngest woman to ever serve in the U.S. Congress. Her district covers part of the Bronx and Queens in New York City.

Before we delve into the Green New Deal, it is important to understand who and what AOC represents.

A graduate of Boston University, she was a bartender and political activist before she ran for Congress. She is one of the first female members of the Democratic Socialists of America (DSA) to serve in Congress.

What exactly does the DSA advocate? "Like most socialist organizations, DSA believes in the abolition of capitalism in favor of an economy run either by 'the workers' or the state—though the exact specifics of 'abolishing capitalism' are fiercely debated by socialists," Vox magazine explained. "In practice, that means DSA [members advocate] ending private ownership of a wide range of industries whose products are viewed as 'necessities,' which they say should not be left to those seeking to turn a profit." The group seeks to "force [private business] owners to give workers control of them—to the greatest extent possible." As a bonus, "DSA members also say that overthrowing capitalism must include the eradication of 'hierarchical systems' that lie beyond the market as well. As a result, DSA supports the missions of Black Lives Matter, gay and lesbian rights, and environmentalism as integral parts of this broader 'anti-capitalist' program."[2]

And the Green New Deal is quite literally the most all-encompassing attack on capitalism, wealth creation, and freedom—and the largest boost to social disruption, toxic racial relations, and central planning. The Green New Deal is NOT about the climate. It was never intended to be about the climate. It is a vehicle for the agendas of the Democratic Socialists of America and other leftist groups.

After her 2018 election victory, AOC became an overnight political and media sensation, feted by the mainstream media and Hollywood. And her promotion of the Green New Deal, perhaps more than anything else, was her ticket to superstardom.

Here is how AOC was introduced to Americans in 2019. She was interviewed by CBS's Anderson Cooper on *60 Minutes*:

> Cooper: You're talking about zero carbon emissions, no use of fossil fuels within 12 years.
>
> AOC: That is the goal. It is ambitious, and …
>
> Cooper: How is that possible? You're talking about everybody having to drive an electric car?
>
> AOC: It's going to require a lot of rapid change that we don't even conceive of as possible right now. What is the problem with trying to push our technological capacities to the furthest extent possible?

And if we don't do all of this? "And we're like, the world is going to end in 12 years if we don't address climate change," AOC explained.

The Green New Deal was officially introduced on February 7, 2019, by Representative Alexandria Ocasio-Cortez and Senator Ed Markey, Democrat of Massachusetts, not as a piece of legislation but as a non-binding resolution entitled, "Recognizing the Duty of the Federal Government to Create a Green New Deal."

The goals of the AOC-Markey GND resolution were global reductions in greenhouse gas emissions of 40 percent to 60 percent from 2010 levels by 2030 and "net-zero" emissions worldwide by 2050. These emission-reduction targets were supposed to keep the global temperatures from rising 1.5 degrees Celsius above pre-industrial levels.

House Resolution 109 cited "adequate health care, housing, transportation, and education" as major tenets of the Green New Deal, which it said would also address "wage stagnation," "socioeconomic mobility," "income inequality," "the racial wealth divide," the "gender earnings gap," a "family-sustaining wage," "family and medical leave," "paid vacations," and many more non-climate issues.

The resolution also called for "building a more sustainable food system that ensures universal access to healthy food" and for remedying "systemic racial, regional, social, environmental, and economic injustices."[3]

The resolution made it clear: the Green New Deal is not really about the climate.

AOC explained, "It's inevitable that we can use the transition to 100% renewable energy as the vehicle to truly deliver and establish economic, social, and racial justice in the United States of America."[4]

The resolution sought a "new national, social, industrial, and economic mobilization on a scale not seen since World War II and the New Deal era."[5]

But critics were quick to dismiss such lofty rhetoric. "There's a world of difference between saying that fighting a world war requires total mobilization of the economy in ways previously unheard of and that we should we fight a world war because we want to mobilize the economy in ways unheard of," Hot Air blog commented.[6]

Unexpected Results

"If climate change were a global ecological crisis, we would expect to find evidence of declining health and well-being over the past 70 years. Instead, we find dramatic improvement in life expectancy, per capita income, food security, and various health-related metrics," explained Marlo Lewis of the Competitive Enterprise Institute. "Global life expectancy increased by 48 percent, from 48 years in 1950 to 71.4 years in 2015, including a 68 percent increase in Africa, the poorest continent....The global child mortality rate fell from 18.2 percent in 1960 to 3.9 percent in 2018."[7]

"Get Rid of Farting Cows and Airplanes"

But a fiasco occurred when, on the same day as the resolution was introduced in Congress, Ocasio-Cortez released an overview of the Green New Deal, including an FAQ that turned out to be too frank about the actual goals of the plan.

The FAQ sheet addressed the methane emissions of cattle: "We set a goal to get to net-zero, rather than zero emissions, in 10 years because we aren't sure that we'll be able to fully get rid of farting cows and airplanes that fast."

When the idea of abolishing airplanes and cows drew ridicule, AOC was defiant, saying, "We need to take a look at factory farming, you know? Period. It's wild." She added, "Maybe we shouldn't be eating a hamburger for breakfast, lunch, and dinner. Like, let's keep it real."[8]

The FAQ also claimed: "We think we can ramp up renewable manufacturing and power production, retrofit every building in America, build the smart grid, overhaul transportation and agriculture, plant lots of trees and restore our ecosystem to get to net-zero."

It promised that the GND would provide "economic security for all who are unable or unwilling to work."

The FAQ also explained that the GND would "build out high speed rail at a scale where air travel stops becoming necessary." A train to Hawaii!

It claimed the GND would "upgrade or replace every building in US for state-of-the-art energy efficiency." Replace every building!

> ### On a War Footing
> Green New Deal advocates "say we are now waging a war to stop catastrophic climate change. So money, sacrifice and disruption are irrelevant," noted David Wojick and Paul Driessen of CFACT in 2020. "The resolution describes the 10-year plan to transform every sector of our economy to remove GHG [greenhouse gases] and pollution. It says it does this through huge investments in renewables, at WW2 scales (which was 40-60% of America's GDP).... The cost of this massive, total transformation of our energy and economic system would easily reach $10 trillion: $30,000 per person or $120,000 per family—on top of those skyrocketing electricity prices. And that's just the intermittent, unreliable energy component of this all-encompassing Green New Deal."[9]

"Massive Waste"

During the Obama administration green stimulus efforts, "$15 billion went to energy efficiency, which turned out to be a massive waste of money," wrote Michael Shellenberger. "Twice as much money was spent weatherizing homes as was saved. The episode disproved the widely parroted myth that efficiency investments always 'pay for themselves.' Determined to learn nothing from history, Green New Dealers are now proposing to spend taxpayer dollars weatherizing every building in America."[10]

"Create affordable public transit available to all, with goal to replace every combustion-engine vehicle." Eliminate all cars!

"Totally overhaul transportation by massively expanding electric vehicle manufacturing, build charging stations everywhere." Litter the landscape with charging stations for expensive cars that run on electricity—from fossil-fuel-powered electric plants!

"We believe the right way to capture carbon is to plant trees and restore our natural ecosystems. CCUS technology to date has not proven effective." Trees will save the planet!

"It's unclear if we will be able to decommission every nuclear plant within 10 years, but the plan is to transition off of nuclear and all fossil fuels as soon as possible." Abolish every reliable form of energy!

The overview GND document was so revealing that AOC had it disappeared quickly. You can still see it online, though. As they say, the internet is forever.[11]

Fact-Checking the Green New Deal

Let's look more closely at the Green New Deal's goals, starting with the most infamous: "to fully get rid of farting cows and airplanes."

Cows and the meat-eating humans who consume them have been demonized by the climate campaigners for a long time. The UN's International Panel on Climate Change (IPCC) published a report in 2019 calling for restrictions on eating meat.[12] Former UN climate chief

Christiana Figueres suggested in 2018 that meat eaters should be treated "the same way that smokers are treated," explaining that "if they want to eat meat, they can do it outside the restaurant."[13]

Nicholas Stern, former climate advisor to the UK government said that a "successful" UN climate pact "would lead to soaring costs for meat and other foods that generate large quantities of greenhouse gases," according to the *Times* of London.[14]

Physicist Thomas P. Sheahen dismissed methane emissions as a climate problem. "Worrying about methane emissions is the greatest waste of time in the entire lexicon of global warming fanaticism," said Sheahen, an MIT-educated physicist, author of the book *An Introduction to High-Temperature Superconductivity*, and co-author of a 2018 peer-reviewed study on methane. He called it "completely false, a nonsense calculation thought up by the IPCC to drum up more concern beyond just CO2.... The tiny increases in methane associated with cows may elicit a few giggles, but it absolutely cannot be the basis for sane regulations or national policy."[16]

Climate activists have been trying for years to remake modern civilization in their centrally planned image. A 2018 UK Committee on Climate Change report warned "airline travel and long-haul shipping are among the 'tough-nut' sectors that will require a radical rethink if humanity is to stand any chance of avoiding climate catastrophe," according to UK *Independent*.[17]

The irony here is that climate alarmists like Al Gore and Leonardo DiCaprio use fossil fuels lavishly with lots of private jet travel. This is

> **Deaths on the Decline**
> "Fewer and fewer people die from climate-related natural disasters," noted Bjørn Lomborg in 2019. "Climate-related deaths have been declining strongly for 70 years.... This is clearly opposite of what you normally hear, but that is because we're often just being told of one disaster after another—telling us how *many* events are happening. The number of reported events is increasing, but that is mainly due to better reporting, lower thresholds and better accessibility (the CNN effect)."[15]

about controlling society with their vision, not about how the airlines' CO_2 emissions somehow change the weather.

According to the GND FAQ, they plan to "build out high speed rail at a scale where air travel stops becoming necessary." In fact, high-speed rail is not panning out like proponents envisioned. "California's high-speed boondoggle is already in $100 billion dollars of debt, and looks to be one of the state's biggest fiscal disasters ever. Amtrak runs billions of dollars in the red (though, as we'll see, trains that run on fossil fuels will also be phased out). Imagine growing that business model out to every state in America?" wrote David Harsanyi at The Federalist.[18]

What about the GND goal "to get to net-zero" emissions? According to Rupert Darwall, the author of *Green Tyranny: Exposing the Totalitarian Roots of the Climate Industrial Complex*, that's a "blueprint for the extinction of capitalism as we know it. Darwall urged everyone to read the fine print of the [UN's] IPCC's 1.5°C report....There was more rationality to Soviet-style central planning, which at least had the aim of producing something of value rather than producing nothing." He added, "Mandating net-zero is the equivalent of imposing multi-trillion dollar tax hikes and with not one cent for deficit reduction, the proceeds going instead to controlling the 'global climate.'"[19]

As Darwall also pointed out, the IPCC report "asserted that emissions must reach net zero by around 2050 and, by 2030, cut emissions by about 45 percent from 2010 levels" and this "2030 timeline unleashed the current wave of heightened climate alarmism. It provoked Rep. Alexandria Ocasio-Cortez (D-N.Y.) to talk of the world ending in 12 years....The 1.5°C target, the report says, creates the opportunity for 'intentional societal transformation.' In language closer to Sanders's than any believer in capitalism, the IPCC says hitting 1.5°C implies 'very ambitious, internationally cooperative policy environments that transform both supply and demand.'"[20]

Meet the Flintstones

And to achieve that "net-zero" target, say good-bye to driving!

The GND is supposed to "replace every combustion-engine vehicle" by "massively expanding electric vehicle manufacturing, build charging stations everywhere." But having any car at all could be a problem if the climate alarmists get their way. "A ban on new roads, gas power plants and incinerators is needed if Wales is to play a leading role in tackling climate change," the BBC reported, citing a report from Friends of the Earth. "To achieve the goal, it wants the government to set a rule for it not to invest in or give permission for any high carbon infrastructure such as new roads."[21]

And according to David Harsanyi of The Federalist, "The GND would like to replace every 'combustion-engine vehicle'—trucks, airplanes, boats, and 99 percent of cars—within ten years.... To be fair, under the GND, everyone will need to retrofit their cars with Flintstones-style foot holes or pedals for cycling. Charging stations for electric vehicles (EV) will be built 'everywhere,' though how power plants will provide the energy needed to charge them is a mystery."[22]

Eliminating private car ownership is now a top priority among the progressive climate activists. Democrat presidential candidate Andrew Yang suggested in 2019 that because of climate change "we might not own our own cars." Yang explained, "Our current car ownership and usage model is really inefficient and bad for the environment." The solution? A "constant roving fleet of electric cars that you would just order up, then you could diminish the impact of ground transportation on our environment very, very quickly."[23]

These proposals are, putting it mildly, out of line with what the public wants. SUVs are still very popular. "Worldwide, some 5.1m electric vehicles were on the world's roads by the end of 2018, an increase of 2 million over the previous year," wrote Nick Butler for the *Financial Times* in 2019. But, Butler noted, the up to "8 million EVs that should be on the road by the end of 2019 represent less than a tenth of 1 percent of the 1.1 billion cars and other light vehicles that use internal combustion engines. Some 85 million internal combustion engine vehicles were sold worldwide in 2018."[24]

Decreasing Your Standard of Living

"None of what the Joe Biden green team has in store will improve the environment; it will only make your life poorer and harder," wrote Steve Milloy of JunkScience.com. According to Milloy, Biden "has married the Green New Deal. If allowed to honeymoon, the couple will bring an end to fracking, national security and your standard of living."[25]

The climate activists endorsing the Green New Deal don't want us to own our own homes either. They're calling for stopping the construction of new houses unless they meet green mandates. During the primary campaign, Democrat senator Elizabeth Warren said she wanted to ban the construction of new homes in America unless they were built with "zero carbon footprint." As she explained, "By 2028, no new buildings, no new houses, without a zero carbon footprint."[26]

UCLA urban planning professor Kian Goh also pushed the green assault on home ownership. "We need to seriously question the ideal of private homeownership," she wrote for *The Nation* in 2019. "Cheap energy is untenable in the face of a climate emergency. And individual homeownership should be seriously questioned.... If we want to keep cities safe in the face of climate change, we need to seriously question the ideal of private homeownership." Goh lamented how the "idealization of individual homeownership has created the scorching landscapes we face today."[27]

Michael Shellenberger, the president of Environmental Progress, ripped the GND's call to "transition off of nuclear and all fossil fuels as soon as possible." The *Time* magazine "Hero of the Environment" tweeted, "I am calling bullshit not just on AOC but on her progressive enablers in the news media who are giving her a pass on the most crucial test of moral and political leadership of our time when it comes to climate change: a person's stance on nuclear power.... I am calling bullshit on climate fakery. Anyone who is calling for phasing out nuclear is a climate fraud perpetuating precisely the gigantic 'hoax' that [Oklahoma] Sen. James Inhofe (R) famously accused environmentalists of perpetuating. If you want to be a self-respecting progressive or journalist who is fairly considering or covering the climate issue, please stop giving

Ocasio-Cortex and other supposedly climate-concerned greens a pass. THEY ARE INCREASING EMISSIONS."[28]

Nuclear energy is considered a "clean" energy source and provided 19.7 percent of U.S. electricity generation in 2019, according to the U.S. Energy Information Administration (EIA).[29]

Under pressure, AOC did partially relent on nuclear energy, calling it "an important element of our energy mix." She claimed, "The Green New Deal does leave the door open for nuclear."[30]

As David Harsanyi at The Federalist pointed out, the "GND calls for the elimination of all fossil fuel energy production, the lifeblood of American industry and life, which includes not only all oil but also natural gas—one of the cheapest sources of American energy, and one of the reasons the United States has been able to lead the world in carbon-emissions reduction."[31]

A Big Bowl of Crazy

I appeared on *Fox and Friends* the day after AOC's Green New Deal resolution came out and called the Green New Deal a "big bowl of crazy."

As I explained on the February 8, 2019, program,

> **Your Lifestyle Is Not "Sustainable"**
>
> "Current lifestyles and consumption patterns of the affluent middle class—involving high meat intake, use of fossil fuels, appliances, air-conditioning, and suburban housing—are not sustainable."
>
> —Maurice Strong, the founder of the UN Environment Programme and architect of the UN's 1992 Rio Earth Summit[32]

This is essentially the environmental Left and the Left wish list over the last 40 years all thrown into one package and they don't want to debate it on the merits of the economics. We're told we need to do all of this, from banning meat to getting rid of airline travel, getting rid of the internal combustion engine—all to save us from a "climate emergency."

And yet we're not told how to expect better weather if we actually pass this thing. It would have no impact on the climate even if you believe Al Gore and the United Nations and all the silliness that they sometimes claim. This plan is plagiarism pure and simple. They borrowed it from the 1960s and 1970s. In my book, I detail how different environmental scares—overpopulation, resource scarcity, even global cooling—had the same solutions: wealth redistribution, central planning, sovereignty limiting, and just a massive government intervention.

... this is the litmus test for the 2020 Democratic contenders. And in a way they have given anyone who cares about free markets, liberty, and science, a grand opening to expose anyone who signs on to this plan.[33]

As Kevin Dayaratna and Nicolas Loris noted in a 2019 Heritage Foundation report, "The Green New Deal is much more than just an energy and climate policy; it is a plan to fundamentally restructure the American economy. To correct those alleged injustices, the plan aims to change how people consume energy, develop crops, construct homes, and produce and transport goods. In other words, the government would use taxes and regulations to control actions and choices made by everyday Americans."[34]

You Have to Laugh

"By the end of the Green New Deal resolution (and accompanying fact sheet) I was laughing so hard I nearly cried. If a bunch of GOPers plotted to forge a fake Democratic bill showing how bonkers the party is, they could not have done a better job. It is beautiful."

—the *Wall Street Journal*'s Kimberley Strassel[35]

"Completely Bonkers"

Congresswoman Alexandria Ocasio-Cortez declared in February 2019, "Yup. If you don't like the Green New Deal, then come up with your own ambitious, on-scale proposal to address the global climate crisis. Until then, we're in charge—and you're just shouting from the cheap seats."[36]

This "we're in charge" declaration by AOC prompted Greenpeace co-founder Patrick Moore to call AOC a "pompous little twit." Moore explained, "You don't have a plan to grow food for 8 billion people without fossil fuels, or get the food into the cities. Horses? If fossil fuels were banned every tree in the world would be cut down for fuel for cooking and heating. You would bring about mass death."[37]

Other critics joined Moore in pointing out how radical and even crazy the Green New Deal is, and how much harm it would do.

"The Green New Deal isn't just un-American, it's also completely bonkers," wrote David Harsanyi. "It is not hyperbole to contend that GND is likely the most ridiculous and un-American plan that's ever been presented by an elected official to voters. Not merely because it would necessitate a communist strongman to institute, but also because the societal costs are unfathomable." The GND attempts to "overhaul modernity by voluntarily destroying massive amounts of wealth and technology."[38]

Robert Bradley wrote at Master Resource that "the Green New Deal was an embarrassment—and, to my knowledge, the most ill-conceived energy proposal in the history of the United States by a wing of a major political party since the oil-industry nationalization proposals of the shortage 1970s (yes, Bernie [Sanders] was part of that)."[39]

Dayaratna and Loris of Heritage summed up the GND as "incredibly costly" for "no meaningful climate benefit": "The plan would introduce a completely new level of cronyism and corporate welfare that would harm consumers multiple times over. The policies proposed in the Green New Deal would disrupt energy markets and skew investment decisions toward politically connected projects."[40]

According to Jamie Spry of the skeptical blog Climatism, "The core objective of the $2 Trillion Climate Crisis Industry has always been the centralized control of human beings and curtailment of free-market, capitalist 'excesses.'... Energy rationing and the control of carbon dioxide (the direct byproduct of cheap, abundant hydrocarbon energy) [is] key to the socialist Left's Malthusian and misanthropic agenda of depopulation and deindustrialisation respectively. A totalitarian ideology enforced through punitive emissions controls under the guise of 'Saving The Planet.'"[41]

And yet some Democrats believe that the Green New Deal is not ambitious enough. "I not only support a Green New Deal, I don't think it goes far enough," declared Senator Warren. "I want to see us move entirely to green."[42]

In July 2020, Biden came out with his own version of the Green New Deal. "There's no more consequential challenge that we must meet in the next decade than the onrushing climate crisis," the Democrat presidential candidate announced. "Left unchecked, it is literally an existential threat to the health of our planet and our very survival."[43]

Biden expressed his determination to permanently undo President Trump's sweeping reversal of Obama's climate legacy. "We're going to lock in progress that no future president can roll back or undercut to take us backward again," he said.[44]

Biden resurrected the climate tipping points. "Science tells us we have nine years before the damage [from climate change] is irreversible," Biden claimed. Meteorologist Dr. Ryan Maue ripped Biden's claim: "Science doesn't say we have '9 years left' to save the planet from climate change. The 'years left' narrative is a complete fraud."[45]

Do As I Say, Not As I Do

During the 2002 presidential race, Joe Biden continued to fly in private jets and be transported in oversized SUVs despite his 2019 call to put fossil fuel executives "in jail" for failing to address climate change. "Holding them liable for what they have done....when they don't deliver, put them in jail. I am not joking about that," Biden said to applause at a town hall in Peterborough New Hampshire on December 29, 2019. One attendee began speaking to Biden, saying, "If we don't stop using fossil fuels..." Biden finished his sentence: "We're all dead."[46] But Biden seemed to be unable to stop using them himself. As CNBC reported, Biden "spent way more on private jets (nearly $924,000) in the third quarter than his top 2020 Democratic rivals."[47]

Biden's 2020 plan, which drew upon the 2019 AOC-Markey version of the Green New Deal, was drafted by a joint task force convened by members of the Bernie Sanders and Ocasio-Cortez campaigns.[48] Biden's Climate Engagement Advisory Council included billionaire climate activist Tom Steyer, former Obama administration EPA chief Carol Browner, and high-profile climate activists. Biden essentially ceded control over his climate policy to the extreme "climate emergency" wing of the Democrat Party.[50]

> **Not So Fast**
>
> "As early as 1864 George Perkins Marsh, sometimes said to be the father of American ecology, warned that the earth was 'fast becoming an unfit home for its "noblest inhabitant,"' and that unless men changed their ways it would be reduced 'to such a condition of impoverished productiveness, of shattered surface, of climatic excess, as to threaten the depravation, barbarism, and perhaps even extinction of the species.'"
> —MIT professor Leo Marx[49]

Biden's two trillion dollar Green New Deal even featured a green crimes division. Biden's plan included a provision for creating an "Environmental and Climate Justice Division" within the Department of Justice.[51]

Bernie Sanders praised the new version of the Green New Deal, noting that it "will make Biden the most progressive president since FDR."[52]

> **Bernie and the Jets**
>
> "Bernie Sanders has made his career out of calling for keeping fossil fuels in the ground. The problem is he can't keep from using fossil fuels lavishly—in the air!" I pointed out on *Fox and Friends* in 2019. "This is rank hypocrisy on the level that only Al Gore could compete. Outside of Al Gore, in electoral politics, Bernie was the guy as the number one 'climate guru.'"[53]
>
> Politico reported: "In the final months of the 2016 campaign, Sanders repeatedly requested and received the use of a carbon-spewing private jet for himself and his traveling staff when he served as a surrogate campaigner for Hillary Clinton."[54]

Slate reviewed Biden's version of the Green New Deal favorably, saying it was the AOC-Markey version "minus the crazy": "It's understandable why Biden might avoid the branding. For many moderates and conservatives, including our president, the phrase 'green new deal' itself has become a shorthand for leftist overreach.... Activists are still clearly happy with Biden's leftward shift."[55]

The delighted left-wing philosopher Noam Chomsky called Biden's climate platform "farther to the left than any Democratic candidate in memory."[56]

To Frack or Not to Frack, That Is the Question

"A Biden administration would move to ban fracking, the oil production technology that has liberated Americans and our gas prices from the shackles of the Organization of the Petroleum Exporting Countries, or OPEC, cartel," Steve Milloy wrote at JunkScience.com. "In no time, American drivers would be facing European-style gas prices and sweating every time Iran, Russia, or Saudi Arabia moved to threaten the global oil supply."[57]

Who Pays the Piper?

"The foundations funding the national litigation effort against energy companies are the same donors supporting the Sunrise Movement, the upstart group behind the recent push for the Green New Deal, according to reporting by Inside Philanthropy," Elena Connolly of Western Wire reported. The Sunrise Movement "received much of its initial financial support from the Rockefeller Family Fund and Wallace Global Fund. Sunrise was founded in 2017 and emerged from a coalescence of alumni from several previous anti-fossil fuel activism efforts like the divestment campaign and protests against energy infrastructure.... Both the Rockefeller Family Fund and the Wallace Global Fund provide substantial financial support to EarthRights International (ERI), the Washington, D.C.-based non-profit representing Boulder County, Boulder City and San Mateo County in their lawsuit against ExxonMobil and Suncor."[58]

But Biden's official position on fracking was actually a bit muddled.

During the primaries in 2020, Biden said "no more—no new fracking" if he won the presidency. Biden also told a voter during the primaries, "Kiddo...look in my eyes. I guarantee you, I guarantee you, we're gonna end fossil fuels."[59] In January 2020, Biden was asked by a New Hampshire voter, "But like, what about, say, stopping fracking?" Biden answered, "Yes." In March 2020 Biden told a CNN debate, "No more, no new fracking."[60]

But by August 2020, Biden was declaring, "I am not banning fracking—no matter how many times Donald Trump lies about me."[61]

Biden's vice presidential pick, Kamala Harris, also seemed to reverse her position on fracking. Harris had promised she would ban fracking during her failed presidential run. "There is no question I am in favor of banning fracking," Harris said during a 2019 CNN town hall. But once she became Biden's running mate, Harris supported Biden's flip-flop, saying that fracking provides "good-paying jobs in places like Pennsylvania."[62]

Alex Epstein, founder of the Center for Industrial Progress, had this reaction to Biden's Green New Deal: "Joe Biden's energy plan calls for outlawing reliable fossil fuel electricity and mandating unreliable solar and wind electricity. This will not stop CO_2 emissions from rising but it will destroy American industry, impoverish American consumers, and jeopardize American security." Epstein added, "Biden says that forcing Americans to rely on unreliable solar and wind will help middle-class Americans. But the cost of energy drives the cost of everything. Skyrocketing energy costs will drive skyrocketing food, housing, healthcare, and transportation costs."[64]

Behavior Modification

The Democrat vice presidential candidate promoted the Green New Deal as a way "we can change human behaviors" in 2019.

"It is a fact that we can change human behaviors without much change to our lifestyle and we can save the future generations of our country and this world," Harris said.[63]

Europe Is Already "Enjoying" Their Version of the Green New Deal—and It's Not Going Well

The European Commission debuted its own "European Green New Deal" in December 2019, declaring, "Climate change and environmental degradation are an existential threat to Europe and the world."[1]

The Euro-version of the GND is being billed as "Europe's man on the moon moment" by European Commission president Ursula von der Leyen.[2]

Convincing or Coercing?

And by the looks of it, Europe is going full bore into their Green New Deal, with a goal of no net greenhouse gas emissions by 2050.[3]

"Cutting the Continent's emissions to 'net zero'—meaning Europe would sequester at least as much greenhouse gases as it produces—by 2050 will require a radical overhaul of nearly every aspect of the modern economy. Dramatic cuts in carbon will wipe out entire industries, transform others and force people to change the way they eat, work, live and travel," reported Politico in a 2020 article entitled "Europe's Climate Goal: Revolution." The gushing article, written by journalist and climate

Meeting Macron

I got the opportunity to challenge French president Emmanuel Macron face-to-face at the UN climate summit in Bonn Germany on November 15, 2017. I shook hands and told President Macron: "President Trump is correct on climate change. I just want to say that. He is,"[5] Macron did a double take, laughed, and smiled. (Macron's own climate policies would result in the rise of the widespread "yellow vest" protests in France in 2018 and 2019.)

Morano confronts Macron[6]

activist Karl Mathiesen, featured this subhead: "To Eliminate Emissions by 2050, the EU Will Have to 'Remake Civilization.'" And it quoted French president Emmanuel Macron calling the European GND vision "the next world."[4]

"We may not know how it can be done, but we do know what needs to be done," *Politico* said.

The media gushes about how the European GND will alter everyday life.

"If Europeans truly mobilize around the delivery of the 2050 goal, every business decision, lifestyle choice, political swing, every hallmark of European culture—from annual ski trips, to Champions League Football matches, to French cheese—will need to be tested against its contribution to climate change," claimed *Politico*.

"The European Climate Law, proposed by the Commission in March, would submit every EU law, past and future, to a test of its compatibility with climate neutrality—a 'tectonic shift,' according to E3G, a think tank that advocates for emission cuts," *Politico* reported.

"No citizen, no industry, no government will reach the goal unchanged. Through carbon pricing and policy nudges, citizens will be coerced or convinced to fly less, eat less red meat and use more trains, buses, trams and bicycles," Politico explained of Europe's GND.[7]

One thing seems certain: whenever governments are given a choice between "coercing" citizens or "convincing" them, "coercing" always seems to win the day.

Europe has been more susceptible to oppressive "climate" regulations like the GND, net-zero emission goals, and the UN Paris Pact than the U.S. European nations generally don't question "the science" behind the claims, for one simple reason—they like the "solutions"! Europeans are used to much more regulatory control of their economies and lives than Americans. So when more climate regulations come along bringing even more central planning and stagnant economic growth, Europeans just accept it as business as usual. Former Soviet bloc Eastern European nations, however, are generally much more skeptical of the climate agenda and its consequences than their Western counterparts.

Americans, on the other hand, have a heritage of comparatively less government intervention in their lives and their economic system. When climate campaigners come along selling their wares, they have had a much tougher time convincing the U.S. of new restrictions to combat an alleged climate "crisis." Americans have historically rejected that kind of government control over their lives. And because Americans have generally been opposed to climate "solutions," they are more motivated to take the time to investigate the scientific claims behind them.

"The Standard Marxist Garbage"

Former Harvard University physicist Dr. Lubos Motl unleashed on the European Green Deal as an "insane suicidal goal of net-zero emissions."

Motl wrote in 2020, "What is amazing is how they mix these unscientific delusions about climate change with tons of other topics that have nothing to do with it and with each other. . . . So we learn that the goal of this 'Green Deal' is actually the standard Marxist garbage plan to 'erase inequalities.' The word 'gender' appears 9 times in this document that pretends to be about the climate."[8]

Europe is looking down the barrel of more central planning via the Green New Deal. And for decades, progressives have used Europe as the model for the U.S. to follow on more government intrusion on issues ranging from childcare to gun rights to health care.

A 2020 Heritage Foundation analysis of Europe's Green New Deal found a woeful number of problems.

"A European Green New Deal would drive energy prices higher, disproportionately harming low-income Europeans, while doing little to improve the climate," noted James Roberts, Nicolas Loris, and Kevin Dayaratna in a Heritage report entitled "Green New Deals: Bad for Americans and Bad for Europeans."

As their analysis found, "The mandates, regulations, and subsidies required to achieve net zero greenhouse gas emissions would drive energy prices higher, disproportionately harming low-income Europeans, and have a negligible impact on climate. Driving out affordable, reliable energy sources for politically preferred ones would reduce living standards and political liberty for everyone living under its decrees, rolling back some of the progress made during two millennia of Western civilization. By inserting more government intervention into the EU economy, a GND would weaken current and future economic freedom."

The "European Climate Law" would transform climate goals "into a legal obligation and a trigger for investment" by mandating "action by all sectors of

The New Totalitarians

I debated climate activists during the UN climate summit which was held in Katowice, Poland, in 2018. I noted that the Polish people have suffered greatly in the past century and are facing a similar threat today. "The history of Poland was one of domination by Germany, then decades under the Soviet Union. Now, a new regulatory body has replaced those old ones and the EU and the UN are now telling Poland how they can do their energy and economy. What I would say to Poland is 'join President Trump, join Brazil, join these other countries that are taking a hard look at leaving the UN Paris Pact.'"[9]

[the EU's] economy," the report noted. "Just as its American cousin would do for Washington, the EU's GND would perforce translate into more centralization of money and power and more economic central planning in Brussels, where the government would determine what types of energy Europeans produce and consume."[10]

In March 2020, IndustriAll, a federation of European trade unions, issued a dire warning that eleven million jobs in the twenty-seven-member EU bloc were in danger because of the Green New Deal.

"We are talking about almost 11 million jobs directly affected in extractive industries, energy intensive industries and in the automotive industry," Luc Triangle, secretary-general of IndustriAll said. "It's easy to say we need to reach ambitious climate targets by 2050 and 2030. But the industrial strategy should give the answer on the 'how' we will get there. And at the moment, we don't have those answers yet."[11]

Caught Cheating

"The U.S. EPA caught Volkswagen cheating red-handed almost exactly one year ago, and in the fallout of that initial accusation the world was taken aback by just how brazen the malfeasance was—engineers deliberately installed software that would run the engine differently when it detected that the vehicle was being driven in a testing situation, so as to keep tailpipe emissions artificially lower than they would in typical road conditions.... Europe has fashioned itself as an eco-friendly paradise, but on closer examination much of that environmental marketing turns out to be merely green lipstick on a pig."

—The American Interest[12]

Pointless Pain

According to the Heritage Foundation report, even if we actually did face a man-made climate problem, the European GND would not have a detectable impact on global temperatures. "As with the U.S. GND, the EU's GND would be climatically meaningless...if the EU reduced its emissions

100 percent by 2030, the climate impact would be no more than 0.046 degrees Celsius of averted warming by 2050 and 0.120 degrees Celsius of averted warming by 2100," the authors noted. "By shrinking the EU's economy by potentially tens of trillions of dollars, the GND will cause lower levels of prosperity and leave Europeans with fewer resources to deal with whatever environmental challenges come their way."

How is Europe Doing?

Europe's "green" path is creating a lot of problems, especially for senior citizens on fixed incomes. "Around 2.8 million people [in the UK] over the age of 65 are set to ration their energy usage out of worry that they cannot afford their energy bills, according to new research by Compare The Market," Energy Live reported in March 2020. "A further 84% think the cost of energy presents a 'real threat' to elderly people living in the UK."[14]

Christopher Monckton, who was an advisor in Margaret Thatcher's government, explained how one particular winter had affected senior citizens. "In the United Kingdom there was a bitterly cold winter—caused by global warming, so the extremists tell us," he said, noting that the UK had seen "seven thousand extra excess deaths, over above the twenty thousand we would normally get in the winter." But the excess deaths occurred "not because the weather was cold so much but as the homes of the people were cold because through the climate policies had vastly increased, in fact doubled the price of electricity. Ordinary working people could not afford to heat their homes."[16]

Other costs may not be so obvious. A 2020 report entitled "The Hidden Cost of Net Zero: Rewiring the UK" from the Global Warming Policy Foundation found that the "UK faces a £200 billion bill to rewire the country if the government follows through on plans to electrify the country's homes and transport systems." Author Mike Travers noted, "Many homeowners will be paying thousands." According to Travers, the existing wiring in the UK will not be able to handle the demand for more power from the installation of electric car chargers and heat pumps.[18]

Europe's green policies are impacting housing. In the UK, green housing plans include a "future homes standard" by 2025 that would seek to slash emissions from new homes by up to 80 percent. Home developers will be "banned from connecting properties to the gas grid and encouraged to roll out air-source heat pumps, solar panels and

> ### They Can't Compete
> "Nobody but nobody in my business seriously invests in Europe. They haven't for a generation. Europe is no longer competitive. It has the world's most expensive energy and labor laws that are uninviting for employers. Worst of all, it has green taxes that, at best, can be described as foolish as they are having the opposite effect to how they were intended."
> —billionaire businessman Sir Jim Ratcliffe, chairman, INEOS Group, "Open Letter to the European Commission President Jean-Claude Juncker," February 12, 2019[17]

Recycling Tedium

"Danes to Sort Trash into Ten Types under New Green Deal," reported the Local in July 2020. "People living in Denmark will need to sort their recycling into ten different containers, under a new deal that aims to cut 0.7m tonnes of emissions and make the country's waste sector carbon neutral by 2030."[20]

better insulation," the *Daily Mail* reported. The UK Home Builders Federation has rejected the "green housing revolution" as "unrealistic."[19]

The auto industry is also getting whacked by green ideology. "Time is running out for European carmakers, which have waited until the last minute to try to meet ambitious EU emissions targets and face billions in fines if they fail to comply," Reuters reported in 2019. By 2020, "CO2 must be cut to 95 grammes per kilometre for 95% of cars from the current 120.5g average—a figure that has risen of late as consumers spurn fuel-efficient diesels and embrace SUVs. All new cars in the EU must be compliant in 2021."

Peugeot CEO Carlos Tavares said, "I'd be surprised if we didn't see a few bankruptcies, considering the amplitude of the coming change."

Will the auto industry fight back? Sadly, no. "The industry has long since given up pushing for the goals to be relaxed—a political impossibility underlined by a resurgent climate protest movement that has added the Frankfurt [auto] show to its target list," according to Reuters.[21]

"Give Prison Sentences to Politicians"

"The European Court of Justice (ECJ) will start examining on Tuesday whether German courts should give prison sentences to politicians who don't enforce bans on heavily-polluting cars....The environmental group Deutsche Umwelthilfe (DUH) is trying to force the Bavarian government to implement measures against air pollution in the state capital of Munich, where nitrogen dioxide levels exceed EU limits," reported EuroNews in 2019.[22]

A May 2020 study from the University of Copenhagen found that up to 61.5 percent of the emissions "saved" by the EU may increase emissions in other parts of the world. [23]

"Part of the emissions that Europe 'saves' through an extensive green transition could possibly be 'leaked' to the rest of the world through, among other things, trade mechanisms, depending on the climate policy of other countries," noted the study's co-author Professor Wusheng Yu of the University of Copenhagen's Department of Food and Resource Economics.

> **Trump's America Is Trumping Europe**
>
> "President Trump must be laughing until his sides hurt," wrote Hank Berrien of the Daily Wire in 2018. CO_2 emissions continued to drop in the U.S., where natural gas was replacing coal, while going up in Europe.[24]
>
> A Rhodium Group study noted the irony that while Trump "continues to unravel Obama-era climate and clean energy policies," natural gas was "keeping U.S. greenhouse gas emissions on the downswing." CO_2 emissions in the United States fell 12 percent from 2005 to 2016.[25]

"If the world beyond the EU does not follow suit and embark on a similar green transition, the decline in global greenhouse gas emissions will effectively be limited and well below the level agreed upon in EU climate policy," added another co-author, Francesco Clora.[26]

A 2019 report by the Office for National Statistics revealed that Britain has effectively outsourced its CO_2 emissions to developing nations: "The impact of globalisation on CO_2 emissions has resulted in service-based economies creating indirect emissions by outsourcing manufacturing products to countries with lower labour costs and less stringent pollution regulations. We find that the UK is a net-importer of CO_2 emissions, with most of the imported CO_2 emissions coming from China. Therefore, any apparent decline in territorial CO_2 emissions is overestimated."[27] Amina Syed of the Office for National Statistics explained: "While directly produced UK emissions have been falling for many years, once you take account of the UK importing products from abroad, the picture doesn't look quite so positive."[28]

A December 2019 report on the EU agenda by the European Environmental Agency was less than glowing. "The European Union is failing at almost every one of its environmental goals, a shock study by the European Environmental Agency has warned," said the UK *Express* newspaper.

The European Environmental Agency report found "serious gaps between the state of the environment and existing EU near- and long-term policy targets." The report, which is issued every five years, noted, "We are hardly reaching any of our goals for 2020."[30]

Also in 2019, a study commissioned by the European Climate Foundation found that "not a single [EU country] is on a pathway to reach net-zero emission by 2050." The study noted that "Spain is the only EU country holding its head above water." The EU nations "do not yet live up to the ambitions set by EU legislators and the Paris Agreement."[31]

In 2020, the EU statistics office Eurostat found that the EU had made "no progress" on climate change since 2015.[32]

The most telling aspect of the so-called climate policy debate is how the U.S. has been reducing emissions while Europe flounders.

Economist Stephen Moore asked in 2018, "Take a wild guess what country is reducing its greenhouse gas emissions the most? Canada? Britain? France? India? Germany? Japan? No, no, no, no, no and no. The answer to that question is the United States of America. Wow! How can that be?" He added, "We never enacted a carbon tax. We don't have a cap and trade carbon emission program. That environmental villain Donald

Trump pulled America out of the Paris climate accord that was signed by almost the entire rest of the civilized world." As Moore concluded, "The countries in the Paris climate agreement have broken every promise they've made and the nation that hasn't signed the treaty is doing more than any other nation to reduce global warming. Yet, we are being lectured by the sanctimonious Europeans and Asians for not doing our fair share to save the planet. It's another case study in how the left cares far more about good intentions than actual results."[34]

Reversing the Industrial Revolution

"UK Chancellor Rishi Sunak has found an ingenious scheme to ensure that Britain never recovers from the economic damage caused by the lockdown: a 'green industrial revolution,'" wrote James Delingpole in 2020. "A green industrial revolution is a bit like the original industrial revolution, except for one or two crucial differences: instead of boosting prosperity, creating jobs and stimulating economic growth, it does the exact opposite.... Meanwhile, as Western nations choose to hobble their recoveries by burdening their economies with more expensive energy, the Eastern powers, led by China, are heading in the opposite direction."[35]

It's a Gas

And these European green failures will likely continue. In 2020, activists' fears grew over whether the goals of the Green New Deal could get watered down due to the poorer European nations' unwillingness to give up fossil fuels.

In May of 2020, eight EU countries declared they were not willing to give up the COVID relief funding for natural gas projects. Bulgaria, Czech Republic, Lithuania, Hungary, Poland, Slovakia, and Greece explained that coal can't be phased out to meet climate goals unless natural gas stepped in. "Moving straight away from coal to something that is completely fossil fuel independent is impossible if you don't transit through something. And that transition, unless other technology becomes available, is natural gas. Of course, this in time also has to be made sustainable in terms of our green goals," said Dragoş Tudorache, Romanian member of the European Parliament.

EuroNews explained, "The central and eastern European countries who are lobbying for natural gas may end up accepting green conditionality in exchange for retaining their place as countries that take more money out of the EU budget then they put in."[36]

> ### "Do Not Believe Them"
> "The biggest threat to Poland today is from the Katowice, Poland (UN climate) conference," I told a large gathering during a speech at the 2018 UN climate summit in Poland. "They will want to convince you that Polish coal mines are destroying the planet—do not believe them. The UN will say that it has the best scientific institution—it is also a lie. They are a political organization that is masquerading as a scientific institution."[37]

China Benefits

The GND comes on top in Europe's previous commitment to the UN Paris Pact. The beneficiary of this green suicide that Europe is committing and the U.S. may or may not reengage in (depending on who is president) is China.

"The Paris Agreement is one of the primary tools with which China is gaming the system. This is because the treaty gives huge benefits to China, still considered a developing country under UN rules, that do not apply to" Europe, Canada, and the U.S., explained Tom Harris, the executive director of the International Climate Science Coalition.

"Under the 2015 agreement, the U.S. committed to reduce its greenhouse gas emissions (about 81% of which is carbon dioxide (CO_2)) by between 26% and 28% below its 2005 levels by 2025. China committed to stop increasing CO_2 emissions by 2030. This asymmetry makes no sense, of course. Allowing China, which now emits about twice as much as America, to increase emissions over this period, while restricting the U.S., would result in even more industries moving to China. Total global CO_2 emissions would then likely rise even faster."[38]

The Green New Deal Plagiarizes the Same "Solutions" from Previous Environmental Scares

E very version of the Green New Deal—including recently touted "Global Green New Deal"—is nothing more than a rehash of the past five decades of environmental activists' wish list of "solutions" to whatever green "crisis" they raised the alarms about in their day. The Green New Deal literally offers the same solutions that were proposed from previous environmental scares.

No matter the environmental problem, the solution is always the same: massive government intervention and control, population control, economic restructuring, wealth redistribution, and limits to national sovereignty. The details of the current environmental "emergency" never really

Climate Change Coincidence?

"Scanning through the plans proposed by Rep. Ocasio-Cortez, the Solving the Climate Crisis report, and now Biden, it's uncanny how fixing the problems associated with man-made climate change just happen to coincide with the exact same economic policies long advocated by political progressives."

—*Reason* magazine's Ron Bailey[1]

matter. They just utilize the old plug and play, changing one environmental scare for another and using the new crisis to push the same agenda.

MIT climate scientist Richard Lindzen has revealed the agenda behind the global warming scare. "Controlling carbon is a bureaucrat's dream. If you control carbon, you control life," Lindzen said in 2007.

In 2020, meteorologist and climate activist Eric Holthaus joined a long line of climate players who have admitted that the climate "emergency" is not about science after all. "The climate emergency isn't about science, it's about justice," Holthaus wrote.[2]

In 2018, Holthaus had expressed his approval for a UN IPCC report's "rigorous backing to systematically dismantle capitalism as a key requirement to maintaining civilization and a habitable planet."[3]

The climate change panic is all about central planning, global governance, planned recessions, and redistributing wealth. In fact, "climate change" is just the most recent in a long chain of eco-scares—overpopulation, deforestation, the coming ice age, the ozone hole, resource scarcity, and others—the "solution" for which is always the same: global regulation by central planners. Climate campaigners are using "the science" as a tool in a partisan political campaign for centralized government planning through the United Nations and the European Union.

Even the *New York Times* has suggested that the Green New Deal is a cover for non-environmental policy ambitions, asking in 2019, "Is the Green New Deal aimed at addressing the climate crisis? Or is addressing the climate crisis merely a cover for a wish-list of progressive policies and a not-so-subtle effort to move the Democratic Party to the left?"[4]

As we have seen, even the proponents the Green New Deal have admitted that the real point of it is not the supposed climate science. As we saw in chapter 1, chief of staff Saikat Chakrabarti has said, "The interesting thing about the Green New Deal is it wasn't originally a climate thing at all. Do you guys think of it as a climate thing? Because we really think of it as a how-do-you-change-the-entire-economy thing."[5]

So the Green New Deal is not really about being "Green." And there's nothing really "New" about it, either.

"Global warming," "climate change," and the "climate emergency" are merely the latest alleged environmental scare being utilized to push the same agenda of more government regulations. Instead of arguing the merits of the economic and political changes they want on their own merits, they are using "torqued up" climate change claims to justify them. The environmental Left has used the same rhetoric and proposed the same remedies for different environmental scares in the 1960s, 70s, and 80s: resource scarcity, overpopulation, global cooling, rainforest clearing, and so forth.

The Green New Deal is essentially the environmental Left's wish list for the last forty years, all thrown into one package. They don't want to debate it on the climate merits or the economics. The public is being told we need to adopt all of these radical proposals—from banning meat to limiting airline travel to eliminating the internal combustion engine—to save us from an alleged climate emergency. We are not even told why we should expect better weather if we actually pass the Green New Deal.

The Green New Deal is plagiarism pure and simple. The plan borrows the same solutions proposed in the 1960s and 1970s.

Redistribute Wealth!

In 1974, future Obama science czar John Holdren proposed fighting environmental degradation with "redistribution of wealth." As he testified to the U.S. Senate Committee on Commerce, "The neo-Malthusian view proposes conscious accommodation to the perceived limits to growth via population limitation and redistribution of wealth in order to prevent the 'overshoot' phenomenon. My own sympathies are no doubt rather clear by this point. I find myself firmly in the neo-Malthusian camp."

The "overshoot problem" Holdren was referring to was the alleged exceeding of the carrying capacity of the environment by modern industrial life. The "neo-Malthusian camp" was a reference to Thomas Malthus, an eighteenth-century economist, who is considered the father of the ideology of limits to growth and fretted that expanding population growth would lead to resource scarcity and starvation.

Top UN IPCC officials have long pushed wealth redistribution as a "solution" to climate change. In 2010, IPCC Working Group 3 vice chair Ottmar Edenhofer publicly admitted that the UN seeks to "redistribute de facto the world's wealth by climate policy."

Edenhofer explained the obvious about "climate" policy: "One has to free oneself from the illusion that international climate policy is environmental policy. This has almost nothing to do with environmental policy anymore, with problems such as deforestation or the ozone hole."[6]

In 2019, the Green New Deal included eerily similar "solutions." As we saw in chapter 3, former Ocasio-Cortez campaign aide Waleed Shahid has admitted that that the Green New Deal is a "proposal to redistribute wealth and power from the people on top to the people on the bottom."[7]

"A Dystopian Malthusian Vision"

"Rich-world scientists in the grip of a dystopian Malthusian vision have, for 40 years, manipulated public fears of the bomb and 'over-population' to promote low-energy, anti-nuclear policies in the name of peace, prosperity, and the environment."
—Climate activist–turned climate apocalypse doubter Michael Shellenberger

"Move to a No-Growth Economy"

Stanford University biologist Paul Ehrlich testified at the same 1974 Senate hearing on the "Domestic Supply Information Act" held by the Committee on Commerce and Committee on Government Operations as John Holdren did.

Ehrlich's testimony will sound familiar to anyone following the modern climate debate. "I think that what is not realized, and it's going to be one of the hardest things to be accepted by the Americans in general, is that the onset of the age of scarcity essentially demolishes current models of economists," he said in 1974. "We are going to move to a no-growth [economy]." He urged the Senate to "do it intelligently through the Government by planning as rapidly as possible."[8]

In 1977, Holdren, Ehrlich, and Ehrlich's wife Anne co-authored a book that demanded "develop[ing] the United States": "A massive campaign must be launched to restore a high-quality environment in North America

The Club of Rome

Former Czech president Vaclav Klaus explained the genesis of much of today's modern green movement. "The Club of Rome was a grouping of very leftists, socialists, intellectuals. At the end of the 1960s, they met in Rome, and they produced their first famous doctrine called 'Limits to Growth,' advocating the dangers of economic growth and the necessity to stop economic growth. It was the beginning of environmental thinking."[9]

and to de-develop the United States....Resources and energy must be diverted from frivolous and wasteful uses in overdeveloped countries to filling the genuine needs of underdeveloped countries. This effort must be largely political."[10]

Researcher Robert Bradley Jr. has delved into the pseudoscience that Holdren and Ehrlich resorted to in their valiant attempts to convince policy makers to unravel the economy of the developed world on the basis of their scare scenario. "Holdren and Paul and Anne Ehrlich put their anti-growth philosophy into a mathematical equation, I=PAT, where a negative environmental impact was linked to any combination of population growth, increasing affluence, and improving technology."[11]

Their "gloomy prognosis" required "organized evasive action: population control, limitation of material consumption, redistribution of wealth, transitions to technologies that are environmentally and socially less disruptive than today's, and movement toward some kind of world government."[12]

They called for the literal "de-development" of the U.S. "Only one rational path is open to us—simultaneous de-development of the

> ### When You've Lost Bill Gates
>
> "University of Illinois economist Julian Simon challenged Paul Ehrlich to put his money where his mouth was and wager up to $1,000 (in 1981) on whether the prices of five different metals would rise or fall over the next decade," Bill Gates has explained. "Ehrlich and Simon saw the price of metals as a proxy for whether the world was hurtling toward apocalyptic scarcity (Ehrlich's position) or was on the verge of creating greater abundance (Simon's).
>
> "Who won the bet? Simon. Definitively. Even as the world population grew from 4.5 to 5.3 billion in the 1980s, the five minerals that were included in the bet—chromium, copper, nickel, tin, and tungsten—collectively dropped in price by almost half. Ehrlich begrudgingly made good on the bet. But to this day he still does not concede that his predictions of Malthusian horrors have been off the mark.... The Bet was a stark reminder to me of how apocalyptic a big part of the environmental movement has been," Gates wrote.
>
> Gates called Paul Ehrlich an "environmental Cassandra": "We know now that Ehrlich was extremely wrong and that following his scientific certainties would have been terrible for the poor."[13]

[overdeveloped countries] and semi-development of the underdeveloped countries (UDC's), in order to approach a decent and ecologically sustainable standard of living for all in between. By de-development we mean lower per-capita energy consumption, fewer gadgets, and the abolition of planned obsolescence," Holdren and Ehrlich had written as early as 1971.[14]

Fast forward to 2019 and we find school-skipper Greta Thunberg screaming at the United Nations in New York: "People are suffering. People are dying. Entire ecosystems are collapsing. We are in the beginning of a mass extinction, and all you can talk about is money and fairy tales of eternal economic growth. How dare you!"[15]

Greta's call for limiting economic growth, which was music to the ears of climate alarmists, echoed Ehrlich and Holdren's rhetoric from fifty years before.

The UN has hosted many calls to limit economic growth and redistribute wealth. As it happens, the current UN secretary-general Antonio Guterres is a former president of the Socialist International.

University of Manchester climate researcher Alice Bows-Larkin has called for "planned recessions" to fight global warming. "Economic growth needs to be exchanged at least temporarily for a period of planned austerity in wealthy nations."

World Government Redux

In 1974, the "problem" was supposed overpopulation. But the proposed "solutions" are eerily familiar. In that year Amherst College professor Leo Marx warned about the "global rate of human population growth. All of this is only to say that, on ecological grounds, the case for world government is beyond argument."[16]

Fast forward to 2009. Former vice president Al Gore expressed satisfaction that the congressional climate bill that had passed the House would help bring about "global governance." Gore explained, "One of the ways it will drive the change is through global governance and global agreements."[17]

In 2009, it was announced that the Obama State Department wanted to form a global "Ecological Board of Directors."[18]

Former French president Jacques Chirac said in 2000 that the UN's Kyoto Protocol on global warming represented "the first component of an authentic global governance."[19]

Alexandria Ocasio-Cortez has acknowledged that her Green New Deal will require "massive government intervention."[20]

Ocasio-Cortez's answer is in line with what the former UN climate chief Christiana Figueres admitted in 2012. Figueres said the UN was seeking a "centralized transformation" that is "going to make the life of everyone on the planet very different" in order to fight climate change. "The Industrial Revolution was also a transformation, but it wasn't a guided transformation from a centralized policy perspective. This is a centralized transformation that is taking place because governments have decided that they need to listen to science. So it's a very, very different transformation and one that is going to make the life of everyone on the planet very different."[21]

People Are the Problem

Population control is another familiar "solution" that has been pushed by the Left for decades.

Prominent environmentalist Paul Ehrlich pushed radical population control measures in the 1960s and 70s as the "solution" to an otherwise disastrous future for humanity and the planet. A November 17, 1967, article by *Los Angeles Times* staff writer George Getze reported, "It is already too late for the world to avoid a long period of famine, a Stanford University biologist said Thursday."

As the newspaper explained, "Paul Ehrlich said the 'time of famines' is upon us and will be at its worst and most disastrous by 1975. He said the population of the United States is already too big, that birth control may have to be accomplished by making it involuntary and by putting sterilizing agents into staple foods and drinking water, and that the Roman Catholic Church should be pressured into going along with routine measures of population control." That "solution" was the only way to ward of "the world famines of the next 20 years" which might "lead to thermonuclear war and the extinction of the human species."[22]

"A Sterility Drug in Food Is Hinted" blared a November 25, 1969, *New York Times* headline. "Biologist Stresses Need to Curb Population Growth," declared the subhead. The article, by Gladwin Hill, reported, "A possibility that the Government might have to put sterility drugs in reservoirs and in food shipped to foreign countries to limit human multiplication was envisioned today by a leading crusader on the population problem. The crusader Dr. Paul Ehrlich of Stanford University, among a number of commentators who called attention to the 'population crisis' as the United States Commission for Unesco opened its 13th national conference here today."[23]

Jacques Cousteau also weighed in on overpopulation. In a November 1991 article in the *UNESCO Courier*, the famed ocean explorer explained, "It's terrible to have to say this. World population must be stabilized and to do that we must eliminate 350,000 people per day."[25]

> ### News Flash: The World Population Didn't Starve to Death in the Eighties
>
> "Despite an explosion in population greater than Malthus could have ever imagined, global living standards are higher than ever."
> —Nigel Lawson in the *Wall Street Journal* in 2015[24]

Be in no doubt, prominent environmentalists wanted to rid the Earth of humans using the coercive powers of the state, based upon their claims that rapid depopulation was necessary.

In our current time, the same push to control population is being promoted in the modern climate debate—though thankfully the population control "solutions" are a bit less radical than Ehrlich's coerced proposals. Limiting population growth was the "solution" proposed to overpopulation concerns in the 1960s and 1970s, but now limiting population is being proposed as the solution to climate change.

"Earth Needs Fewer People to Beat the Climate Crisis, Scientists Say," blared a Bloomberg News headline in 2019. "More than 11,000 experts sign an emergency declaration warning that energy, food and reproduction must change immediately."[27]

> ### What's Your Poison?
>
> "So 50 years ago the UN, the *New York Times*, and academia were openly discussing the possibility of poisoning people's food and water. They quite openly said that the government might have to poison people [to reduce the population]," Tony Heller of RealClimateScience.com has pointed out. "Now let's fast forward to November 2019. Once again we see the same collaboration of the press academia and the UN pushing for far fewer people on the planet."[26]

"A Bit of a Joke"

"I don't believe in overpopulation. I think that's just a kind of a myth the government has thrown out to keep your mind off Vietnam and all the important subjects," former Beatle John Lennon said on the *Dick Cavett Show* in 1971. "I think it's a bit of a joke the way people have made this overpopulation thing into a kind of myth. I don't really believe it. I think whatever happens will balance itself out and work itself out." He added, "I think we've got enough food and money to feed everybody."[28]

In a 2019 letter published in *Bioscience*, more than ten thousand scientists signed on to a letter saying that population "must be stabilized—and, ideally, gradually reduced—within a framework that ensures social integrity." The "profoundly troubling signs from human activities" that led them to that conclusion included "sustained increases in both human and ruminant livestock populations." And, the academics claimed, "Economic and population growth are among the most important drivers of increases in CO_2 emissions from fossil fuel combustion, therefore, we need bold and drastic transformations regarding economic and population policies."[29]

Former vice president Al Gore is also channeling Ehrlich. "In the next 17 years, the population of the global middle class will grow by

"I Regret Having My Kids"

"Fears that climate change will make the Earth uninhabitable are leading some Americans to decide against having kids," according to a study published in the scientific journal *Climatic Change*, the New York Post reported in 2020. "I feel like I can't in good conscience bring a child into this world and force them to try and survive what may be apocalyptic conditions," a twenty-seven-year-old woman told researchers.

Another participant in the study…worried that future weather conditions would "rival world war one in its sheer terror…. 'I regret having my kids because I am terrified that they will be facing the end of the world due to climate change,' a 40-year-old mom said."[30]

3 billion people. How will we accommodate them on a finite planet?" Gore asked.[31]

Representative Alexandria Ocasio-Cortez declared in a 2019 Instagram video, "Our planet is going to face disaster if we don't turn this ship around. And so it's basically like, there is a scientific consensus that the lives of children are going to be very difficult and it does lead, I think young people, to have a legitimate question. You know, should—is it okay to still have children?"[32]

In 2017, *Bill Nye Saves the World* featured a philosophy professor warning that having too many kids is bad for the planet. Bill Nye "the Science Guy" asked him, "So, should we have policies that penalize people for having extra kids in the developed world?" Professor Travis Rieder answered, "I do think that we should at least consider it," and Nye responded, "Well, 'at least consider it' is like 'do it.'"

A 2016 NPR segment titled "Should We Be Having Kids in the Age of Climate Change?" featured Professor Rieder saying, "We should protect our kids by not having them." Rieder proposed "actually penalizing new parents" with a tax that "should be progressive, based on income, and could increase with each additional child. Think of it like a carbon tax, on kids."[34]

In 2014, Al Gore advocated "fertility management" to reduce the number of Africans and help mitigate climate change. In remarks

> ## The Population Bomb Was a Dud
>
> "Research suggests we may actually face a declining world population in the coming years," reported Slate in 2013. "The rate of global population growth has slowed. And it's expected to keep slowing. Indeed, according to experts' best estimates, the total population of Earth will stop growing within the lifespan of people alive today. And then it will fall....It comes down to simple math. According to a 2008 IIASA (International Institute for Applied Systems Analysis) report, if the world stabilizes at a total fertility rate of 1.5—where Europe is today—then by 2200 the global population will fall to half of what it is today. By 2300, it'll barely scratch 1 billion."[33]

"Problem Solved!"

In April of 2018 California governor Jerry Brown warned that climate change was going to kill 3 billion people.[35] "This is a horror," Brown said. "The prospect is 3 billion people on this planet will be subject to fatal lethal heat events—3 billion."[36] Two months later the Berkeley City Council declared a "climate emergency" in 2018 and called for action to "humanely stabilize population."[37]

I appeared on *Varney & Company* on Fox Business Network and explained how these two claims cancel each other out. I explained to host Stuart Varney: "Now here's the problem. The Berkeley California city council is worried that overpopulation will lead to global warming—but their own governor is saying that global warming is going to kill 3 billion people. Problem solved! Global warming will kill the excess population. We just solved it!"[38]

alongside of Bill Gates at a World Economic Forum, the former vice president explained that "making fertility management ubiquitously available" is "crucial" to reduce resource use. "Africa is projected to have more people than China and India by mid-century—more than China and India combined by the end of the century. And this is one of the causal factors that must be addressed.... contraception is a key in controlling the proliferation of unusual weather they say is endangering the world."

As Michael Shellenberger, former climate activist now turned against climate doom, explained in 2020, "It's the same people, the same movement. Climate emerges at exactly the moment when it was clear that overpopulation wasn't going to be the big concern everybody thought it was. When the climate goes away as an apocalyptic concern, something else will emerge. No doubt about it."

Nothing has changed over the decades. The "demands are the same: Don't let poor countries have fossil fuels, for heaven's sake. Don't let them industrialize. How terrible. Don't let them move to cities, keep them in the villages, let's give them a solar panel and a battery, that ought to be good enough. It's pretty dark stuff," said Shellenberger.[39]

Blowing Hot and Cold

Coincidentally, the global cooling–coming ice age scare of the 1970s required the exact same "solutions" as modern climate change!

As Tony Heller, historical researcher at the website Real Climate Science, found, "Every major climate organization endorsed the ice age scare, including NCAR, CRU, NAS, NASA—as did the CIA." In fact, the CIA issued reports warning about the dire implications of the imminent cooling.

A 1975 *Newsweek* article titled "The Cooling World" warned that "the earth's climate seems to be cooling down." The magazine explained that scientists "are almost unanimous in the view that the trend will reduce agricultural productivity for the rest of the century. If the climatic change is as profound as some of the pessimists fear, the resulting famines could be catastrophic. A major climatic change would force economic and social adjustments on a worldwide scale,'" warns a recent report by the National Academy of Sciences.[40]

We're in luck! Geoengineering solves both global cooling AND global warming.

Newsweek noted that one of the "more spectacular solutions proposed" for the coming ice age was "melting the Arctic ice cap by covering it with black soot or diverting arctic rivers." A similar "solution" was also suggested by Leonard Nimoy in a 1978 episode of *In Search Of...*. The man who played Spock presented other such "solutions" for global cooling, including using nuclear energy to "loosen polar ice caps" or blanketing the ice caps in soot to help melt them.[41]

Fast forward to the modern climate change debate, and the same type of ideas are being offered. In 2018, the idea of geoengineering the Earth or its atmosphere was proposed to fight "global warming." A 2018 headline in the UK *Independent* blared: "First Ever Sun-Dimming Experiment Will Mimic Volcanic Eruption in Attempt to Reverse Global Warming."

The article explained, "Plans to geoengineer the atmosphere by blocking out sunlight have been floated before, but an experiment launched

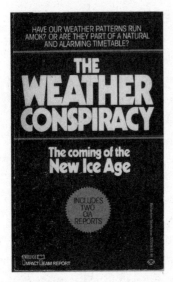

HAVE OUR WEATHER PATTERNS RUN AMOK? OR ARE THEY PART OF A NATURAL AND ALARMING TIMETABLE?

THE **WEATHER CONSPIRACY**

The coming of the **New Ice Age**

INCLUDES TWO CIA REPORTS

IMPACT TEAM REPORT

1977 book warning of the coming ice age.

next year by Harvard researchers will be the first to test the theory in the stratosphere."

Research team member David Keith boasted, "If solar geoengineering is as good as what is shown in these models, it would be crazy not to take it seriously." The experiment "has been partly funded by Bill Gates of Microsoft."[42]

In 2009, Obama White House science advisor John Holdren suggested that we inject pollutants into the atmosphere to cool the planet and cancel out the warming impacts of pollution. As Keith reported, "Holdren told the Associated Press in his first interview since being confirmed last month that the idea of geoengineering the climate is being discussed. One such extreme option includes shooting pollution particles into the upper atmosphere to reflect the sun's rays.... 'It's got to be looked at,' Holdren said. 'We don't have the luxury of taking any approach off the table.'"[43]

A 2012 PJ Media analysis of a 1977 book entitled *The Weather Conspiracy: The Coming of the New Ice Age*, a report by the "Impact Team"[44] demonstrated how the very same "solutions" that are now supposed to cure global warming were proposed over forty years ago to fight global cooling. "In both cases, proponents of the theory-du-jour say that in order to stave off disaster, we must reverse the march of civilization, stop our profligate use of carbon-based fuels, cede power and money from the First World to the Third World, and wherever possible revert to a Luddite pre-industrial lifestyle," PJ Media explained.

The ice age scare book included "two CIA reports" detailing the impacts of the ice age that was reportedly upon us in the 1970s: "The back cover of the book explains: 'From all over the world, frightening accounts of unusual climatic occurrences!... Many of the world's leading climatologists concur: We are slipping towards a new ice age. What can—and can't—we do about it? The answers are in this book!"

As the PJ analysis noted, the 1977 ice age book "spells out all the steps we need to take to survive the upcoming ice age, and—who could have guessed?—they're the exact same steps we now need to take to survive global warming!" noted the analysis. PJ Media summed up the book's message about the coming ice age—a message that will be very familiar:

> There's very little we can do to stop it at this late stage, but we might be able to save ourselves if we immediately take these necessary and drastic steps:
>
> - Increase our reliance on alternative energy sources and stop using so much oil and other carbon-based fuels;
> - Adopt energy-efficient practices in all aspects of our lives, however inconvenient;
> - Impose punitive taxes on inefficient or polluting activities to discourage them;
> - Funnel large sums of money from developed nations like the U.S. to Third World nations;
> - In general embrace all environmental causes.

Opposite Effects

"Fossil fuels are tricky, but evil. In 1975, scientists said that fossil fuels were going to freeze us to death. Forty years later they now know that fossil fuels will burn us up," noted Tony Heller of Real Climate Science, referring to a 1975 article titled "Pollution May Lead to New Ice Age"[45]

In short, before fossil fuels caused global warming, fossil fuels caused…global cooling. Burning fossil fuels was releasing aerosols that were going to block out the Sun and cause the Earth to cool.

The 1977 book reads eerily like an early version of the Green New Deal: "Now we must reduce our standard of living in small ways—lowered room temperatures, fewer gadgets, smaller cars—and in big ways—legislated home improvements, energy-use taxes, and staggered working hours."[46]

"Solutions" That Were Proposed to Fend Off the Coming Ice Age in 1977—and Suspiciously Similar "Solutions" Being Proposed in the Current Climate Change Debate

What follows is my own analysis of the similarities.

The 1977 Ice Age Book: *The Weather Conspiracy: The Coming of the New Ice Age* claimed, "It is probably that only by supplying aid on an unparalleled scale can the rich nations of the world assist the poor in reordering land development priorities and relocating the people this would involve."

The Climate Change Scare Today: This wish from 1977 has become reality. The UN climate fund drains money from wealthy nations to redistribute to poor nations. The Associated Press has described the UN climate fund as a way to "distribute tens of billions of dollars a year to poor countries to help them adapt to changing climate conditions and to move toward low-carbon economic growth." South African development activist Leon Louw criticized the UN's "Green Climate Fund" at the 2011 UN Climate Conference in Johannesburg, South Africa. "Government to government aid is a reward for being better than anyone else at causing poverty," he explained. "It enriches the people who cause poverty....The UN is saying to poor countries: 'Those of you who adopt more anti-prosperity, anti-jobs, and anti-growth policies—under the pretense of environmentalism—we will enrich you.'"

The 1977 Ice Age Book: "The United States government must level with its citizens and explain that all man's reserves are finite. Given the Earth's natural limitations, our current phenomenal rate of waste, inherent in our current consumption of both fossil fuels and food, must stop."

Ice Age Fears

An essay by John Holdren and Paul Ehrlich in the 1971 book *Global Ecology: Readings Toward a Rational Strategy for Man* raised concerns about global cooling. Holdren and Ehrlich noted that since 1940 "the reduced transparency of the atmosphere to incoming light as a result of urban air pollution (smoke, aerosols), agricultural air pollution (dust), and volcanic ash" created a "screening phenomenon" that is "said to be responsible for the present world cooling trend— a total of about .2°C in the world mean surface temperature over the past quarter century. This number seems small until it is realized that a decrease of only 4°C would probably be sufficient to start another ice age."[47]

The Climate Change Scare Today: Concerns about finite resources and government-mandated limits on human behavior are at the heart of the climate debate today. "Global warming is now such a serious threat to mankind that climate change experts are calling for Second World War-style rationing in rich countries to bring down carbon emissions," reported a 2010 UK *Telegraph* article.

"Professor Kevin Anderson, director of the Tyndall Centre for Climate Change Research, said the only way to reduce global emissions enough, while allowing the poor nations to continue to grow, is to halt economic growth in the rich world over the next twenty years," the newspaper reported. "This would mean a drastic change in lifestyles for many people in countries like Britain as everyone will have to buy less 'carbon intensive' goods and services such as long haul flights and fuel hungry cars."[48]

The 1977 Ice Age Book: *The Weather Conspiracy* warned that the "phenomenal rate of waste" from consumption of food "must stop." Fast forward to the twenty-first century, and the UN is warning that "wasted" food is frying the planet. "The food the world wastes accounts for more greenhouse gas emissions than any country except for China and the U.S., the UN said in a report," according to a Reuters story about the

"The Food Wastage Footprint" from the UN Food and Agriculture Organisation. The UN "estimated that the carbon footprint of wasted food was equivalent to 3.3 billion tonnes of carbon dioxide per year."[49]

The Climate Change Scare Today: Leap forward a few decades and voilà: "We have to keep 80 percent of the fossil-fuel reserves that we know about underground. If we don't—if we dig up the coal and oil and gas and burn them—we will overwhelm the planet's physical systems, heating the Earth far past the red lines drawn by scientists and governments," declared activist Bill McKibben, one of the leaders of the "keep it in the ground" movement, in 2016. "We have to do this."[52]

The 1977 Ice Age Book: "Energy prices must be raised to reflect America's energy import bill and the scarcity value of fossil fuels."

The Climate Change Scare Today: The modern climate debate has featured endless attempts—with some success—to raise energy prices.

As the *Vancouver Sun* reported in 2013, "Thomas Stocker suggests the planet might be better off if [gas prices] soared to 'three to four' times its current level. 'This is scandalous, I know,' said Stocker, adding sky-high gasoline could help slow the climate change which world leaders have declared one of the greatest challenges of our time.... He said Canadians, like Americans, could make a significant dent in their emissions by reducing per capita energy use, which is among the highest on the planet."[53]

President Obama's energy secretary Stephen Chu is also on record calling for a huge jump in gas prices. "Somehow we have to figure out how to increase the price of gasoline to the levels in Europe," Chu said in 2008.[54]

The 1977 Ice Age Book: *The Weather Conspiracy: The Coming of the New Ice Age* laid out the supposed "need for major coordinated international efforts to cope with climatic change."

The Climate Change Scare Today: This has happened—in spades! The UN IPCC was formed in 1988, and ever since the world has been subject to a self-interested lobbying organization bent on hyping a "solution" to global warming, all while putting itself in charge of that "solution." The UN's most recent "major coordinated international effort" was the 2015 Paris Agreement.

The 1977 Ice Age Book: *The Weather Conspiracy* said we must seek "to foster research into alternative fuel and food sources and more efficient use of those we already possess."

The Climate Change Scare Today: Statistician Bjørn Lomborg explained in 2017 how spending untold money on renewable energy research has not panned out: "After hundreds of billions of dollars in annual subsidies, we only get, according to the International Energy Agency, 0.5 per cent of the world's energy needs from wind, and 0.1 per cent from solar PV."[55]

But some people have benefited greatly. According to a 2012 *Washington Post* report, "14 green-tech firms in which Gore invested received or directly benefited from more than $2.5 billion in loans, grants and tax breaks, part of Obama's historic push to seed a U.S. renewable-energy industry with public money." The *Post* explained that Gore "benefited from a powerful resume and a constellation of friends in the investment world and in Washington. And four years ago, his portfolio aligned smoothly with the agenda of an incoming administration and its plan to spend billions in stimulus funds on alternative energy. The recovering politician was pushing the right cause at the perfect time.... Gore's orbit extended deeply into the administration, with several former aides winning senior clean-energy posts."

> ### Don't Jump!
>
> "The solution (commit civilizational suicide) always remains the same; all that differs are the wildly divergent purported 'crises' proffered up to justify the imposition of the solution."
> —PJ Media analysis[56]

The 1977 Ice Age Book: "Private dwellings should be taxed according to the efficiency of their energy use. . . . People who carpool would be rewarded, as would those whose housing designs and insulation were energy efficient. The latter may require federal regulations."

The Climate Change Scare Today: At this point, just taxing private dwellings seems positively quaint. Current "solutions" include calls to abolish homes.

The modern global warming debate has gone way beyond taxing houses and is now seeking to ban their construction. In 2019, Senator Elizabeth Warren sought to ban the construction of new homes in America unless they are "Zero Carbon Footprint."[57]

The climate assault on home ownership continued, with UCLA urban planning professor Kian Goh announcing that home ownership may no longer be climate-viable. Goh explained that "cheap energy is untenable in the face of a climate emergency. And individual homeownership should be seriously questioned."[58]

The 1977 Ice Age Book: "Now we must reduce our standard of living in small ways—lowered room temperatures, fewer gadgets, smaller cars—and in big ways—legislated home improvements, energy-use taxes, and staggered working hours."

The Climate Change Scare Today: "Lowered room temperatures?" Again, that's positively quaint.

The current generation of climate alarmists are aiming for full government thermostat control! In 2008, the California state government sought to control home thermostats remotely. The *New York Times* compared this proposal to the 1960s science fiction show *The Outer Limits*. "California state regulators are likely to have the emergency power to control individual thermostats, sending temperatures up or down through a radio-controlled device," the *Times* reported.

The 1977 Ice Age Book: *The Weather Conspiracy: The Coming of the New Ice Age* said we needed to drive "smaller cars" to fight global cooling. Its authors also argued, "It is probable that taxes should be based on the horsepower and corresponding energy efficiency of automobiles."

The Climate Change Scare Today: Once again, the policy proposals that seemed extreme in the seventies now seem quite modest. The current climate scare is being used to justify demands to abolish private car ownership altogether. As we have seen, Andrew Yang, candidate in the 2019 Democratic presidential primaries, warned that climate change may require the elimination of car ownership; Americans would have to depend on a "constant roving fleet of electric cars" instead. "We might not own our own cars. Our current car ownership and usage model is really inefficient and bad for the environment," Yang said.[59] Democrat primary candidate Senator Elizabeth Warren urged, "By 2030, trucks—light-duty trucks and cars, zero carbon footprint."

The 1977 Ice Age Book: *The Weather Conspiracy* authors recommended "energy-use taxes."

Rewriting History

A 2008 paper entitled "The Myth of the 1970s Global Cooling Consensus" attempted to erase the 1970s scare about the coming ice age. But researcher Kenneth Richard of NoTricksZone found in 2016 that there was an overwhelming scientific consensus in the 1960s and 1970s that the planet was on a cooling path. His analysis found "285 papers from 1960s–'80s revealed a robust global cooling scientific 'consensus.'" Richard noted that "220 'cooling' papers published between 1965–'79 could represent an 83.3% global cooling consensus for the era." He concluded, "Concerns about global cooling were quite real, widespread, and scientifically-supported."[60]

The Climate Change Scare Today: In recent decades the U.S. and Europe have been under an onslaught of carbon taxes, not to mention solar and wind energy mandates.

The 1977 Ice Age Book: "Staggered working hours."

The Climate Change Scare Today: Once again, our current age has gone way beyond the proposals from the 1970s. A 2013 study by the Center for Economic Policy and Research, a progressive think tank based in Washington, D.C., claimed "working fewer hours might help slow global warming" and that we should undergo a worldwide switch to a "more European" work schedule. The title of the study was: "Reduced Work Hours as a Means of Slowing Climate Change." According to *U.S. News & World Report*, the study claimed working less "could prevent as much as half of the expected global temperature rise by 2100."[61]

The 1977 Ice Age Book: "Finally, the government should consider imposing a food tax based on the nutritional value of the food we eat. If you want to eat a pound of choice steak, that's fine—but the price should reflect the fact that you are consuming the equivalent of thirteen Asians' daily diet—sixteen pounds of grain."

The Climate Change Scare Today: Current proposals go way beyond a "food tax" and now include a full-scale war on meat-eating and modern agriculture. We have already seen how the Green New Deal goes after "farting cows." The UN came out demanding a war on meat in 2019 in a special report calling for changes in humans diet.[62] The UN had previously claimed, in

> **Ban Veggies Instead?**
>
> "Eating lettuce is over three times worse in greenhouse gas emissions than eating bacon," reported a Carnegie Mellon University 2015 study. Vegetarian diets could be "worse" for climate change than meat, up to three times "more harmful to the environment....Lots of common vegetables require more resources per calorie than you would think. Eggplant, celery and cucumbers look particularly bad when compared to pork or chicken," the study found.[63]

2006, that emissions from cows account for more emissions than all of the transportation sector—airlines, planes, automobiles—combined.[64]

And lest you think it will stop with banning meat…the food police are gunning for more. A study from the Research Institute for Humanity and Nature in Kyoto, Japan, targeted dining out, eating dessert, and drinking alcohol as even worse for the climate worse than meat. "If we are serious about reducing our carbon footprints, then our diets must change," noted study author, associate professor Keiichiro Kanemoto of the Research Institute for Humanity and Nature in Kyoto. "If we think of a carbon tax, it might be wiser to target sweets and alcohol if we want a progressive system…to target less-nutritious foods that are excessively consumed in some population's," Kanemoto added.[65]

University Professor Matthew Liao of the Center for Bioethics at New York University has issued a call to shrink humans as a species to lower our carbon footprint. "I call this human engineering. It involves biomedical modification of humans to better deal with" climate change, Liao explains.[66]

With human engineering "we can make humans smaller," he noted. "By reducing the height of an average man in the U.S. by just 15 cm, it would mean a 23% reduction in metabolic reduction," he calculated. "Another possible and more dangerous possibility is to consider hormone treatments to close growth hormone earlier than normal," he explained. "How can height

"Insects Are Highly Nutritious"

The UN's proposed "solution" to meat eating? NBC News reported in 2017 that the Food and Agriculture Organization of the United Nations "may have a bite-sized solution: insects." In an article titled "How Crickets Could Help Save the Planet," NBC reported that "insects are highly nutritious, and also far more environmentally friendly to raise than conventional livestock." The UN "suggested our current farming and food production practices are unsustainable—but that edible insects are a viable, untapped resource that could help meet the food and water demands of the world's ever-expanding population."[67]

reduction be achieved? One possibility is to use pre-implantation genetics to select shorter children," Liao noted.[68]

He also proposed a meat patch to stop climate-unfriendly meat cravings. Liao has argued that we should "make ourselves allergic to those proteins" in meat so that we suffer an "unpleasant reaction" when we attempt to eat it. "The way we can do that is to create some sort of meat patch," he explained. "Kind of like a nicotine patch where you put it on before you go to dinner go out to restaurant and this will curb your enthusiasm for eating meat."[69]

The 1977 Ice Age Book: To stop the next ice age, "add an ecology tax to each ton [of coal] extracted (experts estimate this at three to six dollars a ton) to repair the damage done."

The Climate Change Scare Today: Today's version of the "ecology tax" is at the heart of all climate proposals over the past several decades and is today known by many names: cap-and-trade, carbon (dioxide) taxes, green energy mandates, and so forth. Many attempts have been made to impose such climate taxes nationwide in the United States, but so far the effort has failed. But the modern-day climate campaigners are not giving up. UN secretary-general Guterres told the climate summit in Madrid that new carbon taxes are needed in 2020.[70]

The 1977 Ice Age Book: "Shower, Don't Bathe. Showers use far less water than tubs. Fine-spray nozzles use far less water than strong-spray ones."

The Climate Change Scare Today: Once again, the "solutions" from the 1970s are downright modest when compared to our present day. Now even showers are a problem! Kevin Anderson, the deputy director of the Tyndall Centre for Climate Change Research in the UK recommended showering less to fight climate change at the 2013 UN climate summit in Poland. "I've cut back on washing and showering—but only to levels that were the norm just a few years back," Anderson told me. "That is why I smell, yes."[71]

And baths are still not recommended. The UN awarded a group of young kids a prize for "best children's global climate change song" in a video timed for release at the 2015 UN Paris climate summit.[72] The video featured children "climate astronauts" singing, "We are astronauts, don't need no bath." The kids also sang, "We don't need no CO2.... We are astronauts of Mother Earth—we don't need no cars."[73]

It's all rather confusing. Are baths bad for the Earth, or good? Al Gore has recommended taking a bath with someone to fight global warming. Gore's 2007 "Live Earth Global Warming Survival Handbook," touts "77 essential skills to fight climate change—or live through it." And "essential skill number #45" is 'Bathe Together.' Gore's booklet urges you to "do it for the planet": "In a matter of just a few decades, millions of people will experience water shortages due to global warming which could be the perfect excuse to share your bath."[74]

CHAPTER 7

The Red New Deal?
The Watermelon Cut Open

The Green New Deal is all about "de-growth" and "planned recessions." Central planning is the real goal.

We have seen how the claim of a "global warming" crisis is merely the latest environmental scare that the progressive Left is using to get their statist agenda implemented. It's a watermelon: green on the outside, red on the inside.

What riles up climate activists more than anything else is the free market economy, particularly the U.S. version. The ideological battle between capitalism and socialism is at the heart of climate alarmism and of proposed "solutions" like the Green New Deal.

Capitalism Is the Real Target

Naomi Klein essentially admits this in her book *This Changes Everything: Capitalism vs the Climate*, in which she claims capitalism "is irreconcilable with a livable climate." According to Klein, "Facing climate change head-on means changing capitalism." Solving climate change is incompatible with our current economic system: "Core inequalities need

to be tackled through redistribution of wealth and technology."

Klein, who serves as an advisor
to Pope Francis, explains, "If climate can be our lens to catalyze
this economic transformation that
so many people need for other
even more pressing reasons, then
maybe that's a winning combination." She is calling for a whole
new system. "I think we might be able to come with a system that is
ecologically rooted that is better than anything that we have tried before."

When I interviewed Klein at the People's Climate March in New York
City in 2014, she admitted that climate activists would be seeking the
same solutions even if there was no global warming issue.

To Klein, "global warming" is definitely not about carbon dioxide.
"Forget everything you think you know about global warming. The
really inconvenient truth is that it's not about carbon—it's about capitalism," Klein explained in her book.

Never let an alleged "crisis" go to waste. "The convenient truth is
that we can seize this existential crisis to transform our failed economic
system and build something radically better," Klein said.[2]

Economist Walter Williams of George Mason University has
explained why capitalism is so unpopular regardless of its successes.
"Despite the miracles of capitalism, it doesn't do well in popularity polls.
One of the reasons is that capitalism is always evaluated against the non-
existent utopias of socialism or communism. Any earthly system pales
in comparison to utopias," Williams pointed out in 2017. "But for the
ordinary person, capitalism, with all of its warts, is superior to any system yet devised to deal with our everyday needs and desires."[3]

But climate activists, particularly those in academia still keep hankering
for something better. Capitalism is allegedly incompatible with the climate,
and it must go. How? The answer is simple: throttle economic growth and

shrink the economy to a level they consider climate-friendly. The throttling mechanism includes economic "degrowth" or "planned recessions."

According to the Degrowth Web Portal, "The beginning of [the degrowth] idea can be dated to the year 1972...the same year, 'The Limits to Growth' was published by the Club of Rome." That was when "social philosopher André Gorz asked: 'Is the earth's balance, for which no-growth—or even degrowth—of material production is a necessary condition, compatible with the survival of the capitalist system?'"

Critics of capitalism like to talk about "degrowth" because the word

Flyer from the People's Climate March in New York City in 2014.

"creates disruption. Disruption in a world where the critique of economic growth is a radical position." The movement has caught on in certain circles, and "more than 100 academic papers on degrowth have been published in international journals since 2008."[4]

University of Manchester climate researcher Alice Bows-Larkin has also called for "planned recessions" to fight global warming. "Economic growth needs to be exchanged" for "planned austerity." She advocates a "whole system change." Bows-Larkin explained: "Economic growth

Dreams Turn into Nightmares

"The green agenda and the environmentalist agenda and the fighting climate agenda is trying to basically stop the existence of the free market system which we were fighting for and we were dreaming about in the communist era for decades."
—former Czech president Vaclav Klaus[5]

needs to be exchanged at least temporarily for a period of planned auster-ity in wealthy nations."

Bows-Larkin said, "This is not about just incremental change. This is about doing things differently, about whole system change, and some-times it's about doing less things.... We really need to make significant change."[6]

Professor Bows-Larkin and her colleague Professor Kevin Ander-son—the fellow who told me at the climate meeting in Poland in 2013 that he had cut back on showering and explained, "That is why I smell, yes"—have written papers calling for "planned recessions" to reduce economic growth and thus emissions in order to fight man-made climate change. They wrote: "Unless economic growth can be reconciled with unprecedented rates of decarbonization (in excess of 6% per year), it is difficult to envisage anything other than a planned economic recession being compatible with stabilization at or below 650ppm CO2."[7]

Bows-Larkin explained, "If we're all constrained by the same amount of carbon budget, that means that if some parts of the world's emissions are needing to rise, then other parts of the world's emissions need to reduce.... So I'd just like to take a quote from a paper by myself and Kevin Anderson back in 2011 where we said that to avoid the two-degree framing of dangerous climate change, economic growth needs to be exchanged at least temporarily for a period of planned austerity in wealthy nations...."

The reductions Bows-Larkin was talking about were drastic: "According to our research, if you're in a country where per cap-ita emissions are really high—so North America, Europe,

> **"Overthrow This System"**
>
> UK environmentalist George Monbiot revealed the true motives of the climate movement:
>
> "We have to overthrow this sys-tem which is eating the planet: perpetual growth," declared Monbiot on a 2019 UK TV show. "We can't do it by just piddling around at the margins of the problem; we've got to go straight to the heart of capitalism and overthrow it."[8]

Australia—emissions reductions of the order of 10 percent per year, and starting immediately, will be required for a good chance of avoiding the two-degree target."[9]

"Terminate Industrial Civilization"

"The only way to stop runaway climate change is to terminate industrial civilization."

—Professor Guy McPherson said on *The Paul Henry Show*, on New Zealand's TV3

The impetus behind the Green New Deal is now quite clear. When you warn that it will be too late to save the planet from the "climate emergency" unless you restrict energy access and manage and plan every aspect of the economy in the name of global warming, you suddenly have the power to create "planned recessions."

Bows-Larkin's colleague Kevin Anderson has written (presumably between his infrequent showers) of the need for "a planned economic recession" to reduce emissions. "Continuing with economic growth over the coming two decades is incompatible with meeting our international obligations on climate change." Anderson, the deputy director of the UK's Tyndall Centre for Climate Change Research, told a UN climate summit that "nations should give up growth obsession."[10]

Anderson's proposals were met with derision from UN IPCC lead author Dr. Richard Tol: "Kevin Anderson, lavishly funded by UK taxpayers, calls for a Greater Depression in the name of climate change."[11]

But Anderson is dead serious. "For humanity it's a matter of life or death....we will not make all human beings extinct, as a few people with the right sort of resources may put themselves in the right parts of the world and survive. But I think it's extremely unlikely that we wouldn't have mass death at 4 degrees," Anderson believes.

Kill or Be Killed

"The world is on fire. This is no time to be patient. If we don't abolish capitalism, capitalism will abolish us."

—Dartmouth College lecturer Mark Bray, "How Capitalism Stokes the Far Right and Climate Catastrophe"[12]

Anderson's outlook is relentlessly grim: "If you have got a population of 9 billion by 2050 and you hit 4 degrees, 5 degrees or 6 degrees, you might have half a billion people surviving."[13]

Former Czech president Vaclav Klaus, who grew up in the former Czechoslovakia under Soviet domination, sees the climate agenda as a grave threat to liberty. I travelled to the Czech Republic to interview Klaus in person for my 2020 film *Climate Hustle 2*. "I'm afraid that there are new '-isms,' which are more and more dangerous than the last era. And I put on the first place that definitely one 'ism' called environmentalism or global warming alarmism," Klaus explained to me.

"Our life under communism increased our sensitivity to all ways of endangering freedom and democracy in the world," he explained. The climate agenda is "more or less nothing new. It's just the quantitative increasing of all the ways of how to block free human activity," Klaus added.[14]

In June 2020, the calls for a climate-crisis-inspired micro-managed economy continued with the journal *Nature Communications* publishing a paper touting "Scientists' Warning on Affluence."

The article in the prestigious journal claims that wealth harms the planet and offers such solutions as "degrowth," as well as "eco-socialism," "maximum income levels," "eco-feminism," and banning "oversized vehicles."

The study avers that the "affluent citizens of the world are responsible for most environmental impacts" and proposed "far-reaching lifestyle changes" to solve the problem. "We provide evidence from the literature that consumption of affluent households worldwide is by far the strongest determinant and the strongest accelerator of increases of global environmental and social impacts.... These solution approaches range from reformist to radical ideas, including degrowth, eco-socialism and eco-anarchism."

Interestingly, the authors of this study freely admit that capitalism and free markets "have increased affluence since World War 2." But the free market has also, the study claims, "led to enormous increases in inequality, financial instability, resource consumption and environmental pressures on vital earth support systems." The solution? "A shift beyond capitalism."

The paper lamented the fact that "low-income groups are rapidly occupying middle- and high-income brackets around the world. This can potentially further exacerbate the impacts of mobility-related consumption,

> ### It Ain't Over Until the Fat Capitalist Sings
> "Capitalism as we know it is over. So suggests a new report commissioned by a group of scientists appointed by the UN Secretary-General."
> —"Scientists Warn the UN of Capitalism's Imminent Demise," Nafeez Ahmend at Vice[15]

which has been shown to disproportionately increase with income.... Affluence needs to be addressed by reducing consumption."

The new goal? "Avoid or to reduce consumption until the remaining consumption level falls within planetary boundaries, while fulfilling human needs." Citizens need to stop "consuming certain goods and services, from living space (overly large homes, secondary residences of the wealthy) to oversized vehicles, environmentally damaging and wasteful food, leisure patterns and work patterns involving driving and flying." Instead we need "'sustainable consumption corridors', i.e. minimum and maximum consumption standards."

The authors of this study also argued,

> Eco-feminist approaches highlight the role of patriarchal social relations and the parallels between the oppression of women and exploitation of nature....
>
> Strengthen equality and redistribution through suitable taxation policies, basic income and job guarantees and by setting maximum income levels, expanding public services and rolling back neoliberal reforms (e.g. as part of a Green New Deal).

"Setting maximum income levels": "The transformation of economic systems can be supported with innovative business models that encourage sharing and giving economies, based on cooperation, communities and localised economies instead of competition."[16]

Patrick Moore, Greenpeace founder–turned climate skeptic, was disgusted: "How does this garbage get published? I have never seen the forests and wild lands so lush with growth. The CO_2 fertilization effect is real, 35% increase in growth, caused by affluence. Can't we teach them just one thing, that the CO_2 we are putting into the atmosphere came from there in the first place? That fossil fuels were made from plants?"[17]

The journal *Nature* has touted "degrowth" for the sake of the climate.

A 2018 study in the journal *Nature Sustainability* also found that economic "degrowth" was needed to fight "global warming." The study claimed the economy needs to be redesigned "within planetary boundaries." The study urged "moving beyond the pursuit of GDP growth to embrace new measures of progress. It could also involve the pursuit of 'degrowth' in wealthy nations and the shift towards alternative economic models such as a steady-state economy."[18]

Wesley J. Smith commented on the study in an article in *National Review*: "In other words, growth is out. We must live within economic and social systems strictly limited by arbitrary boundaries on the use of resources established by 'the experts.'... The environmental movement wants to make the rich West much poorer so that the destitute can become richer."

And, Smith asked, "How are you going to do that, fellows? Confiscation of wealth? Increased socialism? Destruction of democracy for those countries not willing to strip their walls bare? In so many words, all of the above."

Smith slammed the *Nature Sustainability* paper: "In other words, forget creating a world with freedom of opportunity, but tilt at Utopian windmills to force equal outcomes: To each according to his needs, from each according to his ability.... The goal clearly is a technocracy that will undermine freedom, constrain opportunity, not truly benefit the poor, and materially harm societies that have moved beyond the struggle for survival. No thank you! This paper—published in the world's most prestigious science journal!—illustrates why we can never allow these people to be in charge. As I always say, if you want to see what will next go wrong in society, just read the professional journals."[19]

Natasha Chassagne of the University of Tasmania embraced the "degrowth" in the wake of the COVID-19-inspired lockdowns of the global economy in March 2020. "In many ways, what we're seeing now is a rapid and unplanned version of economic 'degrowth'—the transition some academics and activists have for decades said is necessary to address climate change, and leave a habitable planet for future generations," Chassagne wrote for the academic publication The Conversation. "Degrowth is a proposed slowing of growth in sectors that damage the environment, such as fossil fuel industries, until the economy operates within Earth's limits. It is a voluntary, planned and equitable transition in developed nations which necessarily involves an increased focus on the environment, human well-being, and capabilities (good health, decent work, education, and a safe and healthy environment)."[21]

Economist Stephen Moore, a distinguished visiting fellow at the Heritage Foundation, was having none of this. In an article titled "Beware of the Left's 'Degrowth' Movement," Moore asked how we can "ever rely on the left to fix our economy, help the poor and make us all more prosperous if their goal is to shrink the economy, not grow it?"

"What is scary is that many who subscribe to climate change hysteria, as well as the donors who provide the tens of billions of dollars of resources to climate issues, have come to agree that growth is the enemy and that we would all be better off if we were a little poorer," Moore wrote. "It is wrong on so many levels one hardly knows where to start.

> ### It's No Fairy Tale
> "People are suffering. People are dying. Entire ecosystems are collapsing. We are in the beginning of a mass extinction, and all you can talk about is money and fairy tales of eternal economic growth. How dare you!"
> —Greta Thunberg's 2019 speech to the UN[20]

First, economic freedom and growth go hand in hand and have inarguably positive benefits to the poorest citizens of the world and to health and the environment. Nations that have degrowth are much more polluted and have much higher death rates than the United States." For the proponents of "degrowth," though, "Environmental protection is the ultimate 'superior good.' The richer a society becomes, the more they spend on clean air, clean water and nature preservation."

The history of the "degrowth" movement ultimately goes back to Thomas Malthus. As Moore explained, "The origins of the limits to growth and, now, degrowth movements date back to the days of Thomas Robert Malthus, who famously and wrongly predicted that population growth would always outpace food and economic production. These rotten and dangerous ideas are back in vogue, and the *New Yorker* magazine recently highlighted the fad on college campuses and in faculty lounges. It's the latest of leftist extremism—a subversive movement to keep an eye on."

As Moore pointed out, "The philosophy that increased prosperity is the problem and not the solution to our societal problems is not new. In the 1970s, many on the left embraced the 'limits to growth' ideology of too many people, too little food and energy, and imminent ecological disaster. Those ideas were discredited over the ensuing 40 years as innovation and technology, plus a renewed appreciation of economic freedom, advanced rapid growth in living standards around the globe and massive surpluses of food and energy."[23]

Stanford University professor Paul Ehrlich, author of *The Population Bomb*, was one of those proponents of limited growth in the 1970s. In 1974 he predicted that the United States would "move to a no-growth" economy. "I think that what is not realized, and it's going to be one of the hardest things to be accepted by the Americans in general, is that the onset of the age of scarcity essentially demolishes current models of economists. We are going to move to a no-growth" economy, Ehrlich testified to the U.S. Senate Committee on Commerce and Committee on Government Operations.

Ehrlich recommended that we move to economic austerity "intelligently through the government by planning as rapidly as possible." Ehlrich explained to the U.S. Senate the urgency of stifling the economy for environmental reasons before it's too late: "This tendency is perhaps the most dangerous one we face, that somehow people want to wait until the evidence is absolutely overwhelming, that we're in for a catastrophe, before they take action. What worries me is that by the time the evidence is absolutely overwhelming, a good deal of the damage may in fact be irreversible."[25]

The Sierra Club has also touted economic "de-growth." A 2014 article from the environmentalist organization proclaimed, "We have to de-grow our economy." Sierra Club's lifestyle editor Mackenzie Mount wrote, "Reducing individual workloads and distributing the hours among more people could increase personal well-being, temper climate disruption, and foster a stable, equitable world economy, according to the New Economics Foundation in London and the Worldwatch Institute in Washington, D.C."

The article quoted Worldwatch senior fellow Erik Assadourian

> **The Reds Are Now Green**
>
> "As someone who lived under communism for most of his life, I feel obliged to say that I see the biggest threat to freedom, democracy, the market economy and prosperity now is ambitious environmentalism.... This ideology wants to replace the free and spontaneous evolution of mankind by a sort of central (now global) planning."
> —former Czech president Vaclav Klaus[24]

> **What is a Progressive?**
>
> "What is a progressive? A progressive is someone who thinks that [Karl] Marx had a few good ideas at the end of the day."
> —meteorologist Brian Sussman[26]

> ### "Dismantle Capitalism"
>
> "The world's top scientists just gave rigorous backing to systematically dismantle capitalism as a key requirement to maintaining civilization and a habitable planet."
> —climate activist Eric Holthaus welcoming the 2018 UN IPCC's climate report[27]

saying, "There's no such thing as sustainable growth, not in a country like the U.S. We have to de-grow our economy, which is obviously not a popular stance to take in a culture that celebrates growth in all forms. But as the saying goes, if everyone consumed like Americans, we'd need four planets."[28]

Prince Charles has urged a "fundamental transformation of global capitalism" to tackle climate change. In a May 2014 speech, Prince Charles echoed Ehrlich's urgent call: "Over the next eighteen months, and bearing in mind the urgency of the situation confronting us, the world faces what is probably the last effective window of opportunity to vacate the insidious lure of the 'last chance saloon' in order to agree on an ambitious, equitable and far-sighted multilateral settlement in the context of the post-2015 sustainable development goals and the UN Framework Convention on Climate Change."[29]

> ### "The End of Capitalism"
>
> "Ending climate change requires the end of capitalism....Climate change is the result of our current economic and industrial system....the level of disruption required to keep us at a temperature anywhere below 'absolutely catastrophic' is fundamentally, on a deep structural level, incompatible with the status quo."
> —UK *Guardian* columnist Phil McDuff[30]

Charles explained, "I remember when the Iron Curtain came down there was a certain amount of shouting about the triumph of capitalism over communism. Being somewhat contrary, I didn't think it was quite as simple as that. I felt that unless the business world considered the social, community and environmental dimensions, we might end up coming full circle."

Yes, a "last effective window of opportunity...over the next eighteen months"—which expired at the end of 2015. Charles had previously issued expired tipping points of eighteen months, one hundred months, and at one point even granted the world a reprieve by extending his climate doomsday deadline all the way to the year 2050! But in 2020, Charles declared the world is "literally at the last hour" in the fight against climate change.

Other climate activists also railed against economic growth, capitalism, free markets—in other words, modern life.

"The only way to stop runaway climate change is to terminate industrial civilization," according to professor emeritus Guy McPherson of the University of Arizona. McPherson was a natural resources, ecology, and evolutionary biology instructor, but he has since turned into a sort of grief counselor. "I think we are walking around to save our own funeral expenses at this point," he explained.

In 2009 James Hansen, who was NASA's lead global warming scientist at the time, endorsed a book entitled *Time's Up! An Uncivilized Solution to a Global Crisis*, which pondered "razing cities to the ground, blowing up

"Eco-Armageddonism"

"The international far left, having been decisively routed with the collapse of the Soviet Union and of international communism, has attached itself to the environmental movement, usurped the leading positions in it from the bird-watching, butterfly-collecting, and conservation organizations, and is carrying on its anti-capitalist and anarchist crusade behind the cover of eco-Armageddonism."
—publisher Conrad Black in an article titled "How the Post-Soviet Left Latched onto the Climate for Crusade on Capitalism"[31]

Anti-Industrial Revolution

"This is the first time in the history of mankind that we are setting ourselves the task of intentionally, within a defined period of time, to change the economic development model that has been reigning for at least 150 years, since the Industrial Revolution."
—former UN climate chief Christiana Figueres[32]

> ### "We Must Embrace ... Ecological Leninism"
>
> "The whole strategic direction of Lenin after 1914 was to turn World War I into a fatal blow against capitalism. This is precisely the same strategic orientation we must embrace today—and this is what I mean by ecological Leninism. We must find a way of turning the environmental crisis into a crisis for fossil capital itself."
>
> —Lund University academic Andreas Malm[33]

dams and switching off the greenhouse gas emissions machine" as possible solutions to global warming. "The only way to prevent global ecological collapse and thus ensure the survival of humanity is to rid the world of Industrial Civilization," the book explains. "A future outside civilization is a better life; one in which we can actually decide for ourselves how we are going to live." Hansen declared on the book's Amazon page that author Keith Farnish "has it right: time has practically run out, and the system is the problem. Governments are under the thumb of fossil fuel special interests—they will not look after our and the planet's well-being until we force them to do so, and that is going to require enormous effort."

A 2014 study advocated "limits to economic growth" or "degrowth" for the sake of the planet.

The thirty-third report to the Club of Rome, authored by Professor Ugo Bardi of the University of Florence's Earth Sciences Department, called for "a fundamental reorganisation of the way societies produce, manage and consume resources could support a new high-technology civilisation," the UK *Guardian* reported.

According to the report, "This would entail a new 'circular economy' premised on wide-scale practices of recycling across production and consumption chains, a wholesale shift to renewable energy, application of agro-ecological methods to food production, and with all that, very different types of social structures."

But fear not! As the UK *Guardian* reported, "Limits to economic growth, or even 'degrowth,' the report says, do not need to imply an end to prosperity, but rather require a conscious decision by societies to lower their environmental impacts, reduce wasteful consumption, and increase efficiency—changes which could in fact increase quality of life while lowering inequality."[34]

A 2014 study from the Autonomous University of Barcelona supported the "degrowth" movement. "Policies aimed at effectively mitigating climate change through a reduction in economic growth and consumption of fossil fuels would have a monetary impact on the economy, but also an impact on the wellbeing and happiness of individuals," wrote the study author Dr. Filka Sekulova.

He also claimed that lower salaries don't make people less happy. "The reduction in salaries in the two years before the survey, from 1,373 to 1,310 euros monthly in average, did not represent a reduction in the level of happiness," he explained.

What really buys you unhappiness, according to the professor, is too much money. "Up to 1,750 euros we can say that money favors happiness, but after this amount the correlation we observed is negative."

Less is more and, as a bonus, you are fighting climate change when government policies intentionally make you poorer—which will make you so happy! "If we apply these results to climate change mitigation policies, we see that reducing consumption and salaries as well as working hours, while maintaining workplaces, can have a positive effect on people's wellbeing," the researchers claimed.

The study found that your "happiness" can grow even more

CO2 Is Not the Issue

"The people who are running this don't care about CO2, that is merely the pretext for shutting down the hated capitalist West. They want to introduce socialist totalitarianism on a global scale, and the one thing that still stands in the way is the Western love of freedom, and the prosperity the capitalist system brings. They have to tear that down."
—Christopher Monckton, an advisor to Prime Minister Margaret Thatcher[35]

With Christopher Monckton at Versailles, France, on location for *Climate Hustle 2*.

if government policies devalue private ownership and individualism and instead encourage the sharing of cars and living spaces.

According to Professor Sekulova, following these "degrowth" policies is a no-brainer. "Not applying environmental policies to mitigate climate change can have negative consequences when it comes to happiness," he noted.[36]

Maurice Newman, the former advisor to Australian prime minister Tony Abbott, warned that the UN climate agenda was "more about Marxism than science" and lamented that the world is giving in to "bogus science & catastrophism."

Newman said western nations are capitulating to the UN agenda. "They embrace junk science and junk economics and adopt wealth-destroying postmodern pseudo-economics.... Climate change has cowed once great powers into meekly surrendering sovereignty and independent thought to unelected bureaucrats in Geneva. From the White House to the Lodge, private choice now runs a distant second to collectivist visions."

Newman added, "It has its roots in Marxism, and ultimately the Green Fund is presided over by the UN Framework Convention on Climate Change, run by Costa Rican Marxist Christiana Figueres."[37]

The economist Walter Williams, who has spent his career researching and defending the free market, explained how the world fared before capitalism. "Prior to capitalism, the way people amassed great wealth was by looting, plundering and enslaving their fellow man. Capitalism made it possible to become wealthy by serving your fellow man," Williams pointed out.

"Why are leftists soft on communism? The reason leftists give communists, the world's most horrible murderers, a pass is that they sympathize with the chief goal of communism: restricting personal liberty," Williams wrote. "In the U.S., the call is for government control over our lives through regulations and taxation. Unfortunately, it matters little whether the Democrats or Republicans have the political power. The march toward greater government control is unabated. It just happens at a quicker pace with Democrats in charge."

CHAPTER 8

Even Many Environmentalists Are Bailing on the Green New Deal

The Green New Deal made a huge splash in 2019. It went overnight from something that hardly anyone had heard of to front page news that took over the politics of Washington, kids' climate activism, and even popular culture.

Freshman congresswoman Alexandria Ocasio-Cortez shot to instant fame as the face of the Green New Deal.

Conservatives registered the objections they were expected to make to any environmentalist overreach. Pat Buchanan, advisor to Reagan and Nixon, called the Green New Deal a "Democratic suicide note" and noted that the plan "reads like it was written by the college socialists club."[1]

But in a more surprising development, some of the usual suspects, the people who would normally be expected to support the Green New Deal, had some—shall we say—issues with it. Even prominent Democrats recoiled from the plan. From Senator Diane Feinstein to Nancy Pelosi to Democratic Party labor union allies to prominent mainstream media outlets to even former NASA chief "global warming" scientist James Hansen, the Green New Deal garnered some unexpected critics.

Politico quoted Democrats with severe anxiety about the Green New Deal. Representative Elissa Slotkin of Michigan explained why even some Democrats are worried about the GND:

> Even though Slotkin has shown how the climate crisis can be a winning issue, she's not on board with the most prominent progressive effort to make it a national issue, the Green New Deal, backed by her more famous House classmate Rep. Alexandria Ocasio-Cortez. She thinks it's too radical, too polarizing, a gift to President Donald Trump and other Republicans who want to portray Democrats as socialists.
>
> "My district is very worried that Democrats are lurching to the left. I know AOC's face will be on every ad against me in 2020," Slotkin explained....
>
> Slotkin doesn't see why a plan to fix the climate needs to promise universal health care and a federal job guarantee, and she doubts a lefty wish list disguised as an emergency response will play well in her suburban Michigan swing district, which Trump won by seven points....
>
> It's not a coincidence that Trump has vowed to run for re-election against the Green New Deal, or that Senate Republicans gleefully forced a vote on it, or that no Senate Democrats dared to vote yes. Even liberal House speaker Nancy Pelosi, while supporting deep emissions cuts and denouncing Trump's efforts to pull the United States out of the Paris climate accord, has declined to endorse "the green dream or whatever."[2]

Pelosi's rejection of the "green dream" cost her street cred with the climate activists. Extinction Rebellion staged a six-and-a-half-hour climate "hunger strike" in Pelosi's congressional office in D.C. and got arrested. They refused to eat unless they could "talk to Pelosi for one hour—on camera."[3] The group wrote to Pelosi, "Every day the evidence piles up at your desk, but you have yet to pass even symbolic legislation recognizing the climate crisis as a national emergency. With all due respect, you have failed."[4]

At least nine members of Extinction Rebellion were arrested for "unlawful entry" at Pelosi's office. "We entered into the back part of her office which was off limits," explained Russell Gray, an organizer for Extinction Rebellion D.C. "The police stopped us and arrested everybody that was in there."

Another activist, Giovanni Tamacas, explained, "We are hungry and angry. Pelosi's refusal to meet with us just confirms that our leaders are ignoring the emergency. Scientists tell us that the collapse of society is inevitable unless we act now. So we will continue our hunger strike in jail if that's what it takes to prevent this collapse."[5]

"Hungry" after a six-and-half-hour hunger strike? In any case, Pelosi was clearly not winning points with the climate activist base of the Democratic Party and the youth climate movement.

Democratic senator Dianne Feinstein of California was another prominent figure to find herself at odds with Green New Deal activists.

The *Washington Post* reported in February 2019, "An exchange between Sen. Dianne Feinstein (D-Calif.) and a group of schoolchildren petitioning her to advocate for the 'Green New Deal' went viral, drawing criticism and prompting a response from the senator....Her reply? 'I know what I'm doing.'"

Feinstein's confrontation with the activists from the Sunrise Movement—a self-described "army of young people" fighting climate change—was released on Facebook.

According to the *Post*, "Feinstein, who sits on Senate subcommittees on Interior, Environment and related agencies, told the students that she doesn't support the deal, mainly because there is 'no way to pay for it.'"

The teen climate activists were having none of it. "But we have come to a point where our Earth is dying, and it is literally a pricey and ambitious plan that is needed to deal with the magnitude of that issue," replied a sixteen-year-old activist. "So we're asking you to vote 'yes' on the resolution for the Green New Deal because—"

Senator Feinstein stopped the girl mid-sentence and countered: "That resolution will not pass the Senate, and you can take that back to whoever sent you here." Feinstein continued, "I've been in the Senate for a quarter of a century, and I know what can pass, and I know what can't pass." Feinstein instead touted her own climate legislation, which she said had a better chance to pass Congress than the Green New Deal.

But the student activists were not receptive. "Any plan that doesn't take bold, transformative action is not going to be what we need," an activist says in the viral video, which quickly racked up over six million views.

At that point Feinstein let the decorum slip. "Well you know better than I do, so I think one day you should run for the Senate. Then you can do it your way," Feinstein said. "You know what's interesting about this group is I've been doing this for thirty years. I know what I'm doing. You come in here and say, 'It has to be my way or the highway.' I don't respond to that."

Feinstein did hold out the option that she might at some point support the Green New Deal. "I may do that. We'll see. I don't know."

The Sunrise Movement tagged the video with this headline: "This is How @SenFeinstein Reacted to Children Asking Her to Support the #GreenNewDeal Resolution—with Smugness + Disrespect." The group avowed, "This is a fight for our generation's survival. Her reaction is why young people desperately want new leadership in Congress."

Later, Feinstein responded to the brouhaha by writing, "Unfortunately, it was a brief meeting, but I want the children to know they were heard loud and clear. I have been and remain committed to doing everything I can to enact real, meaningful climate change legislation."[6]

In September of 2020, Feinstein was once again targeted by Sunrise Movement activists, this time outside of her home in Washington, D.C. "Protesters began a street blockade outside Feinstein's D.C. home just after 6 a.m. They gathered with noise makers, posters and a large banner reading 'California Needs a Green New Deal," according to a report in the American University *Eagle* newspaper.

"It's really disgusting to look at her house and see complete inaction and complete disrespect of the climate crisis," activist Suzanne Pranger told the paper.[7]

This is perhaps the most unexpected development in the political landscape after the Green New Deal was introduced: how two old party stalwarts like Pelosi and Feinstein found themselves on the outs, lumped together with the climate "deniers."

U.S. Youth Climate Strike leaders Maddy Fernands, Isra Hirsi, Haven Coleman, and Alexandria Villaseñor spelled out the new political reality for Democrats not cheerleading for the Green New Deal. "We are also concerned that top Democrats demonstrate their own lack of urgency about the existential threat of climate change. California senator Dianne Feinstein's recent dismissal of a group of schoolchildren visiting her office to beg her support for the Green New Deal was very disturbing for us young people," the four activists wrote.

"Feinstein will not have to face the consequences of her inaction on climate change. She suggested that the children one day run for the Senate themselves if they wish to pass aggressive climate legislation. Sadly, that may not be an option for us, if she and other Democrats, like House Speaker Nancy Pelosi, continue to dismiss the pleas of our generation. Faced with politicians on both sides of the aisle who belittle and ignore us, we're forced to take a stand, and we're doing it together on a global scale. And that is why we strike."[8]

While Pelosi and Feinstein struggled to grapple with the plan, other Democratic lawmakers spoke out in total opposition. Many elected Democrats met the Green New Deal with resistance the moment it was launched. The *Washington Post* reported on "some members urging caution about setting vague and, at times, impossible-to-achieve goals to only fall short."[9]

Democratic representative Kendra Horn of Oklahoma declared, "I do not support the proposed ban on fracking or the Green New Deal.

The oil and gas industry has fueled economic development and new opportunities in Oklahoma since statehood."[10]

Democratic congressman Max Rose bluntly called the deal a "massive socialist economic policy platform. Just not needed."

Even the civil rights activist Reverend Jesse Jackson, who endorsed Bernie Sanders for president in 2020, seems to realize that the Green New Deal might not be that practical. Despite expressing support for the GND, Jackson publicly contradicted the movement by pushing for a natural gas pipeline.[11] As Axios reported in 2020, "Breaking from other progressives, Rev. Jesse Jackson is calling to build a natural gas pipeline to serve an impoverished community (Pembroke) near Chicago....The community is 80% black and has an average annual income of less than $15,000....Nearly one in five households are forced to go without food to pay their energy bill, the Energy Information Administration noted in a 2018 report."

According to Jackson, the community pays extremely high electric bills in the winter to heat their homes. The residents of Pembroke have no access to natural gas and have been heating their homes with very expensive propane. So Jackson is lobbying local, state, and federal officials in Illinois to support the building of the thirty-mile, $8.2 million natural gas pipeline for Pembroke.

Jackson told Amy Harder of Axios, "I really do support the environmental movement." But he does not seem too concerned that the expansion of fossil fuels he is demanding will violate the Green New Deal or cause more "climate change."[12]

Why doesn't Jackson's support of the Green New Deal cause him to advocate for putting solar panels and windmills in this energy-starved community? Jackson's answer: "When we move to another form of energy, that's fine by me, I support that. But in the meantime, you cannot put the black farmers on hold until that day comes."[13]

Wind and solar may sound great to many politicians touting "green energy," but when push comes to shove, fossil fuels end up answering the call.

Jackson is not alone among his fellow progressive civil rights activists. The Daily Caller reported,

> Revs. Al Sharpton and Jesse Jackson and National Urban League president Marc Morial said they oppose an abrupt move away from fracking, according to an Axios report Monday. They said the technique for producing natural gas helps black people who struggle with high energy prices.
>
> Morial was particularly rough on activists who said their anti-fracking position is tied in with social justice matters. "I would not want to cite a specific instance, but generally speaking, people are debating these issues in some instances without consultation with the leaders of the African-American communities and neighborhoods affected by these issues," Morial told Axios.[14]

Democrat senator Amy Klobuchar of Michigan, who ran for her party's presidential nomination in 2020, also grappled with how to face the Green New Deal. Klobuchar was a cosponsor of the Green New Deal resolution in Congress, but the senator declined to feature it in her presidential climate policy proposals. She seemed to view the Green New Deal as a distant goal, not an immediate action plan. As Klobuchar explained, it is not a good idea to "get rid of all these industries or do this in a few years." Instead, she sought to

"Condescending, Patronizing, and Racist"

The National Urban League's Marc Morial showed a palpable disdain for the environmentalists when he explained why he rejected claims that donations from energy companies to his organization have influenced his stance. "Whenever someone disagrees with what you say, they think, 'Oh, you must be getting paid.' It's condescending, patronizing and racist. I hope you print it. I want them to see it. Because that's the way we feel," Morial said.[15]

"start doing concrete things, and put some aspirations out there on climate change."[16]

Even the usually reliable *New York Times* raised some inconvenient questions about the Green New Deal. The Gray Lady's editorial board asked, "Is the Green New Deal aimed at addressing the climate crisis? Or is addressing the climate crisis merely a cover for a wish-list of progressive policies and a not-so-subtle effort to move the Democratic Party to the left? At least some candidates—Amy Klobuchar of Minnesota among them—seem to think so.... Read literally, the resolution wants not only to achieve a carbon-neutral energy system but also to transform the economy itself."[17]

The *Washington Post* also cast shade on the Green New Deal. "We can't afford bad ideas," the paper's editorial writers asserted. "We favor a Green New Deal to save the planet. We believe such a plan can be efficient, effective, focused and achievable. The Green New Deal proposed by congressional Democrats does not meet that test."

The *Post*'s board was brutal in its takedown of the plan. "They should not muddle this aspiration with other social policy, such as creating a federal jobs guarantee, no matter how desirable that policy might be.... There are a lot of bad ideas out there. The Green New Deal that some Democrats have embraced is case in point."

The paper went on to question the costs associated with the GND. "The plan suggests the country could reach net-zero greenhouse-gas emissions by 2030, an impossible goal. Christopher Clack, the CEO of analysis group Vibrant Clean Energy, estimates it would cost $27 trillion to get there by 2035—a yearly price tag of about 9 percent of 2017 gross domestic product. (Total federal spending is currently a bit more than 20 percent of GDP.) Put another way, that would be more spent every three years than the total amount the country spent on World War II. The plan's proposal to retrofit all existing buildings is also astonishing in its implied scale, and its promise to invest in known fiascos such as high-speed rail reveal deep insensitivity to the lessons of recent government waste."

"They should not muddle this aspiration with other social policy, such as creating a federal jobs guarantee, no matter how desirable that policy might be," the *Post*'s editorial board wrote. The *Post* also called the Green New Deal's goal of reaching "net-zero" greenhouse gas emissions within ten years "impossible" and criticized the resolution's "promise to invest in known fiascos such as high-speed rail."[18]

The Green New Deal also did not sit well with key factions of the Democratic Party base.

A major labor union that endorsed Joe Biden, Hillary Clinton, and President Obama twice for president unloaded on the

The Road to Hell Is Paved with Good Intentions

The *Washington Post* recognized that the Green New Deal was not really about the climate. "The Democratic plan would guarantee every American 'high-quality health care' and 'a job with a family-sustaining wage, adequate family and medical leave, paid vacations, and retirement security.' These expensive aspirations, no matter how laudable, would do nothing to arrest greenhouse-gas emissions," the paper noted. "Good intentions will not solve the global warming crisis. Massive social reform will not protect the climate," the paper continued.

Green New Deal as an "unrealistic manifesto" and said it would "destroy workers' livelihoods" and cause "economic and social devastation."

The Laborers' International Union of North America (LIUNA) represents a half-million members in the construction industry. Terry O'Sullivan, the general president of LIUNA, had this to say on the Green New Deal: "It is exactly how not to win support for critical measures to curb climate change....It is difficult to take this unrealistic manifesto seriously, but the economic and social devastation it would cause if it moves forward is serious and real....[it] threatens to destroy workers' livelihoods, increase divisions and inequality, and undermine the very goals it seeks to reach. In short, it is a bad deal."

O'Sullivan was not finished: "It is exactly how not to successfully enact desperately needed infrastructure investment. It is exactly how not to enact a progressive agenda to address our nation's dangerous income inequality. And it is exactly how not to win support for critical measures to curb climate change. Attaching a laundry list of laudable proposals unrelated to climate change—proposals which LIUNA and other progressive organizations have long fought for—to the sails of fantasy ensures that they all go down on a sinking ship. Infrastructure issues must be addressed in infrastructure legislation, while climate issues must be addressed through climate legislation."[19]

One of the biggest blows to the Green New Deal came when James Hansen, NASA's former lead "global warming" scientist, declared the plan "nonsense." Hansen was the lead voice of climate alarmism for several decades, kicking off the firestorm over man-made climate change during a 1988 Senate hearing. Hansen was such a committed climate activist that he was arrested multiple times protesting climate change. He even accused climate skeptics of "crimes against humanity and nature."

So it surprised some in 2019 when Hansen slammed the Green New Deal during a live Al Jazeera TV debate with Varshini Prakash, co-founder of the Sunrise Movement, the group that has taken the lead in promoting the Green New Deal.

"The Green New Deal as they've defined that is nonsense. We need a real deal which understands how economics works and what we need to do in order to move off of fossil fuels," Hansen said during the TV debate.

"And that requires in addition to this rising carbon fee, with the distribution to the public. We also have to have the technologies we have to help the developing countries," Hansen explained. "And we're going to have to help those countries—they want to raise their standards of living to match ours. And so there, it's a big problem but it's a solvable problem."

The Al Jazeera host turned to the Sunrise Movement's co-founder Varshini Prakash and said, "You and James Hansen both agree on the scale of the challenge but he thinks your solution is nonsense."

Prakash responded, "Well I would say that I don't think that simply putting a price on carbon is going to be enough in this moment. I think if it were 30 years ago that might have been enough."

Hansen replied, "Yeah, it's not enough, but it's the underlying policy that's required to make the price of fossil fuels honest, otherwise people will keep burning them the same way that we did in the West, because people want energy, they're going to raise their standard of living."[20]

Hansen called out other Democratic climate leaders, including Bernie Sanders. "It's time for Bernie Sanders to retire" from the Senate for opposing nuclear energy, Hansen said. "He truly doesn't get it. India and China have no prayer of phasing out coal without the help of nuclear power."[21]

Hansen did not mince his words when it came to the UN Paris Agreement. "[The Paris Agreement] is a fraud really, a fake. It's just bullshit for them to say: 'We'll have a 2C warming target and then try to do a little better every five years.' It's just worthless words. There is no action, just promises. As long as fossil fuels appear to be the cheapest fuels out there, they will be continued to be burned."[22]

That is the reception the Green New Deal received from many Democratic Party leaders, elected officials, and key members of their base. Even more surprising, the biggest opposition came from one of the architects of an earlier Green New Deal—Michael Shellenberger. As we saw in chapter 2, Shellenberger, called a "Hero of the Environment" by *Time* magazine, has come out strongly against the new Green New Deal.

But most shocking of all was when left-wing filmmaker Michael Moore bailed out of the "green" energy movement that is the driving force behind the Green New Deal. As I will reveal in detail in chapter 10, Moore's 2020 film *Planet of the Humans* exposed the so-called renewable energy movement as a slew of crony capitalists making unsustainable claims about wind and solar energy.

"We all want to feel good about something like the electric car, but in the back of your head somewhere you've thought, 'Yeah, but where is the electricity coming from?'" Moore said.[23]

Moore and his director, environmentalist Jeff Gibbs, faced the wrath of the climate campaigners. Breitbart's James Delingpole summed it up: Michael Moore "is now the Green New Deal's worst enemy."[24]

CHAPTER 9

The Costs to End All Costs

The Green New Deal will impose unprecedented costs on the American economy, America's competitiveness, and Americans' quality of life. From the various GND versions' promises of free college or trade school for every citizen to its assurances of "healthy food" and "safe, affordable, adequate housing" to its prescription of guaranteed incomes for all who are "unable or unwilling" to work, the GND covers all aspects of human endeavor. The Green New Deal's plan to end all proven, traditional carbon-based forms of energy in the next ten years is going to be costly.

And for what? As we have seen, all of the so-called "solutions" being proposed to fight global warming—whether they come from the U.S. EPA, the UN Paris Agreement, or the Green New Deal—are purely symbolic. Such planned emissions controls would ultimately serve only to raise energy costs for everyone, they would hit the poor and those on fixed incomes the hardest, and the climate and weather would not change.

The benefits are minimal, but the costs are enormous—par for the course when it comes to climate "solutions." The Paris Agreement

Growing the Government— Shrinking the Economy and Our Freedom

"Its further expansion of the federal government's role in some of the most basic decisions of daily life, however, would likely have a more lasting and damaging impact than its enormous price tag."
—American Action Forum[2]

would theoretically postpone global warming by four years—and cost $100 trillion.[1]

Fossil fuels have been one of the greatest liberators of mankind—and especially of the poor—in the history of our planet. Is it greedy to want heat, A/C, longer lives, and lower infant mortality? If we care about people's lives, fossil fuels are the moral choice in energy.

The immeasurable costs of the Green New Deal will be subtracted from people's living standards, and will decrease lifespans and push the poorest among us deeper into poverty. A 2019 study by the American Action Forum examined the Green New Deal and found its cost to be enormous, almost too large to fathom. As its authors noted, "The GND's proposed goals, 'mobilization,' and specific policy projects encompass social and institutional changes far exceeding the narrow policy goals, but these changes are impossible to quantify at this point."

The study's findings shocked the political establishment. Bloomberg News reported, "Alexandria Ocasio-Cortez's Green New Deal Could Cost $93 Trillion, Group Says": "The so-called Green New Deal may tally between $51 trillion and $93 trillion over 10 years, concludes American Action Forum, which is run by Douglas Holtz-Eakin, who directed the non-partisan CBO from 2003 to 2005. That includes between $8.3 trillion and $12.3 trillion to meet the plan's call to eliminate carbon emissions from the power and transportation sectors and between $42.8 trillion and $80.6 trillion for its economic agenda including providing jobs and health care for all."[3]

As the study reported, in something of an understatement, "The Green New Deal is clearly very expensive."

The $93 trillion number was even cited on *Saturday Night Live*.[4] But the study came under immediate attack by supporters of the Green New Deal and the media. (Is there really any difference between the two?)

Politico pushed back hard on the $93 trillion claim. "The number originated with a report by a conservative think tank, American Action Forum, that made huge assumptions about how Democrats would implement their plan.... To come up with the $93 million total, Republicans added together the cost estimates that the AAF report's authors had placed on various aspects of a Green New Deal platform. Most of those were based on assumptions about universal health care and jobs programs rather than the costs of transitioning to carbon-free electricity and transportation." But, *Politico* countered, the "Green New Deal isn't even a plan yet—at the moment it's a non-binding resolution that calls for major action to stop greenhouse gas pollution while reducing income inequality and creating 'millions of good, high-wage jobs.'"[6]

A 2019 Heritage Foundation study by Kevin Dayaratna and Nicolas Loris concluded that the "Green New Deal would be incredibly costly for American families and businesses—for no meaningful climate benefit." The authors found that "under the most modest estimates, just one

> ## "You Kids Are Going to Give Me $93 Trillion!"
>
> In a 2019 parody skit, *Saturday Night Live* cast member Cecily Strong portrayed California senator Dianne Feinstein interacting with a group of kid climate activists. She tells the kids, "Unfortunately, that deal is not very realistic." One kid responds, "But our planet is dying!"
>
> Strong's Feinstein character asks a group of students if they like to play games. Then she tells them to close their eyes, sticks out her hand, and says, "You kids are going to give me $93 trillion." One child says, "We don't have any money," to which the faux Senator Feinstein replies, "Oh, you don't? Then we all lose." Another student holds up a climate drawing that urges her cooperation. The senator says, "Oh, is that a poster? Then I'm convinced!"[5]

Family Incomes Would Take Major Hit Under Green New Deal

Under the Green New Deal, the typical family of four would lose an average of nearly $8,000 in income every year, or a total of more than $165,000 through 2040.

CHANGE IN ANNUAL INCOME FOR A FAMILY OF FOUR

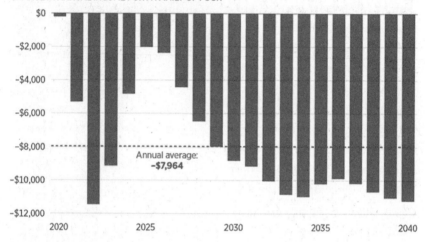

Annual average:
−$7,964

NOTE: Figures shown are differentials between current projections and projections based on the Green New Deal being enacted in 2020.
SOURCE: Authors' calculations based on Heritage Energy Model simulations. For more information, see the methodology in the appendix.

Courtesy of the Heritage Foundation

part of this new deal costs an average family $165,000 and wipes out 5.2 million jobs with negligible climate benefit." Dayaratna and Loris's simulations find that by 2040, the country will incur:

> An overall average shortfall of over 1.1 million jobs;
> A peak employment shortfall of over 5.2 million jobs;
> A total income loss of more than $165,000 for a family of four;
> An aggregate gross domestic product loss of over $15 trillion; and

Increases in household electricity expenditures averaging 30 percent.

The study noted, "These estimates significantly underestimate the costs of the Green New Deal. If policymakers spent, taxed, and regulated energy to truly achieve greenhouse-gas-free emission levels, the costs would almost surely be several orders of magnitude higher. And, more fundamentally, the policies proposed in the Green New Deal are highly regressive. Higher energy costs affect low-income households disproportionately, as they spend a higher percentage of their budget on energy." [7]

A study by another D.C.-based think tank, the Competitive Enterprise Institute (CEI), on the "framework to estimate the minimum costs" of the Green New Deal to different regions of the country found the plan would cost the average household between $74,287 and $76,683 in Colorado, Michigan, and Pennsylvania. The CEI study, by Kent Lassman and Daniel Turner, noted,

> At best, it can be described as an overwhelmingly expensive proposal reliant on technologies that have not yet been invented. More likely, the GND would drive the American economy into a steep economic depression, while putting off-limits affordable energy necessary for basic social institutions like hospitals, schools, clean water and sanitation, cargo shipments, and the production and transport of the majority of America's food supply....
>
> All of the potential benefits and social costs—such as massive increases in land use for the production of energy and food without fossil fuel inputs—are beyond the scope of this analysis. Yet we can conclude that the Green New Deal is an unserious proposal that is at best negligent in its anticipation of transition costs and at worst a politically motivated policy whose creativity is outweighed by its enormous potential for economic destruction. [8]

Statistician Bjørn Lomborg detailed the human cost of higher energy costs in his 2020 book *False Alarm: How Climate Change Panic Costs Us Trillions, Hurts the Poor, and Fails to Fix the Planet.* "So much of climate change policy boils down to limiting access to cheap energy," Lomborg wrote. "When energy becomes more expensive, we all end up paying more to heat our houses. But because the poor use a larger share of their incomes on energy, a price increase burdens them the most....energy poverty means that poorer, elderly people can't afford to keep their homes properly heated, leaving them to stay longer in bed to keep warm."[9]

The 2019 National Bureau of Economic Research study "Inexpensive Heating Reduces Winter Mortality" concluded, "When US home heating costs fell, fewer people died."

Canadian climate analyst Donna Laframboise explained: "In the authors' words, we've known for decades that 'mortality peaks in winter and that cold weather is associated with higher mortality.' When home heating gets expensive, many people—especially the poorest members of our community—turn down the thermostat. But lower indoor temperatures are associated with an uptick in fatal strokes, heart attacks, and infections."

Laframboise added, "There's nothing heroic about a policy that consigns old people to shivering in the dark. That's an attack on our most vulnerable. That's a betrayal."[10]

Attempting to centrally plan energy economies many years or decades into the future—factoring in economic growth, population size, technology, and the needs of a society that far into the future—is simply not realistic.

> ### "The Only Thing That Can Cure Poverty"
>
> "The fraudulence of the left's concern about poverty is exposed by their utter lack of interest in ways of increasing the nation's wealth. Wealth is the only thing that can cure poverty. The reason there is less poverty today is not because the poor got a bigger slice of the pie but because the whole pie got a lot bigger—no thanks to the left."
> —economist Thomas Sowell[11]

International efforts like the UN Paris climate accord will also have no detectable impact on the climate, even if you accept UN science claims and models.

"The Green New Deal's government-managed energy plan poses the risk of expansive, disastrous damage to the economy—hitting working Americans the hardest," the Heritage Foundation study concluded. "The plan would introduce a completely new level of cronyism and corporate welfare that would harm consumers multiple times over."

As the report pointed out, "The policies proposed in the Green New Deal would disrupt energy markets and skew investment decisions toward politically connected projects. Instead of implementing economically destructive policies of more taxes, regulations, and subsidies, federal and state policymakers should remove government-imposed barriers to energy innovation."[12]

Not to be left behind by AOC's original GND or Joe Biden's plan, the U.S. Senate Democrats introduced their own version of the Green New Deal in late summer 2020 which demanded spending $400 billion annually (2 percent of the gross domestic product) in an attempt to achieve "net-zero emissions" by 2050. The Democrats issued a 263-page report that called for boosting federal spending on "climate change" with a focus on climate justice issues with at least 40 percent of the climate "benefits" earmarked to minority communities.

Senate minority leader Charles E. Schumer, Democrat of New York, declared, "The climate crisis is not some distant threat. It is

"A Negligible Impact"

"No matter where one stands on the urgency to combat climate change, the Green New Deal's policies would be ineffective in abating temperature increases and reducing sea-level rise. In fact, even if the U.S. were to cut its CO_2 emissions 100 percent, it would have a negligible impact on global warming."
—"Assessing the Costs and Benefits of the Green New Deal's Energy Policies" by Kevin Dayaratna and Nicolas Loris of the Heritage Foundation, July 2019[13]

here now, and it will be catastrophic if we don't strike back immediately."

What was left unsaid by Senator Shumer was that even if what he said here was true, this plan not only would not impact "climate change," it would not even impact global CO_2 emissions.

> **"Would Only Raise Energy Prices"**
>
> "Democrat plans to 'decarbonize' the economy would only raise energy prices, reduce our standard of living and put our national security in jeopardy without changing, much less improving, the weather."
> —Steve Milloy of JunkScience. com on the Senate Dems' 2020 climate plan[14]

"Regardless of one's views on climate science, U.S. emissions are an ever-shrinking part of global emissions," Steve Milloy of JunkScience.com told the *Washington Times* in response to the Democrats' Green New Deal style plan. EPA data show that between 2005 and 2018, CO_2 emissions dropped 12 percent in the U.S. but rose globally almost 24 percent.[15]

Costs and Benefits

The Competitive Enterprise Institute's report on the cost of the GND noted, "Most provisions of the GND are so broad and open-ended that the list of potential programs necessary to implement the program is only limited by the capacity of legislators to imagine new government programs. Therefore, it is impossible to calculate the maximum cost of the GND."

Even the architects of the GND have conceded that the plan is more of a collection of "values" rather than specific policies.

"The Green New Deal is a non-binding resolution of values. It does not have a price tag or CBO score and costs us $0 if passed," Representative Alexandria Ocasio-Cortez wrote in May 2020.[16]

Democratic senator Ed Markey had also rejected the calls for cost estimates. "Putting a price on a resolution of principles, not policies, is just Big Oil misinformation," Markey claimed in 2019.

Proponents of the GND claim that not enacting the deal would be more costly.

"Not talking about the cost of inaction is incredibly misleading," said Rhiana Gunn-Wright of the climate group New Consensus. "It's about how, when and where you want to spend your money, because you're going to spend it," she added.[17]

Bloomberg News reported in 2019, "Backers of the plan say the cost of [climate] inaction would

"Destroy Our Reliable Electricity"

"It's impossible to have net-zero energy electricity genera-tion without frequent blackouts and substantial economic pain from higher electricity costs, just as a matter of science," James Taylor, president of the Heartland Institute said of the Senate Democrats' Green New Deal–style plan in 2020. "The Democrats would either destroy our reliable electricity grid or they would immediately need to break their campaign promise. It has to be one or the other."[18]

be more expensive. The resolution itself, released earlier this month by Ocasio-Cortez and Massachusetts Democratic Senator Ed Markey points to a major report on global warming released by the United Nations last October that says catastrophic climate change could cost more than $500 billion annually in lost economic output in the U.S. by 2100."[19]

But the assumptions behind this claim are that (a) the world is actually facing "catastrophic climate change" and (b) that global warming is going to cost $500 billion annually.

On point "a" see chapter 3 of this book for a thorough refutation of the dubious climate change "science."

And point "b"—the UN claim that climate change will cost $500 billion per year in "lost economic output in the U.S. by 2100"—is pure modeling nonsense.

Claims from the UN and the Obama administration about the alleged "social cost of carbon"—the supposed huge costs to the econ-omy from "global warming"—have been intensely analyzed and roundly criticized.

Robert Murphy, an economist with the free market Institute for Energy Research, found "little 'science' behind the whopping numbers." As he explained, the "'social cost of carbon' is a very malleable concept that can be inflated or deflated by turning certain wheels."[20]

A 2019 analysis by Marlo Lewis Jr. of the Competitive Enterprise Institute noted the nearly complete omission of the word "cost" from the Green New Deal.

"Perhaps as significant as what the Green New Deal says is what it does not say. The word 'cost' occurs only once—in a provision directing the U.S. government to 'take into account the complete environmental and social costs of emissions.' Although emissions from infrastructure, transportation, manufacturing, and agriculture are to be reduced 'as much as technologically feasible,' the text nowhere states or implies that emission reductions must be cost effective, commercially viable, or reasonably affordable."[22]

Former Harvard University physicist Lubos Motl dismissed Biden's version of the Green New Deal and his plan to spend $75 billion a year on green research and development. "You can't change the laws of physics by throwing seventy-five f*cking billion dollars to something pompously called 'research and development.' Fossil fuels' being the most practical, safe, available concentrated enough source and reservoir of energy—is a demonstrable fact," Motl wrote.

"Hundreds of billions of dollars have already been wasted for something that was pompously called science or research but it was really just a promotion of incompetent, idiotic, and far-left scammers pretending to be useful and scientists. They did nothing useful. Of course, this huge wasted 'R&D' budget is just a tiny part of the trillions that the candidate wants to waste," Motl added.[23]

Representative Alexandria Ocasio-Cortez has declared that addressing climate change through the Green New Deal "is our World War II."[24]

Think about the implications of that statement.

"People tend to interpret Green New Dealer talk of a WW2-like mobilization as a simple metaphor. But these folks mean it as an actual measure of what they are determined to do. So far they have glossed over and ignored the extreme hardships of mobilization," noted David Wojick and Paul Driessen of CFACT in a 2020 op-ed.

"Gasoline, meat and clothing were tightly rationed. Most families were allocated three US gallons of gasoline a week, which sharply curtailed driving for any purpose. Production of most durable goods, like cars, new housing, vacuum cleaners and kitchen appliances, was banned until the war ended. In industrial areas housing was in short supply as people doubled up and lived in cramped quarters. Prices and wages were controlled," Wojick and Driessen wrote.

"No doubt the Green New Deal mobilization would impose different hardships. But all mobilizations are oppressive. You can't commandeer half of the GDP without disrupting or even destroying people's lives."[25]

CHAPTER 10

Energy Mandate Fairy Tale (Michael Moore Shocks the Greens)

D espite the lofty rhetoric and religion-like fervor of its proponents, the Green New Deal will not be able to achieve its objective of eliminating fossil fuels. The government cannot replace energy that works—fossil fuels—with energy that is not ready for prime time—solar and wind.

The fallacies of green energy are being exposed by even some of the most respected voices on the Left. Progressives like Michael Shellenberger and Michael Moore have done yeoman's work exposing the folly of "renewable" energy like solar and wind.

Higher energy costs due to mandates, schemes, and plans to limit CO_2 emissions have absolutely no impact on climate, extreme weather, or global emissions—even if you actually believed all the claims of the UN climate panel and former vice president Al Gore and you should not believe them.

The real success story of energy policy is that U.S. greenhouse gas emissions have actually been declining in recent years, and NOT as a result of the heavy hand of regulation.

Limiting Americans' energy choices and increasing their costs does not "address" climate concerns. There is no need to be opposed to solar or wind power, but the U.S. cannot allow proven, plentiful, and cheap energy from fossil fuels to be banned or taxed for no benefit either to the climate or the economy. If solar and wind power work, let them work on their merits. The U.S. cannot allow frantic calls of a "climate emergency" to force energy policies on a public that otherwise would never accept them.

Achieving Energy Dominance

Under President Trump, the United States has achieved energy dominance by cutting regulations, modernizing infrastructure, supporting innovation, and boosting imports. In a huge victory for sound science, the Trump administration stopped the pretense that "climate change" was a national security concern.[1]

The United States has continued its success in reducing traditional air pollution and is beating most of the European signatories of the UN Paris Agreement in reducing carbon dioxide emissions, despite signaling its intent to withdraw from the Paris Pact in 2017.

Of course, the planet will not care one way or the other about the fate of the UN Paris Pact, because even if it were fully enacted, it would have no measurable impact on global temperatures. And that's on the assumption that the UN is correct about their climate science claims. The UN Paris climate pact—like, of course, the Green New Deal—is pure symbolism: real economic pain for no gain.

Instead of "climate regulations," the Trump administration focused on innovation, technology, improving energy efficiency, and energy dominance.

"The EPA has (mostly) solved the most basic and widespread public health and environmental problems that plagued the U.S. back around the '60s," explained Amy Harder of Axios in 2017. "Climate change is now the top environmental issue in the country. That politicizes the EPA, makes it less of a big deal to average Americans and fuels antipathy from elected Republicans, most of whom don't acknowledge it's a real issue."

Cleaner Air Trumps Critics

"From 2017–2019, the amount of criteria pollutants in our air continued to fall:

Carbon monoxide fell 10 percent.

Lead (3-month average) fell 28 percent.

Since 2010, lead concentrations in the air have fallen by 85 percent.

Ozone fell 4 percent.

NO2 (Nitrogen Dioxide) (annual) fell 4 percent.

Large particulates (24-hour) fell 22 percent.

Fine particulates (24-hour) fell 12 percent.

Sulfur dioxide fell 10 percent.

From 1970 to 2019, combined emissions of criteria air pollutants and their precursors fell by 77 percent while the economy grew 285 percent.

Since 2000, fine particulate matter concentrations in the U.S. have dropped by roughly 40 percent. The U.S. now has some of the lowest fine particulate matter levels in the world."

—the Environmental Protection Agency's "Current List of Achievements" in 2020[2]

According to Harder's astute analysis, "The Obama administration issued a steady stream of major regulations on climate change....It was one of the most aggressive EPAs ever."[3]

President Donald Trump's energy policy boosted U.S. energy to achieve energy dominance in the world—not only ignoring man-made "climate change," but setting to work to undo the Obama administration's climate "legacy," achieved mostly through bypassing democracy with executive orders. By 2018, Trump had won bragging rights when the United States became the largest global crude oil producer, surpassing Russia and Saudi Arabia.[4]

In 2019, as the shale natural gas fracking boom continued unabated, BP reported that the U.S. now led the world in both oil and natural gas production growth. The growth in petroleum output was the largest year-to-year increase ever documented in any country, according to the BP report.[5]

Thank a Fracker

"Pennsylvania has been doing it right by climate policy. If you are concerned about CO2 emissions, Pennsylvania's fracking boom can be thanked....Pennsylvania is a national energy success story. Why would you allow your governor—for purposes of virtue signaling, to threaten this energy success story of helping the U.S. convert to natural gas fracking?...Pennsylvania has a lot to teach the state of New York about energy policy, not the other way around."
—**from my testimony to the Pennsylvania House Environmental Resources and Energy Committee in October 2019 on the governor's seeking to join the Regional Greenhouse Gas Initiative (RGGI)**[6]

Who needs EPA regulations or UN treaties to reduce carbon dioxide emissions when good old market forces and technology-driven efficiency like fracking can reduce them for you? If climate activists were intellectually honest, they would be singing the praises of fracking as the most effective way to reduce emissions. Fracking has put the UN climate agreement out of business. The U.S. does not need the United Nations centrally planning our lives or a Green New Deal forcing wind and solar on the public to reduce emissions.

Back to the 1950s!

According to the U.S. Energy Information Administration (EIA), the United States has now returned to a position of energy dominance for the first time since the 1950s, during the administrations of Harry S. Truman and Dwight D. Eisenhower.

"In 2019, U.S. energy production exceeded energy consumption for the first time since 1957, and U.S. energy exports exceeded energy imports for the first time since 1952," the EIA reported in 2020.[7]

And the U.S. was doing all of this while leading the world in reducing carbon dioxide emissions without a cap-and-trade, carbon (dioxide) taxes, a Green New Deal, or being committed to the UN Paris Agreement.

Meanwhile, the virtue-signaling European nations were failing to meet their targets.[8]

In 2019, President Trump explained the contrast between a pro–fossil fuel energy policy and a Green New Deal energy plan.

"Democrats want to ban shale energy, but shale energy has reduced America's carbon emissions by 527 million metric tons per year. So what are they doing? [This is] a much better record than the European Union, which is always telling us how to do [reduce emissions.] We should be telling them how to do it, based on our economy," Trump said.[9]

What remains to be seen is the impact of the COVID-19 global lockdowns have on energy demand and production. These numbers could see major lockdown impacts as both the global and domestic economy absorb the effects. As we will see in detail in chapters 11 and 14, the COVID-19 lockdowns were welcomed by many proponents of the Green New Deal as "good" for the climate cause.

This energy dominance was very good news to some and not so good news to others. As the Daily Caller reported, "Republicans stood up and cheered the news, while Democrats stayed in their seats," when Trump touted booming American energy production in his 2019 State of the Union address.

Democratic Oregon senator Jeff Merkley was so outraged at this American energy explosion that he said, "The United States is now the

---

"570 Percent More Abundant in 2019"

"The Earth was 570.9 percent more abundant in 2019 than it was in 1980. The world's resources are finite in the same way that the number of piano keys is finite. The instrument has only 88 notes, but those can be played in an infinite variety of ways. The same applies to our planet. The Earth's atoms may be fixed, but the possible combinations of those atoms are infinite. What matters, then, is not the physical limits of our planet, but human freedom to experiment and reimagine the use of resources that we have."

—from an analysis of the "The Simon Abundance Index 2020" by Gale L. Pooley and Marian L. Tupy of Human Progress[10]

number one source of the fossil fuels creating a climate crisis that is literally killing people and destroying Americans' livelihoods."[11]

Climate campaigners fumed over Trump's plan for energy dominance. Former vice president Al Gore led the pack, criticizing Trump for not mentioning so-called renewable energy and complaining that the president was "boasting about more dirty & outdated oil and natural gas projects."[12]

"Deniers" Are Now "Arsonists"

Climate activist Naomi Klein, who claims capitalism is incompatible with a livable climate, wrote, "People claim Trump said not one word about climate change but that's false. He celebrated the US being the world's 'No. 1' oil and gas producer. And the house cheered—they cheered for the knowing destabilization of the planet." She added, "Don't call them deniers, they are arsonists."[13]

The *Los Angeles Times* ran a 2018 story with the headline: "As Global Warming Continues, Trump Wants to Burn Fossil Fuels with an Arsonist's Glee."[14]

But it was former vice president Joe Biden who took the "climate arsonist" smear to a new level during the 2020 presidential campaign. Referring to wildfires and other extreme weather events, Biden claimed in September 2020, "If [Trump] gets a second term, these hellish events will continue to become more common, more devastating and more deadly."

"If you give a climate arsonist four more years in the White House, why would anyone be surprised if we have more America blaze? If we give a climate denier four more years in the White House, why would anyone be surprised when more of America is underwater?"[15]

Biden's blaming deadly fires on the president's climate skepticism is just another example of how the climate activists have been trying to intimidate anyone who dissents on man-made global warming into silence.

"What Joe Biden Said Is You Can Vote Yourself Better Weather"

Joe Biden has declared that Americans can change the weather with their votes.

"We have four more years of Trump's climate denial, how many suburbs will be burned in wildfires?" Biden asked. "How many suburban neighborhoods will have been flooded out? How many suburbs will have been blown away in superstorms?"

As I explained during a September 15, 2020, appearance on *Tucker Carlson Tonight*, "This is climate ambulance chasing at its core, weaponizing weather events to say, 'Look, there's a bad weather event here and we need a Green New Deal.' They are using science to lobby for politics. 'Vote for me and I will make the weather better.'...

"What Joe Biden said is you can vote yourself better weather, President Obama said the same thing in 2012 and people did vote for him. They voted him back in, but guess what, we still have extreme weather. So voting for Obama didn't help and I don't know how voting for Biden is going to stop extreme weather."[16]

Undeterred, President Trump announced in 2020, "Thanks to our bold regulatory reduction campaign, the United States has become the number one producer of oil and natural gas in the world, by far."[17]

Trump summed up the climate issue in his 2020 Davos address, calling the alarmists "prophets of doom" and "heirs of yesterday's foolish fortune-tellers."

"To embrace the possibilities of tomorrow we must reject the perennial prophets of doom and their predictions of the Apocalypse. They are the heirs of yesterday's foolish fortune-tellers, and they want to see us do badly but we won't let that happen. They predicted an overpopulation crisis in the 1960s, mass starvation in the 70s, and an end of oil in the 1990s. These alarmists always demand the same thing: absolute power to dominate, transform and control every aspect of our lives," Trump told the World Economic Forum in January 2020.[18]

The Future Is Hard to Predict

It isn't just that predicted environmental disasters failed to materialize, but also that many agencies and analysts made wrong predictions about energy. An Axios analysis noted that the decade from 2010 to 2019 "blew up energy predictions."[19] Energy reporters Amy Harder and Andrew Witherspoon concluded, "America's energy sources, like booming oil and crumbling coal, have defied projections and historical precedents over the last decade."

The eye-opening Axios analysis revealed how wrong the energy predictions that the U.S. Energy Information Administration (EIA) made in 2010 were. "EIA had projected in 2010 that U.S. energy-related carbon dioxide emissions would continue rising, albeit at a slower pace. In fact, they dropped," wrote Harder and Witherspoon. "In 2010, the U.S. Energy Information Administration projected that in 2019, the U.S. would be producing about six million barrels of oil a day. The reality? We're now producing 12 million barrels of oil a day. Meanwhile, EIA projected oil prices would be more than $100 a barrel. They're currently hovering around $60 a barrel." Fracking is the chief reason.

EIA got it wrong on oil imports as well. "EIA had projected in 2010 that the U.S. would be importing a net eight million barrels of petroleum by now [2019] which includes crude oil and petroleum products like gasoline. In September, the U.S. actually exported a net 89,000 barrels of petroleum," Axios reported, noting that Congress had lifted the forty-year-old ban on crude oil exports in 2015.[20]

"The EIA had projected that coal electricity would remain dominant in the U.S. and natural gas would remain relatively stable—even drop slightly in its share of power supply. The opposite is happening. Coal-fired

Slick Oil Prediction

"Do we really want to threaten to blow up the world over a resource [oil] which we know damn well is going to be gone in 20 or 30 years anyway?"

—overpopulation guru Paul Ehrlich on *The Tonight Show Starring Johnny Carson*—January 31, 1980[21]

power is plummeting and natural gas has risen significantly," the Axios analysis noted. And while solar and wind power "tracked a bit higher" than the 2010 projections, Axios explained, "this is due to the low base on which wind and solar started from, the sporadic nature of federal tax subsidies for these industries and continued support among states."

As John Shanahan, a civil engineer and editor of AllAboutEnergy.net, wrote to me in an email, 2020 research has found "the incredible global importance of fossil fuels, the insignificance of wind and solar energy for generating electricity" in total global energy use. "The data show the total folly of politicians forcing cities, states, countries to be 100% or 50% on wind and solar energy in 30, 50, 100 years. That is 100% unnecessary, 100% wasting limited resources that could be used to solve pressing problems of billions of poor people around the world."[23]

"Embarrassingly Preposterous"

"The U.S. currently gets about 80 percent of its energy from fossil fuels. Promoters of GND imagine we can take that percentage down to zero in only a decade, transitioning fossil fuels to wind and solar. This idea is so embarrassingly preposterous that the GND prophets hastily changed their resolution to simply 'zero emissions.' This idea is equally as ludicrous, but apparently, it sounds better.... Oil and natural gas are also the feedstocks for most products we all use every day. They include plastics, fertilizers, lubricants, fabrics, rubber, asphalt, chemicals, medicines, paint, adhesives, food packaging and the list goes on and on."

—energy analyst Mark Mathis of the Clear Energy Alliance[22]

Even Al Gore has acknowledged the value of fossil fuels. Speaking at the 2017 EcoCity World Summit in Melbourne, the former vice president said, "We have had tremendous benefits from our reliance on fossil fuels. Poverty has declined, living standards have increased and we still depend on them for more than 80% of the world's energy." Gore then asked, "Must we change?" Of course Gore's answer was yes. He devoted

> **"Apple Is Lying to You"**
>
> Apple claims to be using 100 percent renewable energy. But as Alex Epstein, the founder of the Center for Industrial Progress, pointed out in 2020, "Apple is lying to you. They use mostly non-renewable energy, but pay utilities to give them credit for the renewable energy you use—and give you the blame for the non-renewable energy they use."[25]

the remainder of his talk, which I attended in Australia, to the alleged negative effects of carbon dioxide on the climate.[24]

The Same Mix as Before

Let's take a look at the energy mix history of the past hundred years. As this chart from the U.S. Energy Information Administration demonstrates, the U.S. energy consumption mix has not changed all that much in the past century.

In 1908, fossil fuels accounted for 85 percent of U.S. energy consumption. In 2015—more or less the same energy consumption mix as fossil fuels accounted for 81 percent, according to the EIA.[26]

Anderson Cooper of CBS's *60 Minutes* asked AOC:

> Cooper: You're talking about zero carbon emissions, no use of fossil fuels within 12 years.
> AOC: That is the goal. It is ambitious, and...
> Cooper: How is that possible? You're talking about everybody having to drive an electric car?
> AOC: It's going to require a lot of rapid change that we don't even conceive of as possible right now. What is the problem with trying to push our technological capacities to the furthest extent possible?

AOC's question is easy to answer. Banning fossil fuel energy that has proven it works by fueling the Industrial Revolution, improving lives, lowering infant mortality, giving us longer life expectancy, powering modern civilization, and unleashing a technological revolution that helped clean up our environment. Mandating energy that can't fill the

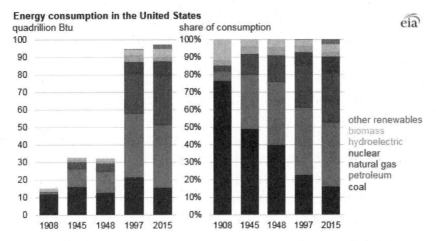

Energy consumption in the United States

This graph helps put things in perspective: the Green New Deal is seeking to obliterate 80 percent plus of our energy consumption by magically shrinking U.S. energy from fossil fuels from 80 percent down to zero CO_2 emissions.

void will needlessly increase energy costs, punish lower income Americans, and bring economic growth to a halt.

A Tiny Fraction

"Fossil fuels currently meet 81% of our global energy needs. And even if every promised climate policy in the 2015 Paris climate agreement is achieved by 2040, they will still deliver 74% of the total. We already spend $129 billion per year subsidizing solar and wind energy to try to entice more people to use today's inefficient technology, yet these sources meet just 1.1% of our global energy needs. The IEA estimates that by 2040—after we have spent a whopping $3.5 trillion on additional subsidies—solar and wind will still meet less than 5% of our needs."

— Bjørn Lomborg, the director of the Copenhagen Consensus Center[27]

The 3–4 Percent Solution

Banning fossil fuel energy to mandate energy like wind and solar that is—to put it politely—not ready to take over the modern world's energy supply, is not rational, moral, or scientific.

BP's "Statistical Review of World Energy 2019" shows oil, coal, and gas supplying 85 percent of global "energy consumption." A study published in the journal *Energies* in September 2020 found, "As of 2018, the world is still generating most (85%) of its energy from fossil fuels (oil, coal, and gas). Nuclear (4%) and one of the renewables, hydroelectricity (7%), also represent significant slices of the pie. However, wind and solar only represent 3%, and other sources only represent 1%." The energy study was titled "Energy and Climate Policy—An Evaluation of Global Climate Change Expenditure 2011–2018."[28]

The U.S. Energy Information Administration estimates for the 2018 global energy mix are very similar to the BP estimates.[29] If you just focus on the U.S.-only energy consumption, the EIA estimated "renewable" consumption in the U.S. at 12 percent in 2018—up one percentage point, from 11 percent in 2017. But the 12 percent "renewable" energy statistic includes hydroelectricity and biomass. If you separate out just wind and solar from that 12 percent "renewable," you end up with…drumroll please: wind and solar met only about 3 percent of U.S. energy needs in 2018, according to the EIA.[30]

And that 3 percent is AFTER $50 billion in subsidies. "Production Tax Credit (PTC) subsidies for renewable solar and wind projects in the U.S. have now reached about $50 billion dollars in cumulative payments through year 2018 with these resources providing about 3% of our countries total energy consumption in that year," wrote Larry Hamlin at *WattsUpWithThat*. "Additionally these annual wind and solar subsidies now total more than $8 billion dollars per year." As Hamlin explained, "Despite more than a decade of government-mandated renewable energy use with lucrative and generous renewable subsidies required, these politically

> **Through the Looking Glass**
> "Even in the Alice in Wonderland energy world of California fossil fuels dominate our states total energy consumption accounting for 82% of energy use with that figure also little changed in the last decade."[31]
> —Larry Hamlin, *WhatsUp WithThat*[32]

driven energy resources have made little progress" in meeting energy needs "largely because of their unreliable and highly limited performance capabilities." Hamlin wrote, "Absent government mandated use and provisions requiring lucrative PTC subsidies, renewables would fall flat on their face in the energy markets."[33]

The BP energy analysis agreed, noting that despite "the large global expenditure on wind and solar projects over the 2011–2018 period" wind and solar went from providing 0.5 percent of world energy in 2010 to 3 percent in 2018, an increase of only 2.5 percentage points.

> ## "Anti-Market Policies"
>
> "Claims that we are in a rapid transition away from fossil fuels are wrong. In the past several decades, solar and wind have gone from providing virtually 0% of American energy to 9.7% of American electricity and just 3.8% of American energy overall (in 2019). Solar and wind's 3.8% market share is not due to the free market but rather anti-market policies that force consumers to use unreliable solar and wind even though they drive up energy costs."
>
> —Alex Epstein, Center for Industrial Progress [34]

The Green New Deal, regardless of the version, has a goal of zeroing out carbon dioxide emissions from the U.S. power sector within a decade to a decade and a half. Biden's 2020 campaign claimed that his $2 trillion Green New Deal plan would zero out CO2 by promoting the installation of "millions of new solar panels and tens of thousands of wind turbines." Biden himself insisted that "these aren't pie-in-the-sky dreams," claiming that he would "move ambitiously to generate clean, American-made electricity to achieve a carbon pollution-free power sector by 2035."[35]

Energy analyst Vijay Jayaraj wrote, "In other words, [Biden] intends to put $2 trillion of irreversible funding into making the American power sector completely devoid of coal, oil, and natural gas, from which America currently generates more than 62 percent of all its electricity. Would Biden's plan usher in a California-like [energy blackout] situation in the rest of the country? The answer to that question is yes."[36]

Name Energy Blackouts

"Like hurricanes, blackouts should be named—for Democrat politicians who are allowing California to burn solely to advance the climate agenda." —Steve Milloy, JunkScience.com[37]

Energy expert Robert Bryce explained, "Californians now rely on an electricity network that looks and acts more like a grid you'd find in Beirut or Africa than ones in Europe or the United States....The bans and restrictions on natural gas are being implemented at the same time California's electricity rates are soaring." Bryce added, "Californians are also paying some of America's highest energy prices....47% higher than the national average."[38]

"Magical Thinking"

Even CNN broadcast skepticism of Green New Deal energy claims. "The Sanders green energy plan is magical thinking," declared CNN host and *Washington Post* columnist Fareed Zakaria in February 2020. Zakaria credited Sanders with "a laudable though ambitious goal." But

Passing Wind

In 2020 climate activist Bill McKibben claimed, "In the last 10 years, engineers have driven the price of sun and wind power down below coal."

But H. Sterling Burnett, an energy policy analyst at the Heartland Institute, explained why McKibben's claim was not accurate. "What McKibben doesn't disclose is that he's only counting the price of wind and solar on days when they are operating at peak capacity, while ignoring their capital costs," Burnett wrote.

"The fact that wind and solar produce so little of the world's electricity mix is proof positive that they are substantially more expensive than conventional energy," Burnett explained. "McKibben also conveniently fails to count the tremendous subsidies wind and solar power received from the government. Indeed, without government subsidies and mandates, wind and solar power would largely be a boutique power supply for the wealthy," Burnett explained.[39]

he ripped the actual plan apart: "It presumes that we can reduce emissions in electricity and transport to zero in ten years while simultaneously shutting down the only two low-emissions, always available sources of power [natural gas fracking and nuclear energy] that collectively provide nearly 60 percent of America's electricity today. And that makes me wonder: Is the real problem that Bernie Sanders will lose or that he might win?"

Zakaria explained, "If we had the means to store electricity on a massive scale, such as in batteries, there would be no longer [any] need for backup power. But we are not even close to having the kind of storage capacity we would need to make this [Sanders's Green New Deal] work." Zakaria also noted that U.S. carbon dioxide emissions fell almost 15 percent between 2005 and 2016 and that "the single largest cause for that" was natural gas replacing coal-fired power, which accounted for 33 percent of the reduction. "The adoption of solar power by contrast, accounted for just 3%," Zakaria said, citing data from Carbon Brief.[41]

> ### "Where Is Fertilizer, Cement, Plastic Going to Come From?"
>
> At Stanford University's 2018 Global Energy Forum, Bill Gates pointed out, "The 'climate is easy to solve' group is our biggest problem." ... "Do you guys on Wall Street have something in your desks that makes steel? Where is fertilizer, cement, plastic going to come from? Do planes fly through the sky because of some number you put in a spreadsheet? The idea that we have the current tools and it's just because these utility people are evil people and if we could just beat on them and put (solar panels) on our rooftop—that is more of a block than climate denial."[40]

Other energy experts agree with CNN's Zakaria about the problems with the GND.

"[Solar and wind power] just depend on when the sun is shining and when the wind is blowing, which is 10 to 40 percent of the year," noted Michael Shellenberger in his critique of the Green New Deal. "The intermittent energy production of wind and solar is a key problem

> ### "Substantially More Subsidies"
>
> "Wind and solar power receive substantially more subsidies than conventional energy sources. Wind power by itself receives more source-specific government subsidies than all conventional energy sources combined. Solar power by itself also receives more source-specific government subsidies than all conventional energy sources combined."
> —the Heartland Institute's Climate Realism website[46]

making them unreliable."[42] As Shellenberger explained, "I spent the last decade looking around the world for alternative models. I quickly discovered two things. First, no nation has decarbonized its electricity supply with solar and wind. Second, the only successful decarbonization efforts were achieved with nuclear."[43]

"Unreliables"

Alex Epstein, the founder of the Center for Industrial Progress and the author of *The Moral Case for Fossil Fuels*, agreed. "In the last 15 years America has become a world energy leader largely through enormous growth in producing the #1 and #3 forms of energy in the world: oil and natural gas," Epstein wrote. "This was only possible because of our unrivaled freedom to develop and innovate." Epstein added, "Energy schemes around the world based on 'unreliables'—solar and wind—have been driving up electricity costs, harming economies, destroying domestic industries, and harming consumers. Germans pay three times the U.S. electricity prices to get just 1/3 of their electricity from solar and wind."[44]

A Green New Deal is not the way to go, given that "America is already too reliant on unreliable solar and wind," Epstein continued. "That's why utilities are already blacking out many of their industrial customers. And grids in Texas and the Northeast are warning of blackouts for everyone if policies don't change. Biden's [Green New Deal] Plan will guarantee blackouts."[45]

In "Why Renewables Can't Save the Planet" at Quillette, Shellenberger explained, "I came to understand the environmental implications of the physics of energy. In order to produce significant amounts of electricity from weak energy flows, you just have to spread them over enormous areas. In other words, the trouble with renewables isn't fundamentally technical—it's natural. Dealing with energy sources that are inherently unreliable, and require large amounts of land, comes at a high economic cost." Shellenberger added, "You can make solar panels cheaper and wind turbines bigger, but you can't make the sun shine more regularly or the wind blow more reliably."[48]

> ### "Overtaxed $50 Billion"
> "Although most countries do offer some subsidies to fossil fuels, the massive taxes imposed by most governments are generally far higher, resulting in a net increase in the price of fossil fuels. Taking into account all taxes and subsidies, fossil fuels in the United States are overtaxed $50 billion per year."
> **—energy expert Bruce Everett of the CO2 Coalition**[47]

Alex Epstein's research found that energy poverty in the U.S. is made worse by solar and wind mandates. "25 million US households say they've gone without food or medicine to pay for energy. 12 million say they've kept their home at an unsafe temperature," Epstein wrote. "US energy poverty should have decreased since 2008, when the price of natural gas—the fuel that powers most home energy use—started plummeting. But energy poverty is going up because we have added so much wasteful, unreliable solar and wind infrastructure to the grid."[49]

The House Democrat version of the Green New Deal in 2020 included provisions to expand the Wind Production Tax Credit (PTC), which Epstein called "a perverse policy that pays utilities to slow down or shut down reliable power plants whenever the wind blows." According to Epstein, "PTC is driving reliable power plants out of business, leading to higher costs and lower reliability." He added, "The only reason utilities buy unnecessary, wasteful wind turbines is government policies that force them to do so or reward them for doing so."[50]

An Iowa wind farm was claimed to "generate more tax credits than electricity" due to the green policies. The Wind XI project "could generate up to $1.8 billion in tax credits for its backers over the next decade," reported Grant Kidwell in *The Hill*. Who benefits from these policies? "Warren Buffett; MidAmerican Energy's other investors; and Facebook, Microsoft, and Google—MidAmerican's biggest customers, who will receive tax benefits of their own for using wind energy. The losers? Taxpayers and other ratepayers footing the bill," Kidwell wrote.[51]

Buffett admitted he really likes the wind incentives: "We get a tax credit if we build a lot of wind farms. That's the only reason to build them."[52]

Alex Epstein explains how unreliable wind power is: "Wind turbines cannot provide the reliable energy that our amazing electrical grid requires 24/7. That's why every place in the world that uses unreliable wind energy depends 24/7 on massive amounts of reliable energy from coal, gas, hydro, or nuclear plants."[53]

When the *New York Times* touted how many more workers the solar industry employed compared to the coal industry, economist Mark Perry of AEI was appalled. "The goal of America's energy sector isn't to create

"Less than a Tenth of 1%"

"Electric Vehicles Are Being Outpaced by the Growth of SUV," read the headline in an analysis by Nick Butler in the *Financial Times* in October 2019. "A casual reader of the media during the past few months could easily get the idea that electric vehicles were in the process of taking over the market," Butler wrote. "Electric vehicle numbers are certainly growing. Worldwide, some 5.1 million electric vehicles were on the world's roads by the end of 2018, an increase of 2 million over the previous year. The 7 million to 8 million electric vehicles that should be on the road by the end of 2019 represent less than a tenth of 1% of the 1.1 billion cars and other light vehicles that use internal combustion engines. Some 85 million internal combustion engines vehicles were sold worldwide in 2018...In the US, SUVs account for 45% of new car sales. But the trend is not limited to the US. In Europe SUVs take 34% of new sales, in China 42% and in India 23%."[54]

as many jobs as possible (as the NYT article would apparently have us believe) especially the politically-favored and heavily-subsidized renewable energy jobs. Rather, the economic goal is to produce as much electric power as possible at the lowest possible cost, and that means we want the fewest number of energy workers!" Perry wrote in 2017. "When it comes to solar energy, we are employing a very large number of workers who produce a very small amount of electric power—a sure sign of economic inefficiency," Perry added.[55]

In 2012, Obama touted his green energy "investments" at the Copper Mountain Solar 1 plant, which relied on $54 million in taxpayer subsidies and had only five full-time employees—amounting to "$10.8 million in tax-dollar subsidies per employee," according to the Nevada Policy Research Institute.[56]

A 2020 study by the Texas Public Policy Foundation found that "wind has received nearly 40 times and solar nearly 200 times more subsidies per unit of electricity generated than oil and gas." As Jason Isaac of Real Clear Energy wrote about the new study, "Over the last decade, wind energy

Swap Independence for Dependence

"The net effect of a Green New Deal distills to replacing domestic energy production (and exports) of hydrocarbons with an unprecedented level of energy mineral imports...China, for example, supplies about 90% of rare-earths for the world. On the cobalt front, China has also quietly gained control over more than 90% of the battery industry's cobalt refining, without which the raw ore is useless. Russia is a massive nickel producer...You don't have to ban fracking to kill the industry; mandating the use of the alternatives has the same effect...If all that weren't enough, there's also the roughly 20 to 100-fold increase in land use that comes with using green machines to replace hydrocarbons. And, of course, there's the mother's milk of a Green New Deal, the trillions of dollars in subsidies, necessarily funded by increased costs and taxes for all consumers."
—energy analyst Mark P. Mills, senior fellow at the Manhattan Institute[57]

received $36.7 billion and solar received $34.4 billion of our tax dollars. Despite this mammoth expenditure, as well as the billions appropriated in the decades prior, wind and solar still only provide 3% of our energy."[58]

"Not Very Earth Friendly"

Energy analyst Vijay Jayaraj wrote, "Both wind and solar are also toxic. The mining of rare earth elements used in them involves processes with toxic waste that has killed people and turned lakes toxic. The recycle value of wind and solar is not great either. As wind blades near end-of-life, they are dumped under the soil and cannot be recycled."[59]

Shellenberger also noted how solar power is not very earth friendly. "Solar panels require 17 times more materials in the form of cement, glass, concrete, and steel than do nuclear plants, and create over 200 times more waste," he wrote. "We tend to think of solar panels as clean, but the truth is that there is no plan anywhere to deal with solar panels at the end of their 20 to 25 year lifespan," he added.

Shellenberger: "Solar and wind farms around the world require at least 300–400 times more land on average than a natural gas or nuclear plant to produce the same quantity of energy."[60]

Epstein also emphasized the importance of nuclear energy. "America can lower emissions and energy costs by decriminalizing nuclear energy. Nuclear is actually the safest source of energy and the only way to

What about the Waste?

"We keep storing it safely and compactly. Because nuclear is such concentrated energy its waste is tiny compared to the alternatives. A better question is: What do we do about solar panel, wind turbine, and battery waste?"

—Alex Epstein, founder of the Center for Industrial Progress[61]

provide reliable non-carbon electricity anywhere in the world. Yet politicians are overregulating it to death."[62]

Bird Blenders

Shellenberger pushed back on wind power advocates' claims that house cats kill more birds than wind turbines. "As for house cats, they don't kill big, rare, threatened birds. What house cats kill are small, common birds, like sparrows, robins and jays," he said. "What kills big, threatened, and endangered birds—birds that could go extinct—like hawks, eagles, owls, and condors, are wind turbines. In fact, wind turbines are the most serious new threat to important bird species to emerge in decades. The rapidly spinning turbines act like an apex predator which big birds never evolved to deal with."

"Birds have evolved over hundreds of years to fly certain paths to migrate," according to environmentalist Lisa Linowes, issuing a warning

Bald Eagle Killed by Wind Turbine

In Ohio, several witnesses saw a large bird tumbling to the ground after colliding with a wind turbine. The severed wing of the bird landed nearby. "We looked around as soon as we heard the turbine hit something, but at first we couldn't tell exactly what it was," a witness told the *Toledo Blade* newspaper in 2020.

"The dead bird was an adult bald eagle, a species safeguarded under the Bald and Golden Eagle Protection Act and the Migratory Bird Treaty Act," the paper reported. "The wing was ripped off," Reid Van Cleve of the Division of Wildlife assigned to Ottawa County said. "It was definitely a turbine strike." Amy Weller, who lives near the wind farm, said, "I was opposed to those windmills from the start because of the impact they could have on wildlife. I had been out to California about 20 years ago and saw the carcasses on the ground under the wind turbines. From an environmental standpoint, I can't believe they would want to do that here, with all of the migration we have in this area and the bald eagles."[63]

> ### Renewables Dig the Earth
>
> "The one million electric vehicles (EVs) now on U.S. roads (courtesy of billions of dollars in subsidies) account for just 0.5% of America's cars but contain, for example, more cobalt than one billion smartphones. In general, fabricating a single EV battery, each of which weighs about 1,000 pounds, requires digging up roughly 500,000 pounds of materials. That's more than a 10-fold increase in the cumulative quantity of materials (liquids) used by a standard car over its entire operating life...The world is literally about to embark on the biggest increase in mineral and metal mining in history."
>
> —energy analyst Mark P. Mills, senior fellow at the Manhattan Institute [65]

about wind power. "You can't throw a turbine up in the way and expect them to adapt. It's not happening."

Kevon Martis, co-founder with Linowes of the Energy and Wildlife Coalition, said, "Democrats have been sold a false narrative by the industrial wind industry." He added, "Many Democrats somehow imagine that industrial wind farms, which take hundreds of times more land than a natural gas plant, are better for the environment."[64]

And the problem with "renewables" isn't just the birds. "In order to build one of the biggest solar farms in California the developers hired biologists to pull threatened desert tortoises from their burrows, put them on the back of pickup trucks, transport them, and cage them in pens where many ended up dying," Shellenberger wrote.

In Scotland, the government revealed in 2020 that nearly 14 million trees have been chopped down to make way for wind turbines. "Statistics, released by Forestry and Land Scotland, show that 13.9 million trees have been axed to make way for 21 wind farm projects since 2000," reported the *Scotland Herald*.

Steve Micklewright, the CEO of Trees for Life, detailed why even climate activists shake their heads at these policies. "It seems deeply ironic that trees are being felled to make way for windfarms when both

---

"Absurd"

"It is absurd for middle-class citizens in advanced economies to tell themselves that eating less steak or commuting in a Toyota TM-0.18% Prius will rein in rising temperatures," noted Bjørn Lomborg. "Electric cars are branded as environmentally friendly, but generating the electricity they require almost always involves burning fossil fuels. Moreover, producing energy-intensive batteries for these cars invariably generates significant CO2 emissions"

Lomborg added, "As IEA Executive Director Fatih Birol has said, 'If you think you can save the climate with electric cars, you're completely wrong.' In 2018, electric cars saved 40 million tons of CO2 worldwide, equivalent to reducing global temperatures by just 0.000018°C—or a little more than a hundred-thousandth of a degree Celsius—by the end of the century."[66]

---

healthy growing forests and renewable energy are important in resolving the global climate emergency."[67]

Neither Clean Nor Green

Another negative environmental impact involves electric vehicles. In the United States, the transportation sector has replaced power plants as the number one source of carbon dioxide emissions, with the majority of the emissions coming from passenger cars and trucks. The Green New Deal sets the goal of an "overhaul" of transportation to get rid of emissions, and the gas-powered internal combustion engine is the target. But electric cars and the batteries they depend on have many environmental and social justice problems.[68]

"Congo's Miners Dying to Feed World's Hunger for Electric Cars," read the headline in the *Sunday Times* of London in 2019. "Exploited by Chinese firms, workers as young as nine risk their lives to feed the world's growing hunger for cobalt," reporter Christina Lamb wrote. "Last year about 70% of the world's supply came from the Democratic

Republic of Congo, one of the poorest, most violent and corrupt places on Earth. Much of its cobalt comes from around this town."

"Without Democratic Republic of Congo there is no electric car industry and no green revolution," said Anneke Van Woudenberg, head of Rights and Accountability in Development (Raid), a UK-based group.

A profile in the *Times* of London exposed the human impact of cobalt mining for electric cars: "Solange Kanena sits on her broken orange sofa, heavily pregnant, resting. Looking around her three-room shack, she wonders how she will feed her eight children. Her husband died in a mining accident 10 days ago. She has never held an iPhone and has no idea what an electric car is. But when the deep, muddy tunnel collapsed on her husband, he was digging for a commodity that is critical to the batteries of both: cobalt"[69]

A 2020 United Nations report warned about the side effects of electric car production. "As demand for rechargeable batteries is forecast to grow rapidly due to EV's becoming more integrated into global transportation, the quantity of the raw materials used in manufacturing them is also expected to increase rapidly," the UN trade body, UNCTAD, explained in their report. And there are "challenges in ensuring that the raw materials are sustainably sourced given that their exploitation is often associated with undesirable environmental footprints, poor human rights and worker protection," the UN report noted. The metals cobalt, lithium, manganese, copper, and minerals like graphite "play a significant role in energy-related technologies such as rechargeable batteries that are used in a variety of applications ranging from electronics to electric vehicles as well as in renewable energies such as nuclear, wind, and solar power."[70]

Energy advocate Paul Driessen, co-author of the book *Energy Keepers, Energy Killers*, summed up the problem with "renewable" energy. "It bears repeating: wind and sun are renewable and sustainable; harnessing them for energy to benefit mankind absolutely is not....How many decades will it take to replace the millions of acres of slow-growth forest that are incinerated each year as a 'carbon neutral' alternative to coal?" he asked. "Wind, solar and biofuel energy are not clean, green, renewable, or sustainable, and they are horrifically destructive to vital ecological values."[71]

Shellenberger echoed Driessen's sentiments. "The most important thing is for scientists and conservationists to start telling the truth about renewables and nuclear, and the relationship between energy density and environmental impact," Shellenberger wrote.[72]

David Wojick and Paul Driessen of CFACT concluded in 2020, "The Green New Deal would force every American to replace their gasoline and diesel cars and trucks with expensive short-haul electric vehicles; their gas furnaces and stoves with electric systems; their home, local and state electrical and transmission systems with expensive upgrades that can handle a totally electric economy. They'll see their landscapes, coast-lines and wildlife habitats blanketed with wind turbines, solar panels, transmission lines and warehouses filled with thousands of half-ton batteries. Virtually every component of this GND nation would be manufactured in China and other faraway places."[73]

Shellenberger asked: "Now that we know that renewables can't save the planet, are we really going to stand by and let them destroy it?"

Prophet or Profit?

The biggest surprise of 2020 came when Oscar-winning filmmaker Michael Moore turned on his fellow progressives over the issue of renewable energy. Moore was a progressive hero for such films as *Bowling for Columbine, Fahrenheit 9/11,* and *Roger and Me.* But Moore's film *Planet of the Humans* sent shockwaves through the climate change debate.

This is how Steven Mosher described Moore's environmental tour de force: "By the midpoint of the movie, Moore has already revealed that each and every form of green energy is a fraud, surviving on popular naiveté, government subsidies and the products of industrial civilization....If he were to have stopped there, his sins against his fellow eco-leftists might one day be forgiven. But he doesn't, instead going on to argue that the fraud extends to the very top of the green-energy movement itself."[74]

Moore and his director, environmentalist Jeff Gibbs, go all the way to the top, exposing the crony capitalism running rampant in the green movement. Al Gore, Bill McKibben of 350.org, Robert F. Kennedy Jr., Richard Branson, Michael Bloomberg, and the Sierra Club, are all presented as green profiteers, swindlers, profiting from the renewable energy cash cow.

"I assumed solar panels would last forever," Moore admitted. "I didn't know what went into the making of them."[75]

"We all want to feel good about something like the electric car, but in the back of your head somewhere you've thought, 'Yeah, but where is the electricity coming from?'" Moore asked.

"It turned out the wakeup call was about our own side," director Gibbs explained. "Everywhere I encountered green energy, it wasn't what it seemed."[76] Follow the money, as they say. "The only reason we've been force-fed the story 'climate change plus renewables equals we're saved' is because billionaires, bankers and corporations profit from it," Gibbs said.

The film shows both new and abandoned industrial wind and solar farms that have clear-cut forests. "It suddenly dawned on me what we were looking at was a solar dead zone," Gibbs explained as he gazed upon a defunct solar farm in California.[77]

Climate skeptic James Delingpole, writing at Breitbart, explained how devastating *Planet of the Humans* was to the climate cause. "We visit a 'solar powered' music festival where we discover that behind the scenes it is largely powered by diesel generators. We visit an ethanol plant—whose wood has to be harvested using fossil fuel–powered equipment and depends for its operational effectiveness on coal. We visit a lovely old wood beloved by hikers and nature lovers in rural Vermont being trashed to build a wind farm. We see 500-year old yuccas in the

Mojave desert being torn up and shredded by diggers to make way for a 'clean' energy solar plant."

"It was enough to make my head explode," as Gibbs said. "Green energy is not going to save us."[78]

Some of the intense gotcha moments in the movie involve green heroes like Bill McKibben dodging questions about how his group was funded. But perhaps the most shocking scene features an interview clip of former vice president Al Gore and Richard Branson laughing about how much Al Gore has enriched himself with his green advocacy.

An unidentified TV interviewer asks Richard Branson, sitting with Al Gore: "Is Al Gore a prophet? Branson replies: "Uhh...ah...How do you spell 'profit'?" Branson, Gore, and the interviewer then all let out a huge, sustained laugh.[79]

Michael Moore Exiled from the Planet of Progressives

It did not take long for Moore's fellow progressives to turn on the film and Moore himself.

Former UN IPCC scientist and climate activist Michael Mann of Penn State went after Moore's film in *Newsweek*, accusing Moore of using "tactics of denial, delay, distraction and deflection." Mann then took a shot at your author, "Fossil fuel industry shills, like Marc Morano of CFACT promoted the film and attacked its critics on social media."[80]

Environmental activist Josh Fox explained that it felt like he had lost a hero when he saw Moore's film. "I will add here, with deep regret and sadness, that my hero has fallen. A multi-millionaire many many many times over, Moore is now attacking environmental heroes like Bill McKibben, Van Jones," Fox wrote. "I cannot sit by and watch that happen. This is not fun, this is terrible."

Mann and Fox joined in an effort to censor Moore's movie. "I just received notice that the distributor of Michael Moore's *Planet of the Humans* is taking the film down due to misinformation in the film.

Thank you to Films For Action [one of the film's distributors] for respond-ing to our demand for a retraction and an apology from Michael Moore," Fox wrote on April 24, 2020.[81]

But the victory lap by Fox was premature, as Moore's film was still available for millions to watch for free on YouTube.

And Film For Action quickly announced their reversal of the decision to censor Moore's film. "We put the film back up on the site," the dis-tributor announced. "We don't want to give the film extra publicity and mystique for getting taken down."

The progressives were briefly successful in getting YouTube to pull Moore's film down from YouTube on the basis of a copyright infringe-ment issue involving one of the photographs in the film.[82]

Moore was livid. "The public now PROHIBITED from watching our film *Planet of the Humans* because it calls out the eco-industrial complex for collaborating with Wall Street and contributing to us losing the battle against the climate catastrophe," Moore wrote on May 28, 2020. "We showed their failure and collusion, they didn't like us for doing that, so instead of having the debate with us out in the open, they chose the route of slandering the film—and now their attempt at the suppression of our free speech. 'Democracy Dies in Darkness.' Fascism is given life when 'liberals' employ authoritarian tactics. Or sit back and say nothing. Who will speak up against blocking the public from seeing a movie that a group of 'green capitalists' don't want you to see? Where is the Academy?" Moore pleaded.[83]

But the YouTube copyright infringement issues were all sorted out and Moore's film was put back up on YouTube two weeks after it was pulled.[84]

Director Gibbs slammed the left-wing critics of the film. "I wish to respond to the eco-industrialists who, in the attempt to 'save the planet,' have gotten into bed with bankers, billionaires, industrialists, and their foundations," Gibbs wrote.

"Solar, wind, and electric technologies are not something separate from a giant fossil-fuel based industrial civilization; they are one and the same.... It's the slave labor in a far away land that lets us all feel so warm and cozy and 'green,'" Gibbs wrote. "Any movement or organization that does not invite self-reflection and instead tries to choke it to death—like the eco-industrial complex is attempting to do to us—is doomed."[85]

Climate skeptic Paul Driessen summed up Moore's film and the progressives' effort to censor it. "The film's key point is the same as my own: wind, solar and biofuel energy are not clean, green, renewable, or sustainable, and they are horrifically destructive to vital ecological values. The censors believe admitting that is sacrilegious," Driessen wrote. "But Moore and Gibbs aren't indicting free-market capitalism. They're indicting government-mandated and subsidized crony corporatist opportunism." He concluded, "Michael Moore and Jeff Gibbs have done us a great service in exposing the environmental degradation from pseudo-renewable energy. Now they just need to reexamine neo-Malthusian doctrines as well."[86]

The COVID–Climate Connection: COVID Lockdowns as Dress Rehearsal for the "Climate Emergency"

America was forever changed by the COVID-19 virus. And so was the climate debate.

The year 2020 saw a drastic shift away from the climate momentum that the Green New Deal was riding when COVID-19 showed up on the global scene. Suddenly the public was genuinely scared about ... not a long-hyped climate "emergency," but viral fears. Most of the world, including the U.S., went into maximum fear and lockdown mode in March of 2020, and climate activists watched helplessly as their issue was supplanted with COVID.

But the climate change alarmists have watched the governments around the world and their responses to the COVID-19 pandemic in awe. Global warming campaigners have been taking notes as the virus-induced societal shutdowns have enacted much of the climate activists' long-sought after agenda. The austere lockdowns and economic collapse have inspired climate activists.

As astrophysicist and philosopher Martín López Corredoira noted, "Neither Greenpeace, nor Greta Thunberg, nor any other individual or collective organization have achieved so much in favor of the health of

IS THE CORONAVIRUS LOCKDOWN **THE FUTURE** ENVIRONMENTALISTS WANT?

the planet in such a short time....It is certainly not very good for the economy in general, but it is fantastic for the environment."[1]

The environmental Left watched as many of the same "solutions" they have advocated for the alleged "climate emergency" were enacted seemingly overnight by governments around the world. Everything the climate campaigners could have ever hoped for has become a (temporary?) reality with the coronavirus-induced shutdown of modern society.

Climate activists...

- Hated airline travel and promoted "flight shaming"... and the airline industry was essentially shut down.[2]
- Hated economic growth, the hallmark of the capitalist system...and growth was wiped out as a recession was created by the lockdowns.[3]
- Called for lower emissions through "planned recession" or "degrowth" policies...and a recession or worse was achieved almost overnight.[4]
- Fretted over the carbon footprint of meals eaten out at restaurants...and restaurants were shuttered, with many small mom-and-pop restaurants closing permanently.[5]
- Called for the end of evil gas-fueled cars...and car production, sales, and driving all took a major hit; global demand for oil dropped dramatically with the lockdowns.[6]
- Wanted to end meat-eating...and there was a national meat shortage with meatpacking plants closing.[7]

- Called for an end to "excess" consumption…and "non-essential" stores, businesses, movie theatres, vacation travel, and so forth were shut down, apparently indefinitely, in response to the coronavirus.[8]
- Wanted kids to skip school to accomplish all of the above climate goals…and almost everywhere the schools were closed.[9]

As Peter Barry Chowka observed at the American Thinker, "Overnight, our society is doing what radical leftist Rep. Alexandria Ocasio-Cortez (D-NY) and her fellow Green New Deal fanatics have demanded: An almost total end to air travel; personal automobile travel down to a trickle; promises of free health care for all quickly becoming the new status quo; and the ability of people to sit at home without working and receive a paycheck from the government. The Democrats want that to continue indefinitely."[10]

Climate campaigners were very excited to see the COVID lockdowns spread globally.

"The brakes placed on economic activities of many kinds, worldwide, have led to carbon emission cuts that would previously have been unthinkable….What was once impossible (socialist, reckless) now turns out not to be, at all," gushed the editors of the UK *Guardian* about the lockdowns.[12]

And prominent climate activists have made it clear that in the future they will not hesitate to mandate these COVID lockdown–types of regulations in the name of climate change.

Oxford University global history professor Peter Frankopan made these approving comments

> **"Far Scarier than Any Virus"**
> "This is what the Left wants. They want people stripped of wealth, isolated, and terrified. They want sources of joy—church, sporting events, vacations, large social gatherings—eliminated. This is how they get control. And it's far scarier than any virus."
> —Julie Kelly of American Greatness on March 12, 2020[11]

about the lockdowns. "One beneficiary will be the climate: after all, the world's lungs are already breathing more easily thanks to the collapse of industrial production. Who is to say that this pandemic does not provide a turning point in world history."[13]

Youth activist Jamie Margolin wrote for *Teen Vogue*, "If we can shut the world down to stop a virus, that also means it is possible to do the same for climate change. Treat all emergencies like emergencies!" In an article entitled "Coronavirus Response Should Be a Model for How We Address Climate Change," Margolin asked, "What would it look like when the world actually decides to take on the climate crisis? It would look like what we're seeing right now....Everyone stopping everything and putting the world on pause to deal with the immediate crisis at hand."[14]

Former vice president Al Gore inserted himself into the COVID–climate discussion. "The scientists have warned us about the coronavirus and they've warned us about the climate crisis, and we've seen the dangers of waiting too late to heed the warnings of the doctors and scientists on this virus....Fossil fuels are a pre-existing condition for COVID-19," Gore explained.[15]

Bill McKibben, founder of the climate group 350.org, sounded downright envious of the global response to COVID. "Who, now that we've seen how fast good governments can move, wouldn't want to use this moment to help avert the even more dangerous crises that global warming is sending our way?"[16]

Joel Kotkin of Chapman University wrote, "The mass

> **"Expect COVID Lockdowns to Morph into Climate Lockdowns"**
>
> "The Joe Biden–Kamala Harris presidential ticket will go all-in on climate absurdity. Promoting 'solutions' like zero-emission goals and the Green New Deal. If elected, their policies would further wreak havoc on the American economy already ravaged by COVID lockdowns and restrictions. If Biden and Harris are elected, expect the COVID lockdowns to morph into the climate lockdowns."
>
> —Marc Morano in August 2020[17]

shutdowns we now experience—likely necessary in a pandemic—could provide a model for imposing harsh actions to curb carbon emissions that activists consider as great or greater threats than the virus itself."[18]

In February of 2020, Democratic presidential primary candidate and mega–climate funder Tom Steyer laid out his plan for a climate police state. "I will declare a state of emergency on climate on the first day of my presidency. I will use the Executive emergency powers of the presidency to tell companies how they can generate electricity, what kind of cars they can build—on what schedule, what kind of buildings we're gonna have, how we are going to use our public lands," Steyer declared. "We need to rebuild this country in a climate-smart way...we don't have a choice on this."[21]

Fly Only if "Morally Justifiable"

In a declared state of "climate emergency," activists don't want you flying commercial airlines unless it is "morally justifiable."

"It turns out, nearly all of those business trips weren't necessary. Seeing loved ones is pretty much the only morally justifiable use for luxury aviation emissions in a climate emergency," declared activist Eric Holthaus in 2020.[19]

And the climate campaigners are targeting U.S. air travelers for having the biggest carbon footprint in the world. "If you want to resolve climate change and we need to redesign [aviation], then we should start at the top, where a few 'super emitters' contribute massively to global warming," said Stefan Gössling at Linnaeus University in Sweden. "We should see the [COVID-19] crisis as an opportunity to slim the air transport system," he added.[20]

There have been calls for military enforcement of climate regulations. In 2019, University of Copenhagen international relations professor Ole Wæver explained, "If there was something that was decided internationally by some more centralized procedure and every country was told 'this is your emission target, it's not negotiable, we can actually take military measures if you don't fulfill it,' then you would basically have to get that down the throat of your population, whether they like it or not."[22]

Other climate activists have demanded a World War II–style climate mobilization that would convert "a large portion of U.S. military into a climate mobilization force."

In 2016 Stan Cox, the author of the book *Any Way You Slice It: The Past, Present, and Future of Rationing,* urged wide-scale rationing to ward off the climate threat. "Necessary steps will include phasing out fossil-fuel use within a decade," Cox claimed, and "deeply cutting meat and dairy consumption; and converting a large portion of the U.S. military into a kind of climate mobilization force." The so-called climate "Victory Plan," according to Cox, "calls for a declaration of a 'national climate and sustainability emergency.'"[24]

The climate activist community had been lobbying for decades for this kind of coercive government intervention in the economy and society.

"Let's not let this crisis go to waste," Professor Mariana Mazzucato of University College London said. Coronavirus offers "a chance to do capitalism differently." She added, "Government has the upper hand, it must seize the moment."[25]

The activists have long sought the opportunity to impose their world view, implement central planning, ban what they deem the non-"climate-friendly" aspects of our lives, and remake society in their image.

"Already, the coronavirus has achieved something that government policies and moral awakening couldn't; it is pushing us into green living.... we'll look back on December 2019 as the all-time peak in global carbon emissions," Simon Kuper, a columnist at the *Financial Times* wrote. "Governments need to make good use of the current pandemic."[26]

Coronavirus "revealed what governments are capable of doing," declared Michael Marmot, the chair of the World Health Organization's Commission on Social Determinants of Health. "With Covid-19, everything went out of the window. It turns out austerity was a choice. The government can spend anything [in the context of the coronavirus crisis], and they have socialised the economy."[28]

> ### "The Absolute Power to Suspend Society"
>
> "The green blob and its 'High Level Climate Action Champions' have wet dreams about Lockdown. They have long sought the absolute power to suspend society: to hold people in their places, and to only permit what is convenient to the blob."
>
> **—UK climate skeptic Ben Pile in July 2020[27]**

Ed Conway, the economics editor of Sky News and a columnist for the *Times* of London could not contain his excitement about the world shutdown. "Don't take this the wrong way but if you were a young, hardline environmentalist looking for the ultimate weapon against climate change, you could hardly design anything better than coronavirus," Conway wrote. "Unlike most other such diseases, it kills mostly the old who, let's face it, are more likely to be climate skeptics. It spares the young. Most of all, it stymies the forces that have been generating greenhouse gases for decades."[29]

In short, if you like living under the COVID lockdowns, then you'll love living under government mandates to "solve" the "climate emergency."

Newsweek magazine reported, "Scientists, activists and religious leaders ranging from Pope Francis to filmmaker Spike Lee are highlighting lockdown reductions in air pollution and nature 'coming alive' as part of a larger call to permanently change industrial and economic behavior after COVID-19."[30]

Former secretary of state John Kerry opined, "It's a tragically teachable moment. I don't say this in a partisan way. But the parallels [between COVID-19 and climate change] are screaming at us, both positive and negative.... You could just as easily replace the words climate change with COVID-19; it is truly the tale of two pandemics deferred, denied, and distorted, one with catastrophic consequences, the other with even greater risk if we don't reverse course.... The long-term parallels between this pandemic and tomorrow's gathering storm of climate crisis are more clear."[31]

Environmental journalist Emily Atkin was more blunt. "I'm sorry, but if you still refuse to see parallels between climate change and coronavirus then honestly you're just stupid." As she explained, "Both are global crises which threaten millions of lives with clear science on how to solve them which governments have been too slow to act on; the same people who promote climate denial are refusing to accept the science of coronavirus, too." Atkins claimed, "Coronavirus makes climate change worse, and vice versa. We can't do our research on climate because of it, we've had to cancel the UN climate summit for international negotiations."[32]

The COVID lockdowns and mandates were a gift to climate activists. The climate movement may now be poised to plan and dictate a new "earth-friendly" world in the aftermath of the heavy-handed government response to the coronavirus. The climate activists quickly began to strategize to use the coronavirus pandemic as a model for the climate scare—as a dry run for what they hope to achieve.

Hall of Shame:
Select Quotations on Not Letting the
COVID-19 Crisis Go to Waste

"Even in the most tragic of times, however, a silver lining prevails. As roads empty and people sequester themselves, the machine of capitalism has slowed dramatically, prompting environmental healing."
—Brooke Russell in the *Santa Barbara Independent*[33]

"We can draw many lessons and opportunities from the current health crisis when tackling planetary warming."
—Professor Natasha Chassagne of the University of Tasmania[34]

"This Crisis Provides a Very Green Opportunity: We Can Accelerate Climate Progress as We Rebuild Society and the Economy": "The
sudden drop in carbon emissions in countries that shut down this
spring initially seemed like a slight silver lining on an otherwise
pitch-black cloud. On reflection, it instead reminds us just how far
we have to go."
—*Boston Globe* article by Professor Peter Fox-Penner, director of the
Institute for Sustainable Energy at Boston University[35]

"During his virtual press conference [UN Secretary-General
António] Guterres gave a nod to the Paris Agreement. He said the pandemic could create an opportunity to rebuild the global economy along
more sustainable lines. [The UN Sec. Gen. said] the pandemic could
create an opportunity to rebuild the global economy along more sustainable lines."
—*Scientific American* article by Nathanial Gronewold[36]

"While COVID-19 is causing untold suffering, the international
response to this unprecedented health crisis in modern times offers an
opportunity to direct finances towards bolstering climate action."
—the UN Green Climate Fund[37]

"When This Pandemic Is Over, It's Time to Dismantle Capitalism":
"extreme weather events connected to climate change are happening
more and more frequently."
—column by Nathalie Olah at Vice[38]

"We've seen all too terribly the consequences of those who denied
warnings of a pandemic. We can't afford any more consequences of
climate denial. All of us, especially young people, have to demand better of our government at every level and vote this fall."
—former president Barack Obama[39]

"There have also been some pleasant surprises [with the COVID lock-
downs]. As many of the world's transportation and industrial sectors
have reduced operations, there has been a remarkable decline in global

levels of carbon dioxide emissions. Of course, the cost in life and liveli-
hood negates any celebration. Nonetheless, there is no denying that we
have gotten a very real glimpse of the potential for global environmental
repair....Clearly, inertia [on green activism] is unacceptable."
—Robert Redford and his son James Redford[40]

"Both the corona crisis and the climate crisis require freedom-limiting measures. The earlier and more vigorously these are defined and
implemented, the sooner the success that is vital for survival can be
expected. In this respect, corona and climate protection measures do
not differ in principle, but only on the time axis."
—public law professor Thomas Schomerus of Leuphana University in
Germany[41]

"Climate action should be central to our response to the COVID-19
pandemic."
—Al Jazeera[42]

"Coronavirus and Climate Change: The Pandemic Is a Fire Drill for
Our Planet's Future."
—op-ed by Professor Adam Frank of the University of Rochester at NBC
News[43]

"Pollution, climate change, and the destruction of our remaining
natural zones has brought the world to a breaking point. For these
reasons, along with increasing social inequalities, we believe it is
unthinkable to 'go back to normal' [after COVID]. The radical transformation we need—at all levels—demands boldness and courage. It will
not happen without a massive and determined commitment. We must
act now."
—letter signed by Hollywood celebrities including Robert De Niro,
Madonna, Cate Blanchett, Barbra Streisand, Jane Fonda, Juliette
Binoche, Ralph Fiennes, Eva Green, Adam Driver, Penélope Cruz, Wil-
lem Defoe, and Joaquin Phoenix[44]

"So if there is a silver lining to this crisis, it's visible in the skies
above China. The dramatic slowdown in manufacturing and driving has

caused a reduction in carbon emissions."
—**PBS/CNN International host Christiane Amanpour**[45]

"The coronavirus may finally cause us to see air travel for what it is, a fuse burning in the climate' bomb.... As it happens, a lot less flying is required if we are to stabilize a non-nightmarish planetary climate for our children, our grandchildren and their children.... We must embrace a world that the coronavirus, perversely, is laying out for us. It is a world of less travel, less consumption...."
—**Christopher Ketcham in the *Los Angeles Times***[46]

"We must seize the opportunity to make the COVID-19 recovery a defining moment in tackling the climate crisis. We say to the Government: 'act courageously—it's there for the taking.'"
—**"2020 Progress Report to Parliament" from the UK Committee on Climate Change**[47]

"Climate change endangers every present and future citizen of this planet. If we truly care about the health of our communities, countries and global commons, we must find ways of powering the planet without relying on fossil fuels. It would be a tragedy to survive the coronavirus but succumb to human-caused climate disruption."
—**Ben Santer, former UN IPCC lead author and atmospheric scientist at Lawrence Livermore National Laboratory**[48]

"The Covid-19 crisis did not make the climate crisis disappear.... If we relaunch the economy in the wrong direction, we will hit the climate crisis wall."
—**Pascal Canfin, chair of the Environment Committee of the European Parliament**[49]

Coronavirus a "win for the environment.... A significant reduction of their carbon footprints.... Where scientists and popular movements have thus far failed to convince the world to act, it seems that Mother Earth may have succeeded, with the never-before-seen COVID-19 virus....
—**Madhvi Ramani in *The Week***[50]

Different Crises, Same "Solutions"

Many measures that governments have taken to control the COVID-19 virus are very similar to climate "solutions" that have been proposed by the UN, the Green New Deal, and climate organizations.[51]

"We should not be intimidated when people say, 'Oh you can't use this COVID crisis to peddle a solution to climate change'—no we have to recognize the necessity of this moment," Washington State governor Jay Inslee said in May 2020 about his plan to rebuild the state's economy with a "green initiative." Inslee added, "These are two things we have to deal with, and we can deal with both, because they're so similar."[52]

New York Times "climate desk" reporter John Schwartz drew parallels between COVID "solutions" and climate "solutions": "Social Distancing? You Might Be Fighting Climate Change, Too," blared the *New York Times* headline. The article cited Kimberly Nicholas, a researcher at the Lund University Center for Sustainability Studies in Sweden saying, "Any time you can avoid getting on a plane, getting in a car or eating animal products, that's a substantial climate savings."

Christopher M. Jones, lead developer at the CoolClimate Network at the UC Berkeley Renewable and Appropriate Energy Laboratory, explained to the *Times* that "many of the actions people are taking in response to the coronavirus outbreak could have a benefit of a reduced carbon footprint."[53]

Climate activist Mark Hertsgaard and Kyle Pope, the editor in chief of the *Columbia Journalism Review*, also drew comparisons to climate and COVID. "The similarities between the causes of and solutions to the coronavirus and the climate crisis are nothing short of eerie," they wrote. "As awful as the coronavirus is, it is something of a test run for the challenges of a climate crisis that continues to accelerate."[54]

Many climate activists also welcomed the economic slowdown. After all, as we saw in chapter 7, the climate alarmists have long wanted "planned recessions." Warmist professor Alice Bows-Larkin, for example, has said, "Economic growth needs to be exchanged" for "planned austerity" and "whole system change."[55]

So climate activists took notes as they saw COVID-19 cause a near-total shutdown of the evil modern life they wage war on and essentially shut down the world economy overnight.

Christiana Figueres noted that slower economic growth from lockdowns "may be good for climate," explaining, "There is less trade, less travel, less commerce."[56] She claimed we need to "converge the solutions" to coro-navirus and climate "because what we cannot afford to do is to jump out of the frying pan of COVID and into the raging fire of climate change."[57]

> ## The Nightmare Is "Only Just Beginning"
>
> "If you thought the nightmare was going to end once the coronavirus scare passed, think again: it's only just beginning. The greens and the globalists aren't about to let a crisis go to waste. This is the moment they have been waiting for. And don't expect much resistance from politicians—even ones wearing the 'Conservative' label, like Boris Johnson. They're part of the problem."
> —James Delingpole in May 2020[58]

Progressive environmentalists lauded the lockdowns as having "ecological benefits" but lamented that they were not in control of the shutdown. Jason Hickel, a lecturer in economic anthropology at Goldsmiths University and member of the advisory board of the Green New Deal for Europe, explained his thoughts on COVID and climate in April 2020: "When you do scale down energy use and industrial production then it does have these ecological benefits but the crucial thing to observe here is that this is happening in an unplanned, chaotic way which is hurting peoples' lives. We would never advocate for such a thing in climate policy. What we need is a planned approach to reducing unnecessary industrial activity that has no connection to human welfare and that also disproportionately benefits already wealthy people as opposed to ordinary people."

"An Opportunity to Reset the Global Economy"

"The recovery from the coronavirus crisis represents an opportunity to reset the global economy and priorities sustainable development without further damaging the planet, Prince Charles said at the opening of a World Economic Forum (WEF) virtual meeting," reported the *Guardian* in June 2020. "'We have a unique but rapidly shrinking window of opportunity to learn lessons and reset ourselves on a more sustainable path,' said Charles, who himself has recovered after suffering mild symptoms of Covid-19."[62]

In other words, while Dr. Hickel likes the "ecological benefits" of the COVID-19 lockdowns, he wants future lockdowns to be more "planned"—so that he and his academic colleagues can be in charge of crafting their vision of a utopian world, which he explains is "reducing unnecessary industrial activity." The climate campaigners envision a post-coronavirus world defined by fear of "climate change," and they are seeking to remake societies from their university offices instead of letting free people and free economies thrive.

As former president Ronald Reagan said: "The more the plans fail, the more the planners plan."

The warmists' repeated calls for "global government" have also been inserted into the coronavirus shutdown debate.[59]

Former UK prime minister Gordon Brown urged world leaders to create "a temporary form of global government" to tackle coronavirus. "This is not something that can be dealt with in one country," he said. "There has to be a coordinated global response."[60]

The goals of the climate activists have been advanced by the total shutdown of society. Climate activists know that if the U.S. government and other Western nations can shut down all aspects of society to deal with a virus, they can do the same for climate change.

Teen climate activist Greta Thunberg explained that COVID demonstrates that action against "climate change" is possible. It's clear we can "change our habits and treat a crisis like a crisis," Thunberg said.[61]

Climate activists must have been pleased to see a conservative Republican president—Donald Trump—at least temporarily support a near-complete shutdown of the economic engines of the U.S. for public safety purposes. The climate campaigners know that a precedent has been set, and they will exploit future presidents and congresses more agreeable to their climate agenda, to impose similar climate-based restrictions for alleged public safety.

The climate movement is also now to increase their focus on linking viruses to "climate change" and thus make fighting climate change a part of fighting deadly viruses.

Former secretary of state and presidential candidate John Kerry, for example, has argued, "Climate change is a threat multiplier for pandemic diseases, and zoonotic diseases—70 percent of all human infections—are impacted by climate change and its effect on animal migration and habitats."[63]

And a science reporter at the *Washington Post* claimed, "Climate change affects everything—even the coronavirus.... No aspect of life on this planet has been untouched by climate change—viruses included."[64]

Actress Jane Fonda waded into the COVID–climate debate. "The melting of the Arctic ice sheet is releasing untold pathogens to which humans are not immune. Climate change guarantees that COVID-19 will not be the last pandemic we will see," she warned.[65]

The activists are now sure to attempt to piggyback efforts like the Green New Deal onto future virus-fighting strategies.

Climate activist Laurie Macfarlane of Open Democracy urged that the COVID response needs to be "a Global Green New Deal" to "decarbonize the global economy as fast as is feasibly possible."[66]

"A crisis is never to be missed as an opportunity to do better," noted International Monetary Fund head Kristalina Georgieva about COVID. "Mother Nature is not going to let us forget that climate change is a major risk to the well-being of people and the well-being of economies.... as we deal with COVID-19 and we restart economies, it is a great opportunity to see what are the policies that we can put in place and even accelerate so we can [see] climate-friendly growth in the future."[67]

The climate alarmists are pouncing on any opportunity to inject climate change into the COVID-19 issue—including attempts to make sure that federal stimulus bills include going in the "right direction toward decarbonization."[68]

A 2013 comment from a former high-level UN climate official sheds light on why climate activists are so enthusiastic about the worldwide COVID-19-inspired lockdowns of the economy. "The only way that a 2015 [UN] agreement can achieve a 2-degree goal is to shut down the whole global economy," Yvo de Boer, former UNFCCC (United Nations Framework Convention on Climate Change) executive secretary said at that time.

As Bloomberg News reported, "There is nothing that can be agreed in 2015 that would be consistent with the 2 degrees," said Yvo de Boer when attempts to reach a deal at a summit in Copenhagen crumbled with a rift between industrialized and developing nations. "The only way that a 2015 agreement can achieve a 2-degree goal is to shut down the whole global economy."[69]

Given the comments of climate campaigners excited about the impact of the COVID lockdowns in 2020, Yvo de Boer's words sound prophetic.

Climate activist Eric Holthaus said on April 22, 2020, about the effect of the COVID lockdowns on global CO_2 emissions: "This is roughly the same pace that the IPCC says we need to sustain every year until 2030 to be on pace to limit global warming to 1.5C and hit the Paris climate goals. This is what 'rapid, far-reaching and unprecedented changes in all aspects of society' looks like."[70] So cheer up, this is good news, right? Just ten more years of full lockdowns, and we can meet our UN Paris climate goals! Hurray!

But the reality is that even with lockdowns and shutdown of most aspects of society, global CO_2 emissions still didn't seem to notice.

Climatologist Dr. Roy Spencer explained why: "It would be difficult to see a downturn in the anthropogenic source of CO_2 unless it was very large (say, over 50%) and prolonged (say over a year or longer)."[71]

"We Need a Green New Deal to... Halt Future Mass Pandemics"

"The coronavirus pandemic makes what we've already known clear: we need a Green New Deal to stop climate change, provide desperately needed jobs, and halt future mass pandemics," claimed the Democratic Socialists of America in March 2020.[72]

DSA party member Alexandria Ocasio-Cortez was also energized by the shutdowns. "You absolutely love to see it (collapse of oil prices). This along with record low-interest rates means it's the right time for a worker-led, mass investment in green infrastructure to save our planet," she wrote.[73]

Activists are also seeking to exploit COVID-19 to remake transportation. "Social planners, ecologists look to exploit coronavirus as opportunity to 'permanently' remove cars from the road and seek 'to save city dwellers...from the auto-centric culture' & 'remake cities,'" explained a *Wired* magazine article in April 2020.[74]

"This is a really heartening trend. All around the world, cities are closing key roads to cars, to make more space for pedestrians and bikes. After the pandemic, this needs to become permanent," argued activist Eric Holthaus.[75]

Many in the climate action community essentially want the public to get used to living under some sort of lockdown. They want at least a portion of these governmental lockdown powers to remain and be used for climate change after the coronavirus pandemic passes. Activists want the public to get used to the travel restrictions, to get used to the quarantines, to get used to limits on their personal freedom—all of which will come in handy as lower emissions are mandated to "solve" the "climate emergency."

Government Lockdowns BAD, COVID Lockdowns GOOD

One of the most ironic facets of the COVID pandemic was how the media and the Left, who freak out when the federal government is shut down for a few days or weeks during a budget battle, fully supported the COVID lockdowns that shut down the entire economy and society for months.

The *New York Times* reported this about the federal government shutdown in 2019: "The standoff is beginning to inflict pain on Americans, whose lives are affected, in one way or another, by the federal government" and "delayed mortgage applications, missed paychecks and stymied farmers are among the repercussions of a shutdown with no end in sight."[77]

There seemed to be no similar concern from the media for Americans whose lives were devastated by the COVID lockdowns in 2020.

The climate activists and progressive Left want you to get used to living a restricted life, where your everyday actions have to be approved by the government or okayed by a bureaucratic official. Our current virus-induced government lockdown is the perfect template for the future the climate campaigners envision, with all of us living under a coercive government that takes the "climate emergency" seriously.

Steve Milloy of JunkScience.com wrote on April 18, "The coronavirus police state is only temporary (I hope!). The climate police state would be permanent."[76]

In reality, further throttling our economy with the punishing climate-based mandates of the Green New Deal is the last thing U.S. businesses need following the COVID shutdowns.

The climate-skeptic Global Warming Policy Forum pointed out in April of 2020, "As Europe's economies are in full lockdown, industries facing total collapse are desperately calling on the EU to water down or at least delay costly climate policies. In this crisis, it is becoming evident that the Green Deal is an existential threat to Europe's economies and the wellbeing of the general public rather than a benefit."[78]

The climate activists at Extinction Rebellion came up with perhaps the most focused message relating COVID to climate. These stickers were seen in March 2020: "CORONA IS THE CURE HUMANS ARE THE DISEASE."

As we shall see in chapter 14, the COVID–climate connection has deepened even more as politicians and the unelected public health bureaucracy refused to relent on their new "emergency" powers over society, and the U.S. and the world made a great leap towards the "Great Reset."

CHAPTER 12

Exploiting the Children

Teen climate activist Greta Thunberg has replaced Al Gore and Leonardo DiCaprio as the celebrity spokesperson for climate change. And she's far from the youngest climate activist. School-age children from around the world have become the go-to spokespersons for climate fears.

Climate campaigners have tried just about everything else to get the public and government to "act" on climate. They failed using scary climate tipping points, blaming every "extreme" weather event somehow on "climate change," warning that polar bears were being driven to extinction, predicting the seas would rise and drown New York City, and so forth. Having failed to convince adults to take "climate action," the climate movement can now use their kids to browbeat society into a Green New Deal. The climate establishment's longtime indoctrination of schoolkids is paying off. These kids have been terrorized with climate doomsday nonsense since kindergarten, and now they are being encouraged to skip school to urge "solutions" for supposed climate change.

The strategic brilliance of this tactic is that anyone who dares question what the children claim about "global warming" is immediately accused of bashing kids: "Pick on someone your own size!" The climate kids have become human shields for the climate lobbying movement to promote the Green New Deal.

"I Want You to Feel the Fear I Feel Every Day"

"This is my cry for help," declared then-fifteen-year-old Greta Thunberg on September 7, 2018, on a "school strike for the climate"—or "Skolstrejk For Klimatet" in her native Swedish.[1]

Greta was taking a stand against global warming by refusing to attend any classes to protest in front of the Swedish parliament building in Stockholm. As she explained in a September 16, 2018, video statement, "Some people say that we should be in school instead, but why should we be studying for a future that's soon to be no more? And when no one is doing anything whatsoever to save that future?" Thunberg asked, "And what is the point of learning facts within the school system when the most important facts given by the finest science of

---

"The Anti-Greta"

"Naomi Seibt is a 19-year-old German who, like Greta, is blond, eloquent and European. But Naomi denounces 'climate alarmism,' calls climate consciousness 'a despicably anti-human ideology,' and has even deployed Greta's now famous 'How dare you?' line to take on the mainstream German media," reported the *Washington Post*, dubbing Naomi "the anti-Greta."

The paper reported that Naomi counters Greta's famous plea of "I want you to panic" with a more hopeful message instead. "I don't want you to panic. I want you to think," Naomi urges.

"I get chills when I see those young people, especially at Fridays for Future. They are screaming and shouting and they're generally terrified. They don't want the world to end," Naomi explained.[2]

that same school system clearly means nothing to our politicians and our society?"[3]

At the 2019 World Economic Forum in Davos, Switzerland, she declared, "I don't want you to be hopeful. I want you to panic. I want you to feel the fear I feel every day. And then I want you to act."[4]

Greta's (inspiring?) message of climate doom made her an international celebrity who has now addressed the EU, the World Economic Forum at Davos, and the United States Congress. She was *Time* magazine's 2019 "Person of the Year."[5]

Greta's climate protest caught the attention of the BBC, the *Guardian*, Greenpeace, and many other organizations. "We urge everyone to do the same wherever you are, to sit outside your parliament's local government building until your nation is on the pathway to a below 2° [temperature] warming targets." She was feted by mainstream media outlets as some sort of climate savior.

More remarkably, Thunberg inspired an international movement of school-age kids to become climate woke and start skipping school and demanding climate "action"—including lawsuits to mandate government policies.

If Greta Went Back to School

"In her Economics class, she might learn that the fossil fuels that she wants to ban are providing reliable, abundant and affordable energy to the planet's growing population."

And in History class she could learn, "A review of human life dating back to the earliest of the great civilizations would reveal that the several previous warming periods (called climate optima) directly correlated to fantastic periods of human prosperity and advances," explained geologist Gregory Wrightstone, the author of *Inconvenient Facts: The Science That Al Gore Doesn't Want You to Know.*

"I am quite sure that Ms. Thunberg has a big heart and wants the best for Earth and humanity, but it is time for her to go back to school to learn what she doesn't know and to unlearn so much of what she has been taught," Wrightstone concluded.[6]

"Mini AOC"

In 2019, an eight-year-old child actor, dubbed "Mini AOC," went viral on social media with her hilarious impersonations of the real Representative Alexandria Ocasio-Cortez. Ava Martinez parodied the Democrat congresswoman from New York in short videos.

Mini AOC, whose real name is Ava Martinez, also appeared in my 2020 film *Climate Hustle 2*. Below is a short excerpt from her part in the movie.

Mini AOC:

I also, like, want to tell you about my plan to single-handedly save the planet. I call it the Green New Deal. I picked green because I'm still learning my colors. I came up with my plan after watching, like, the most important documentary on climate change. It's called *Ice Age 2: The Meltdown*. That's not me saying it, that's science!...

My Green New Deal will cost, like, $93 trillion dollars. Do you know how much that is? Me neither. Because it's totally worth it. If sea levels keep rising, we won't be able to drive to Hawaii anymore....

I used to not believe in climate change either. Like, I thought it meant Mother Nature was transgendering into Father Nature....

Like, socialism is actually short for social media. Did you know that? Like, I use social media so I'm a socialist and, like, three of the most successful countries in the world are socialist too: Venezuela, Facebook, and Twitter.[8]

Greta's message of "panic" resonated with kids across the globe. When a France 24 TV anchor asked teen student Janna Husson, "What brought you out for the march?" her answer was "pure fear."

Janna explained, "Climate change has always been something we learn about in class and things like that. It is a topic we learn about in sophomore year. But now is really starting to affect us and it has been for years."[7]

The International Youth Climate Strike group explained why they were organizing for kids to skip school in March 2019 in the U.S. and the world. "We are striking because if the social order is disrupted by our refusal to attend school, then the system is forced to face the climate crisis and enact change. With our futures at stake, we call for radical legislative action to combat climate change and its countless detrimental effects on the American people," the group said.[9]

Former vice president Al Gore touted the climate-striking kids who skipped school to protest government inaction on the climate. "Today something extraordinary happened," Gore wrote on March 15, 2019. "Today, hundreds of thousands of young people in over 120 countries stood up to fight for their future. Going on strike from school, they spoke with one voice and one message for the adults of the world: Act on climate.'" Gore told the kids, "The future just got a whole lot brighter because of you."

Kids Being Used to "Shame Adults"

"The previous chairman of the Intergovernmental Panel on Climate Change (IPCC), Rajendra Pachauri, has often argued that greens should focus on children. In an interview on Al Jazeera, he said that children should be used to 'shame adults into taking the right steps.' Pachauri's ideas are echoed in UNICEF's manual on climate-change education, which aims to help children become 'agents of change.'"
—Sandy Moor at Spiked Online[10]

"We Don't Want to Die"

The Associated Press dutifully covered the kids' school-skipping protests, reporting in March 2019, "Students across a warming globe pleaded for their lives, future and planet Friday, demanding tough action on climate change. From the South Pacific to the edge of the Arctic Circle, angry students in more than 100 countries walked out of classes to protest what they see as the failures by their governments. . . . Some carried banners that read 'Make Love, Not CO2.'" AP reported, "In Washington, protesters spoke in front of a banner saying 'We don't want to die.'" Meanwhile, "In San Francisco, 1,000 demonstrators descended on the local offices of Sen. Dianne Feinstein and House Speaker Nancy Pelosi, wanting passage of the massive 'Green New Deal' bill proposed in the U.S. Congress," the AP noted.[12]

Gore's group, the Climate Reality Project, had urged children to skip school for the planned global climate protest on March 15, 2019. "They've had enough. And no wonder—it's their future on the line. So if adults aren't going to act on their own, young people will make them," said a Climate Reality Project statement.[11]

But Greenpeace co-founder Patrick Moore, who has turned against his former group and is now a climate skeptic, was having none of Greta's message. "Even if there were an emergency the last thing one should be encouraged to do is panic. That always makes things worse," he pointed out.[13] "This is a fascist tactic. You are using innocent children for your own ends, and this is child abuse of a psychological nature," Moore added. "It's normally called brainwashing. Mao would be proud."[14]

Moore ripped the adult promoters of the kids' protests. "You are clearly projecting your own psychosis on the children. Self-loathing is a heavy burden. Why don't you express it through adults rather than abusing innocents?"[15]

"Better Lives"

"Just a century ago, life was back-breaking. Plentiful energy made better lives possible, without having to spend hours collecting firewood, polluting your household with smoke, achieving heat, cold, transportation, light, food and opportunities. Life expectancy doubled. Plentiful energy, mostly from fossil fuels, has lifted more than a billion people out of poverty in just the past 25 years. That is not evil—it is quite the opposite.

"Ms. Thunberg believes that climate change means people are dying, but the fact is that weather-related disasters just a century ago killed half a million people each year. Today, despite rising temperatures but because of less poverty and more resilience, droughts, floods, hurricanes and extreme temperatures kill just 20,000 people each year—a reduction of 95 per cent. That is a morally commendable achievement."

— **2019 message to Greta Thunberg from statistician Bjørn Lomborg, the president of the Copenhagen Consensus Center**[16]

Climate skeptic Tony Heller of RealClimateScience.com commented, "Greta Thunberg doesn't go to school, because adults around her have convinced her the climate situation is simply too bad....." Heller pointed out, "Greta is scheduled to speak at the UN when her yacht arrives, as their official science expert. In this role she replaces another high school dropout with a 450-foot-long yacht," referring to the UN's previous climate keynote speech by Leonardo DiCaprio.

> **Flying to Save the Planet**
> "I will fly around the world doing good for the environment," Leonardo DiCaprio, who served as the United Nations Messenger of Peace, boldly declared in 2013.[17] A 2017 *Daily Mail* investigation into celebrities' "carbon footprints" found that DiCaprio "flew around 87,609 miles on various business trips and jaunts around the world which burned up 14.8 tonnes of carbon dioxide."[18]

"She has been told that children had a much brighter future when CO_2 levels were lower, like a century ago," Heller wrote. In fact, as he pointed out, life was much more difficult a hundred years ago, with polio outbreaks, extreme weather, and the Spanish flu. "Nothing Greta has been taught has any basis in reality. The Greta situation is a good reminder of how evil the people behind this scam are," Heller wrote.[19]

"The Fear and Despair That My Generation Lives With"

The young climate activists disparage anyone who has hope for the future. Seattle teen Jamie Margolin, co-founder of Zero Hour, testified to Congress in 2019: "I want the entirety of Congress, in fact the whole US government, to remember the fear and despair that my generation lives with every day, and I want you to hold onto it. How do I even begin to convey to you what it feels like to know that within my lifetime the destruction that we have already seen from the climate crisis will only get worse?...Everyone who will walk up to me after this testimony saying I have such a bright future ahead of me, will be lying to my face. It doesn't matter how talented we are, how much work we put in, how many dreams we have, the reality is, my generation has been committed to a planet that is collapsing."

Margolin demanded "urgent climate action" in order to "salvage life on earth" and begin "climate recovery." She added, "You have heard of the Reagan era; the New Deal era. Well, the youth are bringing about the era of the Green New Deal."[20]

A White House climate protest in September 2019 featuring Greta saw activists participating in an eleven-minute "die in" to represent the eleven years that are supposedly left to save the earth. "After marching a short distance toward the White House, numerous protesters lay down on the ground for an 11-minute 'die-in' what one speaker called a 'mass extinction,'" Grist magazine reported.

But despite their attempts to claim that the U.S. Congress can somehow legislate the climate, policies such as the Green New Deal, the UN Paris climate pact, carbon taxes, or EPA regulations, would not be able to "salvage life on earth" even if we actually did face a climate "emergency"—which we don't.[21]

"Rising Eco-Anxiety among Young People"

In 2019 environmentalist Michael Shellenberger, pushed back against scaring kids into climate despair: "I am concerned by the rising eco-anxiety among young people. My daughter is 14 years old. While she herself is not scared, in part because I have explained the science to her, she told me many of her peers are."[22]

In the oil-rich state of Oklahoma, climate activist students walked out of their classes in 2019, demanding a change in American energy. "We have created a system of prioritizing oil and gas over people's lives," the students claimed.[23]

In reality, fossil fuels save and extend human lives. Oil and gas have created a system that maximizes human achievement and environmental improvement. As societies use oil and gas to develop, they create wealth and infrastructure that ultimately clean up the air and water and eliminate slash-and-burn agriculture. Modern societies are not "addicted" to oil or gas—they are "addicted" to longer life, better health, lower infant mortality rates, and resilience to bad weather events.

Thunberg's famous "How dare you?" speech at the UN in September 2019 was her biggest moment thus far.

A tearful, angry Greta screamed, "This is all wrong. I shouldn't be up here. I should be back in school, on the other side of the ocean. Yet you all come to us young people for hope. How dare you!"

Greta was just getting started. "You have stolen my dreams and my childhood with your empty words. And yet I'm one of the lucky ones. People are suffering. People are dying...

"For more than 30 years the science has been crystal clear. How dare you continue to look away, and come here saying that you're doing enough when the politics and solutions needed are still nowhere in sight," she added.

"You are failing us. But the young people are starting to understand your betrayal. The eyes of all future generations are upon you. And if you choose to fail us, I say: We will never forgive you. We will not let you get away with this. Right here, right now is where we draw the line. The world is waking up. And change is coming, whether you like it or not."[24]

My initial reaction was that, as a climate skeptic, I agreed with Greta's assessment of the United Nations' "empty words." I also seconded her observation that "people are suffering" from the UN's incompetence, corruption, and meaningless climate "solutions." In fact, climate skeptics have pointed out for years that the UN's so-called "climate plans" were empty words when it came to actually impacting the climate—even if we were in fact facing a CO_2-driven climate catastrophe.

I appeared on *Fox and Friends* the day after Greta's big UN moment and offered these observations: "If you really want to protest climate, do something challenging. Why would you skip school? That's an easy thing for a kid to do. Give up social media for a couple days. Give up your iPhone and tablet. See how long they go without social media—that would be a protest that would be worthy."

Greta's message of fear sells. Kids in Europe are being treated for "eco-anxiety" because they've been convinced that they are going to die from "climate change." In September of 2019 the *Daily Telegraph* reported, "A group of psychologists working with the University of Bath says it is receiving a growing volume of enquiries from teachers, doctors and therapists unable to cope."

As the UK newspaper reported, "The Climate Psychology Alliance (CPA) told The Daily Telegraph some children complaining of eco-anxiety have even been given psychiatric drugs." Caroline Hickman of Bath explained, "The fear is of environmental doom—that we're all going to die."[25]

The Sunrise Movement's Varshini Prakash has warned that kids are "contemplating suicide" because of the climate crisis. "It's rampant. We'll go to trainings and kids will share really intense stories of contemplating suicide," Prakash said. "People are really, really, really feeling this deep sense of foreboding—a lack of agency, basically."

When Prakash was asked, "You're saying you hear young people contemplating suicide because of climate specifically?" She responded, "Yes. Because of the climate crisis. It's not uncommon."[26]

Greta's message to schoolchildren is that government "climate action" is their salvation. Once the government passes the laws that will fix the climate, the kids can have a future and go back to school.

Just to be very clear: it's not "climate change" that is causing this terrible emotional toll on kids and creating a suicidal environment of hopelessness. It's the fear and the indoctrination kids are receiving from kindergarten through college. Their schools, Hollywood, the media, scientists who should know better,

> ## "A Process of Indoctrination"
>
> "In the schools and colleges, the intelligentsia have changed the role of education from equipping students with the knowledge and intellectual skills to weigh issues and make up their own minds into a process of indoctrination with the conclusions already reached by the anointed."
>
> —Thomas Sowell[27]

and the youth climate movement are creating this desperation with false alarm. These kids are being instilled with fear by the adults in our society. These children believe that they are doomed and only climate "action" can save their future because so many adults want them to think that. Why? Because frightened children are useful for climate-lobbying purposes.

"I Fell into Depression"

Greta revealed her personal path to climate activism in a 2018 TED Talk.

"If burning fossil fuels was so bad that it threatened our very existence, how could we just continue like before? Why were there no restrictions? Why wasn't it made illegal? To me, that did not add up. It was too unreal," Greta recounted.

"So when I was 11, I became ill. I fell into depression, I stopped talking, and I stopped eating. In two months, I lost about 10 kilos of weight. Later on, I was diagnosed with Asperger syndrome, OCD and selective

"A Purely Political Body Posing as a Scientific Institution"

In her testimony to Congress, Greta Thunberg treated the UN IPCC reports as some sort of holy scripture from on high that we must all bow to and follow. But as my previous book, *The Politically Incorrect Guide to Climate Change*, revealed, the UN IPCC is "a purely political body posing as a scientific institution."

The UN IPCC reports hype and distort "climate change" issues for lobbying purposes. The mission of the organization is to examine how CO_2 impacts the climate, so if it fails to find a catastrophe, it fails to have a reason to exist. Naturally, the UN climate panel hypes the climate "problem" and then come up with the "solution" that—guess what?—puts them in charge in perpetuity. As we have seen even Al Gore admitted that the UN IPCC reports were "torqued up" to promote political action. "How [else] do they get the attention of policy-makers around the world?" Gore asked in 2018.[28]

mutism. That basically means I only speak when I think it's necessary—now is one of those moments," she explained.[29]

Greta has admitted that climate activism has helped her find "meaning" in her life. "Before I started school striking I had no energy, no friends and I didn't speak to anyone. I just sat alone at home, with an eating disorder. All of that is gone now, since I have found a meaning, in a world that sometimes seems shallow and meaningless to so many people," she wrote in 2019.[30]

"Learning about climate change triggered my depression in the first place," she told *Time* magazine. "But it was also what got me out of my depression, because there were things I could do to improve the situation. I don't have time to be depressed anymore." Greta's father has said that after she began her school climate strikes, it was as if she "came back to life."[31]

When Greta testified to the U.S. Congress, she was very terse. Instead of giving her own remarks, she submitted the 2018 UN IPCC climate report. "I am submitting this report as my testimony because I don't want you to listen to me," she said. "I want you to listen to the scientists. And I want you to unite behind the science. And then I want you to take action."

"Like Divine Revelation"

Author Michael Fitzpatrick analyzed a speech to the UK parliamentarians in which Greta had claimed, in her opening line, "I speak on behalf of future generations."

As Fitzpatrick wrote in 2019 for Spiked Online, "These are indeed the words of a prophet—one claiming an even bigger constituency than the '99 per cent' of humanity whom the Occupy Movement of 2011/2012, forerunner of today's Extinction Rebellion, claimed to represent."

The government and media "seem to accept without question Thunberg's status as the self-appointed tribune of the yet unborn," Fitzpatrick noted. "Like the millenarian preachers of 19th-century America,

Thunberg has appointed a precise end time: '10 years, 252 days and 10 hours' from the moment of her speech in London."

Fitzpatrick explained, "Like all preachers, Thunberg has a dogma—'the message of the united climate science'. Climate science is here elevated to the status of revealed truth, as The Science....For much of the 20th century, the same could be said about the now discredited racial science and eugenics. Whatever the complexities of the controversy about carbon emissions, it is certain that science, even The Science, cannot predict the future. From Thomas Malthus in the 1790s to the Club of Rome in the 1970s, environmental science has a poor record in its projections of future trends....

"The dogma of 'the united climate science' is, like divine revelation, beyond debate. To question it is the 21st-century equivalent of heresy, or a manifestation of the psychological disorder of 'denialism,'" he added. "Thunberg has been elevated to the status of patron saint," in "the church of impending planetary doom."[32]

Royal Yacht to the Rescue

Greta agonized over how to get to the United Nations conference in New York September 2019. "I don't fly, because of the enormous climate impact of aviation," Greta explained. She ultimately opted to be transported across the Atlantic on an elite racing yacht provided to her by Pierre Casiraghi, a member of Monaco's ruling Grimaldi family and the youngest grandson of Princess Grace Kelly.[33]

Reaction to Greta's solution for her travel dilemma was swift. "After the Green New Deal is

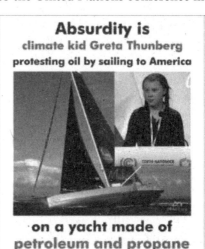

Absurdity is climate kid Greta Thunberg protesting oil by sailing to America

·on a yacht made of petroleum and propane

Greta Would Not Exist without Fossil Fuels

"It was economic growth that lifted Thunberg's ancestors out of agrarian poverty, raised life expectancy from 40 to 70 years, and liberated women and girls from feudal patriarchy. Without Sweden's economic growth, and the fossil fuels upon which it depended, the person who is Greta Thunberg would not exist," environmentalist Michael Shellenberger pointed out in 2020. "Thunberg and other student climate activists even sued Brazil, where per capita incomes are just 25% that of Sweden, for supposedly not doing enough to restrict greenhouse gas emissions."[35]

implemented, and regular people can no longer afford to fly, can we all look forward to crossing oceans on carbon fiber composite racing yachts sponsored by the royal family of Monaco?" asked Craig Rucker, the executive director of the Committee for a Constructive Tomorrow. "The Monaco Yacht Club is among the sponsors paying for the trip. They removed all the corporate sponsor logos from the yacht so as not to be associated with the capitalist prosperity that built it....

"Malizia II, like the rest of the yachts in the Imoca 60 class, is constructed from high-tech

"Humans Developed a New Technology Called the Airplane"

In November of 2019 Greta wrote that she would "need some help" getting from America to the UN Climate Summit in Madrid: "It turns out I've traveled half around the world, the wrong way:) Now I need to find a way to cross the Atlantic in November....If anyone could help me find transport I would be so grateful."

Climate skeptic Tony Heller of RealClimateSceince.com had this response: "Dear Greta, Over 100 years ago, humans developed a new technology called the airplane. They run off fossil fuels and can get you to Madrid in a few hours. If you attended school you might have learned this."[38]

Greta ended up sailing back to Europe aboard *La Vagabonde*, a forty-eight-foot catamaran.[39]

carbon fiber composites to make it ultra-light and fast. It is the ultimate play thing of the wealthy elite. These boats are made of hydrocarbons, not to mention all the energy it took to make them. Carbon fiber composites are primarily made from propane and petroleum. This boat was pumped out of the ground," Rucker added.

"Ending air travel is nihilism. Going back to sailing to cross oceans is a 19th-century solution that cannot meet 21st-century travel needs. This makes no economic, logistical, or ecological sense."[34]

Greta borrowed a page from Al Gore and Leonardo DiCaprio's massive climate hypocrisy with her yacht voyage.

"It turns out that the three westbound crossing crew will be flying back from New York to Europe, while the replacement crew of five will be flying from Europe to New York for the return passage," wrote Michael St. George. "Why can't she just fly to New York with her father? Or even address the United Nations via Skype?"[36]

"Hilarious," wrote Danish statistician Bjørn Lomborg. "Greta's boat trip to the US might emit six times that of a flight, because the five people taking the boat back will fly over to NYC."[37]

Above: We Don't Have Time tweet, August 20, 2018

A "Very Corporate Children's Crusade"

In an article entitled "The Manufacturing of Greta Thunberg," Cory Morningstar detailed Greta's international debut at the website The Wrong Kind of Green:

On August 20, 2018 a tweet featuring a photo of "a Swedish girl" sitting on a sidewalk was released by the tech company, We Don't Have Time, founded by its CEO Ingmar Rentzhog:

"One 15 year old girl in front of the Swedish parliament is striking from School until Election Day in 3 weeks[.] Imagine how lonely she must feel in this picture. People where [*sic*] just walking by. Continuing with the business as usual thing. But the truth is. We can't and she knows it!"

Rentzhog's tweet, via the We Don't Have Time twitter account, would be the very first exposure of Greta Thunberg's now famous school strike.

Tagged in Rentzhog's "lonely girl" tweet were five twitter accounts: Greta Thunberg, Zero Hour (youth movement), Jamie Margolin (the teenage founder of Zero Hour), Al Gore's Climate Reality Project, and the People's Climate Strike twitter account (in the identical font and aesthetics as 350.org).[40]

As Morningstar explained, "It's called marketing and branding....What is going on—is the launch of a global campaign to usher in a required consensus for the Paris Agreement, the Green New Deal and all climate-related policies and legislation written by the power elite—for the power elite." He added, "This is necessary in order to unlock the trillions of dollars in funding by way of massive public demand."[41]

Dominic Green speculated in Standpoint in 2019 that there is much more to Greta's celebrity

Practice What You Preach?

The Tesla that Greta borrowed with Arnold Schwarzenegger's help in Edmonton, Alberta, was littered with garbage and single-use plastics, according to a report from Keean Bexte of Canada's Rebel News in 2019. "The thing was a complete mess—and perfectly illustrates just how Greta preaches one thing while doing another. What a hypocrite!" Bexte said, showing video footage of the car filled with trash.[42]

than the official story. The story of Greta's rise to climate fame is told this way: "Ingmar Rentzhog, founder of the social media platform We Have No Time, happened to be passing [by as Greta was doing her climate school strike]. Inspired, Rentzhog posted Greta's photograph on his personal Facebook page. By late afternoon, the newspaper *Dagens Nyheter* had Greta's story and face on its website. The rest is viral."

But, in a clue that there is more to the Greta story, Rentzhog was trained by Al Gore's Climate Reality Project and set up a We Don't Have Time project in late 2017 to "hold leaders and companies accountable for climate change" by leveraging "the power of social media."

Dominic Green's investigation into Greta's story found a "very corporate children's crusade. Green's research discovered that "the Greta phenomenon has also involved green lobbyists, PR hustlers, eco-academics, and a think-tank founded by a wealthy ex-minister in Sweden's Social Democratic government with links to the country's energy companies." As Green explained, "These companies are preparing for the biggest bonanza of government contracts in history: the greening of the Western economies."

According to his research, "When Greta met the [Gore-trained] Rentzhog, he was the salaried chairman of a private think-tank owned by an ex-Social Democrat minister with a background in the energy sector. Rentzhog's board was stacked with powerful sectoral interests, including career Social Democrats, major union leaders, and lobbyists with links to Brussels. And his board's vice-chair was a member of one of Sweden's most powerful green energy investment groups."[43]

For her part, Greta denies that her path to prominence is anything but authentic. "Many people love to spread rumors saying that I have people 'behind me' or that I'm being 'paid' or 'used' to do what I'm doing. But there is no one 'behind' me except for myself. My parents were as far from climate activists as possible before I made them aware of the situation," she wrote on Facebook in 2019.[44]

Greta's claim that "my parents were as far from climate activists as possible" strains credulity.

> ### "Who Is Paying These Henchmen?"
>
> Journalist Keean Bexte of the Rebel News was harassed by Greta Thunberg's bodyguards in Sweden in 2020. "I flew to Stockholm, Sweden, to watch Greta's so-called 'school strikes' for myself," Bexte explained. "But within minutes of appearing at one of Greta's marches, as I tried to ask her some questions about her protest movement, I was punched in the gut and shoved away by a plain-clothed security guard—in fact, two of them threatened me and told me to 'f–k off!'" said Bexte, who published video footage of the encounter as proof.[45]
>
> "Funnily enough, when it comes to Greta's security—they don't mess around: gasoline vehicles for a reliable getaway. Who is paying these henchmen?" he asked. Bexte had grilled Greta about her climate claims while she was in Canada in 2019.[46]

In March 2016, a full year and half before Greta began her school strike, her mother "stopped flying due to the climate crisis," reported Minnesota Public Radio. " Instead, she and her family typically drive or sail to their destination to reduce their carbon emissions," the article added.[47]

In addition, a full year before Greta began her school strike, her mother received the 2017 WWF Sweden "Environmental Hero" award. These events make Greta's claim that "I made [my parents] aware of the [climate] situation" a little bit harder to accept.[48]

Green found other discrepancies in the storyline of Greta's rise to prominence.

"In emails, media entrepreneur Rentzhog told me that he 'met Greta for the first time' at the parliament, and that he 'did not know Greta or Greta's parents' before then. Yet in the same emails, Rentzhog admitted to meeting Greta's mother Malena Ernman '3–4 months before everything started'—in early May 2018, when he and Malena had shared a stage at a conference called the Climate Parliament. Nor did Rentzhog stumble on Greta's protest by accident. He now admits to having been informed 'the week before' by 'a mailing list from a climate activist' named Bo Thorén, leader of the Fossil Free Dalsland group."

Green explained, "Greta, a child of woke capitalism, is being used to ease the transition to green corporatism." But if you question her parents' "motives, and you risk being accused of 'climate denial', or of bullying a vulnerable child with Asperger's."

The Swiss magazine *Weltwoche* confirmed Green's research, reporting that Greta's "success is largely thanks to the Swedish PR expert Ingmar Rentzhog." *Weltwoche* reported that "environmental activist Bo Thorén had recruited" Greta to start her school strike. Bo Thorén is the founder of Extinction Rebellion in Sweden. As an article on Extinction Rebellion's website entitled "A New Radical Environmental Uprising Starts in Sweden" explained, "So now the uprising is coming to Sweden. Bo Thorén is one of the initiators."[49]

Greta confirmed on Facebook that Bo Thorén had contacted her before her climate school strike ever began. "Bo [Thorén] had a few ideas of things we could do. Everything from marches to a loose idea of some kind of a school strike," Greta said in a February 2, 2019 Facebook post. "I liked the idea of a school strike."

Greta explained how she got involved with Thorén: "In May 2018 I was one of the winners in a writing competition about the environment held by Svenska Dagbladet, a Swedish newspaper. I got my article published and some people contacted me, among others was Bo Thorén from Fossil Free Dalsland. He had some kind of group with people, especially youth, who wanted to do something about the climate crisis."[50]

Greta's connection with the radical and disruptive Extinction Rebellion group led to her musical debut in 2019. Greta appeared on a music track by the British band the 1975. "The proceeds from the track will go to Extinction Rebellion at Thunberg's request," reported the *Guardian*. On the musical track, Greta claims that "solving the climate crisis is the greatest and most complex challenge that homo sapiens have ever faced."[51]

Soros Is Funding the Youth Climate Movement

"While 16-year-old Greta Thunberg has become the face of the climate strike movement, it's no longer gatherings of children. A litany of well-funded, left-wing activist groups have partnered to generate a week of climate protests known as the 'Global Climate Strike,'" wrote Joseph Vazquez at Newsbusters in 2019. "At least 22 of those partners have been funded by liberal billionaire George Soros who spends nearly $1 billion a year on groups pushing a variety of left-wing causes. Together, 22 organizations listed as international or North American partners of the Global Climate Strike received at least $24,854,592 from Soros' Open Society Network between 2000–2017."[52]

Lawsuits filed by schoolchildren against the governments demanding more action on climate change are an integral part of the youth climate movement.

In a report entitled "Genesis of a Shakedown: New Records Expose Children's Marches as Long-Planned Component of Litigation Campaign," David Sassoon of the group Climate Litigation Watch details how the kids are being manipulated by climate activists.

"These demonstrations are a long-planned component of the climate industry's litigation campaign, including particularly *Juliana v. United States*, the 'Climate Kids' suit that is a radical example of the extreme climate activism flooding the courts," Sassoon wrote. "Now comes *Juliana*, a federal case filed in Eugene, Oregon, seeking imposition of the climate agenda by the courts and the subject of a cheerleading CBS News segment. The [climate] agenda has been thwarted by the democratic process," Sassoon explained. The report details how the kids' lawsuit is attempting to "throw aside" the separation of powers in the U.S.

"It meant, as in the *Juliana* case, a demand for federal imposition through the courts" of Green New Deal–style mandates in the U.S. "The entire strategy of the civil and legal disruption we see, of suits, marches and strikes by schoolchildren" has long been a plan of the climate establishment, according to Sassoon.[53]

Kelsey Juliana, the namesake of the *Juliana v. United States*, explained in 2019, "This court case is about establishing a constitutional right to a stable climate system capable of sustaining human life."[54]

Eleven-year-old Avery McRae, who is also part of the lawsuit, declared that her motivation is to go after President Trump. "Trump is not doing anything to help stop climate change. He's a climate change denier, and we're gonna prove that to—to the world," McRae told CBS News.

The lawsuit also features former NASA lead global warming scientist James Hansen as a "guardian for future generations." Hansen is a hardcore activist who has been arrested multiple times protesting climate change. He has accused climate skeptics of "crimes against humanity and nature" and in 2009, when he was still a U.S. government employee at NASA endorsed a book that ponders "razing cities to the ground, blowing up dams and switching off the greenhouse gas emissions machine" as possible solutions to global warming.[55]

"Eco–Child Abuse Pure and Simple"

"The motive behind climate change education is basically to dominate education. It is specifically to take over public education. It is to use alleged nonpartisan, environmental education to politically indoctrinate America's children," Holly Swanson, author of *Training for Treason: The Harmful Political Agenda behind Education for Sustainability*, explained. "It is putting the weight of the world on these children's shoulders, and this is why our children are losing hope. It's eco–child abuse pure and simple."[56]

"Gobbledygook" on *60 Minutes*

The mainstream media has been all too willing to promote the kids' lawsuits against the federal government. The most outrageous propaganda came from *60 Minutes*, where they tossed out any presence of objectivity or balance and went straight to a climate-wacky PR mode.

The CBS program went off the rails in 2019 with kid climate propaganda as it presented viewers with profiles of several teens involved in the climate lawsuits, including one fifteen-year-old school kid who claimed that she had "put her ankle in climate change" after her house flooded.

60 Minutes producer Draggan Mihailovich explained, "There is real fear here. Jayden Foytlin, a 15-year-old from Rayne, Louisiana told me, you know 'when it rains at night, all I can think about is that storm in (In Rayne Louisiana) in August of 2016.'"

"As she puts it she woke up and set foot, put her ankle in climate change basically," Mihailovich said.

The teen activist Jayden Foytlin was defiant about any critique of her activism. "To the people that think that I'm brainwashed, I just usually say I have encountered climate change firsthand," she explained. "And although I am 15, I still know science. I still trust science more than I trust older generations that tell me that I'm wrong."

The program explained that there were twenty-one plaintiffs, ranging in age from eleven to twenty-two years old, years old involved in the lawsuit. According to *60 Minutes*, "Each of them has an individual claim on how they were damaged by 'global warming.'"

The program featured one of the youth's lawyer explaining, "They each have stories about how they were harmed and will testify at trial about that."

When asked if the "kids understand the science here?" producer Mihailovich demurred, "They understand the danger, that is for sure." He defended the children's climate claims: "It's not gobbledygook that they are spewing."

But the reality is that *60 Minutes* featured kids spewing an ocean of climate "gobbledygook"!

A simple check of the scientific evidence would have shown the "put her ankle in climate change" claims to be embarrassing.

As a 2017 study in the *Journal of Hydrology*, which I put up at my website Climate Depot, found, "compelling evidence for increased flooding at a global scale is lacking." The authors reported, "The number of significant trends was about the number expected due to chance alone" and "changes in the frequency of major floods are dominated by multidecadal variability." The study noted that the UN IPCC itself had concluded "that globally there is no clear and widespread evidence of changes in flood magnitude or frequency in observed flood records."[57]

"Worries Me as a Parent and a Citizen"

The kids' climate crusade is proving to be too much even for some who support climate action. In October of 2019 I engaged in a debate on Eric Bolling's TV show about Greta and the youth activists, and—much to my surprise—my debate opponent agreed with me and admitted he does not like the movement either.

Professor Fernando Miralles-Wilhelm of the University of Maryland said, "I have two daughters who are or very engaged and I just I mean I'm still, to be honest, I'm still grappling with how I deal with this....

"I don't think we're conveying the positive side of that equation to the younger generations and that worries me as a parent and as a citizen," Miralles-Wilhelm said. "I don't think people like Al Gore are the best spokespersons for the climate. Neither is Greta."

Surprised by his comments, I responded, "It's really refreshing. I'm happy that you hear the professor here say that. Because many of his colleagues—people like Michael Mann at Penn State—a UN top scientist—just signed a letter urging colleges across America to declare a 'climate emergency' on campuses."

I ended by saying, "We need more scientists like Miralles-Wilhelm because he's the voice of reason against these other ones who are egging these kids on and it's just such a gross disservice to children, robbing them of their innocence in childhood."[58]

CHAPTER 13

Identity Politics Invades the Climate Debate

I dentity politics invaded the climate debate in recent years, and it is now a key component of the various versions of the Green New Deal. Since the death of George Floyd, which triggered the Black Lives Matter movement and created chaos and rioting in cities around the U.S., there has been an increased focus on racially-charged climate issues and identity politics within the climate movement.

AOC has done her best to make the Green New Deal about identity politics. "It's inevitable that we can use the transition to 100% renewable energy as the vehicle to truly deliver and establish economic, social, and racial justice in the United States of America," she said in 2019.

GND cosponsor Ed Markey of Massachusetts has urged, "We should be working to pass a Green New Deal and deliver climate justice."[1]

Al Gore touted Biden's pick of Kamala Harris for vice president because "Kamala has made climate and environmental justice a top priority in her career in public service."

It's Not about the Climate

Climate activist Eric Holthaus admitted that the climate "crisis" or "emergency" is not about the science after all. "The climate emergency isn't about science, it's about justice," Holthaus wrote in July 2020.[2]

Teen climate activist Greta Thunberg has declared that the "climate crisis is not just about the environment. It is a crisis of human rights, of justice, and of political will." She explained, "Colonial, racist, and patriarchal systems of oppression have created and fueled it. We need to dismantle them all."[3]

UK climate skeptic James Delingpole unleashed on the social justice comments. "To anyone familiar with the workings of the green movement, Greta's statement will come as no surprise whatsoever. That's why I called my book on the subject *Watermelons*," Delingpole wrote. "Environmentalists are often green on the outside, red on the inside. Their movement is essentially a global socialistic redistribution exercise hiding behind a mask of green righteousness."[4]

Claims that modern society is dominated by racism and "white privilege" spread from the schoolhouse to the sports world to entertainment to the media to the halls of Congress and presidential candidates. And, yes, to the environmental movement and climate "science." Climate change activism is increasingly being divided into gender, racial, and age categories.

No longer are cap-and-trade, carbon (dioxide) taxes, and more solar and wind the promoted solutions to alleged global warming. Now we can add gender justice and defunding the police!

"The White Man's Own Science"

The activist group Black Land First (BLF)—a "black consciousness revolutionary socialist political party" in South Africa that wants to seize white-owned land "without compensation"—blamed "white people" for the climate change that supposedly caused Tropical Cyclone Idai, which hit Mozambique, Zimbabwe, and Malawi in 2019. BLF demanded the African Union seek reparations from Europe and the U.S. for the cyclone.

As BLF president Andile Mngxitama said, "It's no longer speculation—even the white man's own science corroborates what we blacks know: Africa is paying a heavy price for the actions of the white world."

When we hear climate activists demand that we all "listen to the science," does that mean "white man's own science," or something else?

BLF's Mngxitama said the cyclone was "not a natural disaster but a direct consequence of the white, Western system of ecological assault for profits." He explained, "The multitudes that died as a result of the cyclone are not victims of a natural disaster. This is mass murder which could be prevented if the West abandoned its ways."

BLF is seeking climate reparations from the white world. "BLF calls on the African Union to demand reparations and relief from the European Union and the United States of America for Cyclone Idai. Africa is tired of carrying the burden of the destructive behavior of the global white system of power and consumption.... Black First Land First holds that the destroyers of the ecological balance, through greenhouse gas emissions, must pay for the catastrophe that is caused by their gluttonous cultures and civilization of death," Mngxitama said.

"Cyclone Idai was created by whites and therefore the West must pay," urged the BLF on Twitter.[6]

This is not the first time that white people have been blamed for evil damage to the environment. The *Washington Post* reported in 2019 that according to a new study in the *Proceedings of the National Academy of Sciences,*

"A Virus in His or Her Brain"

"Even the most liberal, well-intentioned white person has a virus in his or her brain that can be activated at an instant," claimed former Obama Green Czar and CNN analyst Van Jones in 2020. "It's not the racist white person who is in the Ku Klux Klan that we have to worry about. It's the white liberal Hillary Clinton supporter walking her dog in Central Park who would tell you right now, you know, people like that—'oh, I don't see race, race is no big deal to me, I see us all as the same, I give to charities,'" Jones said.[5]

"Whites are mainly to blame for air pollution, but blacks and Hispanics bear the burden."[8]

Climate activist Bill McKibben lamented in 2013, "White America has fallen short"—by voting for "climate deniers." In a *Los Angeles Times* op-ed, McKibben complained, "Election after election, nativeborn and long-standing citizens pull the lever for climate deniers."

And aborigines in nineteenth-century Australia blamed the bad climate on "the white man." A March 11, 1846, article in the *Maitland Mercury* explained that "great changes have taken place in the climate of Australia," citing "heavy rains" and "deluging floods" and noted, "The aborigines say that the climate has undergone this change since the white-man came in country."[9]

Woke and Weeping Climate Scientists

NASA, America's (once) hallowed space agency was not far behind in making similar racial claims, with their high-profile scientists going into full political mode.

NASA climate scientist Kate Marvel declared on June 1, 2020, "Climate justice and racial justice are the same thing, and we'll never head off climate catastrophe without dismantling white supremacy." Dr. Marvel, an associate research scientist at NASA Goddard Institute for Space Studies (GISS) in New York City, went political, drawing racially charged links between "climate justice," "racial justice," and "white supremacy."[11] She had previously tweeted out a *Newsweek* article entitled "Science Should Be A Feminist Institution," with the comment, "DAMN RIGHT!"[12]

Marvel is a huge fan of Ocasio-Cortez, the Sunrise Movement, and the Green New Deal. "What I do admire about that is the fact they are using new language. It's not just, 'Look at the sad polar bear,'" Marvel said. "This is not talking about climate change like it's this isolated issue. It's talking about it in the context of all these other things that people care about. And I think that's absolutely the right way to look at it."[13]

NASA climate scientist Peter Kalmus of Jet Propulsion Lab joined Marvel in going woke, linking climate issues and race. On May 30, 2020, Kalmus wrote, "Here's why race justice and climate justice are one and the same: The oppressive extractive plutocracies that colonize and kill black bodies and colonize and kill our planet are one and the same."[14]

Kalmus was responding to the protests and riots springing up across the country in the wake of allegations of racism in law enforcement.[15] "They'd literally rather have a race war than charge even one cop for murdering an innocent black man," Kalmus added.[16]

On his website Kalmus describes himself as "a climate scientist at NASA's Jet Propulsion Lab. I use satellite data and models to study the rapidly changing Earth, focusing on boundary layer clouds and ecological forecasting." He is a member of the American Meteorological Society and the American Geophysical Union. "My awareness of climate breakdown reached the point where I had no choice but to respond in some meaningful way, he explains at his site. "Global warming is happening with a rapidity that leaves me speechless." Kalmus claims he "uses about 1/10th the fossil fuels of the American average."[17]

Climate change literally makes Kalmus cry. In a 2018 article, "Thoughts on Climate Action from a Scientist Who Gave Up Flying," Kalmus recounted how his "tears poured down" when he thought about the calamity of man-made climate change:

> In order to embrace what's coming next, I had to let go of what went before. My grief was like the leap of a trapeze artist, letting go of one trapeze, flying through space, and catching the next one. There were times when tears poured down. I mourned the world I'd known my whole life. I mourned my children's future. I mourned how avoidable this all was. I mourned the strange and hard reality, and I mourned waking up. I mourned every blow struck in anger, and I mourned every bullet fired. I mourned all the species that are leaving us, never to return. I mourned this whole beautiful Earth. But then, through these tears, I accepted reality as it is. Somehow, on the far side of the tears, I found the strength to go forward.

Kalmus envisions "a world where everyone puts others above self and where we live aligned with the biosphere. In such a world, there is no war, crime, hatred, or negativity."[18] And presumably no more tears.

Kalmus's *Being the Change: Live Well and Spark a Climate Revolution* has been endorsed by former NASA lead global warming scientist James Hansen. "A plethora of insights about nature and ourselves, revealed by one man's journey as he comes to terms with human exploitation of our planet," is how Hansen described Kalmus's book.[19]

Hansen, the former director of NASA's Goddard Institute for Space Studies, has a history of endorsing extreme climate books and climate activism. As I detailed in *The Politically Incorrect Guide to Climate Change*:

> In 2009 NASA then–lead global warming scientist James Hansen endorsed a book called *Time's Up! An Uncivilized Solution to a Global Crisis*, which ponders "razing cities to

"Climate Grief"

NASA's Peter Kalmus is not the only woke scientist to be reduced to tears by the coming climate catastrophe.

"I just broke down in tears in the boarding area at SFO [airport] while on phone with my wife. I've never cried because of a science report before," said climate activist Eric Holthaus.

"For Amy Jordan, 40, of Salt Lake City, a mother of three teenage children, the [UN IPCC] report caused a 'crisis.' 'The emotional reaction of my kids was severe,' she told NBC News. 'There was a lot of crying. They told me, 'We know what's coming, and it's going to be really rough,'" wrote Avichai Scher at NBC News.

UN's Yvo de Boer broke down into "flood of tears" after warning that failure to reach a climate deal could "plunge the world into conflict."

Hollywood activist Laurie David recalled of her climate awakening: "I remember crying every day at five in the afternoon."

Bill McKibben, the founder of 350.org said, "My tears started before anyone said a word. As the service started, dozens of choristers from around the world carried three things down the aisle and to the altar: pieces of dead coral bleached by hot ocean temperatures; stones uncovered by retreating glaciers; and small, shriveled ears of corn from drought-stricken parts of Africa."[20]

In 2018 the journal *Nature Climate Change* published a study finding: "'Global warming' causing an increase in 'ecological grief.'"[21]

the ground, blowing up dams and switching off the greenhouse gas emissions machine" as possible solutions to global warming. "The only way to prevent global ecological collapse and thus ensure the survival of humanity is to rid the world of Industrial Civilization," the book explains.

"A future outside civilization is a better life; one in which we can actually decide for ourselves how we are going to live." Hansen declared on the book's Amazon page that author Keith Farnish, "has it right: time has practically run out, and the system is the problem. Governments are under the thumb of fossil fuel special interests—they will not look after our and the planet's well-being until we force them to do so, and that is going to require enormous effort."

Remember, Hansen was NASA's lead global warming scientist, in charge of the temperature dataset, endorsing a book suggesting the solution of calling for ridding the world of industrial civilization. Hansen is a hardcore activist who has been arrested multiple times protesting climate change.

He has accused climate skeptics of "crimes against humanity and nature."[22]

Other NASA climate scientists have also turned science into political activism. NASA's current lead global warming scientist Gavin Schmidt, head of NASA's Goddard Institute for Space Studies, urged in 2016, "We have to have a price on carbon because right now it's still free to put carbon dioxide into the atmosphere. So if you put a price on carbon that is commensurate with the damage that carbon-dioxide emissions cause, then people will be smarter."[23]

There was a political controversy in 2010 when the then–NASA chief Charles Bolden announced that the agency's goal was Muslim outreach. "Perhaps foremost, [President] Obama wanted me to find a way to reach out to the Muslim world and engage much more with dominantly Muslim nations to help them feel good about their historic contribution to science, math and engineering," Bolden said.[26]

Houston, We Have a Problem

NASA's descent into political activism has prompted a group of former NASA scientists and engineers to attempt to bring NASA back to hard science. "We believe the claims by NASA and GISS, that man-made carbon dioxide is having a catastrophic impact on global climate change are not substantiated," the scientists wrote in a letter to NASA.[24]

"The Right Climate Stuff," is a group that includes engineers and scientists from across generations who have taken part in NASA's most high-profile missions dating back to the Apollo program.[25]

And in 2020 NASA began "working with diversity, inclusion, and equity experts" to "address systemic discrimination and inequality" in the agency's "terminology for cosmic objects." NASA announced, "It has become clear that certain cosmic nicknames are not only insensitive but can be actively harmful. NASA is examining its use of unofficial terminology for cosmic objects as part of its commitment to diversity, equity, and inclusion. As an

Former NASA scientists and engineers who formed the "One More Mission" have challenged NASA's allegiance to anthropogenic climate change.

initial step, NASA will no longer refer to planetary nebula NGC 2392 as the 'Eskimo Nebula.' 'Eskimo' is widely viewed as a colonial term with a racist history, imposed on the indigenous people of Arctic regions.... NASA will also no longer use the term 'Siamese Twins Galaxy' to refer to a pair of spiral galaxies," the agency added.[27]

The reaction was swift: "Seriously: Is this what is holding us back in space? Is the Sombrero Galaxy anti-Mexican? Is the Bullet cluster too violent? Should we now say 'holes of color'?" wrote Eric Weinstein. "Isn't this mostly just wallowing?"[28]

"Dwarf stars will henceforth be known as volumetrically challenged stars," a Twitter critique noted.[29]

Not to be left out, ornithologists called for allegedly racist bird names to be changed in 2020 because some names "represent colonialism, racism and inequality."[30]

Gore Goes Full Woke

Former vice president Al Gore linked "climate change" to "white supremacists" in 2020 and decried "the nexus between the climate crisis and racism." Gore wrote, "The one stupid trick that white supremacists have used for 150 years is to accentuate racial division in order to build support among lower-income, majority-white voters for a corporate agenda that actually hurts them." But things are looking up! The former Democrat presidential candidate explained, "I'm optimistic that joining together the climate movement and the racial equality movement will give us strength in numbers that will ultimately lead to success."[31]

Vice magazine has warned about "climate grief, a psychological phenomenon that affects Black and Indigenous peoples, and other people of color, in uniquely devastating ways." As the article's author explained, "We carry the pain of the climate crisis deep inside us.... Our grief—and our anger—is rooted in centuries of painful history, and the current ecological violence hurled at our communities."

The Vice piece quoted Tyffani Dent, a licensed psychologist: "Just like other stressors that people of color experience, ecological grief is often magnified. People of color know...society is going to make sure we're impacted first, and impacted the hardest."

The Vice article cited a report from the American Psychological Association entitled, "Beyond Storms and Droughts: The Psychological

Racist Lawns Are Causing Climate Change

"The ways we maintain [lawns] risk hurting the environment and contributing to climate change. So why do we even have lawns in the first place?" asked David Botti in the *New York Times* in 2019. "We traced their history, starting with early European colonists"—and what did the *Times* investigation reveal? He quotes author Virginia Scott Jenkins explaining how lawns "are a symbol of man's control of, or superiority, over his environment."

"These lawns come on the backs of slaves," as Botti explained in a video that showed a painting of George Washington in a field. "By the 1870s we also see American culture slowly start to embrace lawns for the privileged masses."[32]

Impacts of Climate Change" and claimed, "Research has bolstered the idea that white supremacy has led to the climate crisis."

Vice also quoted Mary Heglar, "a Black climate justice essayist" from Columbia University.

"Hope is such a white concept," said Heglar. "Then there's an extra layer of loneliness that comes with being a climate person of color, because you're just stuck in this perpetual position of trying to save white people from themselves. And it's so fucking exhausting."[33]

The New Climate Fix: "Defund the Police!"

"Defunding the police is very good climate policy," declared Kate Aronoff, a staff writer for the *New Republic* in 2020. "If black lives really do matter to climate advocates, defunding the police should, too," she explained. "An ever-growing number of green groups have released statements expressing solidarity with protesters and denouncing police brutality, white supremacy, and the increasingly warlike rhetoric from the White House." She added, "There's plenty of common cause to be found in calls to defund the police and invest in a more generous, democratic, and green public sphere, well beyond the scope of what any carbon-pricing measure can accomplish."[34]

"The Racism of Climate Change Alarmists"

In his seminal book, *Eco-Imperialism: Green Power, Black Death*, Paul Driessen exposed the racist origins of the European and American nongovernmental organizations', banking institutions', and governments' eco-colonialist, anti-modernity agenda.

"In its introduction, Congress Of Racial Equality national spokesman Niger Innis said the green elites' policies 'prevent needy nations from using the very technologies that developed countries employed to become rich, comfortable, and free of disease. And they send millions of infants, children, men and women to early graves every year.'"

—environmental journalist Duggan Flanakin in 2020[35]

A Vice magazine article entitled, "Why 'Defunding the Police' Is Also an Environmental Issue," urged that defunding the police wasn't "a distraction from organizing mass numbers of people to fight the climate emergency" but rather "part of the same theory of change and political vision" because "Black people suffer more from climate chaos *and* police violence [emphasis in the original]."[36]

Or perhaps we should kill public officials? UK Extinction Rebellion co-founder Roger Hallam believes government officials and big business owners "should have a bullet through their heads" for being "culpable for climate catastrophe." Hallam explained in 2020, "Most days when I get out of bed, I'm saying the people that are culpable are the people who run society, run big business, run governments, run the elites. They are exponentially more culpable for climate catastrophe. [In] 1990 might as well give them six months in prison, now maybe you should put a bullet through their head—or rather someone probably will."[37]

Age and Gender Injected into the Climate Debate

A 2019 study blamed old people for global warming. "Aging Population Increases Energy Use," read the headline in the *Harvard Gazette*. "New research links two of the biggest drivers of global change today: the population's rapid aging and the planet's rising heat." The *Gazette* portrayed old people as a dangerous climate threat. "Using survey data about 'degree days,' which measure heating and cooling demand, [the researchers] showed that the change in demand due to aging was highest in warmer temperatures, spiking among those 70 and older, likely because of cooling needs."[38]

We have been warned. Grammy and Grandpa sitting at home with the air conditioner on in the summer is threatening you and your children's future! So, what is to be done about these pesky old folks?

Bill Nye "the Science Guy" has an idea. Nye suggested in 2017 that older people have to die off for man-made climate change to be taken seriously. "Climate change deniers," Nye explained to the *LA Times*, "are older. It's generational. So we're just going to have to wait for those people to 'age out,' as they say. 'Age out' is a euphemism for 'die.' But it'll happen, I guarantee you — that'll happen."[39]

And kids are getting the message that older people stand in the way of saving the planet. "We are here because our parents trashed the planet and it's up to our generation to save it," screamed eleven-year-old woke climate

> ### "You Are Helping Those People"
>
> "My own daughter looks at me and says, 'You are helping those people (climate skeptics) and I don't know that I want to have children because the world may be gone and you are helping those people.'"
>
> —former Fox News and ABC newsman John Stossel told me during my interview for *Climate Hustle 2*[40]

activist Rosie Clemans-Cope of Maryland from a podium at a Green New Deal rally in front of the U.S. Capitol in September 2019. "The government does nothing, our schools don't teach us and our parents are silent." The sixth-grader urged, "You need to support other social movements too. Because any fight for justice is your fight too. So when kids rally for gun safety or for LGBQT plus rights or when teachers ask for liveable wages, get your butt out there and support them and they will support you. It is called solidarity."

But lest anyone think climate activists are letting younger people off the hook for ruining the planet—think again. Sea Shepherd Conservation Society founder Paul Watson expanded the circle of those who are guilty of harming Mother Earth. "If you have a birth certificate, you are guilty of contributing to the destruction of the planet," Watson said in 2014. "It is indeed our one original sin, being born into a consumer driven world."[41]

"Gender Justice"

"To bolster the role of women in climate change action, [UN] delegates have adopted the first Gender Action Plan at the 23rd 'conference of the parties,'" according to a report from Deutsche Welle. "Climate change is affecting everyone living on this planet. But women in particular will feel its impact, experts say. That's because climate change exacerbates existing gender inequality."[42]

In 2005, I attended the UN climate summit in Montreal Canada and interviewed the spokeslady for "climate gender justice." Here is an excerpt from my report, titled, "Men Warm Globe, Women Feel the Heat, Group Claims": "'Women and men are differently affected by climate change and they contribute differently to climate change,' said Ulrike Rohr, director of the German-based group called 'Genanet-Focal Point Gender, Environment, Sustainability.' Rohr, who is demanding 'climate gender justice,' left no doubt as to which gender she believes was the chief culprit in emitting greenhouse gasses.

"'To give you an example from Germany, it is mostly men who are going by car. Women are going by public transport mostly,' Rohr explained. 'In most parts of the world, women are contributing less

A Sampling of Climate-Identity Politics

"Environmentalists Accuse Leonardo DiCaprio's New HBO Climate Documentary of Promoting 'White Supremacy' & a 'White Savior Complex'"[43]

"Longtime Climate Activist David Roberts Unleashes on Fellow Activists: 'I Am Sick to F*cking Death of Hearing White Men Drone On about Climate, Myself Included'"[44]

"Sierra Club: The Big Problem with Environmentalism Is 'Unsustainable Whiteness'"[45]

"Climate Activist: 'Non-White, Non-Men Climate Experts' Sought for TV & Radio"[46]

NYT climate reporter: "I've been thinking a lot about fossil fuels and white supremacy recently."[47]

"Sierra Club Goes Full Woke: 'We Will Never Survive the Climate Crisis without Ending White Supremacy'—'When the U.S. Pours Carbon Pollution into the Air...That Is White Supremacy'"[48]

"Climate Activists at Sunrise Movement: 'The Fight against Climate Change Exists alongside the Fight against White Supremacy and Colonialism'"[49]

[to greenhouse gasses],' Rohr continued. But it is the women of the world who will feel the most heat from catastrophic global warming, she said."[50]

Recent years have seen some of the biggest names in environmentalism fall from grace.

In 2020 the Sierra Club denounced their own founder John Muir and planned on taking down any monuments to him because of his racist history. Muir, who founded the Sierra Club in 1892, reportedly had ties to white supremacists and made derogatory comments about Blacks and indigenous people.

"As the most iconic figure in Sierra Club history, Muir's words and actions carry an especially heavy weight," said Michael Brune, the organization's executive director. "They continue to hurt and alienate Indigenous people and people of colour who come into contact with the Sierra Club."[51]

The *New Yorker* had detailed Muir's controversial statements in 2015. "[Muir] reported the laziness of 'Sambos.' Later he lamented the 'dirty and irregular life' of Indians in the Merced River valley, near Yosemite. In 'Our National Parks,' a 1901 essay collection written to promote parks

Filipino Activist Quits "Overwhelmingly White" Climate Movement

"The climate movement is overwhelmingly white. So I walked away," Karin Louise Hermes wrote in Vice magazine. "I felt required to tell my Filipino family's experience during speeches and rallies because this form of 'storytelling' was the only thing that would move a mostly white European audience to an emotional response of climate urgency," she explained.

"But after a while I realized I would only be called upon when climate organizations needed an inspiring story or a 'diverse' voice, contacts for a campaign, or to participate in a workshop for 'fun' when everyone else on the (all-white) project was getting paid." She added, "Whenever I would question the whiteness of these spaces and how strategies didn't take race into account, I would be met with uncomfortable silences."[52]

tourism, he assured readers that, 'As to Indians, most of them are dead or civilized into useless innocence.'"

The *New Yorker* article, entitled "Environmentalism's Racist History," also targeted Paul Ehrlich: "This strain of misanthropy seemed to appear again in biologist Paul Ehrlich's 1968 runaway best-seller 'The Population Bomb.' Ehrlich illustrated overpopulation with a scene of a Delhi slum seen through a taxi window: a 'mob' with a 'hellish aspect,' full of 'people eating, people washing, people sleeping....People thrusting their hands through the taxi window, begging. People defecating...People, people, people, people.' He confessed to being afraid that he and his wife would never reach their hotel, and reported that on that night he came to understand overpopulation 'emotionally.'"[53]

Cancel the Original New Deal?

President Franklin D. Roosevelt's original New Deal has been promoted as the model for the Green New Deal. But will the woke turn on the New Deal for purported racism? In 2017, NPR did an analysis titled "A 'Forgotten History' of How the U.S. Government Segregated America" via New Deal policies. "In 1933, faced with a housing shortage, the federal government began a program explicitly designed to increase—and segregate—America's housing stock."

"Author Richard Rothstein says the housing programs begun under the New Deal were tantamount to a 'state-sponsored system of segregation,'" explained NPR's Terry Gross. "The federal government began a program of building public housing for whites only in cities across the country. The liberal instinct of some Roosevelt administration officials led them to build some projects for African-Americans as well, but they were always separate projects; they were not integrated," Gross wrote. "African-Americans and other people of color were left out of the new suburban communities—and pushed instead into urban housing projects."[54]

CHAPTER 14

The Toxic Politics of the Green New Deal

The climate campaigners are on a roll. With little pushback from the media, businesses, or the public on their "climate emergency" narrative, and no pushback from government officials or scientists, the activists are shifting into high gear.

To succeed in achieving their ends, the climate fear establishment has to ramp up the hype and shamelessly manipulate data to make scarier and scarier predictions, especially when current reality fails to alarm. They know the Green New Deal would be the ultimate fulfillment of their decades of activism, a massive all-society-encompassing plan, and that it would not stand a chance of passage without the urgency of the climate fear rhetoric attached to it.

A "Compliant" Public

As we have seen, the COVID-19 lockdowns and suspensions of liberties have only emboldened climate campaigners in their quest to achieve the ultimate progressive vision of planning, monitoring, and controlling the lives of the masses for their "safety," all in the name of "the science."

Lockdowns happened almost overnight and remained in place for months, with constantly moving goalposts for when they could be lifted. The lockdowns were nothing short of a suspension of democracy. There were no votes by legislators or parliaments, just a complete deferral to the expertise of a credentialed class to formulate far-reaching policies at a whim. Public health bureaucrats, whose names no one had ever heard, now wielded massive state powers to enforce every possible rule—quarantines, isolation, mask mandates, restrictions on weddings, funerals, barbeques, playgrounds, and even limits on for how long you are able to leave your house and for what purpose.

And what if you violate any of the edicts of these unelected health bureaucrats? Your friends, neighbors, or even family members could turn you into the authorities. Los Angeles mayor Eric Garcetti encouraged citizens to report violations of the COVID stay at home orders with the phrase, "Snitches get rewards."[1]

"If one lesson from the pandemic is that taking serious action in a timely manner is key—then shouldn't this also be true in terms of climate change?" asked Sir Lindsay Hoyle, the speaker of the House of Commons, at the G7 Speakers' Meeting in 2020. Hoyle expressed his amazement at how readily the public had accepted the COVID lockdowns. "No-one could ever imagine that we would be wearing masks so readily and that we would all be so compliant," he said. "People were prepared to accept limitations on personal choice and lifestyle—for the good of their own family and friends."

Hoyle claimed that the "tragedy is that unlike the pandemic, the climate crisis is not simply an external threat, but one in which we have had a clear hand." He explained, "In other words, it seems that we have brought this on ourselves. While this is again sobering, surely, it is in our hands to rescue it, if we have got the will to do it?"[2]

The "will to do it" means the public has to prepare for climate lockdowns. A compliant public and ambition politicians and bureaucrats are a grave threat to liberty. As I detailed in chapter 11, the COVID lockdowns are being hailed by climate activists as the model for climate lockdowns. Former secretary of state John Kerry noted that "the parallels [between COVID-19 and climate change] are screaming at us, both positive and negative.... You could just as easily replace the words climate change with COVID-19; it is truly the tale of two pandemics deferred, denied, and distorted, one with catastrophic consequences, the other with even greater risk if we don't reverse course."[3]

"Just the Opposite of What's Needed"

Not everyone agrees that the same policies will work equally well to fight both COVID and "climate change."

"Lone drivers commuting to work or heading to shopping malls in massive automobiles, it is argued, waste natural resources and pollute the environment. It would be better for commuters to switch to trains or subways, and for shoppers to walk to neighborhood stores," Michael Barone pointed out. "All these policies, it turns out, are just the opposite of what's needed to stop or slow down a global pandemic. Self-distancing and isolation, not clustering, are necessary. The broad aisles of the suburban supermarket and disposable plastic bags are less likely to transmit disease than the close quarters of the local mini market and oft-used recyclable shopping bags. Heading in your own car to a drive-in testing center is better than riding the subway and waiting in a crowded line."[4]

Technocracy

French president Emmanuel Macron warned, "We must all limit the number of people with who we're in contact with every single day. Scientists say so."[5]

Well if "scientists say so"...

The COVID lockdowns, which the climate activists are hoping to turn into climate lockdowns, herald another step into the "scientism" that is leading us to a technocracy—government by an unelected cadre of experts.

"The lockdown and its consequences have brought a foretaste of what is to come: a permanent state of fear, strict behavioral control, massive loss of jobs, and growing dependence on the state," German economics professor Antony P. Mueller explained in August 2020.

"This coming technocracy involves close cooperation between the heads of the digital industry and of governments. With programs such as guaranteed minimum income and healthcare for all, the new kind of governance combines strict societal control with the promise of comprehensive social justice," he wrote.

"Earlier totalitarian regimes needed mass executions and concentration camps to maintain their power. Now, with the help of new technologies, it is believed, dissenters can easily be identified and marginalized. The nonconformists will be silenced by disqualifying divergent opinions as morally despicable."

Mueller added, "Under the order envisioned by the Great Reset, the advancement of technology is not meant to serve the improvement of the conditions of the people but to submit the individual to the tyranny of a technocratic state. 'The experts know better' is the justification."[6]

Trevor Thomas at the American Thinker quoted C.S. Lewis's prescient warnings against the dangers of technocracy. As Lewis said, "I dread government in the name of science. That is how tyrannies come in."

Lewis explained why government by scientists is so dangerous: "I dread specialists in power because they are specialists speaking outside their special subjects. Let scientists tell us about sciences. But government involves questions about the good for man, and justice, and what things are worth having at what price; and on these a scientific training gives a man's opinion no added value."[7]

Teen school-skipper Greta Thunberg urged the world to "start listening to the science" and "unite behind the science."[8] But just which scientists and which "science" should we be listening to? In the age of COVID lockdowns and a pending Green New Deal, this insight from economist Thomas Sowell's is more valuable than ever: "Experts are often called in, not to provide factual information or dispassionate analysis for the purpose of decision-making by responsible officials, but to give political cover for decisions already made and based on other considerations entirely."[9]

We were warned over fifty years ago about the dangers of being ruled by scientists and experts. President Dwight D. Eisenhower, in his 1961 Farewell Address, bluntly warned that "public policy could itself become the captive of a scientific-technological elite." As Eisenhower explained, "A government contract becomes virtually a substitute for intellectual curiosity" and "the prospect of domination of the nation's scholars by Federal employment, project allocations, and the power of money is ever present and is gravely to be regarded."

Eisenhower added, "We must also be alert to the equal and opposite danger that public policy could itself become the captive of a scientific-technological elite."[10]

In 2020, Eisenhower's "scientific-technological elite" became a very obvious reality in America. COVID lockdowns achieved many of the same goals the climate movement has strived for: central planning, loss of individual freedom, economic pain, obedience to authority, and weakened national sovereignty—all in a virtual blink of the eye.

"A Triumph of the Precautionary Principle"

According to physicist Lubos Motl, "25 million Americans became unemployed in 5 weeks....Many people want this insanity to continue. As far as I know, it has never happened in the history of civilizations that the bulk of a large enough nation, let alone the world, was kept at home for several months....The precautionary principle has only been promoted as a meme since the 1970s when it appeared as the 'Vorsorgeprinzip' in German discussions about deforestation and sea pollution. The precautionary principle is an extremely dangerous fallacy whose purpose is to make an absolutely irrational assumption—namely that some risks must be considered infinitely more critical than all other risks—sound more intelligent or maybe even scientific. You are 'obliged' to do even things that actually make the public health conditions worse."[12]

Healthcare journalist Peter Barry Chowka candidly described the COVID–climate linkage as "a flu d'état…a takeover of our supposedly democratic political process by unelected & unaccountable administrative state medical bureaucrats." Chowka noted that all of the COVID solutions were virtually the same as the Green New Deal solutions.[11]

The Trump administration allowed the health bureaucracy and its failed COVID models to dictate the national policy narrative that led to the lockdowns. Trump economic advisor Larry Kudlow said in April 2020 that it was "up to the health people" when the economy would reopen. "How much longer? I don't really want to forecast. That is up to the health people," Kudlow said on Fox News.[13]

Joe Biden said he would listen to the scientists and go along with a second national lockdown to fight COVID. "Asked specifically whether he would push to shutter economic activity if scientists said it was necessary, Biden replied: 'I would shut it down,'" reported Bill Barrow at ABC News.[14]

The "listen to the science" narrative has been a very effective strategy, cowing Republican politicians, conservatives, and many dissenting scientists into silence or submissiveness when it comes to challenging climate claims. "The science" determines whether or not you are a good, smart person or an evil science denier who deserves to be jailed, according to our mainstream media, government officials, academia, and social media censors.

This "listen to the science" litmus test will also be used to bully Republicans into climate "action." The greatest challenge we may face in fighting the Green New Deal is capitulating Republicans proposing a Green New Deal–light version that is slightly less intrusive.

Cost-Benefit Analysis

As controversy over the COVID lockdowns grew, questions about the costs and benefits of lockdowns were raised.

Economist Sanjeev Sabhlok resigned from his job in the Department of Treasury and Finance in Victoria, Australia, in September 2020 "to protest the outrageous violations of liberty" due to the COVID lockdowns.[16]

> **"Only in Government"**
> "Only in government is any benefit, however small, considered to be worth any cost, however large."
> —economist Thomas Sowell[15]

"Australia's bureaucracy has performed as badly as the world's worst bureaucracy during this pandemic. No one offered any independent advice. Comprehensive groupthink and incompetence has prevailed," he explained.[17] Scientists and politicians are "panting like a mad monster in the excitement of their total power over the people," he added.[18]

"This is like a mass scale bombing of one's own economy," Sabhlok said, referring to lockdowns and phased reopenings.[19] As I detailed in chapter 11, many UN climate supporters and Green New Deal proponents have endorsed the concept of "planned recessions" and economic "degrowth" for climate change. The COVID lockdowns achieved those goals almost overnight.

"Since independent thinking is a punishable offense in all government organizations, science is no longer about advancing the truth but about promoting politically preferred ideas," Sabhlok wrote. "The problem with science today is that it is effectively just another branch of government," Sabhlok explained.[20]

Former UK Supreme Court judge Lord Sumption asked in 2020, "Do we really want to be the kind of society where basic freedoms are conditional on the decisions of politicians in thrall to scientists and statisticians? Where human beings are just tools of public policy?"

Sumption pointed out, "To say that life is priceless and nothing else counts is just empty rhetoric.... There is more to life than the avoidance of death." He added, "To say that there are no limits is the stuff of tyrants. Every despot who ever lived thought that he was coercing his subjects for their own good or that of society at large...."

"A society in which the Government can confine most of the population without controversy is not one in which civilized people would want to live, regardless of their answers to these questions. Is it worth it?" Sumption explained. "The lockdown is without doubt the greatest interference with personal liberty in our history."[21]

Sabhlok believes Western nations need to build in civil liberty protections against future lockdowns: "This pandemic should lead to the rewriting of all textbooks in epidemiology, and should lead to a law (like they have in Sweden) that governments must require court orders for each individual, to restrain them at home for quarantine or lockdown."[22]

> ### A Cure Worse than the Disease
>
> "A group of South African actuaries advised their government that a lockdown would cost 29 lives for every one life saved from the virus. A U.K. government study estimated more conservatively that the ratio would be four-to-one—with lockdowns causing 200,000 fatalities while saving only 50,000 people from death by COVID-19."
>
> —James Lucas at The Federalist[23]

Steve Milloy of JunkScience.com warned that the government response during COVID revealed that "the incompetent, corrupt and politicized public health bureaucracy...wants to create a precedent for permanent control of society via 'public health.'"[24] "As with education, conservatives abandoned public health as a profession decades ago. I don't know any conservatives w/expertise in public health. We are now paying the price," Milloy wrote.[25] "We have ceded the field (of public health) to leftists who have only one tool ... government crackdown. All public health bureaucrats are Dems and worse sorts of leftists.... We can still 'social distance' without devolving into a police state or destroying the economy."[26]

The promoters of the Green New Deal have given anyone who cares about free markets, liberty, and science, an opening to expose the real agenda behind this plan.

"Climate and COVID share the commonality of government control. From electric car and fuel efficiency mandates to the entire economy busting Green New Deal, the 'benevolent' government seeks to control all aspects of our lives," wrote Denver-based physician Brian C. Joondeph. "One can see numerous parallels between COVID and climate policy. Both create fear, to a frenzy level, of the world ending, massive death and destruction, all due to a warming planet or an aggressive flu virus," Joondeph explained. "Question the dogma of either the virus or climate movement and prepare to have your life, if not disrupted, then ruined. There is only one politically correct viewpoint on both issues."[28]

> ### UNICEF Warns Lockdown Could Kill More Than COVID-19
>
> "The risk of children dying from malaria, pneumonia or diarrhoea in developing countries is spiraling due to the pandemic and 'far outweighs any threat presented by the coronavirus', Unicef (UN Children's Fund) has warned," the UK *Telegraph* reported.[27]

Tony Heller, who runs the website RealClimateScience.com, summed up the twin threats of COVID lockdowns and climate "solutions." As Heller wrote, "We have arrived at the end game. Totalitarianism and economic depression. And a compliant public which has begged for it to happen."[29] "The COVID-19 response was the implementation of the Green New Deal," Heller added.[30]

Epidemiologist Knut Wittkowski also slammed the COVID lockdowns and ripped "science" funded to support government policy. "Shutting down schools, driving the economy against the wall—there was no reason for it," Wittkowski explained in a YouTube video. For his honesty, Wittkowski was promptly banned from YouTube, as numerous lockdown dissenters have been by the social media platforms.

"Governments did not have an open discussion, including economists, biologists and epidemiologists, to hear different voices. In Britain, it was

> ### "Torment Us without End"
>
> "Of all tyrannies, a tyranny sincerely exercised for the good of its victims may be the most oppressive. It would be better to live under robber barons than under omnipotent moral busybodies. The robber baron's cruelty may sometimes sleep, his cupidity may at some point be satiated; but those who torment us for our own good will torment us without end for they do so with the approval of their own conscience."
> —C. S. Lewis[31]

the voice of one person—Neil Ferguson—who has a history of coming up with projections that are a bit odd. The government did not convene a meeting with people who have different ideas, different projections, to discuss his projection," Wittkowski pointed out.

Echoing the words of President Eisenhower in 1961, Wittkowski said, "They have the scientists on their side that depend on government funding. One scientist in Germany just got $500 million from the government, because he always says what the government wants to hear. Scientists are in a very strange situation. They now depend on government funding, which is a trend that has developed over the past 40 years. Before that, when you were a professor at a university, you had your salary and you had your freedom. Now, the university gives you a desk and access to the library. And then you have to ask for government money and write grant applications. If you are known to criticise

> ### "Tyranny and Misery"
>
> "Free societies of the kind we've been lucky enough to experience for the last 100, 150 years—are a very rare exception in human history. Most people, most of history ... have lived in tyranny and misery."
> —economist Milton Friedman in 1999[32]

the government, what does that do to your chance of getting funded? It creates a huge conflict of interest."

Eisenhower has been proven correct. The public health bureaucracy and the climate community have become political lobbying organizations and they are using "the science" to support their preferred policies. No researcher looking for government research money would put their name on a study that was against the politically accepted views on either COVID or climate change.

On June 1, 2020, in a discussion of how "the COVID-19 pandemic tells us that everything is connected," UN IPCC chief Hoesung Lee admitted that the UN climate panel he heads is all about using science to lobby for political goals. "Our assessment findings will strengthen the political will of the policy makers for immediate and concrete actions," Lee said on June 1, 2020.[33]

The U.S. is entering into a new phase in which, as Bill Dunne at the American Thinker put it, "the danger of letting lab coats run the world" is palpable. "It should be clear by now that most of the world's leaders were stampeded over the lockdown cliff like so many lemmings. What caused the stampede is even more remarkable: a tiny coterie of obscure, soft-spoken epidemiologists in white lab coats playing with numbers.... the aim was to cause panic," Dunne wrote. "We were plunged into the grandest of experiments in authoritarian paternalism, whereby we plebeians—i.e., those without government jobs—are

❖ » Newsroom » All news » Calls to add 'climate change' to death certificates

Calls to add 'climate change' to death certificates

21 MAY 2020

The Australian National University touts experts' call for climate change to be added to death certificates.

deemed incompetent to judge if it's safe to take a dip in the ocean or a walk in the woods. We can, though, crowd into a Walmart or the local supermarket."[34]

Cause of Death: Climate Change

Say what you will about climate activists, they are a quick study. Seeing the scary and emotional daily COVID-19 death counts on television and all the media attention that the viral fears received inspired climate activists to play copycat in order to draw attention back to their pet climate cause.

Perhaps the wackiest climate story to come out of jealousy over COVID was the call to put "climate change" on death certificates as a cause of death in a study published in May of 2020 in *Lancet Planetary Health.* Academics in Australia were demanding that "climate change" be added to death certificates as a "pre-existing condition."

Arnagretta Hunter of the Australian National University (ANU) Medical School, a co-author of the study, said, "Climate change is a killer, but we don't acknowledge it on death certificates. Climate change is the single greatest health threat that we face globally even after we recover from coronavirus."[35]

The current climate change death toll is 150,000 per year, according to the World Health Organization. Climate change is projected to kill approximately 250,000 per year between 2030 and 2050.[36]

"Far, far more people have died from climate change than are dying from COVID-19—far more," claimed Mary Robinson, the former president of Ireland. "We have to get out of COVID in a way that helps us get out of climate—meaning, go green," she added.[37]

But climate skeptics were having none of it. Ron Clutz of Science Matters ridiculed the study:

"No doubt they noticed how powerful were the Covid-19 death statistics in getting the public to comply with lockdown regulations.

Their logic is clear: When people die with multiple diseases, pick the one that's politically useful. ('Never let a crisis go to waste.')"

Statistician Matt Briggs also ridiculed the study: "They discovered a way to boost fear and keep control!" he said. "Daily body counts blasted from the evil media, 'Over 100 people died from climate change today, raising questions about...blah blah.'"

The possibilities are endless. Federal research has posited a link between "climate change" and "fatal car crashes." A 2016 U.S. Department of Transportation study asked: "How might climate change increase the risk of fatal crashes in a community?"[38] Is it possible that anyone dying in a car crash could be listed as a "climate change" death?

And will cancer deaths be listed on death certificates as a "climate change" death? A 2020 study in the *American Cancer Society Journal* found "climate change is already increasing cancer risk" and even fretted over the "carbon footprint of cancer care."[39]

Organ failure at the time of death could also prompt a climate change death certificate listing. In 2017, Al Gore promoted a link between climate change and health, warning, "Every organ system can be affected by climate change."[40]

If someone dies from a car crash, cancer or organ failure, "climate change" could be listed as a cause on the death certificate. Expect daily "climate change" death tolls to be hyped by the media someday soon.

The science of climate related deaths does not appear to matter. "New data shows the global climate-related death risk has dropped by over 99% since 1920. Despite the near

> **God's Gift to the Left**
> "I just think that COVID is God's gift to the Left."
> —actress and activist Jane Fonda[41]

constant caterwauling from climate alarmists that we are in a 'climate emergency', real-world data, released at the end of 2020 shows that climate related deaths are now approaching zero," reported Meteorologist Anthony Watts.[42]

"Just wait for the headlines about 'Millions killed by climate change.' And 'Climate change death toll mounts.' If it bleeds, it leads. Politicized science is now a fact of life in the Western world, undermining the very foundations of the technological and material progress that liberated the mass of humanity from permanent poverty, the normal state of affairs until the scientific and industrial revolutions changed the state of civilization," Thomas Lifson said at the American Thinker.

"Stalin was the pioneer in bending science in service of a political agenda, and under him, Trofim Lysenko led the charge to corrupt science, which ended disastrously when agriculture was forced to accept practices based on phony science. Lysenkoism is the name given to the practice of bending science to politics," he added.[44]

> ### "It Will Happen"
> "The Great Reset will happen. And I think it will happen with greater speed and with greater intensity than a lot of people might imagine."
> —former secretary of state John Kerry in 2020[43]

"The Great Reset"

COVID and climate have officially melded. WHO director-general Tedros Adhanom Ghebreyesus declared in August 2020 that "the Covid-19 pandemic has given new impetus to the need to accelerate efforts to respond to climate change."[45] In 2020, WHO's director-general claimed,

> ### Happy Slavery
> "You'll own nothing. And you'll be happy ... Whatever you want you'll rent and it'll be delivered by drone...[Meat will be] an occasional treat...The U.S. won't be the world's leading superpower...A billion people will be displaced by climate change ... Polluters will have to pay to emit carbon dioxide...There will be a global price on carbon this will help make fossil fuels history."
> —World Economic Forum's utopian Great Reset video titled "8 Predictions for the World in 2030"[46]

Not All in This Together

"The world's 500 richest people are a combined $813 billion richer now than they were at the beginning of the year," the Bloomberg Billionaires Index reported during the 2020 COVID lockdowns.[47]

NPR reported, "Amazon doubled its profit to $5.2 Billion during the lockdowns as online shopping boomed."[48]

The UK *Guardian* reported, "Tech giants' shares soar as companies benefit from Covid-19 pandemic—Amazon, Apple, Facebook and Google reported positive quarterly results even as overall US economic growth fell by 32.9%."[49]

And CNBC business analyst Jim Cramer explained that the lockdowns led to "one of the greatest wealth transfers in history." He added, "This is the first recession where big business...is coming through virtually unscathed."[50]

"We cannot go back to the way things were," adding "the Covid-19 pandemic has given us a glimpse of our world as it could be: cleaner skies and rivers."

This is the same World Health Organization that warned in 2018 that "climate change is the greatest health challenge of the 21st century, and threatens all aspects of the society in which we live."[51]

Climate activists Mark Hertsgaard and Kyle Pope see COVID and climate as almost one and the same. "The overlaps between the coronavirus crisis and the climate crisis are many.... there is an opportunity for all of us here. As awful as the coronavirus is, it is something of a test run for the challenges of a climate crisis that continues to accelerate," Hertsgaard and Pope wrote. "The similarities between the causes of

"Re-Imagine Economic Systems"

"This pandemic has provided an opportunity for a Reset. This is our chance to accelerate our pre-pandemic efforts to re-imagine economic systems that actually address global challenges like extreme poverty, inequality, and climate change."

—Canadian prime minister Justin Trudeau speaking to UN conference, September 29, 2020[52]

> ### "Build Back Better"
>
> "Build Back Better" is "the latest code phrase for green global tyranny," warned James Delingpole at Breitbart. "'Build back better' is actually a United Nations invented phrase and what it actually means is more world government, more green taxes and regulation, more expensive energy, more identity politics, more corporatism—and, of course, less freedom and entrepreneurialism."[53]

and solutions to the coronavirus and the climate crisis are nothing short of eerie."[54]

Consider yourself warned: COVID and climate—a marriage made in authoritarianism. The melding of the public health bureaucracy and the climate establishment is at hand. Nothing good can come from this arranged marriage.

In June 2020 Klaus Schwab, the chairman and founder of the World Economic Forum in Switzerland, called for "a Great Reset of capitalism" to help fight COVID and climate change. Klaus Schwab said the virus has given us an "opportunity" to pursue "equality and sustainability."

Schwab explained, "The changes we have already seen in response to COVID-19 prove that a reset of our economic and social foundations is possible.... The world must act jointly and swiftly to revamp all aspects of our societies and economies, from education to social contracts and working conditions. Every country, from the United States to China, must participate, and every industry, from oil and gas to tech, must be transformed. In short, we need a 'Great Reset' of capitalism."

Schwab is all in on seizing this "rare but narrow window of opportunity" to shove his "solutions" on the world.[55]

Former vice president Al Gore is also fully committed to "the Great Reset": "I think this is a time for a 'Great Reset,'" Gore said. "We've got to fix a lot of these problems that have been allowed to fester for way too long." Gore added, "So this is a time for a reset to fix a bunch of challenges first among them the climate crisis." Gore-trained activists were set to be featured at the World Economic Forum meeting in

2021 billed as a "twin summit" because it will also feature youth leaders trained at Gore's Climate Reality Project.

"Gore is deeply connected to the 'Great Reset'; and will be closely involved with its rollout in 2021," Justin Haskins, editor-in-chief of StoppingSocialism.com and research fellow at the Heartland Institute wrote.[56]

German economics professor Mueller explained what is behind the "Great Reset," noting, "The ideology of the World Economic Forum is neither left nor right, nor progressive or conservative, it is also not fascist or communist, but outright technocratic. As such, it includes many elements of earlier collectivist ideologies."

He added, "The World Economic Forum's great reset project is social engineering at the highest level. Advocates of the reset contend that the UN failed to establish order in the world and could not advance forcefully its agenda of sustainable development—known as Agenda 2030—because of its bureaucratic, slow, and contradictory way of working. In contrast, the actions of the organizational committee of the World Economic Forum are swift and smart. When a consensus has been formed, it can be implemented by the global elite all over the world."[58]

Maurice Newman, a former advisor to Australian prime minister Tony Abbott, detailed just who is behind the Great Reset. "The World

Russian Collusion

"Two environmental advocacy groups that successfully lobbied against fracking in New York each received more than $10 million in grants from a foundation in California that got financial support from a Bermuda company congressional investigators linked to the Russians, public documents show. The environmental groups Natural Resources Defense Council and the Sierra Club Foundation received millions of dollars in grants from the San Francisco–based Sea Change Foundation. 'Follow the money trail, and this [New York] ban on fracking could be viewed as an example of successful Russian espionage,'" Ken Stiles, a CIA veteran of twenty-nine years who now teaches at Virginia Tech, told the Daily Signal.[57]

Economic Forum, a Geneva-based non-profit foundation whose ranks include Prince Charles and other climate change crusaders like Al Gore and Greta Thunberg, together with the secretary-general of the United Nations, the president of the European Central Bank, the secretary-general of the OECD, the managing director of the IMF, George Soros, world trade union leaders, chief executives of Big Tech and representatives of NGOs like Greenpeace and WWF, believes climate action must be top of the global agenda as we emerge from Covid-19," Newman wrote.

"Much of the World Economic Forum's agenda can be found in America's radical Left's Green New Deal, which addresses climate change and economic inequality," Newman added.[59]

Follow the Money

MIT climate scientist Richard Lindzen explained how climate science became so apocalyptic. "Climate science didn't used to be alarmist prior

---

"A Fake Meat Billionaire"

"Gore's Quest to Become a Fake Meat Billionaire—Lobbies for Climate Policies That Limit Meat While His Firm Invests $200 Million in Meat Substitutes," blared a 2019 headline at my Climate Depot website.

"Gore came out with a list of green tech firms and companies that people should invest in. Obama put $2.5 billion of those into a green stimulus and 14 firms affiliated with Gore got federal money from the Obama administration. Fast forward to 2019: Al Gore invests in the fake meat substitute, Beyond Meat. It's made up of 22 ingredients including bamboo and potato starch, and now it is the most successful IPO this year and at the same time, Gore's associates are writing reports condemning meat and linking eating it to climate. Gore is essentially lobbying for regulations that will enrich him once again. Beyond Meat's IPO was timed on the eve of this big U.N. Report warning about meat-eating."

—Marc Morano on *Tucker Carlson Tonight*, August 15, 2019, with guest host Mark Steyn[60]

Left to right: CFACT's Exec. Dir. Craig Rucker, me, Kevin Sorbo, *Climate Hustle 2* producer Chris Rogers, and CFACT's Adam Houser

to the late 1980s," Lindzen wrote. "That changed during the years 1988–1994, when climate research centered on CO2 and global warming received a 15-fold increase in funding in the US alone. Suddenly there was a great financial incentive to propel alarming global warming scenarios."[61]

And alarming it has become. In 2019, the phrase "climate emergency" swept the world as campaigners, the media, and academia piled on to scare the public into action.

Princeton physicist Freeman Dyson ripped the funding of climate alarmism. "If they did not scare the public they wouldn't get support from the government," Dyson explained in *The Uncertainty Has Settled*, a 2017 documentary. "In the end, everything is decided by who gets the money."

Dyson explained, "I don't say they're dishonest. I think they are inevitably influenced by the fact that they live by scaring the public, that if they did not scare the public they wouldn't get support from the government."[62]

And scaring the public is what they do, relentlessly.

To give just one particularly egregious example, on February 16, 2019, the *New York Times* ran an op-ed by climate activist David Wallace-Wells, author of *The Uninhabitable Earth: Life After Warming*, under this headline: "Time to Panic: The Planet Is Getting Warmer in Catastrophic Ways. And Fear May Be the Only Thing That Saves Us."[63]

University of Colorado extreme weather expert Roger Pielke Jr. explained how the UN helped shape the hysterical nonsense of a "climate emergency." The UN IPCC switched to "extreme scenarios" in its most recent report and thus "helped to create the climate apocalypse, a scary but imaginary future," Pielke explained in 2019.

"The decision by the IPCC to center its fifth assessment report on its most extreme scenario has been incredibly consequential. Thousands

---

"Useful Idiots"

A 2020 report from the UK-based Global Warming Policy Foundation found that "Beijing has coopted western environmental groups through a combination of sticks and carrots" and "western greens have effectively become mouthpieces for President Xi."

"Like all western NGOs, green groups are only allowed to operate in China so long as they bite their tongues and toe the party line. But Beijing is also able to influence their behaviour through funding bodies like Energy Foundation China, a US-based body that distributes money from American billionaire foundations," according to the report's author Patricia Adams.

"They praise the scale of Chinese ambition on climate change, while paying lipservice in criticizing China's massive coal expansion. Meanwhile, the greens turn a blind eye to the obvious; China does not honour its international agreements and has no intention of reducing fossil fuel consumption, quite the opposite. While the world has awakened to China's abuses, western environmentalists are silent," Adams wrote, adding, "China plays them as useful idiots."[64]

of academic studies of the future impacts of climate change followed the lead of the IPCC, and have emphasized the most extreme scenario as 'business as usual' which is often interpreted and promoted as where the world is heading," Pielke explained.

As Donna Laframboise, author of *The Delinquent Teenager Who Was Mistaken for the World's Top Climate Expert*, said, "The IPCC does not do science. The IPCC is a bureaucracy whose purpose is to write reports. The primary function of those reports is to pave the way for UN climate treaties."

She explained, "A set of facts need to be agreed-upon by all parties in advance, so that negotiators can start from the same page. IPCC reports get written by government-appointed scientists, according to predetermined guidelines. Portions of IPCC reports then get re-written by politicians, bureaucrats, and diplomats (in effect, this is an unofficial round of negotiating, in advance of the official negotiations that take place later). International treaties are political instruments."

Laframboise added, "The IPCC exists to make climate treaties possible. The 'science' involved has therefore been selected and massaged to serve a political purpose. Let's ditch the naiveté. How likely is it that experts appointed by governments that have spent billions fighting climate change, would conclude that man-made climate change doesn't exist?"[65]

Professor Ross McKitrick of the University of Guelph in Canada agreed. "The IPCC process I would describe it as it looks to me like when a magician does a card trick and you're watching him shuffle you think he is totally shuffling the cards and actually, he is not shuffling them at all,"

Big Hollywood Funds Climate "Science"

"My Foundation started supporting climate change work in 1989, when I donated a quarter of a million dollars to support the work of environmental scientist Dr. Michael Oppenheimer at EDF [Environmental Defense Fund]. Since then, I, and others have spent countless millions on this issue."

—Barbara Streisand[66]

McKitrick said in my *Climate Hustle* 2 film. "And he knows exactly where the card is that he needs to be on top at the end. The IPCC review process is like that. It looks like a really big formal review process with hundreds of people poring over the data. It's nothing like that."

But exposing who is dealing the decks to the UN IPCC is even more revealing.

Professor Pielke has detailed how billionaires Tom Steyer and Michael Bloomberg "corrupted climate science" and set the stage for extreme "climate emergency" claims.

"In November 2012, one month after stepping down from the hedge fund he led, Steyer gathered environmental leaders and Democratic party leaders around the kitchen table at his ranch in Pescadero, California. Among those in attendance were Bill McKibben, the founder of 350.org, and John Podesta, who had founded the Center for American Progress (CAP) in 2003 to promote progressive causes. Each of Steyer, Bloomberg and Paulson contributed $500,000 to the initial project, which was focused on 'making the climate threat feel real, immediate and potentially devastating to the business world,'" Pielke wrote.

"Climate Porn"

Pielke explained how climate science was corrupted in plain sight:

> The next step was to get the analyses of the project published in the scientific literature where they could influence subsequent research and serve as the basis for authoritative scientific reviews, such as the U.S. National Climate Assessment. For instance, a 2016 paper published in the prestigious journal *Science* from the Risky Business project introduced the erroneous notion of moving from one RCP [Representative Concentration Pathway—a UN IPCC measure of greenhouse gas–forcing] scenario to another via policy, comparing "business as usual" (RCP 8.5) and

"strongest emissions mitigation" (RCP 2.6). That paper has subsequently been cited 294 times in other academic studies, according to Google Scholar. Despite the obvious methodological flaw, the paper passed peer review and has received little or no criticism.[67]

Pielke explained, "I get why [RCP 8.5] is used so much. It offers a great way to get published (results!) and to generate news stories (climate porn!). But every study that uses it eats away a little bit at the credibility of climate science."[68]

Donna Laframboise called the UN high-emission warming scenario known as RCP8.5 a "ridiculous Climate Prophecy": "Incredibly, that 'major scientific report' (National Climate Assessment) takes RCP8.5 seriously. Calling it a 'core scenario,' page 6 of the report presents it as a realistic possibility rather than a farfetched hallucination," Laframboise said in 2020. "This means the report is

"Tech Tyranny"

"Google Promptly Vanishes Greenpeace Co-Founder Dr. Moore from the Enviro Group's History after Trump Tweeted Moore's Skeptical Climate Views," was the headline at Climate Depot on March 16, 2019.

"Oh my! Google has removed my photo and name from the 'Founders of @Greenpeace'. It was still there 2 days ago but now I am erased. Tech Tyranny!!" Patrick Moore wrote.[69]

Trump had tweeted Moore's statements that "the whole climate crisis is not only Fake News, it's Fake Science."

As Moore explained, "I was listed as a founder of Greenpeace on their own websites for 20 years after I left. They only disowned me when I came out in favor of nuclear energy."

He also pointed out, "Greenpeace admits they listed me as a founder for 35 years. Then they took me off the list, as if that makes me 'not a founder'. I was also named a founder in countless media reports. Once you are recognized as a founder it cannot be taken away for political purposes"[70]

> ### Apocalyptic Climate Faith
>
> "It's a faith that, I think, is a characteristic of the modern age; in which we feel good about feeling bad."
> —Mark Steyn, author of "A Disgrace to the Profession": The World's Scientists, in Their Own Words, on Michael E. Mann, His Hockey Stick, and Their Damage to Science [72]

junk. No matter how many federal agencies were involved in its creation. But the *New York Times* didn't tell readers that."[71]

Pielke is incredulous that this was allowed to happen. "Let me be clear about what is going on here. There is no hidden conspiracy, all of this is taking place in plain sight and in public. In fact, what is going on here is absolutely genius. We have a well-funded effort to fundamentally change how climate science is characterized in the academic literature, how that science is reported in the media, and ultimately how political discussions and policy options are shaped," Pielke wrote.

"The corruption of climate science has occurred because some of our most important institutions have let us down. The scientific peer-review process has failed to catch obvious methodological errors in research papers. Leading scientific assessments have ignored conflicts of interest and adopted flawed methods. The media has been selectively incurious as to the impact of big money on climate advocacy," he added.

Actress Barbra Streisand, who has bankrolled climate "science," helped popularize the phrase "climate emergency" back in 2005. As the actress explained, "Al Gore passionately stressed that our world no longer has a climate problem, we are in a climate emergency." Streisand told ABC's Diane Sawyer that we were "in a global warming emergency state."[73]

But any media outlet declaring a "climate emergency" only exposes itself as having no objectivity on this issue. We have reached a point where it is almost irrelevant what the mainstream media reports or claims about the climate issue. Everyone knows their perspective, and some agree with it, while others instinctively realize that they are shilling for climate alarm and the so-called "solutions."

"Devoted to Censorship"

"Facebook has turned its fact-checking in climate and energy over to a partisan group devoted to censorship, not scholarship. They don't fact-check whoppers by the alarmist side, just studies cited by skeptics....Climate Feedback's reasoning is typically superficial and often just plain wrong, and contradicts the data even as compiled by the UN climate change body....It was founded and funded by long-time climate alarmist Eric Michelman for the express purpose of promoting the climate crisis narrative. Indeed, Climate Feedback is tech mogul Michelman's third foray into shutting down a debate that he said, well before he created Climate Feedback, 'is settled.'"
—climate statistician Caleb Rossiter, the executive director of the CO2 Coalition, in testimony to a 2020 hearing of the U.S. Senate Committee on Commerce, Science, and Transportation on social media censorship of climate skeptics[74]

In fact the "climate emergency" declarations spreading throughout news outlets, the corporate world, and academia backfired; they were too much even for many climate activists.

"I Apologize for the Climate Scare"

Prominent climate activist Michael Shellenberger officially recanted his climate alarmism in 2020. "On Behalf of Environmentalists, I Apologize for the Climate Scare," Shellenberger proclaimed. *Time* magazine's former "Hero of the Environment" said, "On behalf of environmentalists everywhere, I would like to formally apologize for the climate scare we created over the last 30 years. Climate change is happening. It's just not the end of the world. It's not even our most serious environmental problem."

Shellengerger admitted, "I may seem like a strange person to be saying all of this. I have been a climate activist for 20 years and an environmentalist for 30. But as an energy expert asked by Congress to provide objective expert testimony, and invited by the Intergovernmental

"Gaslighted the World"
"It isn't shortage of facts or evidence which has caused climate change skeptics to lose the argument. It's quite simply that the mainstream media—led by the BBC—has become such an uncritical propaganda mouthpiece for the Climate Industrial Complex that it has effectively gaslighted the world into believing that there was never an argument in the first place. That is, the skeptical case against 'man-made climate change', though overwhelming, is aired almost nowhere these days outside the fringes of the internet."
—Breitbart's James Delingpole in 2020 [75]

Panel on Climate Change (IPCC) to serve as Expert Reviewer of its next Assessment Report, I feel an obligation to apologize for how badly we environmentalists have misled the public."

He added, "Some people will, when they read this imagine that I'm some right-wing anti-environmentalist. I'm not. At 17, I lived in Nicaragua to show solidarity with the Sandinista socialist revolution.... I became an environmentalist at 16 when I threw a fundraiser for Rainforest Action Network."

But as an honest environmentalist, he had to blow the whistle: "Scientific institutions including WHO and IPCC have undermined their credibility through the repeated politicization of science. Until last year, I mostly avoided speaking out against the climate scare. Partly that's because I was embarrassed. After all, I am as guilty of alarmism as any other environmentalist." Shellenberger confessed, "I remained quiet about the climate disinformation campaign because I was afraid of losing friends and funding. But then, last year, things spiraled out of control. Alexandria Ocasio-Cortez said 'The world is going to end in twelve years if we don't address climate change.' Britain's most high-profile environmental group claimed 'Climate Change Kills Children.'" [76]

Climate skeptics welcomed Shellenbergers's apology with open arms, featuring him on their blogs and in interviews. But Shellenberger's old environmental allies were not happy with his climate conversion; he faced social media censorship and the cancel culture.

My response to Shellenberger was thoughtful and considerate.

"Yes, we accept your apology. Thank you, Michael! But now that prominent climate activists are apologizing and reversing their views, it is time we frankly discuss reparations for the decades of fear, deceit, predictions of doom, poor public policy choices, endless tipping points and tolerating Greta Thunberg forced into our children's lives by the media," I said.

"How about a paycheck to all the falsely slandered climate skeptics from the well-funded climate establishment as a first step toward healing the climate divisions caused by the lies of Al Gore, the UN, academia and the media?" I asked.

"It's also time to:

> **"DROP DEAD"**
>
> I received this hate email from an environmental activist titled "FUCK YOU! DROP DEAD MOTHER-FUCKER!!" following my congressional climate testimony in 2019:
>
> "Whereas you appeared on public at the recent House Natural Resources Committee, and
>
> Whereas you said things that indicate your guilty of Crimes Against Humanity and Ecocide, You are hereby official and irrevocably CURSED:
>
> May you live long enough that your children and grandchildren likewise see the end of ALL LIFE on Planet Earth,
>
> May they, when they understand what they YOU have done,
>
> Ask you, 'How the FUCK could you have done this to us??!!??'
>
> And may they then kill you!
>
> May you die by their hand!
>
> Looking them in the eye as THEY end your miserable life!!!!!"[77]

- Abolish the UN IPCC climate panel. This is long overdue.
- Stop endless taxpayer funding to climate modeling studies that can gin up scare with scant data many years into the future.
- End all climate conferences, especially those in exotic locales that require mega 'carbon footprints' to attend.

- Have the federal government give a climate reparations tax credit to all Americans who are struggling to pay their energy bills due to horrid climate regulations that were based on bad scientific claims.
- Cancel all talk of the Green New Deal & various 'conservative' GOP proposals that commit to 'zero emissions' someday in the future.
- It's time for Al Gore to begin to dismantle his vast real estate empire and cut checks to lower-income American's struggling to pay their energy bills due to his policy advocacy based on the climate con."[78]

"A Proposal to Remake Civilization"

But no climate "reparations" from the activists are likely to ever be paid, because in the end it's not about the science. "Bottom line: the climate activists are decisively winning. The science no longer matters in the public policy debate," wrote Larry Kummer, editor of the FabiusMaximus website, in 2020. "Activists have moved beyond it and the major science institutions no longer defend it against the activists' exaggerations and misrepresentations."

According to Kummer, "RCP8.5 [the UN IPPC's high-emission warming scenario]—and more broadly, climate science—no longer matter. The debate has moved beyond science to the exaggerations of the Climate Emergency and the fictions of the Extinction Rebellion. It is all politics and mass hysteria." He added, "Meanwhile, skeptics are talking to themselves, like characters in Alice in Wonderland—vocal but effectively locked out of the news media."[79]

That is perhaps the most accurate summation of the Green New Deal and its toxic politics: "Climate science—no longer matter[s]."

As I detailed in chapter 1, architects of the Green New Deal admit that it is NOT about the climate—including a former campaign aide to GND-sponsor Alexandra Ocasio-Cortez who revealed that it is really "a proposal to redistribute wealth and power,"[80] and her current chief of staff, who has confessed that "we really think of it as a how-do-you-change-the-entire-economy thing"—and that "it wasn't originally a climate thing at all."[81]

The climate campaigners have been openly admitting for decades that "climate change" is not about the science. In 1993, former U.S. senator Timothy Wirth revealed, "We've got to ride the global warming issue. Even if the theory of global warming is wrong, we will be doing the right thing, in terms of economic policy and environmental policy."[83] And in 2013, Connie Hedegaard, then Europe's climate-action commissioner, said, "Let's say that science, some decades from now, said 'we were wrong, it was not about climate,' would it not in any case have been good to do many of things you have to do in order to combat climate change?"[84]

Vincenzo Balzani, professor emeritus at the University of Bologna, has said that the EU's climate efforts are nothing less than "a proposal to remake civilization."[85]

Simon Bramwell, the co-founder of Extinction Rebellion, wants to go even further. According to him, climate change is about "sabotage" to "take down" civilization. Branwell urges, "We've also got to not only take down civilization but shepherd ourselves and incoming

RICO Investigations

In 2015, twenty climate activist scientists including UN IPCC lead author Kevin Trenberth wrote to President Obama: "We appreciate that you are making aggressive and imaginative use of the limited tools available to you in the face of a recalcitrant Congress. One additional tool—recently proposed by Senator Sheldon Whitehouse—is a RICO (Racketeer Influenced and Corrupt Organizations Act) investigation of corporations and other organizations that have knowingly deceived the American people about the risks of climate change, as a means to forestall America's response to climate change. We strongly endorse Senator Whitehouse's call for a RICO investigation."[82]

generations back into a state of wilding as it were, into like a feral consciousness that is also one of the biggest tasks remaining to us."[86]

And if you raise objections to any of this, you may end up in jail, according to an official UN publication.

The UNESCO (UN Educational, Scientific and Cultural Organization) magazine in 2019 included an article titled "Climate Crimes Must Be Brought to Justice," written by Professor Catriona McKinnon of the University of Exeter.

"The damage that climate deniers do is heinous, and they have no excuses. The time has come to prosecute them," McKinnon wrote. "Climate denial has seriously impeded aggressive mitigation efforts that could have averted our present climate emergency. It has magnified the risk that humanity locks in to catastrophic global climate change. The people in positions of authority in states, or industrial groups whose lies have put us and our descendants in peril, should be held accountable." McKinnon argued that climate denial is "intentional or reckless conduct fit to bring about the extinction of humanity" and that leading climate deniers "should go to trial" at the International Criminal Court.[87]

Other climate activists have echoed these calls to jail climate skeptics. Environmental activist Robert F. Kennedy Jr. told me during an interview in 2014, "I wish there were a law you could punish them with. I don't think there is a law that you can punish those politicians under." Kennedy added, "Do I think the Koch Brothers are treasonous, yes I do.... Do I think they should be in jail, I think they should be enjoying three hots and a cot at the Hague with all the other war criminals."[88]

In 2016 I asked Bill Nye "the Science Guy" about Kennedy's desire to jail skeptics as "war criminals" and Nye replied, "Well, we'll see what happens. Was it appropriate to jail the guys from ENRON?"

Nye's goal is to intimidate dissenting scientists. "That there is a chilling effect on scientists who are in denial—who are in extreme doubt about climate change—I think is good...they are keeping us from getting back to work. They are holding us back," he explained to me.

Robert F. Kennedy Jr. declaring he wants to jail climate skeptics during my interview with him in my 2016 film *Climate Hustle*

Bill Nye pondering the possibility of imprisoning climate skeptics in my 2020 film *Climate Hustle 2*

Nye added, "For me as a taxpayer and voter—the introduction of this extreme doubt about climate change is affecting my quality of life as a public citizen."[89]

As former Czech president Vaclav Klaus told me, the climate agenda is about power. "They want to dictate it, control, regulate, mastermind from above," Klaus said. "This is the way to the end of freedom. This is the way to a brave new world of the future. The brave new world of dictatorship and totalitarianism."[90]

CHAPTER 15

The Ultimate Achievement of the Political Left

S aving the world can be exhausting—and repetitive. In 2015, the
climate establishment cheered as the much-hailed "historic" UN
Paris climate pact was agreed upon in France. But just a few years later,
the world needs saving again. The *Washington Post* reported, "The surge
of optimism that came with Paris has faded," adding that the pact was
"too weak to begin with."[1] The United Nations admitted that the Paris
Agreement did not "save" the planet; it was "not enough" to prevent a
climate change catastrophe. Despite being praised by former vice president Al Gore, former secretary of state John Kerry, and many others, the
UN is now demanding even more climate "action."

The UN IPCC has conceded that cutting CO_2 emissions from transportation and energy was "not enough" and that more saving of the
Earth—along with, naturally more jurisdiction and more power for the
UN—is necessary. "Attempts to solve the climate crisis by cutting carbon
emissions from only cars, factories and power plants are doomed to
failure, scientists will warn this week," the UK *Guardian* reported in
August of 2019.[2]

Former UN IPCC chair Robert Watson has said the Paris Pact was a failure. "Simply, the pledges are far too little, too late," claimed Watson.[3]

Former secretary of state John Kerry, who is serving as the Biden administration's Special Presidential Envoy for Climate, admitted the futility of the UN Paris Pact in December 2020.

"It's not enough," Kerry said. "Even if we did everything that was promised in Paris, the earth's temperature's still going to rise to 3.7 degrees Fahrenheit [*sic*]," Kerry continued. "But because we're not doing anything, we're actually heading to [a rise of] 4.1, 4.5 degrees today. It's beyond catastrophic."[4]

The reality is that these so-called climate "solutions" like the UN Paris Pact, cap-and-trade and carbon (dioxide) taxes, and the Green New Deal will never be enough for climate campaigners. The UN's former IPCC chair Rajendra Pachauri even admitted in 2009 that their previous "historic" and Earth-saving pact, the Kyoto Protocol "did not work" either.[5]

So the UN is now on record admitting both of their recent climate pacts failed to save the climate. And this is despite the fact that every UN climate summit has been hailed as "last chance" to stop "global warming" before it's too late. Previous "last chance" deadlines turned out to be—well—not the "last" chance after all.[6]

At the time, the 2015 Paris Agreement was supposed to have saved the planet and "solved" global warming. Here is a small sampling of praise for the "historic" UN climate pact:

- **The UK *Guardian*:** "World leaders hail Paris climate deal as 'major leap for mankind.'"[7]
- **UN secretary-general Ban Ki-moon** boasted, "History will remember this day," to thunderous applause. He added, "The Paris agreement on climate change is a monumental success for the planet and its people."

- **Al Gore:** "Years from now, our grandchildren will reflect on humanity's moral courage to solve the climate crisis and they will look to December 12, 2015, as the day when the community of nations finally made the decision to act."
- **The *Washington Post*:** "Cheers echoed up and down the tent city where thousands of journalists, activists and business leaders awaited news of the deal, which was sealed during the final 48 hours of nearly non-stop talks."
- **President Obama** hailed the agreement as a "turning point for the world," adding, "We came together around the strong agreement the world needed. Together we've shown what's possible when the world stands as one."
- **Secretary of State John F. Kerry:** "This is a tremendous victory for all of our citizens—not for any one country or bloc, but a victory for all of the planet, and for future generations."
- **British prime minister David Cameron:** "We've secured our planet for many, many generations to come—and there is nothing more important than that."[8]
- **French foreign minister Laurent Fabius:** "On 12 December 2015, we can have a historic day, a major date to go down in the history of mankind. The date can become a message of life."[9]

Newsweek ran an opinion piece under the gushing headline, "The Paris Agreement Will Save Our Lives."[10]

Back in 2015, I was at the "historic" UN climate summit in Paris when they finally "solved" climate change. I premiered my film *Climate Hustle* during the summit, and green groups hung "wanted" posters of me as a "climate criminal" and plastered them around the streets of Paris.

Having attended UN summits annually for nearly two decades, I was not buying any of their celebratory claims about the Paris Pact "saving" squat. "Does this mean we never have to hear about 'solving' global warming again!?" I asked after the Paris summit ended in agreement in December 2015.[11]

"Does this mean we can halt the endless supply of federal tax dollars funding 'climate change' studies? Does this mean we can stop worrying about 'global warming's' ability to end civilization and cause wars, and increase prostitution, bar room brawls, rape, airline turbulence, etc.? Can we finally move on to other issues? I spent the last week in Paris marveling at how so many believe a form of modern witchcraft: That a UN agreement or EPA climate regulations can alter Earth's temperature and the level of storms. But now I realize that if they truly believe the UN has solved 'climate change' even skeptics should rejoice! Now that the UN treaty has 'solved' global warming, can we all just move on to something else?"[13]

This book has been about "the something else" that we have moved on to. It is called the Green New Deal. But even though the GND is newer and has a new spokeswoman, the plan shares the same problems with the UN Paris agreement.

Even if we faced a climate catastrophe, the UN Paris Pact, the Green New Deal, EPA regulations, carbon (dioxide) taxes, cap-and-trade, unplugging your charger, and driving an electric car, would not have any detectable impact on the climate—even if the UN CO_2 science were correct (it's not). All of these measures are not actually about the climate—they are about power, politics, ideology, wealth redistribution and symbolism.

The scientifically meaningless Green New Deal will not impact the global climate in any detectable ways, but it will have huge human impacts measured in economic, sovereignty, and energy harm.[14]

"Somewhere between a Farce and a Fraud"

"The Paris Accord was somewhere between a farce and a fraud....You don't even have to mention greenhouse gases in your commitment if you don't want to. You send in any piece of paper you want, we're going to staple them all together, and we're going to call that the Paris Accord. Everyone sent in a piece of paper. And they stapled it together, and held it up, and said, 'This is amazing!'

"My favorite was Pakistan whose pledge was, 'to reach a peak at some point after which to begin reducing emissions....China promised they will continue increasing their emissions for some time to come....And so, you can staple those together and say we now have a global agreement, but what you have is an agreement to do nothing....The one country that showed up in Paris with a very costly, ambitious target was the United States. So, President Obama took all the zero commitments from everybody else but then threw in a really expensive one for us."

—**Oren Cass** of *City Journal*[15]

And so preventing the pointless and harmful Green New Deal and climate treaties from being imposed on a nation is the right thing to do. As former Thatcher science advisor Lord Christopher Monckton has said, "Climate change is a non-problem. The right answer to a non-problem is to have the courage to do nothing."[16]

But...in political Washington, advocating doing "nothing" about a huge media-hyped issue while an activism-fueled climate "crisis" chorus pounds the airwaves daily linking every possible weather event to "climate change" is hard for many politicians to do. Which means that many on the Republican side of the aisle are highly susceptible to wanting to do "something" about climate change.

"The greatest danger we face right now with the Green New Deal is very simply the Republican Party coming up with the Green New Deal–lite," I testified in 2019 before Congress at a Green New Deal hearing. "We need to oppose it and oppose it firmly. We don't need to come up with the lite version of the plan."

"Doing nothing" on climate is actually an apt description for the climate activists and the UN Paris Agreement, past cap-and-trade bills, carbon taxes, and the Green New Deal. Even Obama's EPA admitted that the Waxman-Markey cap-and trade bill will not have a measurable impact on global CO_2 levels, let alone any measurable or detectable impact on global temperatures. The man-made climate fear promoters have been promoting a do-nothing approach to climate change since the movement's launch by consistently pushing purely symbolic "solutions" to global warming.

Here's a simple question: Would you purchase fire insurance on your home that had a huge upfront premium for virtually no payout if you home burned down? If you answered YES to such an "insurance" policy, then the Green New Deal is an offer you can't refuse. The sponsors of the Green New Deal ought to be able to show that its benefits outweigh its costs—or at least that it has benefits! How much does the proposed new deal allegedly reduce temperature and storminess? Zero!

If we did actually face a man-made climate catastrophe and we were depending on the "solutions" presented in the Green New Deal, we would all be DOOMED!

But politics abhors a vacuum, some are suggesting that it is time to give Republicans and weary more conservative Democrats an alternative to the Green New Deal.

Utah senator Mitt Romney has been "looking at" carbon (dioxide) taxes as a GOP alternative to the Green New Deal. "I would very much like to see us reduce our carbon emissions globally, and we'll see if this might help," Romney said in 2019.[17]

A small number of GOP members of the House are also seeking political cover on climate and pushing a sort of Green New Deal–lite version. Republican representative Matt Gaetz of Florida is supporting a different "Green Real Deal," and GOP senator Lamar Alexander of Tennessee supported a "Manhattan Project" on climate and energy that would force Americans to move to more costly and unreliable alternative energy sources. South Carolina Republican senator Lindsey Graham, who has a long history of waffling on climate, has hinted that he is on board with "solutions" for climate change. "Climate change is real, the science is sound and the solutions are available," Graham said.[18]

GOP House minority leader Kevin McCarthy of California introduced a bill "to put the GOP on the map on climate" in order to appeal to the young voters that many polls show are more woke on climate change.[19]

Climate skeptic Steve Milloy of JunkScience.com lamented that some in the GOP are in "appeasement" mode on climate. "There are many who would gladly try to appease climate alarmists by throwing around limited amounts of taxpayer dollars on various boondoggles to make it look like they take the matter seriously."[20]

Some GOP members of Congress are pushing carbon dioxide capture and storage and promoting "clean" energy, but as of 2020, the plans do not include targets to reduce emission. Geologist Viv Forbes calls it the "carbon capture con." Forbes wrote, "The idea is to capture carbon dioxide from power stations and cement plants, separate it, compress it, pump it long distances and force it underground, hoping it will never escape."

Forbes added, "Carbon-capture-and-storage tops the list of silly schemes to reduce man-made global warming.... Regulating atmospheric carbon dioxide is best left to the oceans and plants— they have been doing it successfully for millennia. The only certain outcome from CCS is more expensive electricity and a waste of energy resources to do all the separation, compressing and pumping."[21]

Former president Trump and some GOP legislators even promoted the planting of one trillion trees by 2030 as part of their environmental plan. The *New York Times* explained that Trump is all in on tree planting. "The idea of planting one trillion trees had one enormous political advantage: It was practically sacrifice-free, no war on coal, no transition from fossil fuels, no energy conservation or investment in renewable sources of power that Mr. Trump loves to mock," the *New York Times* reported in 2020. "Trump never uttered the phrase 'climate change' in his [tree planting] pledge. He described it instead as a plan 'to protect the environment.'"[22]

Chopping Down Tree Claims

Tree planting is not without controversy however.

"Settled Science?! Trees Both Cause & Solve 'Global Warming'?!" read the headline at my Climate Depot website. "Plant or Not Plant Trees to Fight 'Global Warming'?! It's All So Confusing!"

There are many conflicting scientific studies on the climate impact of planting trees. Here is a small sampling of opposite claims about trees:

- "Planting a Trillion Trees Could Be the 'Most Effective Solution' to Climate Change, Study Says" —CBS News, 2019[23]
- "Why Planting Some Trees Could Make Global Warming Worse" —*Christian Science Monitor*, 2016[24]
- "Want to Fight Climate Change? Plant 1 Trillion Trees" —Live Science, 2019[25]
- "We Can't Just Plant Billions of Trees to Stop Climate Change" —*Discover* magazine, 2019[26]
- "Best Way to Fight Climate Change? Plant a Trillion Trees" —AP, 2019[27]
- "Planting Trees Will Not Slow Global Warming" —Climate News Network, 2019[28]
- "Climate Change: Planting New Forests 'Can Do More Harm Than Good" —BBC, 2020[29]

And the tree-planting craze may face other problems as well. "Where are one trillion more trees going to be planted?" the Competitive Enterprise Institute's Myron Ebell asked. "There are major areas of deforestation globally, but quite a bit of that land is now used for farming. Cities occupy other deforested areas. In this country, the problem in our National Forests is far too many thickets of small trees."

The Way Forward

The biggest issue that Republicans who want to appear nice and green on climate have is the language that they use. They need to stop claiming climate is a "problem" or that climate change needs a "solution." Words matter.

They can offer massive spending increases and push technology to attempt to reduce emissions, but they should not concede to the narrative that climate is a "problem." Having worked in Washington for nearly thirty years, there are times when I frankly couldn't care less how much increased funding some in the GOP want to give to boondoggles like carbon capture. I understand that spending money in D.C. is bipartisan and there are very few in Congress who actually care how much money the government spends.

The GOP climate "solutions" gang obviously thinks they need some kind of cover to avoid being labeled a climate "denier." Many Republicans, conservatives, and libertarians loathe being seen as "evil deniers," and they are prepared to avoid that label however they can. In town hall meetings and the social circles around the Washington establishment, they want to fit in, not to be seen as toxic climate deniers who are against "the science." Their spouses or kids may be pressuring them not to be "deniers."

If they appear "reasonable" on climate they're going to be better liked.

My advice to those skittish Republicans is use phrases like "the way forward" or "regardless of your views on climate, our plan is environmentally friendly." But they must avoid claiming that tree planting "solves" climate. If they continue to fall into that claptrap, they are engaging in the same unscientific nonsense the Left does when it claims UN treaties and the Green New Deal "solve" climate change. If the climate-woke Republicans continue to talk of "solving" the climate "problem" it makes them look like they are capitulating, and they appear like nothing more than pandering politicians.

The way forward is to promote free-market environmental policies that make environmental sense regardless of your view on climate change. If some GOP politicians need political cover on climate change, they will inevitably try to spend all the money they can on environmentally friendly legislation, but they should be persuaded to at least not fall into accepting the alarmist narrative.

Energy advocates need to be unapologetic about the moral case for cheap abundant fossil fuels. They need to follow Trump's example of praising the benefits of U.S. energy dominance. They need to be relentless in pointing out the inane anti-energy views of Representative Alexandria Ocasio-Cortez on energy.

AOC told Shell Oil Company in 2020, "I'm willing to hold you accountable for lying about climate change for 30 years when you secretly knew the entire time that fossil fuels emissions would destroy our planet."[30] Setting aside the obvious fact that AOC is wrong about climate change, she is also missing the great benefits of fossil fuels. Shouldn't AOC hold Shell Oil and other fossil fuel companies responsible for helping bring energy and development that has massively improve the lot of human beings? Shouldn't she give them credit for a century-plus of poverty reduction, longer life spans, reduced child mortality, and much improved resilience to extreme weather events?

James Taylor, the president of the Heartland Institute put it best when he turned the tables on the advocates of the Green New Deal and declared, "The world owes U.S. climate reparations."

As Taylor wrote, "The poorest people and the poorest nations of the world have disproportionately enjoyed the benefits of conventional energy use, more atmospheric carbon dioxide, and a warming climate....Global crop yields are up, climate-related deaths are down, extreme weather events are less frequent and severe, and the Earth is a greener place. If anybody owes anybody else climate reparations, nations that have been enjoying these benefits should be sending money to the nation whose carbon dioxide emissions have made much of this possible."[31]

The climate activists continue to openly use climate scare tactics to achieve their ends. And in order to achieve those ends, they have to hype and scare. It's been a very effective strategy; they've bullied

Republican politicians, who should know better, into at least submissiveness and silence.

The relentless attacks on former Trump EPA chief Scott Pruitt, who resigned in 2018, further silenced any potential climate skeptics from speaking out in D.C. Pruitt was singled out by the media, bureaucracy, and activists with daily attacks on his finances, ethics, and policies. And all because of his outspoken skeptical views on climate science.[32]

Young Republican groups have sprung up in recent years advocating climate "action" and carbon taxes to stop climate change. These groups argue that young people are very concerned about climate and therefore the GOP should offer "solutions."

But instead of capitulating to bad policy, bad science, and bad politics, it is time to engage them and reveal to them that what they think they know just ain't so. Republicans are naive to think that the climate activist millennial youth who are skipping school and are all excited about the Green New Deal will become excited if the GOP offers some sort of GND-lite or promotes tree planting.

Opportunity Knocks

The Trump administration was set to launch a presidential climate committee to reexamine the science behind the UN IPCC climate claims. It would have released the first non-consensus federal climate change report with the seal of the U.S. government on it since the UN climate panel's inception in 1988.

Princeton physicist Will Happer joined the Trump administration with the explicit intent of setting up this commission. Happer, who has conducted hundreds of peer-reviewed studies, is considered the foremost expert on the greenhouse effect and its impacts. Former Harvard physicist Lubos Motl explained, "When it comes to the main physical effect that is supposed to drive 'climate change,' Happer's not only an expert. He's one of the world's leading experts."

Reports are that Trump personally okayed the skeptical climate committee, but that the president's staff delayed and delayed until it was too close to the 2020 presidential elections. The president's climate committee was halted, and Happer left the administration in 2019.

This will go down as one of the biggest missed opportunities to challenge Al Gore, the UN IPCC, and the scare-mongering climate "science" establishment. Without this federal challenge led by Dr. Happer, the best opportunity may have been lost for a federal pushback to the absolute scientific crap coming from reports like the federal National Climate Assessment.

Presidential advisors such as Larry Kudlow and science advisor Kelvin Droegemeier, like many officials in Washington, apparently viewed a fight over climate science as a quagmire like the Vietnam War—best avoided at all costs. As for Droegemeier, he proved to be a wasted pick for Trump. Droegemeier is a science bureaucrat who is best known for dodging any opportunity to go on the record with his views on climate change. He clearly does not want to be associated with any challenge to the so-called climate "consensus."

I suspect that none of Trump's cabinet heads would have publicly supported a presidential climate committee, as they appeared to believe that it would not be politically beneficial even to contemplate a public challenge to climate claims. Even if the Trump administration had a second term, the same forces would still have mitigated against any real challenge to the climate "science." The well-funded climate establishment has successfully ensured that anyone questioning any aspect of the "global warming" narrative will face a barrage of ridicule, insults, and bad media. Other than Trump himself, the only cabinet member willing to push back on the climate change scientific claims was former EPA chief Scott Pruitt. The message was clear: challenge the climate narrative, and you will be punished.

President Trump's otherwise awesome "climate legacy"—EPA reforms, Paris Agreement withdrawal, pro-energy policies, and so forth—will almost all be reversed in the first few months or years of the Joe Biden–Kamala Harris administration.

For the Trump administration to have had a lasting legacy on climate change would have required more than just cutting regulations and reversing Obama's climate-related executive orders and EPA policies. Regulations can be reimposed quickly. But a lasting legacy on climate would have included redirecting climate research money to scientists who dissented from the UN IPCC view, defunding the UN IPCC, and withdrawing from the UN climate process. A lasting climate legacy would have required challenging the grossly distorted National Climate Assessment and the United Nations reports. Staffing the federal agencies with scientists who were not beholden to the "consensus" climate view would have resulted in a long-term legacy. The Trump administration never even challenged the CO2 endangerment finding that the Obama administration implemented, regulating carbon dioxide as a pollutant.

In many respects, the Trump administration was an historic opportunity lost for climate skeptics. Having the most climate skeptical U.S. president's administration remain essentially silent on the climate claims emanating from academia, the media, and the United Nations set back the cause of climate skepticism. Climate activists could credibly point out that even the Trump administration never challenged the climate consensus claims—therefore they must be valid.

And without a scientific challenge, they are fighting the Green New Deal with a major handicap. If they don't go after the scientific premises, the GOP is left arguing that the Green New Deal is too expensive.

Still, it needs to be emphasized that President Trump deserves the highest praise for everything he did to restore a rational climate and energy policy in America. And it is unlikely that any future Republican president will attempt to do half of what Trump accomplished on the policy side of climate in the face of massive institutional and media opposition. He stood against the entire climate-industrial complex in the media, government, UN, academia, and political Washington.

With the possible exception of Ronald Reagan, no previous GOP president or nominee could have accomplished what Trump did in taking the heat and having the courage to push back hard on the climate agenda. George H. W. Bush went to the UN Rio Earth Summit and got us into this whole UN climate process. GOP nominee Bob Dole was way too establishment to ever take on the environmentalists. George W. Bush rubber-stamped, funded, and publicly accepted the UN climate claims. GOP presidential nominees John McCain and Mitt Romney were warmists through and through and never would have opposed the climate establishment.

"Put Them in Jail"

Joe Biden has said that fossil fuel executives should be jailed. "We have to set sort of guide rails down now, so between the years 2021 and 2030, it's irreversible—the path we set ourselves on. And one of which is doing away with any substance for fossil fuels—number one.

"Number two, holding them liable for what they have done...when they don't want to deliver, put them in jail. I'm not joking about this," Biden said to applause at a town hall in Peterborough, New Hampshire, in 2019.

"If we don't stop using fossil fuels—" an audience member began to ask, but Biden interrupted, "We're all dead."[34]

"Before Trump, Republicans were losing the energy war by not fighting it," author Rupert Darwall has noted. "As [Trump] sees it, cheap energy powers blue-collar prosperity. It's not surprising, then, that until the Trump presidency, the opponents of cheap energy had the upper hand."[33]

With President Biden in office, the Green New Deal will be a top legislative priority. The Joe Biden–Kamala Harris administration is all in on climate absurdity, promoting "solutions" like zero-emission goals and the Green New Deal. Their policies are going to wreak havoc on the American economy, which is already ravaged by COVID lockdowns and restrictions. "None of what the Joe Biden green team has in store will improve the environment; it will only make your life poorer and harder," aptly noted Steve Milloy of JunkScience.com.[35]

Under Biden and Harris, expect the COVID lockdowns to morph into climate lockdowns. Expect the groundwork established by the COVID lockdowns to be used to declare a "public health crisis" for climate change in order to trample all manner of freedoms. For societal control, planned recessions, central planning, and stifling fossil fuels, COVID lockdowns have proved way more effective than the climate scare.

This is a political and economic movement. It has nothing to do with the actual climate. As we have seen throughout this book, the "climate" activists are deliberately terrifying people, including children, to push through planned recessions, lockdowns, and a host of other destructive policies that they really want for other reasons. And as we've seen in Europe, where they are the most advanced in terms of implementing these policies, they're utterly failing.

Even if you believe we face a "climate crisis," we would all be doomed if we had to rely on the United Nations and EPA to save us

COVID Lockdowns to Climate Lockdowns?

"Progressive environmentalists" urged "President-elect Joe Biden to go beyond naming a climate czar and declare an environmental national emergency," reported Bloomberg News in December 2020.

"Invoking a climate emergency could give Biden the authority to circumvent Congress and fund clean energy projects, shut down crude oil exports, suspend offshore drilling and curtail the movement of fossil fuels on pipelines, trains, and ships, according to a research note by consulting firm ClearView Energy Partners. 'The president's powers to address climate change through an emergency are very, very large,' said Kassie Siegel, an attorney with the environmental group Center for Biological Diversity, which is lobbying Biden's team to act. 'This is No. 1 on the list of things the Biden administration should do.'"[36]

through climate taxes. We need an innovative free market approach to environmental policy. As statistician Bjørn Lomborg noted, "For the most important environmental issues, economic growth has solved problems, not created them." He explained, "The cleanest places are not the poorest countries, but the richer economies that have cleaned up their act. As societies become richer, individuals can afford to stop worrying about food and sanitation, and to start worrying about the environment."[37]

Whether it's the U.S. government or the UN with the Green New Deal or the UN with a global climate pact, we cannot regulate and tax our way to a better climate. A resurrection of a Soviet-like system of massive regulations on every aspect of our lives will crush America. As I have extensively demonstrated, climate "solutions" will do nothing for the climate, but they will do severe damage to the economy and people's lives, and greatly benefit nations like China. The sooner we can eliminate the Green New Deal and UN climate and energy policies, the better off energy distribution and the developing world's poor will be. The world needs energy initiatives, not anti-energy initiatives, and as we go forward, the less we think about Green New Deals, the better for both energy and the Earth.

Scientific truth and reality-based economics are always "dangerous" to climate charlatans peddling their coming climate catastrophe. It used to be that people who stood on street corners warning of the end times were recognized as nutcases. Now, with the climate "emergency" and the proposed "solutions" to it in Green New Deal, those same apocalyptic predictions are coming from the "scientific community" and the halls of Congress.

The way forward is already clear. Improving technologies, expanding energy access, and growing economies in the developing world are already improving the environment in the United States and across the globe more than any Green New Deal, UN treaty, or carbon (dioxide) taxes ever conceivably could.

Let's expose this dangerous charade. The Green New Deal is not green. It's not new. And it's not a good deal for America.

Acknowledgments

This book was greatly aided by the tireless efforts of a band of climate-skeptical bloggers, public policy experts, and vocal scientists who have devoted themselves to revealing the truth behind the climate claims put forth by the UN, Al Gore, the Green New Deal, the media, and academia. Here is a partial honor roll of those whose work was invaluable in writing this book:

Kevin Dayaratna
Tom Nelson
Anthony Watts
Tony Heller
Craig Rucker
Paul Driessen
Pierre Gosselin
Joanne Nova
Tim Ball
William Briggs
Tom Harris
Caleb Rossiter
James Taylor
Steve Milloy
Will Happer
Paul Homewood
Benny Peiser
David Legates
Donna Laframboise
Willie Soon
John Stossel
Joe Bastardi

Patrick Moore
Judith Curry
Lubos Motl
Alex Epstein
James Delingpole
Christopher Monckton
Roger Pielke Jr.
Roy Spencer

Notes

Chapter 1: The Green Raw Deal

1. Tom Elliott, "Ocasio-Cortez on Millennials: 'We're Like the World Is Going to End in 12 Years If We Don't Address Climate Change,'" Grabien News, January 21, 2019, https://news.grabien.com/story-ocasio-cortez-millennials-were-world-going-end-12-years-if-w.

2. Nicolas Loras, "Green New Deal Would Barely Change Earth's Temperature. Here are the Facts," The Heritage Foundation, February 8, 2019, https://www.heritage.org/energy-economics/commentary/green-new-deal-would-barely-change-earths-temperature-here-are-the; "What Build Back Better and the Green New Deal Propose," BOSS Magazine, n.d., https://thebossmagazine.com/build-back-better/; Robert Bradley Jr., "'Green New Deal FAQ,' (the Infamous AOC Post for Posterity)," MasterResource, April 10, 2019, https://www.masterresource.org/green-new-deal/green-new-deal-faq-the-infamous-aco-post-for-posterity/; Nate Madden, "'Free' College? Green New Deal? Socialist Health Care? Study Finds It's Impossible to Pay for Them by Only Squeezing the Rich," The Blaze, August 16, 2019, https://www.theblaze.com/conservative-review/free-college-green-new-deal-socialist-health-care-study-finds-impossible-pay-squeezing-rich; Rachel Gold, "Gold '19: Earth's History Shows We Need a Green New Deal," *The Brown Daily Herald*, April 24, 2019, https://www.browndaily herald.com/2019/04/24/gold-19-earths-history-shows-need-green-new-deal/.

3. Loras, "Green New Deal."

4. Douglas Holtz-Eakin, Dan Bosch, Ben Gitis, Dan Goldbeck, and Philip Rossetti, "The Green New Deal: Scope, Scale, and Implications," American Action Forum, February 25, 2019, https://www.americanaction forum.org/research/the-green-new-deal-scope-scale-and-implications/.

5. Klaus Schwab, "Now Is the Time for a 'Great Reset,'" World Economic Forum, June 3, 2020, https://www.weforum.org/agenda/2020/06/now-is-the-time-for-a-great-reset/.

6. Marc Morano, "AOC's Chief-of-Staff Admits Green New Deal about Implementing Socialism—'It Wasn't Originally a Climate

Thing at All'—It's a 'Change-the-Entire-Economy Thing,'" Climate Depot, July 12, 2019, https://www.climatedepot. com/2019/07/12/aocs-chief-of-staff-admits-green-new-deal-about-implementing-socialism-it-wasnt-originally-a-climate-thing-at-all-its-a-change-the-entire-economy-thing/.

7. David Montgomery, "AOC's Chief of Change," *Washington Post Magazine,* July 10, 2019, https://www.washingtonpost.com/news/ magazine/wp/2019/07/10/feature/ how-saikat-chakrabarti-became-aocs-chief-of-change/.

8. Michael Bastasch, "Liberal Campaigner Calls 'Green New Deal' a Plan to 'Redistribute Wealth and Power' from Rich to Poor," Daily Caller, February 5, 2019, https://dailycaller.com/2019/02/05/ ocasio-cortez-green-deal-redistribute-wealth/.

9. Michael Bastach, "Trump's National Security Plan: 'Energy Dominance,' Not 'Anti-Growth' Climate Policies," Daily Caller, December 18, 2017, https://dailycaller.com/2017/12/18/trumps-national-security-plan-energy-dominance-not-anti-growth-climate-policies/?utm_source=site-share.

10. Candace Dunn and Tim Hess, "The United States Is Now the Largest Global Crude Oil Producer," The Global Warming Policy Forum, December 9, 2018, https://www.thegwpf.com/ the-united-states-is-now-the-largest-global-crude-oil-producer/.

11. "Fossil Fuels Account for the Largest Share of U.S. Energy Consumption," Energy Information Administration, September 14, 2020, https://www.eia.gov/todayinenergy/detail.php?id=45096.

12. Michael Bastasch, "Green Revolution? Solar and Wind Produced Just 3% of Global Energy," Daily Caller, June 12, 2019, https:// dailycaller.com/2019/06/12/ green-revolution-solar-and-wind-produced-just-3-of-global-energy/.

13. "Editorial: As Global Warming Continues, Trump Wants to Burn Fossil Fuels with an Arsonist's Glee," *Los Angeles Times,* September 29, 2018, http://www.latimes.com/opinion/editorials/la-ed-global-warming-paris-agreement-south-korea-20180929-story.html.

14. Bart Jansen, "'Is This Doomsday': Biden Says Wildfires Show Trump Doesn't Deserve Reelection, Calls Him 'Climate Arsonist,'" *USA TODAY,* https://www.usatoday.com/story/news/politics/elections /2020/09/14/wildfires-joe-biden-calls-donald-trump-climate-arsonist-over-fire-damage/5790418002/.

15. Chris Talgo, "Joe Biden and the Green New Deal," Townhall, October 5, 2020, https://townhall.com/columnists/ christalgo/2020/10/05/joe-biden-and-the-green-new-deal-n2577385.

16. Rob Byrne (@RobByrneDC), "Here's a Clip of Biden...[footage from CNN]," Twitter, September 30, 2020, 8:26 p.m., https://twitter.com/i/status/1311462496583266306.

17. Tyler O'Neil, "Kamala Harris: 'It Is a Fact That We Can Change Human Behaviors' on Climate Change," PJ Media, March 11, 2019, https://pjmedia.com/video/tyler-o-neil/2019/03/11/kamala-harris-it-is-a-fact-that-we-can-change-human-behaviors-on-climate-change-n9 2136.

18. Talgo, "Joe Biden."

19. JAS Foundation, "Professor Guus Berkhout: Stop the Doom-and-Gloom Mongering," The Global Warming Policy Forum, January 29, 2019, https://www.thegwpf.com/prof-guus-berkhout-stop-the-doom-and-gloom-mongering/.

20. The Global Warming Policy Forum, "Donald Trump Rejects Environmental 'Prophets of Doom' in Davos Address," GWPF Newsletter, January 21, 2020, https://mailchi.mp/441bd7b44842/donald-trump-rejects-environmentalprophets-of-doom-in-davos-address?e=f4e33fdd1e.

21. Julia Manchester, "Romney Urges Trump to Support Paris Climate Deal," The Hill, May 31, 2017, https://thehill.com/blogs/blog-briefing-room/news/335834-romney-tweets-support-for-paris-climate-deal; Ben Doherty, "John McCain Urges Action on Great Barrier Reef and Paris Climate Deal", Guardian, May 30, 2017, https://www.theguardian.com/australia-news/2017/may/30/john-mccain-urges-action-on-great-barrier-reef-and-paris-climate-deal..

22. Marc Morano, "Move Over Rachel Carson! Morano's Politically Incorrect Climate Book Outselling 'Silent Spring' at Earth Day," Climate Depot, April 27, 2018, https://www.climatedepot.com/2018/04/27/move-over-rachel-carson-moranos-politically-incorrect-climate-book-outselling-silent-spring/.

23. Roger Helmer, "Climate Hustle Comes to Brussels," blog post, October 19, 2016, https://rogerhelmermep.wordpress.com/2016/10/19/climate-hustle-comes-to-brussels-2/.

24. Marc Morano, "President Trump's Tweet Promotes Climate Hustle 2 Film & Morano's Praising of Trump's 'Energy Dominance,'" November 25, 2020, https://www.climatedepot.com/2020/11/25/trump-tweet-promote-climate-hustle-2-film-moranos-praising-of-trumps-energy-dominance/.

25. Marc Morano, "Watch: Morano Testifies at Wild Pennsylvania Climate Hearing —Compared to Racist, a Holocaust Denier, Tin Foil Hats, and Heckled—Dem Legislator Walks Out," Climate Depot, October 29, 2019, https://www.climatedepot.

com/2019/10/29/watch-morano-testifies-at-wild-pennsylvania-climate-hearing-compared-to-racist-a-holocaust-denier-heckled-dem-legislator-walks-out/.

26. Ted MacDonald, "Two of Fox's Favorite Climate Deniers Testified before Congress on U.N. Extinction Report," Media Matters, May 22, 2019, https://www.mediamatters.org/fox-news/two-foxs-favorite-climate-deniers-testified-congress-un-extinction-report..

27. Marc Morano, "Environmentalist David Suzuki Calls Morano 'an Evil Person' and a 'Bad-ass' at UN While Urging Overthrow of Capitalism," Climate Depot, December 12, 2019, https://www.climatedepot.com/2019/12/12/environmentalist-david-suzuki-calls-morano-an-evil-person-a-bad-ass-at-unwhile-touting-overthrow-of-capitalism/; Marc Morano, "Skeptical Climate 'Talking Points' 36-Page Report Released at UN Climate Summit in Madrid," Climate Depot, December 10, 2019, https://www.climatedepot.com/2019/12/10/skeptical-climate-talking-points-36-page-report-released-at-un-climate-summitin-madrid/..

28. Noel Sheppard, "UN IPCC Official Admits 'We Redistribute World's Wealth by Climate Policy,'" Newsbusters, November 18, 2010, https://www.newsbusters.org/blogs/nb/noel-sheppard/2010/11/18/un-ipcc-official-admits-we-redistribute-worlds-wealth-climate.

29. Suzanne Goldenberg, "IPCC Chairman Dismisses Climate Report Spoiler Campaign," *Guardian*, September 19, 2013, https://www.theguardian.com/environment/2013/sep/19/ipcc-chairman-climate-report?CMP=twt_fd.

30. Marc Morano, witness, "Responding to the Global Assessment Report of the Intergovernmental Science-Policy Platform on Biodiversity and Ecosystem Services," House Natural Resources Committee, Subcommittee on Water, Oceans, and Wildlife, May 22, 2019, https://naturalresources.house.gov/hearings/wow-oversight-hearing.

31. Marc Morano, interview by Bret Baier, "UN Report Warns 1 Million Living Species Face Extinction," Fox News Channel, May 6, 2019, https://video.foxnews.com/v/6033531126001#sp=show-clips.

32. E. S. Brondizio, J. Settele, S. Diaz, and H. T. Ngo, "Global Assessment Report on Biodiversity and Ecosystem Services," Intergovernmental Science-Policy Platform on Biodiversity and Ecosystem Services, 2019, https://ipbes.net/global-assessment.

33. Seth Borenstein (@borenbears), "You don't pay attention to reality….," Twitter, April 22, 2020, 3:02 p.m., https://twitter.com/borenbears/status/1253036579905560579.

34. Ted MacDonald, "Two of FOX's Favorite Climate Deniers Testified before Congress on U.N. Extinction Report," Media Matters, May 22, 2019, https://www.mediamatters.org/fox-news/two-foxs-favorite-climate-deniers-testified-congress-un-extinction-report; Marc Morano, "Climate Skeptics Hijack House Dem Hearing—Dominate Discussion—Warmists Lament: 'How Did These Two Dominate a Hearing Run by Democrats?,'" Climate Depot,May22,2019,https://www.climatedepot.com/2019/05/22/climate-skeptics-hijack-house-dem-hearing-dominate-discussion-warmists-lament-how-did-these-two-dominate-a-hearing-run-by-democrats/.

35. Randy Showstack, "Congress Hears Biodiversity Warning During a Charged Hearing," EOS, May 23, 2019, https://eos.org/articles/congress-hears-biodiversity-warning-during-a-charged-hearing.

36. Jimmy Tobias, "Republicans Aren't Just Climate Deniers. They Deny the Extinction Crisis, Too," *Guardian*, May 23, 2019, https://www.theguardian.com/commentisfree/2019/may/23/republicans-arent-just-climate-deniers-they-deny-the-extinction-crisis-too.

37. Gavin Schmidt (@ClimateOfGavin), "A reminder…," Twitter, September 12, 2020, 12:17 p.m., https://twitter.com/ClimateOfGavin/status/1304816472930291720..

38. Steve Milloy (@JunkScience), "No problem. Thanks for having a hearing…," Twitter, May 22, 2019, 9:37 p.m., https://twitter.com/JunkScience/status/1131373449664974850..

39. Marc Morano, "Update: Morano's Facebook Video Goes Viral with over 10.2 Million Views—Prompts Efforts to Ban 'Climate Deniers' & Attack Zuckerberg," Climate Depot, August 14, 2018, https://www.climatedepot.com/2018/08/14/moranos-skeptical-facebook-climate-video-goes-viral-with-7-4-million-views-prompts-warmists-try-to-ban-all-climate-deniers-attack-zuckerberg/; Dana Nuccitelli, "Facebook Video Spreads Climate Denial to 5 Million Users," *Guardian*, July 25, 2018, https://www.theguardian.com/environment/climate-consensus-97-per-cent/2018/jul/25/facebook-video-spreads-climate-denial-misinformation-to-5-million-users.

40. Shannon Osaka, "A Climate Denial Video Has 6 Million Views. Facebook Doesn't Care," Grist, July 31, 2018, https://grist.org/article/a-climate-denial-video-has-6-million-views-facebook-doesnt-care/.

41. Alexander Petersen, Emmanuel Vincent, and Anthony Westerling, "Discrepancy in Scientific Authority and Media Visibility of Climate Change Scientists and Contrarians," *Nature Communications* 10, no. 3502 (2019), https://doi.org/10.1038/s41467-019-09959-4.

42. Craig Rucker, "Journal 'Nature Communications' Climate Blacklist," CFACT, August 16, 2019, https://www.cfact.org/2019/08/16/journal-nature-communications-climate-blacklist/.

43. Steven Hayward, "Steve and John Make the Climate Blacklist!," Powerline Blog, August 15, 2019, https://www.powerlineblog.com/archives/2019/08/steve-and-john-make-the-climate-blacklist.php.

44. Randy Olson (@ABTagenda), "Does climate community…," Twitter, August 14, 2019, 3:37 p.m., https://twitter.com/ABTagenda/status/1161723447463911424.

45. Randy Olson (@ABTagenda), "2007 I had…," Twitter, August 14, 2019, 1:11 p.m., https://twitter.com/ABTagenda/status/1161686797136490496.

46. Will Johnson, "Amid COVID-19, Americans Don't Care about Climate Change Anymore," *Fortune*, August 10, 2020, https://fortune.com/2020/08/10/climate-change-global-warming-coronavirus/.

47. Valerie Richardson, "Polls Show Climate Change Issue Going Down in Flames as Coronavirus Steals Spotlight," *Washington Times*, August 11, 2020, https://www.washingtontimes.com/news/2020/aug/11/polls-voter-concern-climate-change-sinking-covid19/.

48. James Corbett, "Richard Lindzen on the State of Climate Change" (interview), The Corbett Report, Transcript of Interview by James Corbett of Professor Richard Lindzen, November 22, 2010, embedded at Jamie Spy, "Bureaucratic Dioxide," Climatism, August 28, 2013, https://climatism.blog/2013/08/28/bureaucratic-dioxide/..

49. Marc Morano, "Prominent Geologist Dr. Robert Giegengack Dissents—Laments 'Hubris' of Those Who 'Believe That We Can 'Control' Climate—Denounces 'Semi-Religious Campaign,'" Climate Depot, November 11, 2019, https://www.climatedepot.com/2019/11/11/prominent-geologist-dr-robertgiegengack-dissents-laments-the-hubris-that-leads-us-to-believe-that-we-cancontrol-climate-denounces-semi-religious-campaign/; Marc Morano, "Skeptical Climate 'Talking Points' 36-Page Report Released at UN Climate Summit in Madrid," Climate Depot, December 10, 2019, https://www.climatedepot.com/2019/12/10/skeptical-climate-talking-points-36-page-report-released-at-unclimate-summit-in-madrid/.

50.   Philip Stott, "Global Warming Politics," JunkScience.com, October 15, 2007, http://junksciencearchive.com/oct07.html.

Chapter 2: A History: Every New Crisis Has the Same "Solution": Expanding the Size and Power of Government

1.   "New Deal," History.com, November 27, 2019, https://www.history.com/topics/great-depression/new-deal.

2.   Steve Fraser, "The Greening of the New Deal," *The Nation*, October 18, 2019, https://www.thenation.com/article/archive/green-new-deal-history/.

3.   Brian Sussman, "Green Students Root for Red," blog post, March 14, 2019, https://www.briansussman.com/commentary/green-students-root-for-red/.

4.   David A. Ridenour, "A Green New Deal Would Fail, Just Like the Original New Deal," *Orange County Register*, August 12, 2019, https://www.ocregister.com/2019/08/12/a-green-new-deal-would-fail-just-like-the-original-new-deal/.

5.   Fraser, "The Greening of the New Deal."

6.   Ibid.

7.   Samuel Miller McDonald, "The Green New Deal Can't Be Anything Like the New Deal," *New Republic*, May 31, 2019, https://newrepublic.com/article/153996/green-new-deal-cant-anything-like-new-deal.

8.   Olivia B. Waxman, "How FDR's New Deal Laid the Groundwork for the Green New Deal—in Good Ways and Bad," *Time*, February 8, 2019, https://time.com/5524723/green-new-deal-history/.

9.   Patrick J. Buchanan, "Green New Deal: A Democratic Suicide Note," *WND*, February 11, 2019, https://www.wnd.com/2019/02/green-new-deal-a-democratic-suicide-note/.

10.   Noah, "Major Union Boss Unloads on AOC's New Green Deal: 'Will Destroy Workers' Livelihoods," We Love Trump, 2019, https://welovetrump.com/2019/02/10/major-union-boss-unloads-on-aocs-new-green-deal-will-destroy-workers-livelihoods/; "LIUNA Endorses Joe Biden for President," Laborers' International Union of North America, September 7, 2020, https://www.liuna.org/news/story/liuna-endorses-joe-biden-for-president.

11.   "Walter Williams: Good Economists Deal with Reality," *Orange County Register*, April 22, 2012, ttps://www.ocregister.com/2012/04/22/walter-williams-good-economists-deal-with-reality/.

12. UN General Assembly, Resolution 70/1, The 2030 Agenda for Sustainable Development, A/RES/70/1 (September 25, 2015), https://www.un.org/ga/search/viewm_doc.asp?symbol=A/RES/70/1..

13. Tony Morley, "The Great Decline in Poverty over Time," HumanProgress, August 24, 2020, https://www.humanprogress.org/the-great-decline-in-poverty-over-time/.

14. Steve Milloy, "Did Hugo Chavez Write the Green New Deal?," Breitbart, October 19, 2019, https://www.breitbart.com/politics/2019/10/19/steve-milloy-did-hugo-chavez-write-the-green-new-deal/.1.

15. Tom DeWeese, "Green New Deal Reveals the Naked Truth of Agenda 21," American Policy Center, February 25, 2019, https://americanpolicy.org/2019/02/25/green-new-deal-reveals-the-naked-truth-of-agenda-21/.

16. Nancy Pelosi, "Agenda 21—1992," C-SPAN, October 2, 1992 (user-created clip, March 24, 2020), https://www.c-span.org/video/?c4863326/user-clip-agenda-21-1992-nancy-pelosi#.

17. Audrea Ang, "Associated Press: Pelosi Appeals for China's Help on Climate Change," Nancy Pelosi: Speaker of the House, May 28, 2009, https://www.speaker.gov/newsroom/associated-press-pelosi-appeals-chinas-help-climate-change.

18. DeWeese, "Green New Deal Reveals the Naked Truth."

19. Ron Clutz, "Greenland Glaciers: History vs. Hysteria" Climate Impacts, August 25, 2019, https://rclutz.wordpress.com/2019/08/25/greenland-glaciers-history-vs-hysteria/.

20. Alexander C. Kaufman, "What's the 'Green New Deal'? The Surprising Origins Behind a Progressive Rallying Cry," Grist, June 30, 2018, https://grist.org/article/whats-the-green-new-deal-the-surprising-origins-behind-a-progressive-rallying-cry/.

21. Liyu Woldemichael, "What's the Deal: FDR to the Green New Deal," The Kenan Institute for Ethics at Duke University, January 31, 2020, https://kenan.ethics.duke.edu/whats-the-deal-fdr-to-the-green-new-deal-january/.

22. Patrick Wood, "Fraud: Green New Deal Plagiarized from 2009 UN Environment Programme Report," Canada Free Press, March 20, 2019, https://canadafreepress.com/article/fraud-green-new-deal-plagiarized-from-2009-un-environment-programme-report.

23. Jason Hopkins, "Environmentalist Tells Tucker Carlson: Renewables Can't Save the Planet," Daily Caller, March 1, 2019, https://dailycaller.com/2019/03/01/tucker-carlson-wrecks-renewable-energy/.

24. Shellenberger, "If Bernie Sanders Is So Progressive, Why Is the Green New Deal So Regressive?"

25. Alexander C. Kaufman, "What's the 'Green New Deal'? The Surprising Origins behind a Progressive Rallying Cry," Grist, June 30,2018,https://grist.org/article/whats-the-green-new-deal-the-surprising-origins-behind-a-progressive-rallying-cry/.

26. Michael Shellenberger, "If Bernie Sanders Is So Progressive, Why Is the Green New Deal So Regressive?," *Forbes*, February 25, 2020, https://www.forbes.com/sites/michaelshellenberger/2020/02/25/if-bernie-sanders-is-so-progressive-why-is-the-green-new-deal-so-regressive/#232817d110c4.

27. Kaufman, "What's the 'Green New Deal'?"

28. Declan McCullagh, "Physicists Stick to Warming Claim Post-ClimateGate," CBS News, December 8, 2009, https://www.cbsnews.com/news/physicists-stick-to-warming-claim-post-climategate/.

29. Michael Shellenberger, "The Only Green New Deals That Have Ever Worked Were Done with Nuclear, Not Renewables," *Forbes*, February 8, 2019, https://www.forbes.com/sites/michaelshellenberger/2019/02/08/the-only-green-new-deals-that-have-ever-worked-were-done-with-nuclear-not-renewables/#416cca027f61.

Chapter 3: Man-Made Climate Change Is Not a Threat

"If You Believe in Magic…" John Sebastian, "Do You Believe in Magic," from The Lovin Spoonful, Do You Believe in Magic, Kama Sutra, 1965.

"Rivers and Seas Are Boiling!" Dan Aykroyd and Harold Ramis, Ghostbusters, Columbia-Delphi Productions, 1984.

"It's Like a Heat Wave!" Brian Holland, Lamont Dozier, and Eddie Holland, "(Love Is Like a) Heat Wave," from Martha and the Vandellas, Heat Wave, Hitsville U.S.A., 1963.

"Melting, Melting—Oh What a World" Noel Langley, Florence Ryerson, and Edgar Allan Woolf, The Wizard of Oz (based on The Wonderful Wizard of Oz by Frank L. Baum), Metro-Goldwyn-Mayer, 1939.

"Go to Jail, Go Directly to Jail" Charles Darrow, Monopoly, Parker Brothers, 1935 (based on The Landlord's Game, created in 1903 by Lizzie Maggie, which included the phrase "Go to Jail"). Board Game.

1. Thomas Richard, "Seattle judge says kids can sue government for climate change inaction," Blasting News, December 23, 2016,

https://us.blastingnews.com/news/2016/12/seattle-judge-says-kids-can-sue-government-for-climate-change-inaction-001348747.html.

2. Lukas Mikelionis, "Ocasio-Cortez, Sanders call for climate change emergency mobilization, seeks a re-do of failed Green New Deal," Fox News, July 9, 2019, https://www.foxnews.com/politics/ocasio-cortez-sanders-call-climate-change-emergency-mobilization-green-new-deal.

3. Will Happer, "Can Climate Models Predict Climate Change?," Praguer U, February 5, 2018, https://www.prageru.com/videos/can-climate-models-predict-climate-change#.WnipiKqCoGk.twitter.

4. Joshua Caplan, "Al Gore: 99.9 Percent of Scientists Agree with Me on Climate Change," Breitbart, March 16, 2019, https://www.breitbart.com/politics/2019/03/16/al-gore-99-9-percent-of-scientists-agree-with-me-on-climate-change/.

5. Richard Tol, witness, "Examining the UN Intergovernmental Panel on Climate Change Process," House Committee on Science and Technology, May 29, 2014, https://science.house.gov/hearings/.examining-the-un-intergovernmental-panel-on-climate-change-process?1.

6. Lawrence Solomon, "Lawrence Solomon: 97% Cooked Stats," *Financial Post*, January 4, 2011, https://financialpost.com/opinion/lawrence-solomon-97-cooked-stats.

7. Joseph Bast and Roy Spencer, "The Myth of the Climate Change '97%,'" *Wall Street Journal*, May 26, 2014, https://www.wsj.com/articles/SB10001424052702303480304579578462813553136.

8. Marc Morano, "MIT Climate Scientist Dr. Richard Lindzen Mocks 97% Consensus: 'It Is Propaganda,'" Climate Depot, February 15, 2016, https://www.climatedepot.com/2016/02/15/.mit-climate-scientist-dr-richard-lindzen-mocks-97-consensus-it-is-propaganda/.

9. Patrick Moore, witness, "Natural Resource Adaptation: Protecting Ecosystems and Economies," Senate Committee on Environment and Public Works, Subcommittee on Oversight, February 25, 2014, https://www.epw.senate.gov/public/index.cfm/2014/2/.updated-time-subcommittee-on-oversight-hearing-entitled-natural-resource-adaptation-protecting-ecosystems-and-economies.

10. Marc Morano, "Relax. It's Not Global Warming 'End Times,'" *Human Events*, May 14, 2013, https://humanevents.com/2013/05/14/global-warming/.

11. Marc Morano, "Flashback: Prominent Dutch Scientist: 'I Find the Doomsday Picture Al Gore Is Painting—a 6M Sea Level Rise 15 Times IPCC Number—Entirely without Merit," Climate Depot, February 12, 2016, https://www.climatedepot.com/2016/02/12/.flashback-prominent-

dutch-scientist-i-find-the-doomsday-picture-al-gore-is-painting-a-6m-sea-level-rise-15-times-ipcc-number-entirely-without-merit/.

12. Kenneth Richard, "MIT's Dr. Lindzen Pokes Fun at the 'Naïve,' Well-Funded 'Scientific Reasoning' That 1 Factor—CO_2—Controls Climate," NoTricksZone, June 15, 2020, https://notrickszone.com/2020/06/15/mits-dr-lindzen-pokes-fun-at-the-naive-well-funded-scientific-reasoning-that-1-factor-co2-controls-climate/.

13. William Happer, "Trump Adviser William Happer Talks Climate Alarmism During COP25 in Madrid," The Heartland Institute, December 3, 2019, YouTube, https://youtu.be/j8KxVQFoyTo.

14. Roger Pielke, "The Incredible Story of How Climate Change Became Apocalyptic," *Forbes*, December 6, 2019, https://www.forbes.com/sites/rogerpielke/2019/12/06/the-incredible-story-of-how-climate-change-became-apocalyptic/#440e7510789d.

15. "Streisand Sings Praises of Clinton's Global Initiative," Newsmax, October 6, 2005, https://www.newsmax.com/pre-2008/streisand-sings-praises-clinton-s/2005/10/06/id/681427/.

16. "About NCA4 Vol. II," GlobalChange.gov, U.S. Global Change Research Program, November 2018, https://www.globalchange.gov/content/nca4-planning.

17. Tom Elliott, "Ocasio-Cortez on Millenials: 'We're Like the World Is Going to End in 12 Years If We Don't Address Climate Change,'" Grabien News, January 21, 2019, https://news.grabien.com/.story-ocasio-cortez-millennials-were-world-going-end-12-years-if-w.

18. Michael Armstrong, "Man and Nature: George Perkins Marsh," *Adirondack Explorer*, September 23, 2014, https://www.adirondackexplorer.org/book_reviews/man-nature-george-perkins-marsh.

19. Elizabeth May, "'We Have Hours' to Prevent Climate Disaster," *Star*, March 24, 2009, https://www.thestar.com/news/gta/2009/03/24/we_have_hours_to_prevent_climate_disaster.html.

20. "PM Warns of Climate 'Catastrophe,'" BBC News, October 19, 2009, http://news.bbc.co.uk/2/hi/uk_news/8313672.stm.

21. Robert Verkaik, "Just 96 Months to Save World, Says Prince Charles," *Independent*, July 9, 2009, https://www.independent.co.uk/environment/green-living/just-96-months-to-save-world-says-prince-charles-1738049.html.

22. Robin McKie, "President 'Has Four Years to Save Earth,'" *Guardian*, January 17, 2009, https://www.theguardian.com/environment/2009/jan/18/jim-hansen-obama.

23. Reuters, "Ecological Disaster Feared," *Vancouver Sun*, May 11, 1982, https://news.google.com/newspapers?id=05tlAAAAIBAJ&sjid

=TYwNAAAAIBAJ&pg=5103,351973&dq=ecological+holocaust&
hl=en.

24. John Harris, "Hay Festival: 'Climate Change Is a Long Struggle,'"
Guardian, May 31, 2010, https://www.theguardian.com/
books/2010/may/31/hay-festival-climate-change-debates.

25. Marc Morano, "Earth 'Serially Doomed': The Official History of
Climate 'Tipping Points' Began in 1864—a New 'Global Warming'
12-Year Deadline from Rep. Ocasio-Cortez," Climate Depot,
January 22, 2019, https://www.climatedepot.com/2019/01/22/earth-serially-
doomed-the-official-history-of-climate-tipping-points-began-in-
1864-a-new-global-warming-12-year-deadline-from-rep-osasio-
cortez/.

26. Kenneth Richard, "Recent Studies Indicate Species Extinctions
Decline with Warming—Mass Extinction Events Due To
COOLING," NoTricksZone, May 16, 2019, https://notrickszone.
com/2019/05/16/recent-studies-indicate-species-extinctions-decline-
with-warming-mass-extinction-events-due-to-cooling/.

27. Richard Lindzen, "Thoughts on the Public Discourse over Climate
Change," Merion West, April 25, 2017, https://merionwest.
com/2017/04/25/richard-lindzen-thoughts-on-the-public-discourse
-over-climate-change/.

28. Marc Morano, "Prominent Princeton Scientist Dr. Happer Testifies
to Congress: 'Warming and increased CO_2 will be good for
mankind,'" Climate Depot, May 20, 2010, https://www.
climatedepot.com/2010/05/21/prominent-princeton-scientist-dr-happer-
testifies-to-congress-warming-and-increased-co2-will-be-good-for-
mankind/.

29. Marc Morano, "Prominent Scientists Declare Climate Claims ahead
of UN Summit 'Irrational'—'Based on Nonsense'—'Leading Us
Down a False Path,'" Climate Depot, November 19, 2015, https://
www.climatedepot.com/2015/11/19/scientists-declare-un-climate-summit-
goals-irrational-based-on-nonsense-leading-us-down-a-false-path/.

30. Roy W. Spencer, "Global Satellites: 2016 Not Statistically Warmer
Than 1998," blog post, January 3, 2017, https://www.drroyspencer.
com/2017/01/global-satellites-2016-not-statistically-warmer-than-1998/.

31. Marc Morano, "More Than 700 Scientists from 400 Institutions in
40 Countries Have Contributed Peer-Reviewed Papers Providing
Evidence That the Medieval Warm Period Was Real, Global, and
Warmer Than the Present," https://www.climatedepot.
com/2013/03/08/more-than-700-scientists-from-400-institutions-
in-40-countries-have-contributed-peerreviewed-papers-providing-

evidence-that-the-medieval-warm-period-was-real-global-warmer-than-the-present/

32. Patrick Michaels, interview in Marc Morano, *Climate Hustle* (film), 2015, https://www.climatehustle.org/.

33. "New York Times Hysterical over Global Greening," CFACT, August 13, 2018, https://www.cfact.org/2018/08/13/new-york-times-hysterical-over-global-greening/.

34. Tony Heller, "100% Predictable Fraud from Government Climate Scientists," Real Climate Science blog, February 14, 2017, https://realclimatescience.com/2017/02/100-predictable-fraud-from-government-climate-scientists/.

35. Anthony Watts, "While NOAA/NASA Claims 2019 As the 'Second Warmest Year Ever,' Other Data Shows 2019 Cooler Than 2005 for USA.," Watts Up With That?, January 15, 2020, https://wattsupwiththat.com/2020/01/15/while-noaa-nasa-claims-2019-as-the-second-warmest-year-ever-other-data-shows-2019-cooler-than-2005-for-usa/.

36. "State of the Climate 2018: Global Warming Is Not Accelerating," Global Warming Policy Foundation, press release, April 3, 2019, https://www.thegwpf.org/new-report-global-warming-is-not-accelerating/.

37. "The Reassuring Facts about the Climate in 2019," Global Warming Policy Foundation, press release, May 26, 2020, https://www.thegwpf.org/the-reassuring-facts-about-the-climate-in-2019/ (internal citation omitted).

38. David Whitehouse, "2016 Global Temperature: The Pause Never Went Away," The Global Warming Policy Forum, January 19, 2017, https://www.thegwpf.com/2016-global-temperature-the-pause-never-went-away/.

39. Lennart Bengtsson, quoted in Peter Ferrara, "As the Economy Recesses, Obama's Global Warming Delusions Are Truly Cruel," *Forbes*, February 22, 2013, https://www.forbes.com/sites/peterferrara/2013/02/22/.as-the-economyrecesses-obamas-global-warming-delusions-aretruly-cruel/#53f78db3a779.

40. Marc Morano, "Nobel Prize-Winning Scientist Who Endorsed Obama Now Says Prez. Is 'Ridiculous' and 'Dead Wrong' on 'Global Warming,'" Climate Depot, July 6, 2015, https://www.climatedepot.com/2015/07/06/.nobel-prize-winning-scientist-who-endorsed-obama-now-says-prez-is-ridiculous-dead-wrong-on-global-warming/.

41. Anastasios Tsonis, "The Overblown and Misleading Issue of Global Warming," *Washington Times*, January 2, 2019, https://www.

washingtontimes.com/news/2019/jan/2/
the-overblown-and-misleading-issue-of-global-warmi/.

42. Michael Shellenberger, "On Behalf of Environmentalists, I
Apologize for the Climate Scare," Environmental Progress, June 29,
2020, https://environmentalprogress.org/big-news/2020/6/29/
on-behalf-of-environmentalists-i-apologize-for-the-climate-scare.
See also Marc Morano, "Prominent Climate Activist Shellenberger
Officially Recants: 'On Behalf of Environmentalists, I Apologize for
the Climate Scare,'" Climate Depot, June 29, 2020, https://www.
climatedepot.com/2020/06/29/prominent-climate-activist-
shellenberger-officially-recants-on-behalf-of-environmentalists-
i-apologize-for-the-climate-scare/.

43. Marc Morano, "UN Scientists Who Have Turned on the UN IPCC
and Man-Made Climate Fears—a Climate Depot Flashback Report,"
Climate Depot, August 21, 2013, https://www.climatedepot.com/
2013/08/21/un-scientists-who-have-turned-on-unipcc-man-made-
climate-fears-a-climate-depot-flashback-report/.

44. Marc Morano, "UN IPCC Lead Author Dr. Richard Tol Bolts
Warmist Narrative: Calls Gore's Claims 'Complete Madness,'"
Climate Depot, January 7, 2016, https://www.climatedepot.
com/2016/01/07/un-ipcc-lead-author-dr-richard-tol-bolts-warmist-
narrative-calls-gores-claims-complete-madness/.

45. "The Scientists Who Sat Governor Rick Scott Down and Explained
the CAGW Scam," Hockey Schtick blog, August 24, 2014, https://
hockeyschtick.blogspot.com/2014/08/meet-scientists-who-sat-
governor-rick.html.

46. "State of the Climate 2018: Global Warming Is Not Accelerating,"
Global Warming Policy Foundation, March 4, 2019, https://www.
thegwpf.org/new-report-global-warming-is-not-accelerating/.

47. Roy W. Spencer, "Hillary Clinton Boards the Climate Crisis Train
to Nowhere," *Forbes*, October 25, 2016,https://www.forbes.com/
sites/realspin/2016/10/25/hillary-clinton-boards-the-climate-crisis-train-
to-nowhere/#7fc88e67371e.

48. John Marchese, "SCIENCE: Al Gore Is a Greenhouse Gasbag,"
Philadelphia, February 2, 2007, http://www.phillymag.com/articles/
science-al-gore-is-a-greenhouse-gasbag/.

49. "Polar Bear Numbers Could Have Quadrupled," Global Warming
Policy Foundation, press release, March 19, 2019, https://www.
thegwpf.org/polar-bear-numbers-could-have-quadrupled/.

50. Marc Morano, "STUDY: Polar Bear Numbers Reach New
Highs—Population Increases to the Highest Levels in Decades,"

Climate Depot, March 5, 2019, https://www.climatedepot.com/2019/03/05/study-polar-bear-numbers-reach-new-highs-population-increases-to-the-highest-levels-in-decades/.

51. Susan J. Crockford, "State of the Polar Bear Report 2018," Global Warming Policy Foundation, 2018, https://www.thegwpf.org/content/uploads/2019/02/State-of-the-polar-bear2018.pdf (internal citation omitted).

52. Susan Crockford, "Polar Bears Have Not Been Harmed by Sea Ice Declines in Summer—the Evidence," Polar Bear Science, August 18, 2013, https://polarbearscience.com/2013/08/18/polarbears-have-not-been-harmed-by-sea-icedeclines-in-summer-the-evidence/.

53. Valerie Richardson, "Polar Bear Zoologist Blasts Obama's Climate Alarmism: 'Sensationalized Nonsense,'" *Washington Times*, January 9, 2017, https://www.washingtontimes.com/news/2017/jan/9/polar-bear-conservation-group-blasts-obama-admin/.

54. Marc Morano, "Scientist to Congress: 'No Evidence' That Hurricanes, Floods, Droughts, Tornadoes Are Increasing," Climate Depot, March 29, 2017, https://www.climatedepot.com/2017/03/29/scientist-to-congress-no-evidence-that-hurricanes-floods-droughts-tornadoes-are-increasing/.

55. Roger Pielke Jr. (@RogerPielkeJr), "Important New Paper Pielke, Jr., R. 2021 (in press). Economic 'Normalization' of Disaster Losses 1998-2020: A Literature Review and Assessment A few years in the making, a robust peer review process Now accepted," Twitter, sixteen-tweet thread, July 7, 2020, 2:56 p.m., https://twitter.com/RogerPielkeJr/status/1280576376836206592.

56. Michael Bastasch, "UN's New Report Shows There's 'Little Basis' for a Favorite Claim of Climate Activists," Daily Caller, October 8, 2018, https://dailycaller.com/2018/10/08/un-climate-report-global-warming/.

57. Roger Pielke, witness, "Climate Change: It's Happening Now," Senate Committee on Environment and Public Works, July 18, 2013, https://www.epw.senate.gov/public/_cache/files/a6df9665-e8c8-4b0f-a550-07669df48b15/71813hearingwitnesstestimonypielke.pdf.

58. Michael Bastasch, "Consensus: Still No Connection between Global Warming and Floods," Daily Caller, August 30, 2017, https://dailycaller.com/2017/08/30/consensus-still-no-connection-between-global-warming-and-floods/?utm_source=site-share.

59. Glenn A. Hodgkins, et al., "Climate-Driven Variability in the Occurrence of Major Floods across North America and Europe,"

Journal of Hydrology 552 (September 2017): 704–17, https://doi.
org/10.1016/j.jhydrol.2017.07.027.

60. Giuseppe Formetta and Luc Feyen, "Empirical Evidence of
Declining Global Vulnerability to Climate-Related Hazards,"
Global Environmental Change 57 (July 2019): 101920, https://doi.
org/10.1016/j.gloenvcha.2019.05.004.

61. Marc Morano, "'Massively Incorrect': Point-by-Point Rebuttal to
Michael Mann's Newsweek Smear of Trump, Greenpeace
Co-Founder Dr. Moore, and Princeton's Dr. Happer—Update:
Michael Mann Responds," Climate Depot, March 14, 2019, https://
www.climatedepot.com/2019/03/14/massively-incorrect-point-by-
point-rebuttal-to-michael-manns-newsweek-smear-of-trump-
greenpeace-co-founder-dr-moore-princetons-dr-happer/.

62. Paul Homewood, "Another Quiet Year for Tornadoes," Not a Lot of
People Know That (blog), November 12, 2016, https://notalotofpeople
knowthat.wordpress.com/2016/11/12/another-quiet-year-for-tornadoes/.

63. Dennis Mersereau, "2019 Was an Incredibly Active Year for
Tornadoes," *Forbes*, December 31, 2019, https://www.forbes.com/
sites/dennismersereau/2019/12/31/2019-was-an-incredibly-active-
year-for-tornadoes/#4a3627a86bc5.

64. Persepcta Weather, "A Look Back at Global Tropical Activity and
US Tornadoes in 2020 . . . Global Tropical Activity Below Normal .
. . US Tornado Activity Below Normal and No Reported EF-5s,"
December 31, 2020, https://www.perspectaweather.com/blog/a-look-
back-at-global-tropical-activity-and-us-tornadoes-in-2020global-
tropical-activity-below-normalus-tornado-activity-below-normal-
and-no-reported-ef-5s.

65. Marc Morano, "NOAA: 'It Is Premature to Conclude … That
Global Warming Has Already Had a Detectable Impact on
Hurricane Activity'—U.S. Landfalling Hurricanes 'Show a Slight
Negative Trend' since 'late 1800s,'" Climate Depot, August 31,
2019, https://www.climatedepot.com/2019/08/31/noaa-it-is-premature-
to-conclude-global-warming-has-already-had-a-detectable-impact-
on-hurricane-activity-u-s-landfalling-hurricanes-show-a-slight-
negative-trend-since-late-1800s/no-evidence-that-climate-change-
causes-weather-extremes-4-tornadoes-31.

66. Ralph Alexander, "No Evidence That Climate Change Causes
Weather Extremes: (4) Tornadoes," Science Under Attack (blog),
July 29, 2019, https://www.scienceunderattack.com/blog/2019/7/29/
no-evidence-that-climate-change-causes-weather-extremes-4-
tornadoes-31.

67. "The Reassuring Facts about the Climate in 2019," Global Warming Policy Foundation, press release, May 26, 2020, https://www. thegwpf.org/the-reassuring-facts-about-the-climate-in-2019/.

68. Roger Pielke, "When Is Climate Change Just Weather? What Hurricane Dorian Coverage Mixes Up, On Purpose," *Forbes*, September 4, 2019, https://www.forbes.com/sites/rogerpielke/ 2019/09/04/when-is-climate-change-just-weather-what-hurricane-dorian-coverage-mixes-up-on-purpose/#6251541e6a15.

69. Thomas Knutson, et al., "Tropical Cyclones and Climate Change Assessment: Part I: Detection and Attribution," *Bulletin of the American Meteorological Society* 100, no. 10 (October 2019): 1987–2007, https://doi.org/10.1175/BAMS-D-18-0189.1.

70. Andrew B. Hagen and Christopher W. Landsea, "On the Classification of Extreme Atlantic Hurricanes Utilizing Mid-Twentieth-Century Monitoring Capabilities," *Journal of Climate* 25, no. 13 (July 2012): 4461–4475, https://doi.org/10.1175/ JCLI-D-11-00420.1.

71. Marc Morano, "Extreme Weather Expert Dr. Roger Pielke Jr.: '13 Years Ending 2018 Had Fewest Cat3+ USA Landfalls Since 1900 with 3,'" Climate Depot, September 16, 2019, https://www. climatedepot.com/2019/09/16/extreme-weather-expert-dr-roger-pielke-jr-13-yrs-ending-2018-had-fewest-cat3-usa-landfalls-since-1900-with-3/.

72. Perspecta Weather, "A Look Back."

73. Pierre Gosselin, "US Atmospheric Scientist Sees No Link between Accumulated Cyclone Energy and Global Warming over Past 30 Years," NoTricksZone, September 20, 2016, https://notrickszone. com/2016/09/20/us-atmospheric-scientist-sees-no-link-between-accumulated-cyclone-energy-and-global-warming-over-past-30-years/#sthash.DzmD9uYt.dpbs.

74. Roger Pielke Jr., "Drought and Climate Change," Roger Pielke Jr.'s blog, September 24, 2012, http://rogerpielkejr.blogspot. com/2012/09/drought-and-climate-change.html.

75. "Drought," Global Warming Policy Forum factsheet, January 31, 2020, https://www.thegwpf.com/are-droughts-getting-worse/.

76. "New Drought Atlas Maps 2,000 Years of Climate in Europe," Earth Institute at Columbia University, November 6, 2015, https:// www.earth.columbia.edu/articles/view/3264.

77. Stefan H. Doerr and Cristina Santin, "Global Trends in Wildfire and Its Impacts: Perceptions Versus Realities in a Changing World," *Philosophical Transactions of the Royal Society B: Biological*

Sciences 371, no. 1696 (June 2016): 20150345, https://dx.doi.
org/10.1098%2Frstb.2015.0345.

78. Morano, *The Politically Incorrect Guide to Climate Change* (Washington, D.C.: Regnery Publishing, 2018), 211, 212, citing Doerr and Santin, "Global Trends in Wildfire."

79. Sebastian Lüning and Fritz Vahrenholt, "No Long-Term Trend in Heatwaves in North America" trans. Pierre Gosselin, NoTricksZone (blog), August 31, 2018, https://notrickszone. com/2018/08/31/media-claims-of-more-heat-waves-refuted-by-multiple-recent-studies-longterm-data/.

80. Evan M. Oswald and Richard B. Rood, "A Trend Analysis of the 1930–2010 Extreme Heat Events in the Continental United States," *Journal of Applied Meteorology and Climatology* 53, no. 3 (March 2014): 565–582, https://doi.org/10.1175/JAMC-D-13-071.1.

81. John R. Christy, House Energy and Power Subcommittee, September 20, 2012, http://energycommerce.house.gov/sites/ republicans.energycommerce.house.gov/files/Hearings/ EP/20120920/HHRG-112-IF03-WStateChristyJ-20120920.pdf.

82. "Climate Change Indicators: High and Low Temperatures," Environmental Protection Agency, last updated August 2016, https://www.epa.gov/climate-indicators/ climate-change-indicators-high-and-low-temperatures.

83. Maria-Jose Viñas, "NASA Study: Mass Gains of Antarctic Ice Sheet Greater Than Losses," NASA, October 30, 2015, https://www.nasa. gov/feature/goddard/nasa-study-mass-gains-of-antarctic-ice-sheet-greater-than-losses.

84. CFACT Ed, "NASA Researcher: Antarctica Still Gaining Ice," CFACT, June 17, 2018, https://www.cfact.org/2018/06/17/ nasa-researcher-antarctica-still-gaining-ice/.

85. Michael Bastasch, "NASA Has More Evidence Volcanic Activity is Heating Up Antarctica's Ice Sheet," Daily Caller, November 7, 2017, https://dailycaller.com/2017/11/07/nasa-has-more-evidence-volcanic-activity-is-heating-up-antarcticas-ice-sheet/.

86. Anthony Watts, "Taking Down the Latest *Washington Post* Antarctic Scare Story on 6x Increased Ice Melt," Watts Up with That? (blog), January 15, 2019, https://wattsupwiththat. com/2019/01/15/taking-down-the-latest-washington-post-antarctic-scare-story-on-6x-increased-ice-melt/.

87. Marc Morano, "Update: AP's Seth Borenstein at It Again Hyping Antarctic Melt Fears—Recycles Same Claims from 2014, 1990, 1979, 1922, and 1901!—Climate Depot's Point-by-Point Rebuttal,"

Climate Depot, February 28, 2015, https://www.climatedepot.
com/2015/02/28/aps-seth-borenstein-at-it-again-hyping-antarctic-
melt-fears-climate-depots-point-by-point-rebuttal/.

88. Andrzej Araźny, Przemysław Wyszyński, and Rajmund Przybylak,
"A Comparison of Bioclimatic Conditions on Franz Josef Land (the
Arctic) between the Turn of the Nineteenth to Twentieth Century
and Present Day," *Theoretical and Applied Climatology* 137, nos.
3–4 (August 2019): 2623–2638, https://doi.org/10.1007/s0070
4-018-02763-y.

89. Kenneth Richard, "6 New Papers Link Arctic/North Atlantic
Climate Changes to Natural Factors," NoTricksZone (blog),
October 1, 2018, https://notrickszone.com/2018/10/01/in-the-arctic-
amo-nao-predominantly-force-ocean-temperatures-and-cause-
major-melting-events/.

90. Ronan Connolly, Michael Connolly, and Willie Soon,
"Re-Calibration of Arctic Sea Ice Extent Datasets Using Arctic
Surface Air Temperature Records," *Hydrological Sciences
Journal*, May 22, 2017, https://www.tandfonline.com/doi/pdf/10.
1080/02626667.2017.1324974.

91. "The Reassuring Facts about the Climate in 2019" (press release)
Global Warming Policy Foundation, May 26, 2020, https://www.
thegwpf.org/the-reassuring-facts-about-the-climate-in-2019/.

92. Pierre Gosselin, "Max Planck Institute for Meteorology Director
Not Worried about Climate Tipping Points ... Worried about
Panic," NoTricksZone (blog), August 14, 2020, https://notrickszone.
com/2020/08/14/max-planck-institute-for-meteorology-director-
not-worried-about-climate-tipping-points-worried-about-
panic/?utm_source=rss&utm_medium=rss&utm_campaign=max-
planck-institute-for-meteorology-director-not-worried-about-
climate-tipping-points-worried-about-panic.

93. Kenneth Richard, "A New 1796-2013 Greenland Reconstruction
Shows It Was Warmer in the 1920s-1940s – and No Hockey Sticks,"
NoTricksZone blog, April 6, 2020, https://notrickszone.
com/2020/04/06/a-new-1796-2013-greenland-reconstruction-shows-
it-was-warmer-in-the-1920s-1940s-and-no-hockey-sticks/.

94. Patrick J. Michaels and Paul C. Knappenberger, "Taming the
Greenland Melting Global Warming Hype," Cato Institute, June 10,
2016, https://www.cato.org/blog/
taming-greenland-melting-global-warming-hype.

95. Associated Press, "Key Greenland Glacier Growing Again after
Shrinking for Years, NASA Study Shows," NBC News, March 25,

2019, https://www.nbcnews.com/mach/science/key-greenland-glacier-growing-again-after-shrinking-years-nasa-study-ncna987116.

96.   B. M. Vinther, et al., "Extending Greenland Temperature Records into the Late Eighteenth Century," Journal of Geophysical Research vol. 111, D11105, June 6, 2006, https://crudata.uea.ac.uk/cru/data/greenland/vintheretal2006.pdf

97.   "Latest Scientific Studies Refute Fears of Greenland Melt," Senate Environment and Public Works Committee, July 30, 2007, https://www.epw.senate.gov/public/index.cfm/pressreleases-all?ID=175b568a-802a-23ad-4c69-9bdd978fb3cd

98.   Michael E. Mann, "Climate Catastrophe Is a Choice," Foreign Affairs, April 21, 2017, https://www.foreignaffairs.com/articles/2017-04-21/climate-catastrophe-choice.

99.   "World Climate Predictors Right Only Half the Time," The New Zealand Climate Science Coalition, June 7, 2007, http://nzclimatescience. net/index.php?option=com_content&task=view&id=23&Itemid=32.

100. Steven Goddard, "CIA 1974 National Security Threat: Global Cooling/Excess Arctic Ice Causing Extreme Weather," Real Science (blog), February 26, 2013, https://stevengoddard.wordpress.com/2013/02/26/cia-1974-national-security-threat-global-coolingexcess-ice-causing-extreme-weather/.

101. Anthony Watts, "Debunked: The 'Climate Change Causes Wars' Myth," Watts Up with That? (blog), August 29, 2011, https://wattsupwiththat.com/2011/08/29/debunked-the-climate-change-causes-wars-myth/.

102. Robert F. Kennedy Jr., "It's Time to Find Our Common Ground and Fight the Deep State," The Defender, December 16, 2020, https://childrenshealthdefense.org/defender/fight-the-real-deep-state/.

103. "Fossil Fuels Account for the Largest Share of U.S. Energy Production and Consumption," Energy Information Administration, September 14, 2020, https://www.eia.gov/todayinenergy/detail.php?id=45096.

104. Tony Heller (@Tony_Heller), "Shutting down US energy supplies means dependence on Middle East oil, which means a permanent state of war for the Military Industrial Complex," Twitter, November 27, 2020, 5:17 p.m., https://twitter.com/Tony__Heller/status/1332493881506553856.

105. Mark P. Mills, "The Green New Deal Can't Break the Laws of Physics," Daily Caller, October 27, 2020, https://dailycaller.com/2020/10/27/green-new-deal-laws-of-physics/.

106. Benjamin Zycher, "The Green New Deal: Economics and Policy Analytics," American Enterprise Institute, April 24, 2019, https://www.aei.org/research-products/report/the-green-new-deal-economics-and-policy-analytics/.

107. Michael Bastasch, "Ocasio-Cortez's 'Green New Deal' Would Avert a 'Barely Detectable' Amount of Global Warming. That's According to EPA's Climate Model," Daily Caller, January 7, 2019, https://dailycaller.com/2019/01/07/ocasio-cortez-green-new-deal-warming/.

108. Marc Morano, "2016 State of the Climate Report," CFACT, November 2016, https://www.cfact.org/wp-content/uploads/2016/11/2016-State-of-the-Climate-Report.pdf.

109. Gina McCarthy, "'One One-Hundreth of a Degree?' EPA's McCarthy Admits Obama Regs Have No Measurable Climate Impact," The HARRY READ ME File, YouTube, July 15, 2015, https://youtu.be/hkkeLpbzo-Y.

110. Charles McConnell, "Former Obama Energy Chief Eviscerates President's Climate Reg: 'Falsely Sold As Impactful,'" The HARRY READ ME File, YouTube, May 26, 2016, https://youtu.be/jMxjHvoCPec.

111. Bill Nye, "Bill Nye Jailing Skeptics," CFACT, YouTube, April 14, 2016, https://youtu.be/xlk4Lt__Sno.

112. Simon Kent, "Danish Academic: U.N. Might Use Military to Enforce Climate Agenda," Breitbart, December 3, 2019, https://www.breitbart.com/environment/2019/12/03/danish-academic-u-n-might-use-military-to-enforce-climate-agenda/.

113. Farz Edraki and Ann Arnold, "Could Climate Change Become a Security Issue—and Threaten Democracy?" ABC News, December 2, 2019, https://www.abc.net.au/news/2019-12-03/climate-change-international-security-risk/11714284.

114. Bernard Potter, "IPCC Official: 'Climate Policy Is Redistributing the World's Wealth,'" Global Warming Policy Forum, November 18, 2010, https://www.thegwpf.com/ipcc-official-climate-policy-is-redistributing-the-worlds-wealth/.

115. Marc Morano, "Flashback: Gore: U.S. Climate Bill Will Help Bring About 'Global Governance,'" Climate Depot, July 10, 2009, https://www.climatedepot.com/2009/07/10/flashback-gore-us-climate-bill-will-help-bring-about-global-governance-2/.

116. Reuters, "UN Climate Change Chief Steps Down after Historic Paris Deal," *Guardian*, February 19, 2016, https://www.theguardian.com/environment/2016/feb/19/un-climate-change-chief-steps-down-after-historic-paris-deal.

117. Greta Thunberg, Luisa Neubauer, and Angela Valenzuela, "Why We Strike Again," Project Syndicate, November 29, 2019, https://www.project-syndicate.org/commentary/climate-strikes-un-conference-madrid-by-greta-thunberg-et-al-2019-11?barrier=accesspaylog.

118. Tony Heller, "George Monbiot Explains Climate Science," Real Climate Science (blog), April 12, 2019, https://realclimatescience.com/2019/04/george-monbiot-explains-climate-science/.

119. Judith Curry, "Madrid," Climate Etc. (blog), December 2, 2019, https://judithcurry.com/2019/12/02/madrid/?mc_cid=c314390c89&mc_eid=d5e6b5270d#more-25458.

120. Roy W. Spencer, "Hillary Clinton Boards the Climate Crisis Train to Nowhere," *Forbes*, October 25, 2016, https://www.forbes.com/sites/realspin/2016/10/25/hillary-clinton-boards-the-climate-crisis-train-to-nowhere/#3c5dce3d371e.

Chapter 4: The Details of the Deal

1. Tom Elliott, "Ocasio-Cortez: Fixing Global Warming Requires 'Massive Government Intervention,' Grabien News, February 7, 2019, https://news.grabien.com/story-ocasio-cortez-fixing-global-warming-requires-massive-governm.

2. Jennie Neufeld, "Alexandria Ocasio-Cortez Is a Democratic Socialists of America Member. Here's What That Means," Vox, June 27, 2018, https://www.vox.com/policy-and-politics/2018/6/27/17509604/alexandria-ocasio-cortez-democratic-socialist-of-america.

3. Recognizing the Duty of the Federal Government to Create a Green New Deal., H.R. 109, 116th Cong. (2019).

4. AllahPundit, "AOC's Chief of Staff: We Don't Think of The Green New Deal as a Climate Thing but as a 'Change the Entire Economy' Thing," HotAir (blog), July 12, 2019, https://hotair.com/archives/allahpundit/2019/07/12/aocs-chiefstaff-dont-think-green-new-deal-climate-thing-change-entire-economy-thing/.

5. Marlo Lewis, Jr., "A Citizen's Guide to Climate Change," Competitive Enterprise Institute, June 11, 2019, https://cei.org/content/citizens-guide-climate-change.

6. Joe Newby and Jeff Dunetz, "Alexandra Ocasio-Cortez: Fixing Climate Change Will End Racism," The Lid, December 7, 2018, https://lidblog.com/ocasio-cortez-climate-change-racism/.

7. Zack Colman and Anthony Adragna," 'Green New Deal' lands in the Capitol," *Politico*, February 7, 2019, https://www.politico.com/story/2019/02/07/green-new-deal-resolution-1155146..

8. Yaron Steinbuch, "AOC Explains Why 'Farting Cows' Were Considered in Green New Deal," New York Post, February 22, 2019, https://nypost.com/2019/02/22/aoc-explains-why-farting-cows-were-considered-in-green-new-deal/..

9. David Wojick and Paul Driessen, "Green New Deal Disruption and Destruction," CFACT, August 21, 2020, https://www.cfact.org/2020/08/21/green-new-deal-disruption-and-destruction/?utm_source=rss&utm_medium=rss&utm_campaign=green-new-deal-disruption-and-destruction..

10. Michael Shellenberger, "The Only Green New Deals That Have Ever Worked Were Done with Nuclear, Not Renewables," *Forbes*, February 8, 2019, https://www.forbes.com/sites/michaelshellenberger/2019/02/08/the-only-green-new-deals-that-have-ever-worked-were-done-with-nuclear-not-renewables/#1f2e7927f61c.

11. See, for example, "Green New Deal FAQ," https://apps.npr.org/documents/document.html?id=5729035-Green-New-Deal-FAQ.

12. Andrew Stuttaford, "With Meat We Shall Not Inherit the Earth," National Review, October 27, 2009, https://www.nationalreview.com/corner/meat-we-shall-not-inherit-earth-andrew-stuttaford/..

13. Bjørn Lomborg, "Fewer and fewer people die from climate-related natural disasters…," Facebook, January 23, 2019, https://www.facebook.com/bjornlomborg/photos/a.221758208967/10157523426118968/?type=3&theater..

14. Justin Worland, "If We Want to Stop Climate Change, Now Is a Moment of Reckoning for How We Use the Planet, Warns U.N. Report," Time, August 8, 2019, https://time.com/5646787/ipcc-climate-change-land-report/.

15. Bjørn Lomborg, "Where's the Beef? Ask Green Campaigners," Shine, November 3, 2018, https://www.shine.cn/opinion/1811305941/?mc_cid=d873354042&mc_eid=bcd216d9bf.

16. Marc Morano, "Green New Deal's False Scientific Premise Exposed: Physicist Rips Cow Farting Climate Fears: 'Worrying about Methane Emissions Is the Greatest Waste of Time,' Climate Depot, February 20, 2019, https://www.climatedepot.com/2019/02/20/green-new-deal-false-scientific-premise-exposed-physicist-rips-cow-farting-climate-fears-worrying-about-methane-emissions-is-the-greatest-waste-of-time/.

17. Josh Gabbatiss, "Shipping and Airline Travel Must Be Eliminated in Their Current Forms to Stop Climate Change, Scientists Warn," *Independent*, June 28, 2018, https://uk.news.yahoo.com/shipping-airline-travel-must-eliminated-195745838.html?.

18. David Harsanyi, "The 10 Most Insane Requirements of the Green New Deal," The Federalist, February 7, 2019, https://thefederalist.com/2019/02/07/ten-most-insane-requirements-green-new-deal/.

19. Rupert Darwall, "Biden's 'Building Back Better' Is a Fable—One That Will Ruin Any Post-Covid Recovery," RealClear Energy, September 10, 2020, https://www.realclearenergy.org/articles/2020/09/10/bidens_building_back_better_is_a_fable__one_that_will_ruin_any_post-covid_recovery_576736.html

20. Rupert Darwall, "Growth Will Be a Thing of the Past If Businesses Choose 'Net Zero,'" The Hill, March 7, 2020, https://thehill.com/opinion/energy-environment/486409-growth-will-be-a-thing-of-the-past-if-businesses-choose-net-zero.

21. Steffan Messenger, "Climate change: Call to Ban New Roads As Part of Challenge," BBC News, September 3, 2020, https://www.bbc.com/news/uk-wales-54002555.

22. Harsanyi, "The 10 Most Insane Requirements."

23. Graham Piro, "Yang: Climate Change May Require Elimination of Car Ownership," Washington Free Beacon, September 19, 2019, https://freebeacon.com/politics/yang-well-eliminate-car-ownership-to-fight-climate-change/.

24. Nick Butler, "Electric Vehicles Are Being Outpaced by the Growth of SUVs," *Financial Times*, October 7, 2019, https://www.ft.com/content/24fffce8-e52a-11e9-9743-db5a370481bc?.

25. Steve Milloy, "Joe Biden's Green Dreams Are about Controlling You, Not the Climate," *Federalist*, August 3, 2020, https://thefederalist.com/2020/08/03/joe-bidens-green-dreams-are-about-controlling-you-not-the-climate/.

26. C. Douglas Golden, "Warren Says She's Willing to Ban Construction of New Homes in America," *Western Journal*, January 12, 2020, https://www.westernjournal.com/warren-says-willing-ban-construction-new-homes-america/.

27. Kian Goh, "California's Fires Prove the American Dream Is Flammable," *Nation*, December 23, 2019, https://www.thenation.com/article/archive/california-fires-urban-planning/.

28. Mike Shellenberger (@ShellenbergerMD), "2. I am calling bullshit…," Twitter, February 7, 2019, 2:23 p.m., https://twitter.com/ShellenbergerMD/status/1093591020615262208.

29. "What Is U.S. Electricity Generation by Energy Source," Energy Information Administration, last updated February 27, 2020, https://www.eia.gov/tools/faqs/faq.php?id=427&t=3EIA.

30. Third Way Climate & Energy (@ThirdWayEnergy), "Last night during the #NY14 debate, @AOC made it clear that the door is open for nuclear energy in the #GreenNewDeal "The GND leaves the door open for nuclear," but community input & vetting new technologies is key. 1/," Twitter, May 19, 2020, 1:51 p.m., https://twitter.com/ThirdWayEnergy/status/1262803166053183488.

31. Harsanyi, "10 Most Insane Requirements."

32. John Izzard, "Maurice Strong, Climate Crook," Quadrant, December 2, 2015, https://quadrant.org.au/opinion/doomed-planet/2010/01/discovering-maurice-strong/.

33. Marc Morano, "Fox and Friends," Fox News Channel, February 8, 2019, https://video.foxnews.com/v/5999961462001#sp=show-clips.

34. Kevin Dayaratna and Nicolas Loris, "Assessing the Costs and Benefits of the Green New Deal's Energy Policies," Heritage Foundation, July 24, 2019, https://www.heritage.org/energy-economics/report/assessing-the-costs-and-benefits-the-green-new-deals-energy-policies (internal citation omitted).

35. Kimberley Strassel (@KimStrassel), "1) By the end of the Green New Deal resolution. . .," Twitter, February 7, 2019, 5:57 p.m., https://twitter.com/kimstrassel/status/1093644987256909824?lang=en.

36. Alexandria Ocasio-Cortez (@AOC), "Yup…," Twitter, February 22, 2019, 8:59 p.m., https://twitter.com/AOC/status/1099126500924760064.

37. Patrick Moore (@EcoSenseNow), "Pompous little twit…," Twitter, February 23, 2019, 10:36 a.m., https://twitter.com/EcoSenseNow/status/1099332287282307072.

38. Harsanyi, "10 Most Insane Requirements."

39. Robert Bradley, Jr., "The Green New Deal: The 'Farting Cow' Fiasco Turns One," Master Resource (blog), March 5, 2020, https://www.masterresource.org/green-new-deal/green-new-deal-faq2/.

40. Dayaratna and Loris, "Assessing the Costs and Benefits of the Green New Deal's Energy Policies."

41. Jamie Spry, "Methane Mendacity: Cows, Farts, and New Green Lies," Climatism (blog), February 20, 2019, https://climatism.blog/2019/02/20/methane-mendacity-cows-farts-and-new-green-lies/.

42. RNC Research (@RNCResearch), "Elizabeth Warren: the Green New Deal doesn't go 'far enough'…" Twitter, February 20, 2020,

9:50 p.m., https://twitter.com/RNCResearch/status/12306861 83346331648

43.   Chris Woodward, "Morano: Bernie Sanders, AOC Ghostwriters of Biden's Energy Plan," One News Now, July 15, 2020, https://onenewsnow.com/science-tech/2020/07/15/morano-bernie-sanders-aoc-ghostwriters-of-bidens-energy-plan.

44.   Ronald Bailey, "Biden's New Green New Deal Is the Same as the Old Green New Deal," Reason, July 16, 2020, https://reason.com/2020/07/16/bidens-new-green-new-deal-is-the-same-as-the-old-green-new-deal/.

45.   Yelena Dzhanova, "Joe Biden Spent Way More on Private Jets in the Third Quarter Than His Top 2020 Democratic Rivals," CNBC, October 17, 2019, https://www.cnbc.com/2019/10/17/joe-biden-spent-more-on-private-jets-in-3qthan-2020-democratic-rivals.html..

46.   Marc Morano, "Biden: We're Down to 9 Years to Save Earth from Global Warming," Climate Depot, July 14, 2020, https://www.climatedepot.com/2020/07/14/biden-were-down-to-9-years-to-save-earth-from-global-warming/..

47.   "Joe Biden Town Hall in Peterborough, New Hampshire," C-SPAN, December 29, 2019, https://www.c-span.org/video/?467685-1/joe-biden-holds-town-hall-peterborough-hampshire.

48.   Julian Brave NoiseCat, "Joe Biden Has Endorsed the Green New Deal in All but Name," The Guardian, July 20, 2020, https://www.theguardian.com/commentisfree/2020/jul/20/joe-biden-has-endorsed-the-green-new-deal-in-all-but-name..

49.   Michael Armstrong, "Man and Nature: George Perkins Marsh," Adirondack Explorer, September 23, 2014, https://www.adirondackexplorer.org/book_reviews/man-nature-george-perkins-marsh..

50.   Adam Aton, "Biden Launches 'Climate Engagement' Council to Target Voters," Energy and Environment News Climate Wire, July 6, 2020, https://www.eenews.net/climatewire/stories/1063511913?t=https%3A%2F%2Fwww.eenews.net%2Fstories%2F1063511913.

51.   Joe Biden, "The Biden Plan to Secure Environmental Justice and Equitable Economic Opportunity," BidenHarris campaign website, accessed October 3, 2020, https://joebiden.com/environmental-justice-plan/#.

52.   Bernie Sanders, "Fox and Friends," AIR.TV, Fox News Channel, July 18, 2020, https://www.air.tv/watch?v=cKy2MX6NTByKJRFi7AbVkQ.

53.   "Bernie Sanders Criticized for 'Rank Hypocrisy' on Climate Change after Private Jet Use Revealed," Fox News Insider, July

26, 2019, https://insider.foxnews.com/2019/02/26/bernie-sanders-private-jet-use-candidate-accused-hypocrisy-climate-change-global-warming.

54. Daniel Lippman, "Ex-Clinton Staffers Slam Sanders over Private Jet Flights," *Politico*, February 25, 2019, https://www.politico.com/story/2019/02/25/bernie-sanders-hillary-clinton-private-jet-flights-1182793.

55. Jordan Weissmann, "Joe Biden Is Campaigning on the Green New Deal, Minus the Crazy," Slate, July 15, 2020, https://slate.com/business/2020/07/joe-bidens-climate-plan-is-the-green-new-deal-minus-the-crazy.html.

56. Milloy, "Joe Biden's Green Dreams."

57. Elena Connolly, "New Reporting Sheds Light on Who Is Funding Sunrise," Western Wire, January 10, 2019, https://westernwire.net/new-reporting-sheds-light-on-who-is-funding-sunrise/.

58. Anand Giridharadas, "Noam Chomsky Wants You to Vote for Joe Biden and Then Haunt His Dreams," The.Ink, August 11, 2020, https://the.ink/p/noam-chomsky-wants-you-to-vote-for.

59. GOP War Room, "Biden: 'I Guarantee You We're Going to End Fossil Fuel,'" Youtube, September 6, 2019, https://www.youtube.com/watch?v=Slszva6kk9o

60. Jeff Dunetz, "Video Proof Biden Said He Would Ban Fracking," The Lid, October 22, 2020, https://lidblog.com/video-biden-ban-fracking/.

61. Chris White, "'No New Fracking': Biden Calls for High Speed Rail to Move U.S. away from Oil Drilling," Daily Caller, March 15, 2020, https://dailycaller.com/2020/03/15/joe-biden-new-fracking-ban-high-speed-rail/.

62. Matt Margolis, "Kamala Harris Flip-Flops on Fracking after Polls Tighten in Pennsylvania," PJ Media, September 7, 2020, https://pjmedia.com/election/matt-margolis/2020/09/07/kamala-harris-flip-flops-on-fracking-after-polls-tighten-in-pennsylvania-n899077.

63. The Hill (@thehill), "It is a fact that we can change human behaviors…," Twitter, March 10, 2019, 11:33 a.m., https://twitter.com/thehill/status/1104767114605342722.

64. Alex Epstein, "2020 Talking Points on Joe Biden's Energy Plan," Energy Talking Points, https://energytalkingpoints.com/bidens-energy-plan/

Chapter 5: Europe Is Already "Enjoying" Their Version of the Green New Deal—and It's Not Going Well

1. European Commission, "A European Green Deal," https://ec.europa.eu/info/strategy/priorities-2019-2024/european-green-deal_en.
2. Karl Mathiesen, "Europe's Climate Goal: Revolution," Politico, June 17, 2020, https://www.politico.eu/article/europe-climate-goal-revolution-net-zero-emissions/.
3. European Commision, "The European Green Deal," December 11, 2019, https://g8fip1kplyr33r3krz5b97d1-wpengine.netdna-ssl.com/wp-content/uploads/2019/12/The-European-Green-Deal-Communication.pdf.
4. Mathiesen, "Europe's Climate Goal."
5. Marc Morano, "Morano Confronts Pres. Macron at UN Climate Summit: 'Trump Is Correct on Climate Change,'" CFACT, November 15, 2017, YouTube, https://youtu.be/6iEMyr9g44E.
6. Ibid.
7. Mathiesen, "Europe's Climate Goal."
8. Lubos Motl, "European Green Deal: 120 Silly Demands," The Reference Frame blog, January 23, 2020, https://motls.blogspot.com/2020/01/european-green-deal-120-silly-demands.html.
9. Marc Morano, "COP24: Why Is the World Struggling to Quit Coal?," The Newsmakers, December 7, 2018, YouTube, https://youtu.be/-_6EDvXgDR0, from The Newsmakers, TRT World TV, Dec 6, 2018..
10. James Roberts, Nicolas Loris, and Kevin Dayaratna, "Green New Deals: Bad for Americans and Bad for Europeans," Heritage Foundation, August 7, 2020, https://www.heritage.org/energy-economics/report/green-new-deals-bad-americans-and-bad-europeans..
11. Frederic Simon, "Eleven Million Jobs at Risk from EU Green Deal, Trade Unions Warn," Euractiv, March 10, 2020, https://www.euractiv.com/section/energy-environment/news/eleven-million-jobs-at-risk-from-eu-green-deal-trade-unions-warn/.
12. "US Calls Out Europe for Emissions Cheating," *The American Interest*, September 28, 2016, The Global Warming Policy Forum, https://www.thegwpf.com/green-fraudsters-us-calls-out-europe-for-emissions-cheating/.
13. Motl, "European Green Deal: 120 Silly Demands."

14. Dimitris Mavrokefalidis, "Almost 3m Elderly People Turn Off Heating As 'They Cannot Afford Energy Bills,'" Energy Live News, March 10, 2020, https://www.energylivenews.com/2020/03/10/almost-3m-elderly-people-turn-off-heating-as-they-cannot-afford-energy-bills/.

15. Ronald Stein, "Democrats [*sic*] Climate Policy Follows Germany's Failed Plan," CFACT, |July 9th, 2020, https://www.cfact.org/2020/07/09/democrats-climate-policy-follows-germanys-failed-plan/?utm_source=feedly&utm_medium=rss&utm_campaign=democrats-climate-policy-follows-germanys-failed-plan.

16. Christopher Monckton, interview with Marc Morano, *Climate Hustle* (film), 2015, https://www.climatehustle.org/.

17. Jim Ratcliffe, "Open Letter to the European Commission President Jean-Claude Juncker," INEOS Group, February 12, 2019, https://www.ineos.com/news/ineos-group/letter-to-the-european-commission-president-jean-claude-juncker/.

18. Mike Travers, "The Hidden Cost of Net Zero: Rewiring the UK," Global Warming Policy Foundation, July 16, 2020, https://www.thegwpf.org/content/uploads/2020/07/Travers-Net-Zero-Distribution-Grid-Replacement.pdf.

19. Matt Oliver, "Government's Green Housing Plan under Fire As Developers Claim It Is 'Unworkable,'" This Is Money, March 6, 2020, https://www.thisismoney.co.uk/money/markets/article-8084233/Developers-claim-Governments-Green-housing-plan-unworkable.html..

20. Ritzau/The Local, "Danes to Sort Trash into Ten Types under New Green Deal," The Local, June 17, 2020, https://www.thelocal.dk/20200617/danes-to-sort-trash-into-ten-types-under-new-green-deal.

21. Laurence Frost and Edward Taylor, "Carmakers Near CO2 Cliff-Edge in Electrification Race," Reuters, September 9, 2019, https://www.reuters.com/article/us-autoshow-frankfurt-carbon/carmakers-near-co2-cliff-edge-in-electrification-race-idUSKCN1VU2IF.

22. Cristina Abellan Matamoros, "Bavarian MPs Who Don't Enforce Environmental Rules 'Could Face Jail,'" EuroNews, September 2, 2019,https://www.euronews.com/2019/09/02/bavarian-mps-who-don-t-enforce-environmental-rules-could-face-jail.

23. "Ambitious EU Climate Efforts Could Increase Greenhouse Gas Emissions in the Rest of the World," University of Copenhagen, May 18, 2020, https://news.ku.dk/all_news/2020/05/ambitious-eu-

climate-efforts-could-increase-greenhouse-gas-emissions-in-the-rest-of-the-world/.

24. Hank Berrien, "HAHAHA: Greenhouse Gas Emissions Falling in U.S., Climbing in Europe," The Daily Wire, July 3, 2018, https://www.dailywire.com/news/hahaha-greenhouse-gas-emissions-falling-us-hank-berrien?amp.

25. John Larsen, Kate Larsen, Whitney Herndon, Peter Marsters, Hannah Pitt, and Shashank Mohan, "Taking Stock 2018," Rhodium Group, June 28, 2018, https://rhg.com/research/taking-stock-2018/.

26. Wusheng Yu and Francesca Clora, "Implications of Decarbonizing the EU Economy on Trade Flows and Carbon Leakages," February 2020, https://european-calculator.eu/wp-content/uploads/2020/04/EUCalc_PB_n07_Trade.pdf.

27. George Agbugba, et al., "The Decoupling of Economic Growth from Carbon Emissions: UK Evidence," Office for National Statistics, last updated October 21, 2019, https://www.ons.gov.uk/economy/nationalaccounts/uksectoraccounts/compendium/economicreview/october2019/thedecouplingofeconomicgrowthfromcarbonemissionsukevidence#toc.

28. Richard Partington, "Britain Now G7's Biggest Net Importer of CO2 Emissions Per Capita, Says ONS," *Guardian*, October 21, 2019, https://www.theguardian.com/uk-news/2019/oct/21/britain-is-g7s-biggest-net-importer-of-co2-emissions-per-capita-says-ons.

29. Justin Worland, "How Europe's Border Carbon Tax Plan Could Force the U.S. to Act on Climate Change," *Time*, March 4, 2020, https://time.com/5793918/european-union-border-carbon-tax/.

30. Joe Barnes, "EU Crisis: Bloc Admits Failing at Almost Every Green Goal—'Get Our Own House in Order,'" *Express*, December 4, 2019, https://www.express.co.uk/news/world/1212809/EU-news-European-Environmental-Agency-climate-emergency-latest-update.

31. Frederic Simon, "EU National Climate Plans Well below Par, Study Reveals," Euractiv, May 16, 2019, updated March 4, 2020, https://www.euractiv.com/section/climate-strategy-2050/news/eu-national-climate-plans-well-below-par-study-shows/.

32. Dimitris Mavrokefalidis, "Progress Towards the EU's Climate and Energy Targets Has Stalled," Energy Live News, June 23, 2020, https://www.energylivenews.com/2020/06/23/progress-towards-the-eus-climate-and-energy-targets-has-stalled/.

33. Steve Milloy (@JunkScience), "The EU has yet to meet any climate target...," Twitter, September 5, 2020, https://twitter.com/ JunkScience/status/1302257344517214208.

34. Stephen Moore, "'Who's the Cleanest of Them All,'" *Washington Times*, August 19, 2018, https://www.washingtontimes.com/ news/2018/aug/19/ the-united-states-didnt-sign-the-paris-climate-acc/.

35. James Delingpole, "Britain Unleashes a Green New Deal to Kill What's Left of the Economy," Breitbart, June 3, 2020, https://www. breitbart.com/europe/2020/06/03/ britain-unleashes-green-new-deal-to-kill-whats-left-of-the-economy/.

36. Sandor Zsiros, "Eco Groups Fear Green Recovery May Get Watered Down," EuroNews, June 11, 2020, https://www.euronews. com/2020/06/11/eco-groups-fear-green-recovery-may-get-watered-down.

37. "Konferencja o ekoideologii: „ONZ chce jeszcze większej kontroli," Polonia Christiana, https://www.pch24.pl/konferencja-o-ekoideologii—onz-chce-jeszcze-wiekszej-kontroli,64775,i.html.

38. Tom Harris, "Biden Can't Have it Both Ways on Paris Climate Accord," The Post & Email, October 16, 2020, https://www. thepostemail.com/2020/10/16/ biden-cant-have-it-both-ways-on-paris-climate-accord/.

Chapter 6: The Green New Deal Plagiarizes the Same "Solutions" from Previous Environmental Scares

1. Ronald Bailey, "Biden's New Green New Deal Is the Same as the Old Green New Deal," *Reason*, July 16, 2020, https://reason. com/2020/07/16/ bidens-new-green-new-deal-is-the-same-as-the-old-green-new-deal/.

2. Eric Holthaus (@EricHolthaus), "The climate emergency isn't about science, it's about justice...," Twitter, July 28, 2020, 8:45 a.m., https://twitter.com/EricHolthaus/status/1288093160829341697.

3. Anthony Watts, "@EricHolthaus—New IPCC Report Calls For '...Rigorous Backing to Systematically Dismantle Capitalism,'" Watts Up With That (blog), October 9, 2018, https:// wattsupwiththat.com/2018/10/09/ericholthaus-new-ipcc-report-calls-for-rigorous-backing-to-systematically-dismantle-capitalism/.

4. The Editorial Board, "The Green New Deal Is Better Than Our Climate Nightmare," *New York Times*, February 23, 2019, https://

www.nytimes.com/2019/02/23/opinion/green-new-deal-climate-democrats.html.

5. David Montgomery, "AOC's Chief of Change," *Washington Post Magazine*, July 10, 2019, https://www.washingtonpost.com/news/magazine/wp/2019/07/10/feature/how-saikat-chakrabarti-became-aocs-chief-of-change/.

6. Marc Morano, "Flashback: UN IPCC Official Admits UN Seeks to 'Redistribute De Facto the World's Wealth by Climate Policy,'" Climate Depot, September 10, 2015, http://test.climatedepot.com/2015/09/10/flashback-un-ipcc-official-admits-un-seeks-to-redistribute-de-facto-the-worlds-wealth-by-climate-policy/.

7. Michael Bastach, "Liberal Campaigner Calls 'Green New Deal' a Plan to 'Redistribute Wealth and Power' from Rich to Poor," Daily Caller, February 5, 2019, https://dailycaller.com/2019/02/05/ocasio-cortez-green-deal-redistribute-wealth/.

8. United States Senate Committee on Commerce, *Domestic Supply Information Act: Joint Hearings before the Committee on Commerce and Committee on Government Operations, United States Senate, Ninety-third Congress, Second Session…* (Washington, D.C.: U.S. Government Printing Office, 1974).

9. Vaclav Klaus, interview in Marc Morano, *Climate Hustle 2* (film), 2020, www.ClimateHustle.com.

10. John Holdren, Anne Ehrlich, and Paul Ehrlich, *Human Ecology: Problems and Solutions* (San Francisco: W.H. Freeman and Company, 1973), 279.

11. Robert Bradley, Jr., "John Holdren: White House Malthusian," Master Resource blog, March 3, 2011, https://www.masterresource.org/holdren-john/holdren-malthusian/#more-14268.

12. Holdren, Ehrlich, and Ehrlich, *Human Ecology*, 5.

13. Bill Gates, "An Economist and a Biologist Test a Theory," GatesNotes, December 12, 2013, https://www.gatesnotes.com/books/the-bet.

14. Bradley, Jr., "John Holdren: White House Malthusian."

15. NPR Staff, "Transcript: Greta Thunberg's Speech at the U.N. Climate Action Summit," NPR, September 23, 2019, https://www.npr.org/2019/09/23/763452863/transcript-greta-thunbergs-speech-at-the-u-n-climate-action-summit.

16. Leo Marx, "American Institutions and Ecological Ideals: Scientific and Literary Views of Our Expansionary Life-Style Are Converging," November 27, 1970, http://dlc.dlib.indiana.edu/dlc/

bitstream/handle/10535/2461/LMAM70AA.pdf.txt?sequence=2 for full text.

17. Marc Morano, "Flashback: Gore: U.S. Climate Bill Will Help Bring About 'Global Governance,'" Climate Depot, July 10, 2009, http://www.climatedepot.com/2009/07/10/flashback-gore-us-climate-bill-will-help-bring-about-global-governance-2/.

18. Adam Brickley, "Global 'Ecological Board of Directors' Envisioned by State Department's Climate Czar," CNSNews.com, September 4, 2009, https://www.cnsnews.com/news/article/global-ecological-board-directors-envisioned-state-department-s-climate-czar.

19. Christopher C. Horner, "Chirac: Kyoto 'First Step Toward Global Governance,'" Competitive Enterprise Institute, November 19, 2000, https://cei.org/content/chirac-kyoto-first-step-toward-global-governance

20. Michael Palicz, "Green New Deal: 'Air Travel Stops Becoming Necessary,'" Americans for Tax Reform, February 7, 2019, https://www.atr.org/green-new-deal-air-travel-stops-becoming-necessary.

21. Elizabeth Kolbert, "Global Warming Talks Progress Is 'Slow but Steady'—UN Climate Chief," *Guardian*, November 21, 2012, https://www.theguardian.com/environment/2012/nov/21/global-warming-talks-progress-un-climate-chief.

22. George Getze, "Dire Famine Forecast by '75," *Los Angeles Times*, November 17, 1967, https://latimes.newspapers.com/image/382441164/?.

23. Gladwin Hillspecial, "A Sterility Drug in Food Is Hinted," *New York Times*, November 25, 1969, https://www.nytimes.com/1969/11/25/archives/a-sterility-drug-in-food-is-hinted-biologist-stresses-need-to-curb.html.

24. Nigel Lawson, "Apocalypse Later," *Wall Street Journal*, July 27, 2015, https://www.wsj.com/articles/apocalypse-later-1438039375?.

25. Bahgat Elnadi and Adel Rifaat, "Interview: Jacques-Yves Cousteau," *UNESCO Courier*, November 1991, https://unesdoc.unesco.org/ark:/48223/pf0000090256.

26. Tony Heller, "UN Depopulation Agenda," YouTube, July 22, 2020, https://youtu.be/5JBrVY4-h7U.

27. Eric Roston, "Earth Needs Fewer People to Beat the Climate Crisis, Scientists Say," Bloomberg, November 5, 2019, https://www.bloomberg.com/news/articles/2019-11-05/scientists-call-for-population-control-in-mass-climate-alarm.

28. John Lennon, "John & Yoko on Overpopulation," Thenewsurvivalist, YouTube, October 18, 2010, https://youtu.be/EASoPHn2CWs.2.

29. William J. Ripple, et al., "World Scientists' Warning of a Climate Emergency," BioScience 70, no. 1 (January 2020): 8-12, https://doi.org/10.1093/biosci/biz088. A correction has been published, "Corrigendum: World Scientists' Warning of a Climate Emergency," BioScience 70, no. 1 (January 2020): 100, https://doi.org/10.1093/biosci/biz152..

30. Bruce Golding, "Climate Change Fears Keep Some Americans from Having Kids, Study Finds," *New York Post*, November 27, 2020, https://nypost.com/2020/11/27/climate-change-fears-keep-americans-from-having-kids-study/

31. Steve Milloy, "Gore Goes Malthusian: Frets about Accommodating Growing Middle Class 'on a Finite Planet,'" JunkScience.com, February 4, 2013, https://junkscience.com/2013/02/gore-goes-malthusian-frets-about-growing-middle-class-on-a-finite-planet/.

32. Ying Ma, "Alexandria Ocasio-Cortez's Latest Climate Fix—No Children for You," Fox News, February 26, 2019, https://www.foxnews.com/opinion/alexandria-ocasio-cortezs-latest-climate-fix-no-children-for-you.

33. Jeff Wise, "About That Overpopulation Problem," Slate, January 9, 2013, https://slate.com/technology/2013/01/world-population-may-actually-startdeclining-not-exploding.html..

34. Jennifer Ludden, "Should We Be Having Kids in the Age of Climate Change?," NPR, August 18, 2016, https://www.npr.org/2016/08/18/479349760/should-we-be-having-kids-in-the-age-of-climate-change?.

35. Gregg Re, "Berkeley Declares 'Climate Emergency' Worse than World War II, Demands 'Humane' Population Control," Fox News, June 13, 2018, https://www.foxnews.com/politics/berkeley-declares-climate-emergency-worse-than-world-war-ii-demands-humane-population-control.

36. Melanie Arter, "Jerry Brown: 3 Billion Will Die from Global Warming," CNSNews.com, April 19, 2018, https://www.cnsnews.com/news/article/melanie-arter/california-governor-predicts-billions-will-die-heat-because-climate.

37. Re, "Berkeley Declares 'Climate Emergency.'"

38. Marc Morano, "Watch: Morano on Fox Debunking New Antarctic Ice Melt Scare & Explaining How 'Global Warming' Will Solve Alleged Overpopulation Problem," Climate Depot, June 15,

2018,https://www.climatedepot.com/2018/06/15/watch-morano-on-fox-debunking-new-antarctic-ice-melt-scare-explaining-how-global-warming-will-solve-alleged-overpopulation-problem/.

39. Valerie Richardson, "Ex-Alarmist Disputes Climate Narrative in New Book," *Washington Times*, July 1, 2020, https://www.washingtontimes.com/news/2020/jul/1/michael-shellenberger-ex-alarmist-disputes-climate/.

40. Peter Gwynne, "The Cooling World," *Newsweek*, April 28, 1975, https://www.scribd.com/doc/225798861/Newsweek-s-Global-Cooling-Article-From-April-28-1975.

41. Rob Verger, "Newsweek Rewind: Debunking Global Cooling," *Newsweek*, May 23, 2014, https://www.newsweek.com/newsweek-rewind-debunking-global-cooling-252326.

42. Josh Gabbatiss, "First Ever Sun-Dimming Experiment Will Mimic Volcanic Eruption in Attempt to Reverse Global Warming," *Independent*, December 4, 2018, https://www.independent.co.uk/news/science/sun-dimming-solar-geoengineering-volcano-eruption-global-warming-climate-change-harvard-a8667141.html.

43. Keith Johnson, "Team Obama: We'll Consider Geoengineering to Fight Climate Change," *Wall Street Journal*, April 8, 2009, https://www.wsj.com/articles/BL-EB-4019.

44. Impact Team, *The Weather Conspiracy: The Coming of the New Ice Age* (New York: Ballantine Books, 1977), 127.

45. Tony Heller, "Before Fossil Fuels Caused Global Warming, They Caused Global Cooling," Real Climate Science (blog), June 6, 2016, https://realclimatescience.com/2016/06/before-fossil-fuels-caused-global-warming-they-caused-global-cooling/..

46. Zombie, "The Coming of the New Ice Age: End of the Global Warming Era?" PJ Media, January 31, 2012, https://pjmedia.com/zombie/2012/01/31/the-coming-of-the-new-ice-age-end-of-the-global-warming-era-n137133..

47. John P. Holdren and Paul R. Ehrlich, "Overpopulation and the Potential for Ecocide," in *Global Ecology: Readings toward a Rational Strategy for Man*, eds. Holdren and Ehrlich (New York: Harcourt Brace Jovanovich, 1971), 76–77.

48. Louise Gray, "Cancun Climate Change Summit: Scientists Call for Rationing in Developed World," *Telegraph*, November 29, 2010, https://aftermathnews.wordpress.com/2010/11/30/cancun-climate-change-summit-scientists-call-for-rationing-in-developed-world/.

49. Reuters, "Third Biggest Greenhouse Gas Emitter? Word's Wasted Food," NBC News, September 11, 2013, https://www.nbcnews.

com/science/wasted-food-third-biggest-greenhouse-gas-culprit-after-china-us-8C11128871.

50. Rachel Sharp, "Bill Gates Is Accused of Hypocrisy after Joining Bidding War to Buy the World's Largest Private Jet Operator," UK Daily Mail, January 8, 2021, https://www.dailymail.co.uk/news/article-9128203/Bill-Gates-bids-private-jet-operator-one-month-releases-climate-change-book.html. .

51. Marc Morano, "Watch: Morano on Fox and Friends on Bill Gates Private Jet & COVID Lockdown Hypocrisy," Climate Depot, January 10, 2021, https://www.climatedepot.com/2021/01/10/watch-morano-on-fox-and-friends-on-bill-gates-private-jet-covid-lockdown-hypocrisy-gates-is-1-carbon-footprint-of-all-celebrity-climate-activists-30k-a-month-electricity-bill-at-his-home/..

52. Marc Morano, Fox & Friends, Fox News Channel, February 26, 2019, https://www.climatedepot.com/2019/02/26/watch-morano-on-fox-friends-bernie-theprivate-jets-sanders-wants-fossil-fuels-kept-in-the-ground-but-he-cant-keepfrom-using-fossil-fuels-lavishly-in-the-air/..

53. Margaret Munro, "Quadruple Gas Price to Save Planet, Climatologist Urges," *Vancouver Sun*, June 9, 2011, https://vancouversun.com/news/quadruple-gas-price-to-save-planet-climatologist-urges.

54. 155 Cong. Rec. 10553 (2009), https://www.govinfo.gov/content/pkg/CRECB-2009-pt8/html/CRECB-2009-pt8-issue-2009-04-23.htm.

55. Bjørn Lomborg, "Trump Is Right to Reject Paris Climate Deal: It's Likely to Be a Costly Failure," *Daily Telegraph*, June 1, 2017, https://www.telegraph.co.uk/news/2017/06/01/donald-trump-right-reject-paris-climate-change-treaty-likely/.

56. Kian Goh, "California's Fires Prove the American Dream Is Flammable," The Nation, December 23, 2019, https://www.thenation.com/article/archive/california-fires-urban-planning/..

57. Zombie, "The Coming of the New Ice Age: End of the Global Warming Era?".

58. C. Douglas Golden, "Warren Says She's Willing to Ban Construction of New Homes in America," Western Journal, January 12, 2020, https://www.westernjournal.com/warren-says-willing-ban-construction-new-homes-america/.

59. Graham Piro, "Yang: Climate Change May Require Elimination of Car Ownership," *Washington Free Beacon*, September 19, 2019, https://freebeacon.com/politics/yang-well-eliminate-car-ownership-to-fight-climate-change/.

60. Kenneth Richard, "Massive Cover-Up Exposed: 285 Papers from 1960s–80s Reveal Robust Global Cooling Scientific 'Consensus,'" NoTricksZone, September 13, 2016,http://notrickszone.com/2016/09/13/

61. Jason Koebler, "Study: Global Warming Can Be Slowed by Working Less," *U.S. News & World Report*, February 4, 2013, https://www.usnews.com/news/articles/2013/02/04/-study-global-warming-can-be-slowed-by-working-less; David Rosnick, "Reduced Work Hours as a Means of Slowing Climate Change," Center for Economic and Policy Research, February 2013, https://www.cepr.net/documents/publications/climate-change-workshare-2013-02.pdf.

62. Marc Morano, "Eat Insects? 'Meat Patch' to Stop Cravings? New UN Report Takes Aim at Meat Eating—UN Seeks Expansion of Climate Agenda to Regulate What You Eat," Climate Depot, August 8, 2019, https://www.climatedepot.com/2019/08/08/poop-burgers-meat-patch-to-stop-cravings-new-un-report-takes-aim-at-meat-eating-un-seeks-expansion-of-climate-agenda-to-regulate-what-you-eat/

63. Michelle S. Tom, Paul S. Fischbeck, and Chris T. Hendrickson, "Energy Use, Blue Water Footprint, and Greenhouse Gas Emissions for Current Food Consumption Patterns and Dietary Recommendations in the U.S.," Environment Systems and Decisions 36, no. 1 (March 2016): 92–103, https://doi.org/10.1007/s10669-015-9577-y..

64. Geoffrey Lean, "Cow 'Emissions' More Damaging to Planet than CO2 from Cars," Independent, December 10, 2006, https://www.independent.co.uk/environment/climate-change/cow-emissions-more-damaging-to-planet-thanco2-from-cars-427843.html..

65. Rachel Koning Beals, "Eating Out, Ice Cream, and Booze May Be Worse for Climate Change Than Meat," Market Watch, January 6, 2020, https://www.marketwatch.com/story/dining-out-dessert-and-booze-may-be-worse-for-climate-change-than-meat-2019-12-26.

66. S. Matthew Liao, "Human Engineering and Climate Change," S. Matthew Liao (blog), February 9, 2012, http://www.smatthewliao.com/2012/02/09/human-engineering-andclimate-change/; Marc Morano, "NYU Prof. S.Matthew Liao of Center for Bioethics Promotes 'Solution of Human Engineering. It Involves the Biomedical Modification of Humans to Make Them Better at Mitigating Climate Change,'" Climate Depot, https://test.climatedepot.com/2012/03/12/nyu-prof-s-matthew-liao-of-center-for-bioethics-promotes-solution-of-human-engineering-it-involves-the-

biomedical-modification-of-humans-to-make-them-better-at-mitigating-climate-change/.

67. Joseph Bennington-Castro, "How Crickets Could Help Save the Planet," NBC News, February 16, 2017, https://www.nbcnews.com/mach/environment/how-eating-crickets-could-help-save-planet-n721416.

68. Marc Morano, "Climate Depot Round Up: Flashback 2012: Meet Man Who Wants to Engineer a Master Climate Race?! NYU Prof. Matthew Liao: Humans Genetically Engineered to Combat Global Warming—'Pharmacological Enhancement,'" Climate Depot, February 28, 2014, http://www.climatedepot.com/2014/02/28/climate-depot-round-up-flashback-2012-meetman-who-wants-to-engineer-a-master-climaterace-nyu-prof-matthew-liao-humans-geneticallyengineered-to-combat-global-warmingpharmac/; Sydney Opera House Talks & Ideas, "Matthew Liao—Engineer Humans to Stop Climate Change (Ideas at the House)," YouTube, June 25, 2013, https://www.youtube.com/watch?v=KzBVtmyN6_Y.

69. Marc Morano, "NYU Bioethicist Prof. Liao on Eating Meat: Seeks to 'Make Ourselves Allergic to Those Proteins…Unpleasant Reaction…the Way We Can Do That Is to Create Some Sort of Meat Patch,'" Climate Depot, October 20, 2012, https://www.climatedepot.com/2012/10/20/nyu-bioethicist-prof-liao-on-eating-meat-seeks-to-make-ourselves-allergic-to-those-proteinsunpleasant-reactionthe-way-we-can-do-that-is-to-create-some-sort-of-meat-patch/.

70. Sumaira FH, "UN Chief Tells Climate Summit Huge Carbon Cuts, New Carbon Taxes Needed in 2020," UrduPoint, December 11, 2019, https://www.urdupoint.com/en/world/un-chief-tells-climate-summit-huge-carbon-cut-784708.html.

71. Marc Morano, "Global Warming Professor Kevin Anderson 'Cuts back on Washing and Showering' to Fight Climate Change—Admits at UN Climate Summit: 'That is Why I Smell'—Defends His Call for 'a Planned Economic Recession,'" Climate Depot, November 19, 2013, https://www.climatedepot.com/2013/11/19/global-warming-professor-kevin-anderson-cuts-back-on-washing-and-showering-to-fight-climate-change-admits-at-un-climate-summit-that-is-why-i-smell/.

72. Marc Morano, "'We Don't Need No CO2'—'Don't Need No Bath': Children 'Astronauts' Awarded by UN for 'Climate Song,'" Climate Depot, February 22, 2016, https://www.climatedepot.com/2016/02/22/we-dont-need-no-co2-dont-need-no-bath-children-astronauts-awarded-by-un-for-climate-song/.

73. Bernadette la Hengst, "Climate Astronauts Feat. Climate Fairy," YouTube, October 14, 2015, https://youtu.be/krFjP3cOoeU.

74. Rustybx "Al Gore Takes Private Jet—9/9/07 (Complete Version), rustybx, September 9, 2007, YouTube, 3:45, https://youtu.be/2VV309lbB8c.

Chapter 7: The Red New Deal? The Watermelon Cut Open

1. Michael Winship, "Naomi Klein: 'There are no non-radical options left before us,'" Salon, FEBRUARY 4, 2016, https://www.salon.com/2016/02/04/naomi_klein_there_are_no_non_radical_options_left_before_us_parner/.

2. Geoff, "Naomi Klein Admits That It's Not about Carbon—It's about Capitalism," The Australian Climate Sceptics Blog, February 21, 2017, https://theclimatescepticsparty.blogspot.com/2017/02/naomi-klein-admits-that-its-not-about.html.

3. Walter E. Williams, "Fascism and Communism," *Patriot Post*, December 20, 2017, https://patriotpost.us/opinion/53010.

4. "What Is Degrowth?," Degrowth Web Portal, https://www.degrowth.info/en/what-is-degrowth/.

5. Vaclav Klaus, interview in Marc Morano, *Climate Hustle* 2 (film), 2020, www.ClimateHustle2.com.

6. Alice Bows-Larkin, "Climate Change Is happening. Here's How We Adapt," TedGlobalLondon, June 2015, https://www.ted.com/talks/alice_bows_larkin_climate_change_is_happening_here_s_how_we_adapt?language=en.

7. Kevin Anderson and Alice Bows, "Reframing the Climate Change Challenge in Light of Post-2000 Emission Trends," *Philosophical Transactions of the Royal Society A: Mathematical, Physical and Engineering Sciences* 366, no. 1882 (November 2008): 3863–82, https://doi.org/10.1098/rsta.2008.0138.

8. Tom Rogan, "George Monbiot and the Climate Change Heart of Darkness," *Washington Examiner*, April 19, 2019, https://www.washingtonexaminer.com/opinion/george-monbiot-and-the-climate-change-heart-of-darkness.

9. Alice Bows-Larkin, "Climate Change Is Happening. Here's How We Adapt," TEDGlobalLondon, June 2015, TED video, https://www.ted.com/talks/alice_bows_larkin_climate_change_is_happening_here_s_how_we_adapt/details?.

10. John Vidal, "Make the Rich Change Their Ways to Avoid a 2C Rise, Says Top Scientist," *Guardian*, November 21, 2013, https://www. theguardian.com/environment/2013/nov/21/climate-change-2c-rise.

11. Richard Tol (@RichardTol), "Kevin Anderson…," Twitter, November 21, 2013, 2:53 p.m., https://twitter.com/RichardTol/ status/403612173521272833.

12. Mark Bray, "How Capitalism Stokes the Far Right and Climate Catastrophe," Truthout, October 30, 2018, https://truthout.org/ articles/how-capitalism-stokes-the-far-right-and-climate-catastrophe/.

13. Tom Nelson, "Warmist Kevin Anderson: 'I Think It's Extremely Unlikely That We Wouldn't Have Mass Death at 4 Degrees," Tom Nelson blog, July 9, 2011, http://tomnelson.blogspot.com/2011/07/ warmist-kevin-anderson-think-its.html.

14. Vaclav Klaus, interview.

15. Nafeez Ahmed, "Scientists Warn the UN of Capitalism's Imminent Demise," Vice, August 27, 2018, https://www.vice.com/en/ article/43pek3/scientists-warn-the-un-of-capitalisms-imminent- demise.

16. Thomas Wiedmann, et al., "Scientists' Warning on Affluence," *Nature Communications* 11, no. 3107 (June 2020): https://doi. org/10.1038/s41467-020-16941-y.

17. Marc Morano, "'Scientists' warning on affluence': Study: Wealth harms the planet! Solutions? 'Degrowth'; 'Eco-socialism'; Banning 'oversized vehicles'; 'Eco-feminism'; 'Maximum income levels,'" Climate Depot, June 20, 2020, https://www.climatedepot. com/2020/06/20/scientists-warning-on-affluence-study-wealth- harms-the-planet-solutions-degrowth-eco-socialism-banning- oversized-vehicles-eco-feminism-maximum-income-levels/.

18. Daniel W. O'Neill, et al., "A Good Life for All within Planetary Boundaries," *Nature Sustainability* 1, no. 2 (February 2018): 88–95, https://doi.org/10.1038/s41893-018-0021-4.

19. Wesley J. Smith, "Environmentalists Push Global Wealth Redistribution," *National Review*, February 6, 2018, https://www. nationalreview.com/corner/environmentalists-push-global-wealth- redistribution/.

20. NPR Staff, "Transcript: Greta Thunberg's Speech at the U.N. Climate Action Summit," NPR, September 23, 2019, https://www. npr.org/2019/09/23/763452863/transcript-greta-thunbergs- speech-at-the-u-n-climate-action-summit.

21. Natasha Chassagne, "Here's What the Coronavirus Pandemic Can Teach Us about Tackling Climate Change," The Conversation,

March 26, 2020, https://theconversation.com/heres-what-the-coronavirus-pandemic-can-teach-us-about-tackling-climate-change-134399.

22. Stephen Moore, "Beware the Left's 'Degrowth' Movement," RealClearPolitics, April 15, 2020, https://www.realclearpolitics. com/articles/2020/04/15/beware_the_lefts_degrowth_ movement_142942.html.

23. Stephen Moore, "Beware the Left's 'Degrowth' Movement," RealClearPolitics, April 15, 2020, https://www.realclearpolitics. com/articles/2020/04/15/beware_the_lefts_degrowth_ movement_142942.html.

24. Vaclav Klaus, "Freedom, Not Climate, Is at Risk," Financial Times, June 13, 2007, https://www.ft.com/ content/9deb730a-19ca-11dc-99c5-000b5df10621#axzz2wKiaXK90..

25. Roger Pielke Jr., "1974 Ehrlich and Holdren Senate Testimony," Roger Pielke Jr.'s Blog, SEPTEMBER 3, 2013, http://rogerpielkejr. blogspot.com/2013/09/1974-ehrlich-and-holdren-senate.html

26. Brian Sussman, interview in Marc Morano, Climate Hustle 2 (film), 2020, www.ClimateHustle2.com..

27. Nicolas Loris, "UN's Solution to Climate Change: End Capitalism," The Daily Signal, October 19, 2018, https://www.dailysignal. com/2018/10/19/uns-solution-to-climate-change-end-capitalism/..

28. Mackenzie Mount, "Work Less to Live More," Sierra Magazine, March 6, 2014, https://www.sierraclub.org/sierra/2014-2-march-april/green-biz/work-less-live-more..

29. Emily Gosden, "Prince Charles: reform capitalism to save the planet," UK Telegraph, May 27, 2014, http://www.telegraph.co.uk/news/uknews/prince-charles/10859230/Prince-Charles-reform-capitalism-to-save-the-planet.html/

30. Phil McDuff, "Ending Climate Change Requires the End of Capitalism. Have We Got the Stomach for It?," *Guardian*, March 18, 2019, https://www.theguardian.com/commentisfree/2019/mar/18/ending-climate-change-end-capitalism.

31. Conrad Black, "How the Post-Soviet Left Latched onto the Climate for Crusade on Capitalism," *New York Sun*, December 5, 2015, https://www.nysun.com/foreign/how-the-post-soviet-left-latched-onto-the-climate/89372/.

32. Nicolas Loris, "U.N. Climate Report Merely a Blueprint for Destroying the World Economy," Heritage Foundation, October 17th, 2018, https://www.heritage.org/energy-economics/commentary/un-climate-report-merely-blueprint-destroying-the-world-economy.

33. Dominic Mealy, "'To Halt Climate Change, We Need an Ecological Leninism': An Interview with Andreas Malm," Jacobin, June 15, 2020, https://www.jacobinmag.com/2020/06/andreas-malm-coronavirus-covid-climate-change.

34. Nafeez Ahmed, "Scientists Vindicate 'Limits to Growth'—Urge Investment in 'Circular Economy,'" The Guardian, June 4, 2018, https://www.theguardian.com/environment/earth-insight/2014/jun/04/scientists-limits-to-growth-vindicatedinvestment-transition-circular-economy?CMP=twt_gu..

35. Christopher Monctkon, interview in Marc Morano, Climate Hustle 2 (film), 2020, www.ClimateHustle2.com..

36. "Economic Degrowth Compatible with Wellbeing if Work Stability Is Maintained," Science Codex, March 12, 2014, https://www.sciencecodex.com/economic_degrowth_compatible_with_wellbeing_if_work_stability_is_maintained-129540..

37. Gabrielle Chan, "Climate Sceptic Maurice Newman Says World Leaders Embracing Junk Science," *Guardian*, December 27, 2015, http://www.theguardian.com/australia-news/2015/dec/28/climate-sceptic-maurice-newman-says-world-leaders-embracing-junk-science.

Chapter 8: Even Many Environmentalists Are Bailing on the Green New Deal

1. Patrick J. Buchanan, "Green New Deal: A Democratic Suicide Note," WND, February 11, 2019, https://www.wnd.com/2019/02/green-new-deal-a-democratic-suicide-note/.

2. Michael Grunwald, "Climate Change Could Be a Problem in 2020…for Democrats," Politico, September 3, 2019, https://www.politico.com/magazine/story/2019/09/03/climate-change-democratic-candidates-2020-227910.

3. Emily Holden, "Young Activists Kick Off a Climate Hunger Strike by Occupying Nancy Pelosi's Office," Mother Jones, November 18, 2019, https://www.motherjones.com/environment/2019/11/young-activists-kick-off-a-climate-hunger-strike-by-occupying-nancy-pelosis-office/.

4. Victor Skinner, "'Climate' Activists Take Supplements, Drink Salt Water from Stemmed Glasses during 6.5-Hour 'Hunger Strike' in Pelosi's Office," American Mirror, November 19, 2019, https://www.theamericanmirror.com/blog/2019/11/19/climate-activists-take-supplements-drink-salt-water-from-stemmed-glasses-during-6-5-hour-hunger-strike-in-pelosis-office/.

5. Michael Brice-Saddler, "Schoolchildren Debate Dianne Feinstein on 'Green New Deal.' Her Reply? 'I Know What I'm Doing,'" Washington Post, February 23, 2019, https://www.washingtonpost. com/politics/2019/02/23/schoolchildrendebate-dianne-feinstein-green-new-deal-her-reply-i-know-what-im-doing/..

6. Marc Morano, "Extinction Rebellion Climate Activists Arrested in Pelosi's Office," Climate Depot, November 22, 2019, www. climatedepot.com/2019/11/22/extinction-rebellion-climate-activists-arrested-in-pelosis-office/..

7. Abbie Veitch and Asher Weinstein, "AU Sunrise Hub Protests outside Sen. Feinstein's House in Response to West Coast Wildfires," *Eagle*, October 15, 2020, https://www.theeagleonline. com/article/2020/10/au-sunrise-hub-protests-outside-sen-feinsteins-house-in-response-to-west-coast-wildfires.

8. Maddy Fernands, et al., "Adults Won't Take Climate Change Seriously. So We, the Youth, Are Forced to Strike," Bulletin of the Atomic Scientists, March 7, 2019, https://thebulletin.org/ 2019/03/adults-wont-take-climate-change-seriously-so-we-the-youth-are-forced-to-strike/.

9. Brice-Saddler, "Schoolchildren Debate Dianne Feinstein."

10. Chris White, "Exclusive: We Asked Battleground Dem Lawmakers about Sen. Sanders' Anti-Fracking Promises. Only One Responded," Daily Caller, February 28, 2020, https://dailycaller.com/2020/02/28/ bernie-sanders-conor-lamb-green-new-deal/.

11. Chris White, "Rev. Jesse Jackson Bucks Environmentalists, Pushes Natural Gas Pipeline As Black Neighborhoods Struggle with Sky High Energy Prices," Daily Caller, May 4, 2020, https://dailycaller. com/2020/05/04/ jesse-jackson-natural-gas-energy-prices-climate-change/.

12. Amy Harder, "Inside Rev. Jesse Jackson's Push for a Natural Gas Pipeline," Axios, May 4, 2020, https://www.axios.com/jackson-natural-gas-3e1af88d-a823-4096-975d-c9b0ad207806.html.

13. Ibid.

14. Chris White, "Civil Rights Leaders Rail against Enviro Activists, Say Natural Gas Benefits Black Communities," Daily Caller, March 30, 2020, https://dailycaller.com/2020/03/30/ natural-gas-civil-rights-fracking/.

15. Ibid.

16. Dan Gearino, "Amy Klobuchar on Climate Change: Where the Candidate Stands," Inside Climate News, January 5, 2020,

https://insideclimatenews.org/news/24062019/amy-klobuchar-climate-change-global-warming-election-2020-candidate-profile.

17. "Want a Green New Deal? Here's a Better One (editorial)," Washington Post, February 24, 2019, https://www.washingtonpost.com/opinions/want-a-greennew-deal-heres-a-better-one/2019/02/24/2d7e491c-36d2-11e9-af5bb51b7ff322e9_story.html.

18. The Editorial Board, "The Green New Deal Is Better Than Our Climate Nightmare," *New York Times*, February 23, 2019, https://www.nytimes.com/2019/02/23/opinion/green-new-deal-climate-democrats.html..

19. LIUNA (@LIUNA), "Statement of #TerryOSullivan, General President of the Laborers' International Union of North America, On the 'Green New Deal' #LIUNA #GreenNewDeal," Twitter, February 8, 2019, 9:40 a.m., https://twitter.com/LIUNA/status/1093882327577567232.

20. Marc Morano, "Climate Movement Grandpa James Hansen Declares the Green New Deal Is 'Nonsense'—'We Need a Real Deal Which Understands How Economics Works,'" Climate Depot, April 26, 2019, https://www.climatedepot.com/2019/04/26/climate-movement-grandpa-james-hansen-says-the-green-new-deal-is-nonsense/.

21. Eleanor Clift, "Top Climate Scientist to Bernie: You're Killing People in India," The Daily Beast, September 20, 2019, https://www.thedailybeast.com/top-climate-scientist-to-bernie-sanders-youre-killing-people-in-india.

22. Oliver Milman, "James Hansen, Father of Climate Change Awareness, Calls Paris Talks 'A Fraud,'" *Guardian*, December 12, 2015, https://www.theguardian.com/environment/2015/dec/12/james-hansen-climate-change-paris-talks-fraud.

23. "Michael Moore-backed Doc, 'Planet of the Humans,' Tackles 'False Promises' of Green Energy," Breitbart, August 8, 2019, https://www.breitbart.com/entertainment/2019/08/08/michael-moore-backed-doc-planet-of-the-humans-tackles-false-promises-of-green-energy/.

24. James Delingpole, "Michael Moore Is Now the Green New Deal's Worst Enemy," Breitbart, April 23, 2020, https://www.breitbart.com/entertainment/2020/04/23/delingpole-michael-moore-is-now-the-green-new-deals-worst-enemy/.

Chapter 9: The Costs to End All Costs

1. Marc Morano, "Statistician: UN climate treaty will cost $100 trillion—to Have No Impact—Postpone Warming by Less than Four Years by 2100," Climate Depot, January 17, 2017, https://www.climatedepot.com/2017/01/17/danish-statistician-un-climate-treaty-will-cost-100-trillion-to-postpone-global-warming-by-less-than-four-year-by-2100/.

2. Douglas Holtz-Eakin, et al., "The Green New Deal: Scope, Scale, and Implications," American Action Forum, February 25, 2019, https://www.americanactionforum.org/research/the-green-new-deal-scope-scale-and-implications/.

3. Ari Natter, "Alexandria Ocasio-Cortez's Green New Deal Could Cost $93 Trillion, Group Says," Bloomberg, February 25, 2019, https://www.bloomberg.com/news/articles/2019-02-25/group-sees-ocasio-cortez-s-green-new-deal-costing-93-trillion.

4. "Cut for Time: Dianne Feinstein Message–SNL," *Saturday Night Live*, March 2, 2019, YouTube, 0:55, https://youtu.be/kP_iVlEyp5M?t=55

5. Zack Colman, "The Bogus Number at the Center of the GOP's Green New Deal Attacks," Politico, March 10, 2019, https://www.politico.com/story/2019/03/10/republican-green-new-deal-attack-1250859.

6. Edmund DeMarche, "'SNL' Posts Dianne Feinstein Spoof after Meeting with Children Over Green New Deal," Weather Internal, March 4, 2019, https://weatherinternal.com/snl-posts-dianne-feinstein-spoof-after-meeting-with-children-over-green-new-deal/.

7. Kevin Dayaratna and Nicolas Loris, "Assessing the Costs and Benefits of the Green New Deal's Energy Policies," Heritage Foundation, July 24, 2019, https://www.heritage.org/energy-economics/report/assessing-the-costs-and-benefits-the-green-new-deals-energy-policies.

8. Kent Lassman and Daniel Turner, "What the Green New Deal Could Cost a Typical Household," Competitive Enterprise Institute, July 30, 2019, https://cei.org/content/what-green-new-deal-could-cost-typical-household.

9. Bjørn Lomborg (@BjornLomborg), "Climate alarmism doesn't just waste trillions of dollars. It also harms the poor. It means more old people that can't keep their homes heated. Climate change is…,"

Twitter, August 22, 2020, 9:40 a.m., https://twitter.com/BjornLomborg/status/1297166669962530820.

10. Donna Laframboise, "Canada's Carbon Tax Will Kill People," Big Picture News blog, April 8, 2019, https://nofrakkingconsensus.com/2019/04/08/canadas-carbon-tax-will-kill-people/.

11. Thomas Sowell, Twitter, October 27, 2020, https://twitter.com/ThomasSowell/status/1321091969330909189

12. Kevin Dayaratna and Nicolas Loris, "Assessing the Costs and Benefits of the Green New Deal's Energy Policies," Heritage Foundation, July 24, 2019, https://www.heritage.org/energy-economics/report/assessing-the-costs-and-benefits-the-green-new-deals-energy-policies.

13. Dayaratna and Loris, "Assessing the Costs and Benefits."

14. Valerie Richardson, "Senate Dems Unveil California-Style $400B Per Year Climate-Change Plan," *Washington Times*, August 25, 2020, https://www.washingtontimes.com/news/2020/aug/25/senate-democrats-400billion-climate-change-plan/.

15. Ibid.

16. Alexandria Ocasio-Cortez (@AOC), "Hey there! Totally get it if you've never bothered to read the legislation you're commenting so authoritatively on," Twitter, May 14, 2020, 4:07 p.m., https://twitter.com/AOC/status/1261025403071803393.

17. Richardson, "Senate Dems Unveil Climate Change Plan."

18. Zack Colman, "The Bogus Number."

19. Ari Natter, "AOC's Green New Deal Could Cost $93 Trillion."

20. Robert P. Murphy, "White House Revises Dubious 'Social Cost of Carbon,'" Institute for Energy Research, June 6, 2013, https://www.instituteforenergyresearch.org/uncategorized/white-house-revises-dubious-social-cost-of-carbon/.

21. Francis Menton, "Annals of Government Fraud: The 'Social Cost of Carbon,'" Manhattan Contrarian, June 12, 2016, https://www.manhattancontrarian.com/blog/2016/6/11/annals-of-government-fraud-the-social-cost-of-carbon.

22. Marlo Lewis Jr., "How Much Will the Green New Deal Cost Your Family?," Competitive Enterprise Institute, February 26, 2019, https://cei.org/blog/how-much-will-green-new-deal-cost-your-family.

23. Lubos Motl, Twitter, October 26, 2020, https://twitter.com/lumidek/status/1320745420755243009.

24. Tom Rogan, "No, Alexandria Ocasio-Cortez, This Ain't World War II," *Washington Examiner*, January 22, 2019, https://www.

washingtonexaminer.com/opinion/no-alexandria-ocasio-cortez-this-aint-world-war-ii.

25. David Wojick and Paul Driessen, "Green New Deal Disruption and Destruction," CFACT, August 21, 2020, https://www.cfact.org/2020/08/21/green-new-deal-disruption-and-destruction/?.

Chapter 10: Energy Mandate Fairy Tale (Michael Moore Shocks the Greens)

1. Michael Bastasch, "Trump's National Security Plan: 'Energy Dominance,' Not 'Anti-Growth' Climate Policies," Daily Caller, December 18, 2017, https://dailycaller.com/2017/12/18/trumps-national-security-plan-energy-dominance-not-anti-growth-climate-policies/?.

2. Molly Block (deputy associate administrator at the Environmental Protection Agency), email to the author, October 7, 2020; see Marc Morano, "EPA Touts Achievements: 'The U.S. Became the Number One Energy Producer in the World,' under Trump Admin," Climate Depot, October 22, 2020, https://www.climatedepot.com/2020/10/22/epa-touts-achievements-the-u-s-becamethe-number-one-energy-producer-in-the-world-under-trump-admin/..

3. Amy Harder, "How America Got Its Most Powerful EPA Boss," Axios, July 31, 2017, https://www.axios.com/how-america-got-its-most-powerful-epa-boss1513304511-a47ee79d-e604-4ce7-ac51-b20d167fa990.html..

4. "The United States Is Now the Largest Global Crude Oil Producer," Energy Information Administration, September 12, 2018, https://www.eia.gov/todayinenergy/detail.php?id=37053&src.

5. Michael Bastasch, "Green Revolution? Solar and Wind Produced Just 3% of Global Energy," Daily Caller, June 12, 2019, https://dailycaller.com/2019/06/12/green-revolution-solar-and-wind-produced-just-3-of-global-energy/.

6. Marc Morano, witness, "Pennsylvania CO_2 and Climate," Pennsylvania House Environmental Resources and Energy Committee Hearing, October 28, 2019, http://www.climatedepot.com/wp-content/uploads/2019/10/Marc-Morano-Testimony-PA-House-October-28-2019.pdf.

7. "Fossil Fuels Account for the Largest Share of U.S. Energy Production and Consumption," Energy Information Administration, September 14, 2020, https://www.eia.gov/todayinenergy/detail.php?id=45096.

8. James Barrett, "Study: U.S. Leads World in Reducing CO2 Emissions, While UN Paris Accord Nations Break Promises," Daily Wire, August 22, 2018, https://www.climatedepot. com/2018/08/22/study-u-s-leads-world-in-reducing-co2-emissions-while-un-paris-accord-nations-break-promises/.

9. Donald Trump, "Remarks by President Trump at 9th Annual Shale Insight Conference: Pittsburgh, PA," White House Remarks, October 23, 2019, https://www.whitehouse.gov/briefings-statements/remarks-president-trump-9th-annual-shale-insight-conference-pittsburgh-pa/.

10. Gale L. Pooley and Marian L. Tupy, "The Simon Abundance Index 2020," Human Progress, April 22, 2020, https://www. humanprogress.org/the-simon-abundance-index-2020/.

11. Michael Bastasch, "Democrats Didn't Clap As Trump Touted American Energy Boom in SOTU," Daily Caller, February 5, 2019, https://dailycaller.com/2019/02/05/democrats-energy-sotu-clap/.

12. Al Gore (@algore), "The President doesn't get it. Solar & wind represent the fastest growing job sectors. Costs of renewable electricity are declining rapidly.," Twitter, February 5, 2019, 9:44 p.m., https://twitter.com/algore/status/1092977206001917953.

13. Naomi Klein (@NaomiAKlein), "People claim Trump said not one word about climate change but that's false.," Twitter, February 6, 2019, 7:01 a.m., https://twitter.com/NaomiAKlein/status/1093117426508664832.

14. Editorial Board, "Editorial: As Global Warming Continues, Trump Wants to Burn Fossil Fuels with an Arsonist's Glee," *Los Angeles Times*, September 29, 2018, https://www.latimes.com/opinion/editorials/la-ed-global-warming-paris-agreement-south-korea-20180929-story.html.

15. Daily Wire News, "Biden: Voting for 'Climate Arsonist' Trump Could Cause Suburbs to Be 'Blown Away in Superstorms,'" Daily Wire, September 15, 2020, https://www.dailywire.com/news/biden-voting-for-climate-arsonist-trump-could-cause-suburbs-to-be-blown-away-in-superstorms?.

16. Marc Morano, "Watch: Morano on Tucker Carlson on Fox News: Biden Is 'Weaponizing Weather Events'—'Using Science to Lobby for Politics. Vote for Me and I Will Make the Weather Better,'" Climate Depot, September 16, 2020, https://www.climatedepot. com/2020/09/16/watch-morano-on-tucker-carlson-on-fox-news-biden-is-weaponizing-weather-events-using-science-to-lobby-for-politics-vote-for-me-and-i-will-make-the-weather-better/.

17. Penny Starr, "Trump: Ending Obama-Era Regs Made USA #1 Producer of Oil and Gas," Climate Dispatch, February 5, 2020, https://climatechangedispatch.com/trump-obama-regs-oil-gas-sotu/.

18. Marc Morano, "Trump Rejects Climate 'Prophets of Doom' in Davos Address—Declares Climate Fear Promoters 'Heirs of Yesterday's Foolish Fortune-Tellers,'" Climate Depot, January 21, 2020, https://www.climatedepot.com/2020/01/21/trump-rejects-climate-prophets-of-doom-in-davos-address-declares-climate-fear-promoters-heirs-of-yesterdays-foolish-fortune-tellers/, citing "Donald Trump Addresses World Leaders at Davos Forum," SBS News, January 21, 2020, https://www.sbs.com.au/news/donald-trump-addresses-world-leaders-at-davos-forum and Donald Trump, "Donald Trump Attacks the Climate Change Prophets of Doom," GWPF, YouTube, January 21, 2020, https://youtu.be/_lpVPh6LeU8.

19. Mike Allen, "1 Big Thing: The Decade That Blew Up Energy Predictions," Axios, December 23, 2019, https://www.axios.com/newsletters/axios-am-b9b10d24-23d0-4a19-8c38-b328f194a24e.html?.

20. Amy Harder and Andrew Witherspoon, "The Decade That Blew Up Energy Predictions," Axios, December 23, 2019, https://www.axios.com/energy-predictions-reality-check-524b9be9-2c0c-407e-86cb-37b11aa72ed2.html.

21. Marc Morano, "Flashback 1980: Paul Ehrlich Calls Oil 'a Resource Which We Know Damn Well Is Going to Be Gone in 20 or 30 Years' (By Year 2000 or 2010)," Climate Depot, October 2, 2017, https://www.climatedepot.com/2017/10/02/flashback-1980-paul-ehrlich-calls-oil-a-resource-which-we-know-damn-well-is-going-to-be-gone-in-20-or-30-years-by-year-2000-or-2010/.

22. Mark Mathis, "Green New Deal: Impossible," Clear Energy Alliance, YouTube, March 1, 2019, https://www.youtube.com/watch?v=-sPsYycBGVo.

23. John A. Shanahan, "Astounding Facts about Energy for the World Today: Fossil Fuels, Nuclear, Hydro-Electric, Wind and Solar," email to the author, September 10, 2020.

24. Marc Morano, "Surprise: Gore Praises Fossil Fuels for Having 'Tremendous Benefits'—'Poverty Has Declined, Living Standards Increased,'" Climate Depot, July 13, 2017, https://www.climatedepot.com/2017/07/13/surprise-gore-praises-fossil-fuels-for-having-tremendous-benefits-poverty-has-declined-living-standards-increased/.

25. Alex Epstein (@AlexEpstein), "Q: Isn't @Apple 100% renewable? That's what they tell us.," Twitter, September 16, 2020, 7:40 p.m., https://twitter.com/AlexEpstein/status/1306377463182684160.

26. "U.S. Energy Production, Consumption Has Changed Significantly Since 1908," Energy Information Administration, November 1, 2016, https://www.eia.gov/todayinenergy/detail.php?id=28592.

27. Bjørn Lomborg, "Your Electric Car and Vegetarian Diet Are Pointless Virtue Signaling in the Fight against Climate Change," Market Watch, December 28, 2019, https://www.marketwatch.com/amp/story/guid/90B2547C-25CB-11EA-8ACF-1E53DFC48893?.

28. Coilín ÓhAiseadha, et al., "Energy and Climate Policy—An Evaluation of Global Climate Change Expenditure 2011–2018," *Energies* 13, no. 18 (September 2020): 4839, https://doi.org/10.3390/en13184839.

29. U.S. Energy Information Administration, *International Energy Outlook 2019* (Washington, DC: U.S. Energy Information Administration, Office of Energy Analysis, U.S. Department of Energy, 2019), 85

30. "In 2018, the United States Consumed More Energy Than Ever Before," Energy Information Administration, December 23, 2019, https://www.eia.gov/todayinenergy/detail.php?id=42335.

31. Larry Hamlin, "EIA Data Show Wind & Solar Met 3% of U.S. Energy after $50 Billion in Subsidizes," Watts Up With That? (blog), June 6, 2019, https://wattsupwiththat.com/2019/06/06/eia-data-shows-wind-solar-met-3-of-u-s-energy-after-50-billion-in-subsidizes/.

32. Ibid.

33. Ibid.

34. Alex Epstein, "Energy Transition," EnergyTalkingPoints.com, https://energytalkingpoints.com/energy-transition/.

35. Katie Glueck and Lisa Friedman, "Biden Announces $2 Trillion Climate Plan," *New York Times*, July 14, 2020, updated August 11, 2020, https://www.nytimes.com/2020/07/14/us/politics/biden-climate-plan.html.

36. Vijay Jayaraj, "California Now, America Next: Courtesy of Unreliable and Toxic Renewables," Clash Daily, September 6, 2020, https://clashdaily.com/2020/09/california-now-america-next-courtesy-of-unreliable-and-toxic-renewables/.

37. Steve Milloy (@JunkScience), "Like hurricanes, blackouts should be named…," Twitter, October 25, 2020, 6:45 p.m., https://twitter.com/JunkScience/status/1320496819395268610.

38. Robert Bryce, "Blackouts Expose Perils and Costs of California's 'Electrify Everything' Push," *Forbes*, August 18, 2020, https://www. forbes.com/sites/robertbryce/2020/08/18/blackouts-expose-perils-and-costs-of-californias-electrify-everything-push/#6b69f56f7a01.

39. H. Sterling Burnett, "Bill McKibben Caught Lying about Wind and Solar Costs," Climate Dispatch, April 29, 2020, https://climatechangedispatch.com/bill-mckibben-caught-lying-wind-solar-costs/.

40. Mark Golden, "Cheap Renewables Won't Stop Global Warming, Says Bill Gates," Precourt Institute for Energy at Stanford University, November 15, 2018, https://energy.stanford.edu/news/cheap-renewables-won-t-stop-global-warming-says-bill-gates..

41. John Sexton, "Fareed Zakaria: 'The Sanders Green Energy Plan Is Magical Thinking,'" Hot Air, February 17, 2020, https://hotair. com/archives/ john-s-2/2020/02/17/fareed-zakaria-sanders-green-energy-plan-magicalthinking/. See also Zeke Hausfather, "Analysis: Why US Carbon Emissions Have Fallen 14% Since 2005," Carbon Brief, August 15, 2017, https://www. carbonbrief.org/analysis-why-us-carbon-emissions-have-fallen-14-since-2005..

42. Jason Hopkins, "Environmentalist Tells Tucker Carlson: Renewables Can't Save the Planet," Daily Caller, March 1, 2019, https://dailycaller. com/2019/03/01/ tucker-carlson-wrecks-renewable-energy/.

43. Michael Shellenberger, "The Only Green New Deals That Have Ever Worked Were Done with Nuclear, Not Renewables," *Forbes*, February 8, 2019, https://www.forbes.com/sites/michaelshellenberger/2019/02/08/the-only-green-new-deals-that-have-ever-worked-were-done-with-nuclearnot-renewables/#55b8d1077f61..

44. Alex Epstein, "2020 Talking Points on American Energy Policy," Energy Talking Points, https://energytalkingpoints.com/energy-policy/.

45. Alex Epstein, "2020 Talking Points on Joe Biden's Energy Plan," Energy Talking Points, https://energytalkingpoints.com/bidens-energy-plan/.

46. H. Sterling Burnett, "Bill McKibben Caught Lying about Wind and Solar Costs," Climate Realism, April 27, 2020, https://climate realism.com/2020/04/bill-mckibben-caught-lying-about-wind-and-solar-costs/.

47. Bruce Everett, "Do Government Policies Favoring Fossil Fuels Hamper the Development of Wind and Solar Power," CO2 Coalition, July 23, 2020, http:// co2coalition.org/publications/do-government-policies-favoring-fossil-fuels-hamper-the-development-of-wind-and-solar-power/..

48. Michael Shellenberger, "Why Renewables Can't Save the Planet," *Quillette* , February 27, 2019, https://quillette.com/2019/02/27/why-renewables-cant-save-the-planet/..

49. Alex Epstein, "2020 Talking Points on Energy Poverty," Energy Talking Points, https://energytalkingpoints.com/energy-poverty/.

50. Catherine Morehouse, "House Democrats Unveil Major Clean Energy Bill As Senate GOP Mulls Timeline for Economic Stimulus," Utility Dive, July 2, 2020, https://www.utilitydive.com/news/house-democrats-unveil-major-clean-energy-bill-as-senate-gop-mulls-timeline/580680/. Alex Epstein, "2020 Talking Points on Wind Production Tax Credit," Energy Talking Points, https://energytalkingpoints.com/wind-production-tax-credit/.

51. Grant Kidwell, "Iowa Wind Farm Generates More Tax Credits Than Electricity," *The Hill*, October 6, 2019, https://thehill.com/blogs/congress-blog/energy-environment/299405-iowa-wind-farm-generates-more-tax-credits-than.

52. Alex Epstein, "2020 Talking Points on Wind Production Tax Credit," Energy Talking Points, https://energytalkingpoints.com/wind-production-tax-credit/.

53. Ibid.

54. Nick Butler, "Electric Vehicles Are Being Outpaced by the Growth of SUVs," *Financial Times*, October 7, 2019, https://www.ft.com/content/24fffce8-e52a-11e9-9743-db5a370481bc?.

55. Mark J. Perry, "Inconvenient Energy Fact: It Takes 79 Solar Workers to Produce Same Amount of Electric Power As One Coal Worker," American Enterprise Institute, May 3, 2017, https://www.aei.org/carpe-diem/inconvenient-energyfact-it-takes-79-solar-workers-to-produce-same-amount-of-electric-poweras-one-coal-worker/..

56. Kyle Gillis, "Obama to Tout Green Energy 'Investments' at Solar Facility Employing 5 Workers, Relying on $54 Million in Taxpayer Subsidies," *Nevada Journal*, March 21, 2012, https://www.npri.org/nevadajournal/obamatout-green-energy-investments-solar-facility-employing-5-workers-relying-54- million-taxpayer-s/.

57. Mark P. Mills, "The Green New Deal Can't Break the Laws of Physics," Daily Caller, October 27, 2020, green-new-deal-laws-of-physics.

58. Jason Isaac, "Earth Day Hangover? Wait Until You See the Tab," Real Clear Energy blog, April 28, 2020, https://www.realclearenergy.org/ articles/2020/04/28/earth_day_hangover_wait_until_you_see_the_tab_490235. html.

59. Jayaraj, "California Now, America Next."

60. Michael Shellenberger, "Democrats' New Climate Plan Will Kill Endangered Species, Environmentalists Fear," *Forbes*, June 30, 2020, https://www.forbes.com/sites/michaelshellenberger/2020/06/30/democrats-climate-plan-will-kill-endangered-species-environmentalists-fear/#5fcaa6507571.

61. Alex Epstein (@AlexEpstein), "Q: What do we do about nuclear waste?," Twitter, September 17, 2020, 6:57 p.m., https://twitter.com/AlexEpstein/status/1306728899326480385.

62. Alex Epstein, "2020 Talking Points on CO2 Emissions," Energy Talking Points, https://energytalkingpoints.com/co2-emissions/.

63. Matt Markey, "Bald Eagle Killed by Wind Turbine at Wood County Site," *Toledo Blade*, May 1, 2020, https://www.toledoblade.com/local/environment/2020/05/01/

64. Michael Shellenberger, "Democrats' New Climate Plan Will Kill Endangered Species."

65. Mills, "The Green New Deal Can't."

66. Bjørn Lomborg, "Your Electric Car and Vegetarian Diet Are Pointless Virtue Signaling in the Fight against Climate Change," Market Watch, December 28, 2019, https://www.marketwatch.com/story/your-electric-car-and-vegetarian-diet-are-pointless-virtue-signalling-in-fighting-climate-change-2019-12-26. .

67. David Bol, "14m Trees Have Been Cut Down in Scotland to Make Way for Wind Farms," Scotland Herald, February 29, 2020, https://www.heraldscotland.com/news/18270734.14m-trees-cut-scotland-make-way-wind-farms/

68. "Transportation Replaces Power in U.S. As Top Source of CO2 Emissions," Yale Environment 360, December 4, 2017, https://e360.yale.edu/digest/transportation-replaces-power-in-u-s-as-top-source-of-co2-emissions.

69. Christina Lamb, "Congo's Miners Dying to Feed World's Hunger for Electric Cars," UK *Times*, March 10, 2019, https://www.thetimes.co.uk/article/congos-miners-dying-to-feed-worlds-hunger-for-electric-cars-jcrvj37vr.

70. "Commodities at a Glance: Special Issue on Strategic Battery Raw Materials," United Nations Conference on Trade and Development, 2020, https://unctad.org/system/files/official-document/ditccom2019d5_en.pdf.

71. Paul Driessen, "Wind, Solar, and Biofuel Energy are Devastating Planet Earth," Climate Dispatch, May 7, 2020, https://climatechangedispatch.com/wind-solar-biofuel-energy-devastating-planet-earth/.

72. Michael Shellenberger, "Why Renewables Can't Save the Planet."

73. David Wojick and Paul Driessen, "Green New Deal Disruption and Destruction," CFACT, August 21, 2020, https://www.cfact. org/2020/08/21/green-new-deal-disruption-and-destruction/.

74. Steven W. Mosher, "Why Eco-Leftists Are Suddenly Turning on Michael Moore," *New York Post*, May 2, 2020, https://nypost. com/2020/05/02/ why-eco-leftists-are-suddenly-turning-on-michael-moore/.

75. Anthony Watts, #EarthDay EPIC! Michael Moore's New Film Trashes 'Planet Saving' Renewable Energy," Watts Up With That?, April 22, 2020, https://wattsupwiththat.com/2020/04/22/earthday-epic-michael-moores-new-film-trashes-planet-saving-renewable-energy-full-movie-here/#:~:text=%E2%80%9CPlanet%20of%20the%20Humans%20was,but%20after%20cutting%20down%20forests.

76. AP, "Michael Moore-Backed Doc, 'Planet of the Humans,' Tackles 'False Promises' of Green Energy," Breitbart, August 8, 2019, https://www.breitbart.com/entertainment/2019/08/08/michael-moore-backed-doc-planet-of-the-humans-tackles-false-promises-of-green-energy/.

77. Valerie Richardson, "Michael Moore Turns on Climate Left with Film Skewering Green Energy," *Washington Times*, April 24, 2020, https://www.washingtontimes.com/news/2020/apr/24/michael-moore-turns-climate-left-film-skewering-gr/.

78. James Delingpole, "Michael Moore Is Now the Green New Deal's Worst Enemy," Breitbart, April 23, 2020, https://www.breitbart. com/entertainment/2020/04/23/delingpole-michael-moore-is-now-the-green-new-deals-worst-enemy/.

79. Tom Nelson (@tan123), "Moore's movie 9:40: Richard Branson will allegedly spend $3 billion to fight global warming!," Twitter, April 21, 2020, 3:44 p.m., https://twitter.com/tan123/status/1252684 773388095492.

80. Michael E. Mann, "Michael Moore's New Film Turns Heroes into Villains and Villains into Heroes," Newsweek, May 7, 2020, https:// www.newsweek.com/ michael-moore-planet-humans-film-climate-change-1502554.

81. Josh Fox BlackLivesMatter (@joshfoxfilm), "1) I just received notice that the distributor of Michael Moore's #PlanetoftheHumans...," Twitter thread, April 24, 2020, 2:33 a.m., https://twitter.com/ joshfoxfilm/status/1253572812591247360.

82. James Delingpole, "Finally YouTube Cancels Michael Moore-Produced Documentary," Breitbart, May 26, 2020, https://www.

breitbart.com/europe/2020/05/26/delingpole-finally-youtube-cancels-michael-moore-produced-documentary/.

83. "Coordinated Censorship Campaign against Planet of the Humans Leads to It Being Taken Down from YouTube Where It Had Been Viewed 8.3 Million Times," Planet of the Humans website, May 28, 2020, https://planetofthehumans.com/2020/05/28/coordinated-censorship-campaign-against-planet-of-the-humans-leads-to-it-being-taken-down-from-youtube-where-it-had-been-viewed-8-3-million-times/.

84. Bob Meinetz, "Censor 'Planet of the Humans'? Josh Fox Tried. He Failed.," Energy Central, June 8, 2020, https://energycentral.com/c/cp/censor-planet-humans-he-tried-he-failed.

85. Jeff Gibbs, "'Old Data' Is a Lie," Planet of the Humans website, May 18, 2020, https://planetofthehumans.com/2020/05/18/old-data-is-a-lie/.

86. Driessen, "Wind, Solar, and Biofuel Energy."

Chapter 11: The COVID–Climate Connection: COVID Lockdowns as Dress Rehearsal for the "Climate Emergency"

1. Martín López Corredoira, "The Benefits of Coronavirus for the Health of the Planet," Science 2.0 (blog), March 4, 2020, https://www.science20.com/martin_lopez_corredoira/the_benefits_of_coronavirus_for_the_health_of_the_planet-245939.

2. Johannes Ledel, "'Flight Shame' Has Swedes Rethinking Air Travel," Yahoo News, April 9, 2019, https://news.yahoo.com/flight-shame-swedes-rethinking-air-travel-032414475.html.

3. Krishnan Guru-Murthy, "Expect More Disease Outbreaks 'If We Continue to Deny, Delude, and Delay on Climate Change'—Christiana Figueres," Channel 4 News, March 2, 2020, https://www.channel4.com/news/expect-more-disease-outbreaks-if-we-continue-to-deny-delude-and-delay-on-climate-change-christiana-figueres.

4. Alice Bows-Larkin, "Climate Change Is Happening. Here's How We Adapt," TEDGlobalLondon, June 2015, TED video, https://www.ted.com/talks/alice_bows_larkin_climate_change_is_happening_here_s_how_we_adapt/details?.

5. Rachel Koning Beals, "Eating Out, Ice Cream, and Booze May Be Worse for Climate Change Than Meat," Market Watch, January 6, 2020, https://www.marketwatch.com/story/dining-out-dessert-and-booze-may-be-worse-for-climate-change-than-meat-2019-12-26.

6. Graham Piro, "Yang: Climate Change May Require Elimination of Car Ownership," *Washington Free Beacon*, September 19, 2019, https://freebeacon.com/politics/yang-well-eliminate-car-ownership-to-fight-climate-change/.

7. Bjørn Lomborg, "Where's the Beef? Ask Green Campaigners," Shine, November 30, 2018, https://www.shine.cn/opinion/1811305941/.

8. Michael Bastasch, "Professor: 'Terminate Industrial Civilization' to Save Earth from Global Warming," Daily Caller, October 22, 2014, https://dailycaller.com/2014/10/22/professor-terminate-industrial-civilization-to-save-earth-from-global-warming/.

9. Marc Morano, "Marc Morano on Fox & Friends on Climate Strikes: 'Greta Is Instilling Fear in Millions of Kids,'" Seasonspass33, September 23, 2019, YouTube video, https://youtu.be/_5WWWYswS-E.

10. Peter Barry Chowka, "Will the Covid-19 PsyOp Succeed?," American Thinker, April 19, 2020, https://www.americanthinker.com/blog/2020/04/will_the_covid19_psyop_succeed.html.

11. Julie Kelly (@julie_kelly2), "This is what the Left wants … ," Twitter, March 12, 2020, 4:46 p.m., https://twitter.com/julie_kelly2/status/1238204694885007360.

12. Editorial, "The Guardian View on the Climate and Coronavirus: Global Warnings," *Guardian*, April 12, 2020, https://www.theguardian.com/commentisfree/2020/apr/12/the-guardian-view-on-the-climate-and-coronavirus-global-warnings.

13. Steven Milloy, "Never Waste a Crisis: Climate Alarmism Surfs Coronavirus," Heartland Institute, April 7, 2020, no. 6, https://www.heartland.org/news-opinion/news/never-waste-a-crisis-climate-alarmism-surfs-coronavirus.

14. Jamie Margolin, "Coronavirus Shows Us Rapid Global Response to Climate Change Is Possible," Teen Vogue, March 18, 2020, https://www.teenvogue.com/story/coronavirus-response-climate-crisis.

15. Al Gore, "Al Gore: The Climate Connection: Real Time with Bill Maher (HBO)," Real Time with Bill Maher, April 10, 2020, YouTube video, https://youtu.be/2IbdTnID7sU.

16. Valerie Richardson, "'Dress Rehearsal'? Climate Activists Say Tackle Climate 'Crisis' with Vigor of Pandemic," *Washington Times*, April 22, 2020, https://www.washingtontimes.com/news/2020/apr/22/earth-day-climate-activists-treat-climate-coronavi/.

17. Marc Morano, "COVID Lockdowns to Morph into Climate Lockdowns: Biden's VP Pick Kamala Harris Seeks Green New Deal So 'We Can Change Human Behaviors,'" Climate Depot, August 11, 2020, https://www.climatedepot.com/2020/08/11/bidens-vp-pick-kamala-harris-seeks-green-new-deal-so-we-can-change-human-behaviors-to-fight-climate-change/.

18. Joel Kotkin, "Oligarchy and Pestilence," Real Clear Energy, April 10, 2020, https://www.realclearenergy.org/articles/2020/04/10/oligarchy_and_pestilence_488761.html.

19. Eric Holthaus (@EricHolthaus), "1% of peoplle cause half of global aviation emissions...," Twitter, November 18, 2020, 11:18 a.m., https://twitter.com/EricHolthaus/status/1329096682932461574?ref_

20. Damian Carrington, "1% of People Cause Half of Global Aviation Emissions—Study," *Guardian*, November 17, 2020, https://www.theguardian.com/business/2020/nov/17/people-cause-global-aviation-emissions-study-covid-19

21. Tom Steyer (@TomSteyer), "To get climate right, let's start with listening to communities of color... ," Twitter, February 24, 2020, 11:44 p.m., https://twitter.com/TomSteyer/status/1232164461613465600.

22. Farz Edraki and Ann Arnold, "Could Climate Change Become a Security Issue—and Threaten Democracy?," ABC News, December 2, 2019, https://www.abc.net.au/news/2019-12-03/climate-change-international-security-risk/11714284.

23. Martin Durkin (@Martin_Durkin), "Lockdown feels like the new Climate Change ...," Twitter, June 17, 2020, 1:27 p.m., https://twitter.com/Martin_Durkin/status/1273306347627589633.

24. Stan Cox, "If There's a World War II-Style Climate Mobilization, It Has to Go All the Way—and Then Some," Counterpunch, September 22, 2016, https://www.counterpunch.org/2016/09/22/if-theres-a-world-war-ii-style-climatemobilization-it-has-to-go-all-the-way-and-then-some/.

25. Mariana Mazzucato, "The Covid-19 Crisis Is a Chance to Do Capitalism Differently," *Guardian*, March 18, 2020, https://www.theguardian.com/commentisfree/2020/mar/18/the-covid-19-crisis-is-a-chance-to-do-capitalism-differently.

26. Simon Kuper, "Coronavirus Could Help Push Us into a Greener Way of Life," *Financial Times*, March 19, 2020, https://www.ft.com/content/9d0d917e-68aa-11ea-800d-da70cff6e4d3.

27. Ben Pile (@clim8resistance), "The green blob and its 'High Level Climate Actions' have wet dreams about Lockdown. . . .," Twitter,

July 9, 2020, 8:07 a.m., https://twitter.com/clim8resistance/status/1281198376579719170.

28. James Taylor, "WHO Official: Coronavirus Shows What Is Possible for Climate Restrictions," Climate Realism, March 29, 2020, https://climaterealism. com/2020/03/who-official-coronavirus-reveals-what-measures-are-possiblefor-climate-restrictions/.

29. Ed Conway, "Coronavirus Can Trigger a New Industrial Revolution," UK Times, March 5, 2020, https://www.thetimes. co.uk/article/ coronavirus-has-a-silver-lining-cz8wpc6xjo.

30. Benjamin Fearnow, "Scientists Cite Pollution Decrease in Calls to 'Flatten the Curve' of Climate Change Post-Coronavirus," *Newsweek*, April 11, 2020, https://www.newsweek.com/scientists-cite-pollution-decrease-calls-flatten-curve-climate-change-post-coronavirus-1497430.

31. Rachel Koning Beals, "Covid-19 and Climate Change: 'The Parallels Are Screaming at Us,' Says John Kerry," Market Watch, April 22, 2020, https://www.marketwatch.com/story/covid-19-and-climate-change-the-parallels-are-screaming-at-us-says-john-kerry-2020-04-22.

32. Michael Segalov, "The Parallels Between Coronavirus and Climate Crisis Are Obvious," *Guardian*, May 4, 2020, https://www.theguardian.com/environment/2020/may/04/parallels-climate-coronavirus-obvious-emily-atkin-pandemic.

33. Brooke Russell, "Boiling the Frog: Covid-19 and Climate Change," *Independent*, April 10, 2020, https://www.independent. com/2020/04/10/boiling-the-frog-covid-19-and-climate-change/.

34. Daniel Cusick, "Outbreak Reveals Radical Climate Idea: Economic 'Degrowth,'" E&E News, March 31, 2020, https://www.eenews. net/stories/1062743761.

35. Peter Fox-Penner, "This Crisis Provides a Very Green Opportunity," *Boston Globe*, April 19, 2020, https://www.bostonglobe. com/2020/04/19/opinion/this-crisis-provides-very-green-opportunity/?event=event25.

36. Nathanial Gronewold, "U.N. Shifts from Climate Change to Coronavirus," Scientific American, March 23, 2020, https://www. scientificamerican.com/article/u-n-shifts-from-climate-change-to-coronavirus/.

37. Jack Houghton, "UN Climate Change Fund Calls Coronavirus an 'Opportunity' to Reshape the World," Sky News, April 20, 2020, https://www.skynews.com.au/details/_6150659462001.

38. Nathalie Olah, "When This Pandemic Is Over, It's Time to Dismantle Capitalism," Vice, April 6, 2020, https://i-d.vice.com/en_

uk/article/n7jgkg/coronavirus-covid-19-capitalism-productivity-
tories-nhs-economy.

39. Joe Kovacs, "Obama Drops Coronavirus Bombshell: It's All Due to
Climate Change!," WND, March 31, 2020, https://www.wnd.
com/2020/03/obama-drops-coronavirus-bombshell-due-climate-
change/.

40. Douglas Ernst, "Robert Redford: Pandemic Provides 'Pleasant
Surprises' for Eco-Warriors," Climate Dispatch, May 1, 2020,
https://climatechangedispatch.com/robert-redford-pandemic-provides-
pleasant-surprises-for-eco-warriors/.

41. Thomas Schomerus, "Corona und Klima—Krise als Chance,"
Verfassungsblog, March 24, 2020, https://verfassungsblog.de/
corona-und-klima-krise-als-chance/. See English translation at Pierre
Gosselin, "German Public Law Professor, High Court Judge:
Climate Crisis 'Requires Freedom-Limiting Measures,'" NoTricks
Zone blog, April 4, 2020, https://notrickszone.com/2020/0
4/04/german-public-law-professor-judge-climate-crisis-requires-
freedom-limiting-measures/.

42. Vijay Kolinjivadi, "The Coronavirus Outbreak Is Part of the Climate
Change Crisis," Al Jazeera, March 30, 2020, https://www.aljazeera.
com/opinions/2020/3/30/the-coronavirus-outbreak-is-part-of-the-
climate-change-crisis/.

43. Adam Frank, "Coronavirus and Climate Change: The Pandemic Is a
Fire Drill for Our Planet's Future," NBC News, March 27, 2020,
https://www.nbcnews.com/think/opinion/coronavirus-climate-
change-pandemic-fire-drill-our-planet-s-future-ncna1169991.

44. James Barrett, "Hollywood Stars Demand 'Radical Transformation'
of World, No 'Return to Normal' after Covid Crisis," The Daily
Wire, May 6, 2020, https://www.dailywire.com/news/read-it-
hollywood-stars-demand-radical-transformation-of-world-no-
return-to-normal-after-covid-crisis.

45. Brad Wilmouth, "PBS's Amanpour Finds Eco 'Silver Lining' in
Covid-19 Outbreak," Climate Dispatch, March 13, 2020, https://
climatechangedispatch.com/amanpour-silver-lining-covid-19/.

46. Christopher Ketcham, "Op-Ed: Coronavirus Has Something to
Teach Us about How to Save the Planet—by Staying Put," Los
Angeles Times, March 14, 2020, https://www.latimes.com/opinion/
story/2020-03-14/
coronavirus-travel-ban-air-travel-climate-change-carbon-emissions.

47. "Reducing UK Emissions: 2020 Progress Report to Parliament," UK
Committee on Climate Change, June 25, 2020, https://www.theccc.

org.uk/publication/reducing-uk-emissions-2020-progress-report-to-parliament/.

48. Ben Santer, "How Covid-19 Is Like Climate Change," Scientific American, March 17, 2020, https://blogs.scientificamerican.com/observations/how-covid-19-is-like-climate-change/.

49. Gabriela Baczynska and Kate Abnett, "European Politicians, CEOs, Lawmaker Urge Green Coronavirus Recovery," Reuters, April 14, 2020, https://www.reuters.com/article/us-health-coronavirus-climatechange-reco/european-politicians-ceos-lawmakers-urge-green-coronavirus-recovery-idUSKCN21W0F2.

50. Madhvi Ramani, "Coronavirus Is an Environmental Wake-Up Call," *Week*, March 5, 2020, https://theweek.com/articles/899439/coronavirus-environmental-wakeup-call.

51. Guru-Murthy, "Expect More Disease Outbreaks 'If We Continue to Deny, Delude, and Delay on Climate Change'—Christiana Figueres."

52. Ed Dawson, "Gov Inslee Calls Covid Crisis 'an Opportunity' to Move State to More 'Green' Economy," 610Kona News Radio, May 20, 2020, https://www.610kona.com/gov-inslee-calls-covid-crisis-an-opportunity-to-move-state-to-more-green-economy/.

53. John Schwartz, "Social Distancing? You Might Be Fighting Climate Change, Too," *New York Times*, March 13, 2020, https://www.nytimes.com/2020/03/13/climate/coronavirus-habits-carbon-footprint.html.

54. Mark Hertsgaard and Kyle Pope, "The Coronavirus Has Lessons for Journalists Covering the Climate Crisis," *The Nation*, April 20, 2020, https://www.thenation.com/article/environment/coronavirus-climate-crisis-journalism/.

55. Alice Bows-Larkin, "Climate Change Is Happening. Here's How We Adapt," TEDGlobalLondon, June 2015, TED video, https://www.ted.com/talks/alice_bows_larkin_climate_change_is_happening_here_s_how_we_adapt/details?.

56. Guru-Murthy, "Expect More Disease Outbreaks."

57. NBC News (@NBCNews), "What we cannot afford...," Twitter, April 17, 2020, 3:43 p.m., https://twitter.com/NBCNews/status/1251234966454796289.

58. James Delingpole, "'Build Back Better'—the Latest Code Phrase for Green Global Tyranny," Breitbart, May 31, 2020, https://www.breitbart.com/europe/2020/05/31/delingpole-build-back-better-the-latest-code-phrase-for-green-global-tyranny/.

59. James Tucker Jr., "Global Elite Wants U.S. to Sign Treaty," *American Free Press*, July 2, 2005, https://www.americanfreepress.net/html/kyoto.html.

60. Larry Elliott, "Gordon Brown Calls for Global Government to Tackle Coronavirus," *Guardian*, March 26, 2020, https://www.theguardian.com/politics/2020/mar/26/gordon-brown-calls-for-global-government-to-tackle-coronavirus.

61. Reuters, "Greta Thurnberg: Coronavirus Shows Action Against Climate Change Possible," *Jerusalem Post*, March 24, 2020, https://www.jpost.com/International/Greta-Thurnberg-Coronavirus-shows-action-against-climate-change-possible-622164.

62. Phillip Inman, "Pandemic Is Chance to Reset Global Economy, Says Prince Charles," *Guardian*, June 3, 2020, https://www.theguardian.com/uk-news/2020/jun/03/pandemic-is-chance-to-reset-global-economy-says-prince-charles.

63. Rachel Koning Beals, "COVID-19 and Climate Change: 'The Parallels Are Screaming at Us,' Says John Kerry," Market Watch, April 22, 2020, https://www.marketwatch.com/story/covid-19-and-climate-change-the-parallels-are-screaming-at-us-says-john-kerry-2020-04-22.

64. Sarah Kaplan, "Climate Change Affects Everything—Even the Coronavirus," *Washington Post*, April 15, 2020, https://www.washingtonpost.com/climate-solutions/2020/04/15/climate-change-affects-everything-even-coronavirus/.

65. Jane Fonda, "COVID-19 Has Created a Pivotal Time When the Future May Be Decided," Jane Fonda blog, March 31, 2020, https://www.janefonda.com/2020/03/covid-19-has-created-a-pivotal-time-when-the-future-may-be-decided/.

66. Laurie Macfarlane, "Governments Must Act to Stop the Coronavirus—But We Can't Return to Business As Usual," Open Democracy, March 12, 2020, https://www.opendemocracy.net/en/oureconomy/we-must-act-to-contain-the-coronavirus-but-we-cant-return-to-business-as-usual/.

67. Douglas Ernst, "IMF Chief Echoes AOC on Using Pandemic As 'Great Opportunity' to Push Green Agenda," *Washington Times*, April 27, 2020, https://www.washingtontimes.com/news/2020/apr/27/kristalina-georgieva-echoes-aoc-on-using-coronavir/.

68. Scott Waldman and Maxine Joselow, "Democrats Eye Climate Policy in Economic Relief Bill," E&E News, March 12, 2020, https://www.eenews.net/stories/1062581379.

69. Alex Morales, "Kyoto Veterans Say Global Warming Goal Slipping Away," Bloomberg, November 4, 2013, https://www.bloomberg.

com/news/articles/2013-11-04/kyoto-veterans-say-global-warming-goal-slipping-away.

70. Eric Holthaus (@EricHolthaus), "This is roughly the pace ... ," Twitter, April 22, 2020, 9:27 a.m., https://twitter.com/EricHolthaus/status/1252952128131342336.

71. Roy Spencer, Ph.D., "Why the Current Economic Slowdown Won't Show Up in the Atmospheric CO2 Record," Roy Spencer blog, May 15, 2020, https://www.drroyspencer.com/2020/05/why-the-current-economic-slowdown-wont-show-up-in-the-atmospheric-co2-record/.

72. Democratic Socialists of America (@DemSocialists), "The coronavirus pandemic ...," Twitter, March 18, 2020, 9:05 a.m., https://twitter.com/DemSocialists/status/1240262981973422080.

73. Bill Bostock, "Alexandria Ocasio-Cortez Deleted a Tweet about the Negative Oil Price That Said, 'You Absolutely Love to See It,'" Business Insider, April 21, 2020, https://www.businessinsider.com/oil-price-negative-aoc-tweet-absolutely-love-see-it-deleted-2020-4.

74. Alex Davies, "The Pandemic Could Be an Opportunity to Remake Cities," *Wired*, April 13, 2020, https://www.wired.com/story/pandemic-opportunity-remake-cities/.

75. Eric Holthaus (@EricHolthaus), "This is a really heartening trend ... ," Twitter, April 21, 2020, 12:36 p.m., https://twitter.com/EricHolthaus/status/1252637224413339655.

76. Steve Milloy (@JunkScience), "This is true ...," Twitter, April 18, 2020, 11:38 a.m., https://twitter.com/JunkScience/status/1251535611976126468.

77. Jim Tankersley, Matthew Goldstein, and Glenn Thrush, "As Government Shutdown Persists, Americans Feel the Bite," *New York Times*, January 7, 2019, https://www.nytimes.com/2019/01/07/us/politics/govenment-shutdown-impact-effects.html.

78. "SOS: EU Urged to Put Economic Survival Ahead of Green Deal," Global Warming Policy Forum, April 4, 2020, https://www.thegwpf.com/sos-eu-urged-to-put-economic-survival-ahead-of-green-deal/.

Chapter 12: Exploiting the Children

1. "Greta Thunberg: Our Lives Are in Your Hands," Medium, September 7, 2018, https://medium.com/wedonthavetime/greta-thunberg-our-lives-are-in-your-hands-b5a7b1e24a97.

2.   Desmond Butler, Juliet Eilperin, "The Anti-Greta: A Conservative Think Tank Takes on the Global Phenomenon," Washington Post, February 23, 2020, https://www.washingtonpost.com/climate-environment/2020/02/23/ meet-anti-greta-young-youtuber-campaigning-against-climate-alarmism/.

3.   Greta Thunberg (@GretaThunberg), "Fridays for future. The school strike continues!," Twitter, September 16, 2018, 12:55 p.m., https://twitter.com/ GretaThunberg/status/1041369960436703232..

4.   Rebel News (@RebelNewsOnline), "She sums all climate change activists up in one sentence: 'I don't want you to be hopeful, I want you to panic.'," Twitter, September 8, 2019, 4:47 p.m., https://twitter.com/RebelNewsOnline/ status/1170800883610849280.

5.   Safia Samee Ali and Elizabeth Chuck, "Greta Thunberg is Time's 2019 Person of the Year," NBC News, December 11, 2019, https://www.nbcnews.com/news/ us-news/ greta-thunberg-time-s-2019-person-year-n1099396.

6.   Gregory Wrightstone, "The Education of Greta Thunberg: Naivety Meets Reality for the Teen Climate Alarmist," PJ Media, June 1, 2019, https://pjmedia.com/columns/gregory-wrightstone/2019/06/01/ the-education-of-greta-thunberg-naivety-meets-reality-for-the-teen-climate-alarmist-n120309.

7.   "Climate Change: Students to Skip School This Friday to Demand Action," FRANCE 24 English, March 14, 2019, YouTube video, https://youtu.be/Q5bTE-t49WI.

8.   Ava Martinez, a.k.a. Mini AOC, in Marc Morano, *Climate Hustle 2* (film), 2020, www.ClimateHustle2.com.

9.   "Richmond Climate Strike," The Action Network, December 6, 2019, https://actionnetwork.org/events/ richmond-youth-climate-strike-2.

10. Sandy Moor, "Keep Kids out of the Climate Debate," Spiked, March 7, 2019, https://www.spiked-online.com/2019/03/07/ keep-kids-out-of-the-climate-debate/.

11. Valerie Richardson, "Al Gore–Led Group Encourages Students to Ditch School for Climate Strike, *Washington Times*, March 13, 2019, https://www.washingtontimes.com/news/2019/mar/13/ al-gore-led-group-encourages-students-ditch-school/.

12. Frank Jordans and Seth Borenstein, "Students Globally Protest Warming, Pleading for Their Future," AP News, March 15, 2019, https://apnews.com/article/e53351b075884886937f78e3b2118621.

13. Patrick Moore (@EcoSenseNow), "Greta, 'I want you to panic.,'" Twitter, September 8, 2019, 11:24 a.m., https://twitter.com/EcoSenseNow/status/1170719530915516416.

14. Patrick Moore (@EcoSenseNow), "You don't seem to get it...," Twitter, March 15, 2019, 4:20 p.m., https://twitter.com/EcoSenseNow/status/1106651355425456131.

15. Patrick Moore (@EcoSenseNow), "You are clearly projecting...," Twitter, March 15, 2019, 4:50 p.m., https://twitter.com/EcoSenseNow/status/1106658890488471554.

16. Bjørn Lomborg, "On Climate Change, Humanity Is Not 'Evil,'" *Globe and Mail*, September 26, 2019, https://www.theglobeandmail.com/opinion/article-on-climate-change-humanity-is-not-evil/.

17. Jim Treacher, "Leo DiCaprio: 'I Will Fly Around the World Doing Good for the Environment,'" Daily Caller, January 21, 2013, http://dailycaller.com/2013/01/21/leo-dicaprio-i-willfly-around-the-world-doing-good-for-theenvironment/.

18. Gareth Davies, "Carbon Footprints of the Telethon Stars: The Hand in Hand Hurricane Fund-Raiser Started with a Lecture about Global Warming—Then Celebrities with Multiple Homes, Cars and Private Jets Starting Soliciting Much Needed Money," *Daily Mail*, September 13, 2017, http://www.dailymail.co.uk/news/article-4880930/Leo-Bieber-s-jet-setting-addedIrma.html.

19. Tony Heller, "Greta's Dire Straits," Real Climate Science blog, August 22, 2019, https://realclimatescience.com/2019/08/gretas-dire-straits/.

20. Jamie Margolin, witness, "Voices Leading the Next Generation on the Global Climate Crisis," House Foreign Affairs Committee, Subcommittee on Europe, Eurasia, Energy, and the Environment Hearing, September 18, 2019, https://foreignaffairs.house.gov/hearings?ID=206DAC73-8EAB-41CA-96F7-2C2FD5B47E46.

21. Chris D'Angelo, "'Never Give Up': Greta Thunberg Takes Climate Strike to the White House," Grist, September 13, 2019, https://grist.org/article/never-give-up-greta-thunberg-takes-climate-strike-to-the-white-house/.

22. Michael Shellenberger, "Why Climate Alarmism Hurts Us All," *Forbes*, December 4, 2019, https://www.forbes.com/sites/michaelshellenberger/2019/12/04/why-climate-alarmism-hurts-us-all/amp/?.

23. Lacey Lett, "Oklahoma Students Plan to Walk Out of School Demanding Better Policies on Climate Change," KFOR News,

December 3, 2019, https://kfor.com/news/oklahoma-students-plan-to-walk-out-of-school-demanding-better-policies-on-climate-change/.

24. "Transcript: Greta Thunberg's Speech at the U.N. Climate Action Summit, NPR, September 23, 2019, https://www.npr.org/2019/09/23/763452863/transcript-greta-thunbergs-speech-at-the-u-n-climate-action-summit.

25. Henry Bodkin, "Parents Told Not to Terrify Children over Climate Change As Rising Numbers Treated for 'Eco-Anxiety,'" *Telegraph*, September 15, 2019, https://www.telegraph.co.uk/news/2019/09/15/parents-told-not-terrify-children-climate-change-rising-numbers/?

26. Anand Giridharadas, "To Solve Everything, Solve Climate," The Ink, September 1, 2020, https://the.ink/p/to-solve-everything-solve-climate.

27. Thomas Sowell (@ThomasSowell), "In the schools and colleges…," Twitter, August 7, 2020, 4:27 p.m., https://twitter.com/ThomasSowell/status/1291833412114931718.

28. Al Gore, "Al Gore Calls Trump's Deregulation Proposals 'Literally Insane,'" PBS NewsHour, October 12, 2018, YouTube video, 2:00, https://youtu.be/CT-x-j1FeSQ?t=120.

29. Greta Thunberg, "School Strike for Climate–Save the World by Changing the Rules | Greta Thunberg | TEDxStockholm," TEDx Talks, December 12, 2018, YouTube video, https://youtu.be/EAmmUIEsN9A.

30. Greta Thunberg (@GretaThunberg), "Before I started school striking…," Twitter, August 31, 2019, 5:47 p.m., https://twitter.com/GretaThunberg/status/1167916944520908800.

31. Charlotte Alter, Suyin Haynes, and Justin Worland, "Time 2019 Person of the Year: Greta Thunberg," *Time*, December 23–30, 2019, https://time.com/person-of-the-year-2019-greta-thunberg/?.

32. Michael Fitzpatrick, "Greta Thunberg: Autistic Prophet?," Spiked, May 7, 2019, https://www.spiked-online.com/2019/05/07/greta-thunberg-autistic-prophet/.

33. CFACT Ed, "Greta's 'Green' Coming to America Was via Petrochemicals Worthy of a Royal," CFACT, September 26, 2019, https://www.cfact.org/2019/09/26/watch-this-cool-time-lapse-a-greta-green-yacht-is-born-from-petrochemicals/?.

34. Craig Rucker, "Climate Kid Greta Protesting Oil on Yacht Made of Hydrocarbons," CFACT, July 31, 2019, https://www.cfact.

org/2019/07/31/
climate-kid-greta-protesting-oil-on-yacht-made-of-hydrocarbons/.

35. Michael Shellenberger, "New Documentary Film, 'Juice,' Challenges Elitism of Anti-Growth Environmentalism," *Forbes*, August 7, 2020, https://www.forbes.com/sites/michaelshellenberger/2020/08/07/new-documentary-film-juice-challenges-elitism-of-anti-growth-environmentalism/#23c6c33a5669.

36. Michael St. George, "How Green is St. Greta's Ark? Er, Not Very," Conservative Woman, August 20, 2019, https://www.conservativewoman.co.uk/how-green-is-st-gretas-ark-er-not-very/.

37. Bjørn Lomborg (@BjornLomborg), "Hilarious…," Twitter, August 16, 2019, 6:33 a.m., https://twitter.com/BjornLomborg/status/1162311408144531457.

38. Tony Heller (@Tony_Heller), "Dear Greta,…," Twitter, November 1, 2019, 3:27 p.m., https://twitter.com/Tony__Heller/status/1190349783950450688.

39. Doyle Rice, "Greta Thunberg Is Sailing Back across the Atlantic. Here's What She Accomplished While in the U.S.," *USA Today* November 13, 2019, https://www.usatoday.com/story/news/nation/2019/11/13/climate-activist-greta-thunberg-sails-back-europe-la-vagabonde/4178195002/.

40. Cory Morningstar, "The Manufacturing of Greta Thunberg—For Consent: The Political Economy of the Non-Profit Industrial Complex (Act 1)," Wrong Kind of Green blog, January 17, 2019, http://www.wrongkindofgreen.org/2019/01/17/the-manufacturing-of-greta-thunberg-for-consent-the-political-economy-of-the-non-profit-industrial-complex/.

41. Morningstar, "The Manufacturing of Greta Thunberg—For Consent."

42. Keean Bexte, "United Nations Reacts: What Do You Think of Greta Thunberg's Plastic-Garbage-Filled Tesla?," Rebel News, December 11, 2019, https://www.rebelnews.com/united_nations_reacts_greta_thunberg_garbage_filled_tesla.

43. Dominic Green, "Greta's Very Corporate Children's Crusade," Standpoint, May 30, 2019, https://standpointmag.co.uk/issues/june-2019/gretas-very-corporate-childrens-crusade/?.

44. Greta Thunberg, "Recently I've seen many rumors circulating about me and enormous amounts of hate…," Facebook, February 2, 2019, https://www.facebook.com/gretathunbergsweden/posts/recently-ive-seen-many-rumors-circulating-about-me-and-enormous-amounts-of-hate-/767646880269801/.

45. "Journalist Allegedly Harassed by Greta Thunberg's Bodyguards in Sweden," Daily Sabah, January 28, 2020, https://www.dailysabah. com/ europe/2020/01/28/ journalist-allegedly-harassed-by-greta-thunbergs-bodyguards-in-sweden.

46. Keean Bexte (@TheRealKeean), "I went to Greta Thunberg's 'school strike.' I was greeted by a city block full of undercover security. Funnily enough ... ," Twitter, January 24, 2020, 12:55 p.m., https:// twitter.com/TheRealKeean/ status/1220767206562099201.

47. Brooke Knoll, "Mother of Activist Greta Thunberg Gave Up Opera Career to Fight Climate Change," Classical Minnesota Public Radio, September 25, 2019, https://www.classicalmpr.org/ story/2019/09/25/ malena-ernman-opera-greta-thunberg.

48. "Artisten Malena Ernman och biologen Rebecka Le Moine utsedda till Årets Miljöhjältar av WWF," WWF press release, October 5, 2017, https://www.wwf. se/pressmeddelande/artisten-malena-ernman-och-biologen-rebecka-le-moineutsedda-till-arets-miljohjaltar-av-wwf-2689982/.

49. Ansgar Neuhof, "De milj ardairs achter Greta Thunberg, het Zweedse klimaatorakeltje" [The billionaires behind Greta Thunberg, the Swedish climate oracle], ClimateGate.NL blog, https://www.climategate.nl/2020/01/ de-miljardairs-achter-greta-het-zweedse-klimaatorakeltje/.

50. Greta Thunberg, "Recently I've seen many rumors circulating about me and enormous amounts of hate. ...," Facebook, February 2, 2019, https://www.facebook.com/gretathunbergsweden/posts/recently-ive-seen-many-rumors-circulating-about-me-and-enormous-amounts-of-hate-/767646880269801/.

51. Laura Snapes, "'Time to Rebel': Greta Thunberg Adds Voice to New Song by the 1975," *Guardian*, July 24, 2019, https://www. theguardian.com/music/2019/jul/25/time-to-rebel-greta-thunberg-makes-musical-debut-on-the-1975-track.

52. Joseph Vazquez, "Soros Gave Global Climate Strike Partners More Than $24M," MRC Business blog, September 26, 2019, https:// www.newsbusters.org/blogs/business/joseph-vazquez/2019/09/26/ soros-gave-global-climate-strike-partners-more-24m.

53. David Sassoon, "Genesis of a Shakedown: New Records Expose Children's Marches as Long-Planned Component of Litigation Campaign," Climate Litigation Watch, March 13, 2019, https:// climatelitigationwatch.org/genesis-of-a-shakedown-new-records-expose-childrens-marches-as-long-planned-component-of-litigation-campaign/. See also H. Sterling Burnett, "Appeals Court Places Hold

on Activist-Backed Youth Climate Lawsuit," Heartland Institute, September 11, 2017, https://www.heartland.org/news-opinion/news/appeals-court-places-hold-on-activist-backed-youth-climate-lawsuit.

54. Pat Dooris, "Who Is Kelsey Juliana? Meet the Woman Whose Name Is on the Federal Climate Change Lawsuit," KGW8, June 4, 2019, https://www.kgw.com/article/tech/science/environment/who-is-kelsey-juliana-meet-the-woman-whose-name-is-on-the-federal-climate-change-lawsuit/283-1bce7dea-4f0d-4b32-881b-efef3706aa6c.

55. Bill Blakemore, "Climate Canard No. 1: A 'Crime against Humanity' (and the Central Fear about Global Warming)," ABC News, April 15, 2012, https://abcnews.go.com/blogs/technology/2012/04/climate-canard-no-1-a-crime-against-humanity-and-the-central-fear-about-global-warming; James Delingpole, "James Hansen: Would You Buy a Used Temperature Data Set from THIS Man?," *Telegraph*, January 22, 2010, https://www.climatedepot.com/2010/01/22/time-for-meds-nasa-scientist-james-hansen-endorses-book-which-calls-for-ridding-the-world-of-industrial-civilization-ndash-hansen-declares-author-has-it-rightthe-system-is-the-problem/.

56. Holly Swanson, interview in Marc Morano, *Climate Hustle* 2 (film), 2020, www.ClimateHustle2.com.

57. Glenn A. Hodgkins et al., "Climate-Driven Variability in the Occurrence of Major Floods across North America and Europe," *Journal of Hydrology* 552 (September 2017): 704–17, https://doi.org/10.1016/j.jhydrol.2017.07.027.

58. Eric Bolling, Marc Morano, and Fernando Miralles-Wilhelm, "Watch: Climate Skeptic Morano Debates Warmist Professor about Kids Climate School Strikes," Seasonspass33, October 22, 2019, YouTube video, https://youtu.be/ZQjh6Fy9418. See also Jean S. Renouf et al., "Why Universities Need to Declare an Ecological and Climate Emergency," Times Higher Education, September 27, 2019, https://www.timeshighereducation.com/blog/why-universities-need-declare-ecological-and-climate-emergency.

Chapter 13: Identity Politics Invades the Climate Debate

1. Scott Waldman and Maxine Joselow, "Democrats Eye Climate Policy in Economic Relief Bill," E&E News, March 12, 2020, https://www.eenews.net/stories/1062581379.

2. Eric Holthaus (@EricHolthaus), "The climate emergency isn't about science, it's about justice. ... ," Twitter, July 28, 2020, 8:45 a.m., https://twitter.com/EricHolthaus/status/1288093160829341697.

3. Greta Thunberg, Luisa Neubauer, and Angela Valenzuela, "Why We Strike Again," Project Syndicate, November 29, 2019, https://www.project-syndicate.org/commentary/climate-strikes-un-conference-madrid-by-greta-thunberg-et-al-2019-11.

4. James Delingpole, "Greta the Teenage Climate Puppet Goes Full Marxist," Breitbart, November 29, 2019, https://www.breitbart.com/politics/2019/11/29/greta-thunberg-goes-full-marxist/.

5. Adam Ford, "CNN's Van Jones: 'Even the Most Well-Intentioned White Person Has a Virus in His or Her Brain," Disrn, May 30, 2020, https://disrn.com/news/cnns-van-jones-even-the-most-well-intentioned-white-person-has-a-virus-in-his-or-her-brain.

6. TimesLive, "Whites Created Cyclone Idai and Must Therefore Pay, Says BLF," DispatchLive, March 24, 2019, https://www.dispatchlive.co.za/news/2019-03-24-whites-created-cyclone-idai-and-must-therefore-pay-says-blf/.

7. Michael Mann, "Yes, Tucker Carlson is both a climate denier...," Twitter, September 11, 2020, 9:09 p.m., https://twitter.com/MichaelEMann/status/1304587858779529216; also see Marc Morano, "Former UN Lead Scientist Michael Mann: 'Tucker Carlson Is Both a Climate Change Denier and a Racist F#ck,'" Climate Depot, September 12, 2020, https://www.climatedepot.com/2020/09/12/former-un-lead-scientist-michael-mann-rants-tucker-carlson-is-both-a-climate-change-denier-and-a-racist-fck/.

8. Isaac Stanley-Becker, "Whites Are Mainly to Blame for Air Pollution, but Blacks and Hispanics Bear the Burden, Says a New Study," *Washington Post*, March 12, 2019, https://www.washingtonpost.com/nation/2019/03/12/whites-are-mainly-blame-air-pollution-blacks-hispanics-bear-burden-says-new-study/.

9. "On the Change of Climate," *Maitland Mercury & Hunter River General Advertiser*, March 11, 1846, http://trove.nla.gov.au/newspaper/article/679787?searchTerm=climate%20change&searchLimits=; see also Steven Goddard, "Was Captain Cook the First Climate Wrecking White Man?," Real Climate, May 21, 2013, https://stevengoddard.wordpress.com/2013/05/21/was-captain-cook-the-firstclimate-climate-wrecking-white-man/.

10. Roger Pielke Jr., "Pielke on Climate #5," The Climate Fix blog, September 18, 2017, https://theclimatefix.wordpress.com/2017/09/18/pielke-on-climate-5/.

11. Kate Marvel (@DrKateMarvel), "I've been off social media because global pandemic+ schools closed+ full-time job etc. Just popping back to say that climate justice and racial justice are the same thing,

... ," Twitter, June 1, 2020, 12:03 p.m., https://twitter.com/DrKateMarvel/status/1267486848340893697.

12. Kate Marvel (@DrKateMarvel), "DAMN RIGHT @SarahEMyhre," Twitter, January 23, 2018, 2:23 p.m., https://twitter.com/DrKateMarvel/status/955883674888736769.

13. Mark Hand, "Scientists Stand Behind Youth Climate Activists in Support of Green New Deal," Think Progress, December 14, 2018, https://archive.thinkprogress.org/climate-scientists-welcome-the-rise-of-youth-activists-fighting-for-a-green-new-deal-b78bbd3cb061/.

14. Peter Kalmus (@ClimateHuman), "Here's why race justice and climate justice are one and the same...," Twitter, May 30, 2020, 11:58 a.m., https://twitter.com/ClimateHuman/status/1266760903405350912.

15. Tim Sullivan and Stephen Groves, "Protests Over Police Killings Rage in Dozens of U.S. Cities," AP News, May 30, 2020, https://apnews.com/article/c743eaecd9a5948a4576565b12e3230d.

16. Peter Kalmus (@ClimateHuman), "They'd literally rather have a race war...," Twitter, May 29, 2020, 2:09 a.m., https://twitter.com/ClimateHuman/status/1266250341114212355.

17. Peter Kalmus, "About Me," Peter Kalmus blog, https://peterkalmus.net/about/.

18. Peter Kalmus, "Thoughts on Climate Action from a Scientist Who Gave Up Flying," Sierra, March 9, 2018, https://www.sierraclub.org/sierra/thoughts-climate-action-scientist-who-gave-flying.

19. James Hansen, "Read by Chapter," Peter Kalmus blog, https://peterkalmus.net/ books/read-by-chapter-being-the-change/.

20. Marc Morano, "Crying over 'Climate Change'—Tears, Sobbing, & 'Climate Grief' Is an Actual Thing for Activists—Special Report," Climate Depot, June 3, 2020, https://www.climatedepot.com/2020/06/03/crying-over-climate-changetears-sobbing-climate-grief-is-an-actual-thing-for-activists-special-report/. See, for example, "Yvo de Boer's Career As UN Climate Chief," Guardian, February 18, 2010, https://www.theguardian.com/environment/gallery/2010/feb/18/yvode-boer-resigns-un; Peter Kiefer, "Hollywood Is Gearing Up for Environmental Activism," Hollywood Reporter, April 21, 2017, https://www. hollywoodreporter.com/news/ hollywood-is-gearing-up-a-week-science-enviromental-activism-996473.2.

21. Ashlee Cunsolo and Neville Ellis, "Ecological Grief as a Mental Health Response to Climate Change-Related Loss," Nature Climate Change 8, no. 4, (April 2018), https://doi.org/10.1038/s41558-018-0092-2.

22. Marc Morano, *The Politically Incorrect Guide to Climate Change* (Washington, D.C.: Regnery, 2018), 234–35, internal citations omitted.

23. Gerry Bellett, "Global Warming Is Here to Stay, Says NASA Scientist," *Vancouver Sun*, April 17, 2015, https://www.vancouversun.com/technology/Global+warming+here+stay+says+NASA+scientist+with+video/10978871/story.html.

24. "Astronauts and Scientists Send Letter to NASA: Stop Global Warming Advocacy," CFACT, April 10, 2012, https://www.cfact.org/2012/04/10/ astronauts-and-scientists-send-letter-to-nasa-stop-global-warming-advocacy/..

25. The Right Climate Stuff, https://www.therightclimatestuff.com/..

26. Clara Moskowitz, "NASA Chief Says Agency's Goal Is Muslim Outreach, Forgets to Mention Space," Christian Science Monitor, July 14, 2010, https:// www.csmonitor.com/Science/2010/0714/NASA-chief-says-agency-s-goal-is-Muslim-outreach-forgets-to-mention-space.

27. "NASA to Reexamine Nicknames for Cosmic Objects," NASA press release, August 5, 2020, https://www.nasa.gov/feature/nasa-to-reexamine-nicknames-for-cosmic-objects..

28. Eric Weinstein (@EricRWeinstein), "I suppose naming something the 'Eskimo Nebula' was pretty CounterIntuitive. ...," Twitter, August 7, 2020, 9:31 p.m., https://twitter.com/EricRWeinstein/status/1291909852575313920..

29. Viashino (@TheViashino), "Dwarf stars...," Twitter, August 7, 2020, 9:38 p.m., https://twitter.com/TheViashino/status/1291911686853726213.

30. Gabriel Foley and Jordan Rutter, "The Stench of Colonialism Mars These Bird Names. They Must Be Changed.," *Washington Post*, August 4, 2020, https://www.washingtonpost.com/opinions/2020/08/04/american-bird-names-colonialism-audubon/.

31. Emily Atkin, "An Interview with Al Gore," Heated, June 3, 2020, https://heated.world/p/an-interview-with-al-gore.

32. David Botti, "The Great American Lawn: How the Dream Was Manufactured," *New York Times*, August 9, 2019, https://www.nytimes.com/2019/08/09/video/ lawn-grass-environment-history.html.

33. Nylah Burton, "People of Color Experience Climate Grief More Deeply Than White People," Vice, May 14, 2020, https://www.vice.com/en/article/v7ggqx/ people-of-color-experience-climate-grief-more-deeply-than-white-people..

34. Kate Aronoff, "Defunding the Police Is Good Climate Policy," New Republic, June 4, 2020, https://newrepublic.com/article/157984/defunding-police-good-climate-policy.

35. Duggan Flanakin, "The Racism of Climate Change Alarmists," Townhall, September 3, 2020, https://townhall.com/columnists/dugganflanakin/2020/08/25/the-racism-of-climate-change-alarmists-n2575020.

36. Geoff Demcicki, "Why 'Defunding the Police' Is Also an Environmental Issue," Vice, June 18, 2020, https://www.vice.com/en/article/akz3vz/why-defunding-the-police-is-also-an-environmental-issue.

37. Brittany Vonow and Sascha O'Sullivan, "Fury As Extinction Rebellion Founder Say MPs and Business Owners 'Should Have Bullet Put Through Their Heads,'" UK Sun, September 2, 2020, https://www.thesun.co.uk/news/12559571/extinction-rebellion-founder-mps-business-bullet/. See also Roger Hallam, "XR Founder Calls for Government and Business Owners to Be Shot," Christian Calgie, September 1, 2020, https://youtu.be/NP75tN9K7Kk.

38. Alvin Powell, "Aging Population Increases Energy Use," Harvard Gazette, June 6, 2019, https://news.harvard.edu/gazette/story/2019/06/harvard-research-shows-energy-use-climbs-with-age-and-temperature/.

39. Patt Morrison, "Bill Nye on the Terrifying Ascendancy of American 'Dingbatitude,'" *Los Angeles Times*, July 19, 2017, https://www.latimes.com/opinion/op-ed/la-ol-patt-morrison-bill-nye-science-20170719-htmlstory.html.

40. John Stossel, Interview Climate Hustle 2, September 2020, www.ClimateHustle2.com

41. Paul Watson, "'V.' V stands for Verity, Virtue, Valor, Validity and Veganism…," Facebook, May 6, 2014, https://www.facebook.com/captpaulwatson/posts/10152354821425932.

42. Katharina Wecker and Irene Banos Ruiz, "To Combat Climate Change, Increase Women's Participation," Deutsche Welle, November 20, 2017, https://www.dw.com/en/to-combat-climate-change-increase-womens-participation/a-41427366.

43. Rowan Institute (@rowan_institute), "Please read @rowan_institute's collective statement…," Twitter, June 12, 2019, 7:56 p.m., https://twitter.com/rowan_institute/status/1138958406323073024.

44. Tom Nelson (@tan123), "Sad: @drvox has lost his youthful enthusiasm about saving the world from a completely imaginary

climate crisis? ...," Twitter, June 8, 2019, 9:34 a.m., https://twitter. com/tan123/status/1137352119143587804.

45. Nikhil Swaminathan, "The Unsustainable Whiteness of Green," Grist, June 20, 2017, https://grist.org/feature/ the-unsustainable-whiteness-of-green/..

46. Eric Holthaus (@EricHolthaus), "Who are your favorite (non-white non-men) climate experts you'd like to see on TV and hear on the radio?," Twitter, November 25, 2018, 2:12 p.m., https://twitter.com/ EricHolthaus/ status/1066771611041312778.

47. Michael McKenna, "New York Times Asleep at the Switch over Journalistic Ethics," *Washington Times*, October 28, 2020, https://m.washingtontimes.com/ news/2020/oct/28/ new-york-times-asleep-at-the-switch-over-journalis/8.

48. Hop Hopkins, "Racism Is Killing the Planet," Sierra, June 8, 2020, https:// www.sierraclub.org/sierra/racism-killing-planet.

49. Mattias Lehman, "The Climate Justice Movement Must Oppose White Supremacy Everywhere—By Supporting M4BL," Medium, May29,2020,https://medium.com/sunrisemvmt/the-climate-justice-movement-mustoppose-white-supremacy-everywhere-by-supporting-m4bl-4e338cf91b19..

50. Marc Morano, "Men Warm Globe, Women Feel the Heat, Group Claims," Free Republic, December 6, 2005, http://freerepublic.com/ focus/f-news/1534943/ posts.

51. Oliver O'Connell, "The Sierra Club: America's Oldest Conservation Group Denounces Racism of Its Founder," *Independent*, July 22, 2020, https://www.independent.co.uk/news/world/americas/sierra-club-john-muir-racism-white-supremacy-monuments-conservation-a9633036.html.

52. Jedediah Purdy, "Environmentalism's Racist History," New Yorker, August 13, 2015, https://www.newyorker.com/news/news-desk/ environmentalisms-racist-history.

53. Karin Louise Hermes, "Why I Quit Being a Climate Activist," Vice, February 6, 2020, https://www.vice.com/en/article/g5x5ny/ why-i-quit-being-a-climate-activist.

54. Terry Gross, "A 'Forgotten History' of How the U.S. Government Segregated America," NPR, May 3, 2017, https://www.npr.org /2017/05/03/526655831/a-forgotten-history-of-how-the-u-s-government-segregated-america.

Chapter 14: The Toxic Politics of the Green New Deal

1. Brooke Singman, "LA Mayor Garcetti Encourages Residents to Report Violators of Stay-at-Home Order: 'Snitches Get Rewards,'" Fox News, April 3, 2020, https://www.foxnews.com/politics/la-mayor-garcetti-residents-report-violators-stay-at-home-order.

2. David Williamson, "'Dream On!' Speaker Lindsay Hoyle Slapped Down for Lockdown-Style Climate Change Rules," *UK Express*, September 12, 2020, https://www.express.co.uk/news/politics/1334816/climate-change-rules-lindsay-hoyle-G7.

3. Rachel Koning Beals, "COVID-19 and Climate Change: 'The Parallels Are Screaming at Us,' Says John Kerry," Market Watch, April 22, 2020, https://www.marketwatch.com/story/covid-19-and-climate-change-the-parallels-are-screaming-at-us-says-john-kerry-2020-04-22?.

4. Michael Barone, "Anti-Pandemic Rules the Opposite of Anti-Climate Change Rules," Rasmussen Reports, March 27, 2020, https://www.rasmussenreports.com/public_content/political_commentary/commentary_by_michael_barone/anti_pandemic_rules_the_opposite_of_anti_climate_change_rules.

5. Rebecca Klar, "France's Macron Calls for All Citizens to Remain Confined in Homes: 'We're at War,'" The Hill, March 16, 2020, https://www.msn.com/en-us/news/politics/frances-macron-calls-for-all-citizens-to-remain-confined-in-homes-were-at-war/ar-BB11gYQa.

6. Antony P. Mueller, "From Lockdowns to 'The Great Reset,'" Mises Wire, August 1, 2020, https://mises.org/wire/lockdowns-great-reset.

7. Trevor Thomas, "The Wuhan Virus Reminds Us: Beware Scientism and the Technocrats," American Thinker, April 8, 2020, https://www.americanthinker.com/articles/2020/04/the_wuhan_virus_reminds_us_beware_scientism_and_the_technocrats.html.

8. Penny Starr, "Watch Live: Climate Kid Greta Thunberg Testifies in Congress," Breitbart, September 18, 2019, https://www.breitbart.com/politics/2019/09/18/watch-live-climate-kid-greta-thunberg-testifies-in-congress/.

9. Thomas Sowell (@ThomasSowell), "Experts are often called in…," Twitter, August 29, 2020, 8:12 a.m., https://twitter.com/ThomasSowell/status/1299681372185993216.

10. Dwight D. Eisenhower, "Farewell Address," ourdocuments.gov, 1961, https://www.ourdocuments.gov/doc.php?flash=false&doc=90&page=transcript.

11. Peter Barry Chowka, "Will the Covid-19 PsyOp Succeed?," *American Thinker*, April 19, 2020, https://www.americanthinker. com/blog/2020/04/will_the_covid19_psyop_succeed.html.

12. Lubos Motl, "Lockdown Madness Is a Triumph of the Precautionary Principle," the reference frame blog, April 29, 2020, https://motls.blogspot.com/2020/04/lockdown-madness-is-triumph-of.html?.

13. Larry Kudlow, "Kudlow Predicts the Unemployment Numbers 'Will Continue to Be Poor' in Weeks Ahead," Fox News Channel, April 3, 2020, https://video.foxnews.com/v/6146876412001#sp=show-clips.

14. Bill Barrow, "Biden Says He'd Shut Down Economy If Scientists Recommended," ABC News, August 23, 2020, https://abcnews. go.com/Politics/wireStory/ biden-hed-shut-economy-scientists-recommended-72559926.

15. David Catron, "A Mitigation Disaster," American Spectator, April 6, 2020, https://spectator.org/a-mitigation-disaster/.

16. Sanjeev Sabhlok, "Who Am I?," Sanjeev Sabhlok's blog, https:// www. sabhlokcity.com/who-am-i/..

17. Sanjeev Sabhlok, Pope @Church of Reason & Liberty (@sabhlok), "Australia's bureaucracy has performed as badly...," Twitter, July 28, 2020, 2:52 a.m., https://twitter.com/sabhlok/status/1288004318 499491840..

18. Sanjeev Sabhlok, Pope @Church of Reason & Liberty (@sabhlok), "The only thing we know for sure today is that "scientists" and politicians are wrong...," July 25, 2020, 6:15 a.m., https://twitter. com/sabhlok/ status/1286968218892943362..

19. Sanjeev Sabhlok, Pope @Church of Reason & Liberty (@sabhlok), "Absolutely. Small retailers and hospitality establishments, gyms and fitness industry and many others can't possibly recover. This is like mass scale bombing of one's own economy," Twitter, August 2, 2020, 7:04 a.m., https://twitter.com/sabhlok/ status/1289879789830983682.

20. Sanjeev Sabhlok, Pope @Church of Reason & Liberty (@sabhlok), "The Problem with Science Today Is That It Is Effectively Just Another Branch of Government," Twitter, Jul 16, 2020, 6:03 a.m., https://twitter.com/sabhlok/ status/1283703789111795714..

21. Lord Sumption, "Locking Up the Elderly Until Coronavirus Is Defeated Is a Cruel Mockery of Basic Human Values," *Daily Mail*, May 2, 2020, https://www.dailymail.co.uk/debate/article-8281007/ amp/Former-Supreme-Court-judge-LORD-SUMPTION-gives-withering-critique-Governments-lockdown.html?.

22. Sanjeev Sabhlok, Pope @Church of Reason & Liberty (@sabhlok), "This pandemic…," Twitter, May 5, 2020, 7:07 p.m., https://twitter.com/sabhlok/status/1257809057420677120.

23. James Lucas, "How to Show Americans Lockdowns Are Killing More People Than the Virus," The Federalist, October 21, 2020, https://thefederalist.com/2020/10/21/how-to-show-americans-lockdowns-are-killing-more-people-than-the-virus/.

24. Steve Milloy (@JunkScience), "We need herd immunity and for the virus to burn itself out. The incompetent…," Twitter, August 2, 2020, 11:51 a.m., https://twitter.com/JunkScience/status/1289952045122727936.

25. Steve Milloy (@JunkScience), "Conservative politicians are now at the mercy of the leftist-run public heath [sic] bureaucracy. As with education…," Twitter, March 22, 2020, 10:51 a.m., https://twitter.com/JunkScience/status/1241739320546988034.

26. Steve Milloy (@JunkScience), "We can still 'social distance' without devolving into a police state or destroying the economy," April 12, 2020, 5:58 p.m., https://twitter.com/JunkScience/status/1249456832046936067.

27. Sarah Newey, "UNICEF Warns Lockdown Could Kill More Than Covid-19 As Model Predicts 1.2 Million Child Deaths," *Telegraph*, May 13, 2020, https://www.telegraph.co.uk/global-health/science-and-disease/unicef-warns-lockdown-could-kill-covid-19-model-predicts-12/.

28. Brian C. Joondeph, "COVID and Climate Policy Following the Same Playbook," American Thinker, August 17, 2020, https://www.americanthinker.com/articles/2020/08/covid_and_climate_policy_following_the_same_playbook.html.

29. Tony Heller (@Tony_Heller), "We have arrived at the end game.," Twitter, March 18, 2020, 12:27 a.m., https://twitter.com/Tony__Heller/status/1240132755574394880.

30. Tony Heller (@Tony_Heller), "I've been saying this for the past four months. The COVID-19 response…," Twitter, July 29, 2020, 8:22 a.m., https://twitter.com/Tony__Heller/status/1288449867455504387.

31. "C.S. Lewis: Quotable Quote," Goodreads, https://www.goodreads.com/quotes/19967-of-all-tyrannies-a-tyranny-sincerely-exercised-for-the-good.

32. BasicEconomics, "Milton Friedman vs Bill Clinton (1999)," YouTube, May 28, 2012, https://youtu.be/UlNxIc9gUMc.

33. IPCC (@IPCC_CH), "'The COVID-19 pandemic tells us that everything is connected…," Twitter, June 1, 2020, 5:30 a.m., https://twitter.com/IPCC_CH/status/1267388037199269889.

34. Bill Dunne, "The Danger of Letting Lab Coats Run the World," American Thinker, May 14, 2020, https://www.americanthinker.com/articles/2020/05/the_danger_of_letting_lab_coats_run_the_world.html.

35. "Calls to Add 'Climate Change' to Death Certificates," The Australian National University, May 21, 2020, https://www.anu.edu.au/news/all-news/calls-to-add-%E2%80%98climate-change%E2%80%99-to-death-certificates; Thomas Longden et al., "Heat-Related Mortality: An Urgent Need to Recognise and Record," *The Lancet Planetary Health* 4, no. 5 (May 2020): e171, https://doi.org/10.1016/S2542-5196(20)30100-5.

36. NowThis (@nowthisnews), "Former Irish President Mary Robinson says we must address the climate crisis with the same tenacity as the coronavirus pandemic," Twitter, June 23, 2020, 11:13 a.m., https://twitter.com/nowthisnews/status/1275446766196809728.

37. Ibid.

38. DJ Patil and Mark Rosekind, "2015 Traffic Fatalities Data Has Just Been Released: A Call to Action to Download and Analyze," Obama White House Archives, August 29, 2016, https://obamawhitehouse.archives.gov/blog/2016/08/29/2015-traffic-fatalities-data-has-just-been-released-call-action-download-and-analyze.

39. Leticia M. Nogueira, K. Robin Yabroff, and Aaron Bernstein, "Climate Change and Cancer," *CA: A Cancer Journal for Clinicians* 70, no. 4 (July/August 2020): 239–244, https://doi.org/10.3322/caac.21610.

40. Al Gore, *An Inconvenient Sequel: Truth to Power* (New York: Rodale, 2017), 110.

41. Graham Piro, "Biden Surrogate Jane Fonda Calls COVID 'God's Gift to the Left,'" Washington Free Beacon, October 7, 2020, https://freebeacon.com/2020-election/biden-surrogate-jane-fonda-calls-covid-gods-gift-to-the-left/.

42. Anthony Watts, "After 100 Years of Climate Change, 'Climate Related Deaths' Approach Zero," Climate Realism, January 2, 2021, https://climaterealism.com/2021/01/after-100-years-of-climate-change-climate-related-deaths-approach-zero/.

43. Justin Haskins, "John Kerry: 'Great Reset Will with Greater Speed and Greater Intensity Than A Lot of People Might Imagine,'" Climate Depot (blog), December 1, 2020, https://www.climatedepot.

com/2020/12/01/john-kerry-great-reset-will-with-greater-speed-and-with-greater-intensity-than-a-lot-of-people-might-imagine/

44. Thomas Lifson, "Latest Warmist Scheme: Record 'Climate Change' As Cause of Death on Death Certificates," American Thinker, May 23, 2020, https://www.americanthinker.com/blog/2020/05/latest_warmist_scheme_record_climate_change_as_cause_of_death_on_death_certificates_.html.

45. Berkeley Lovelace, Jr., "WHO Warns Coronavirus Vaccine Alone Won't End Pandemic: 'We Cannot Go Back to the Way Things Were,'" CNBC, August 21, 2020, updated August 23, 2020, https://www.cnbc.com/amp/2020/08/21/who-warns-a-coronavirus-vaccine-alone-will-not-end-pandemic.html?.

46. Marc Morano, "Watch 2016 Video: World Economic Forum's Utopian Great Reset Vision of 2030…,"Climate Depot (blog), November 3, 2020, https://www.climatedepot.com/2020/11/03/watch-2016-video-world-economic-forums-utopian-great-reset-vision-of-2030-youll-own-nothing-and-youll-be-happy-whatever-you-want-youll-rent-itll-be-delivered-by-drone-meat/.

47. "'Great Polarization' May Be Next for World's Richest, UBS says," Mint, October 7, 2020, https://www.livemint.com/news/world/-great-polarizationmay-be-next-for-world-s-richest-ubs-says-11602031975218.html. .

48. Alina Selyukh, "Amazon Doubles Profit to $5.2 Billion As Online Shopping Spikes," NPR, July 30, 2020, https://www.npr.org/sections/coronavirus-live-updates/2020/07/30/897271729/amazon-doubles-profit-to-5-8-billion-as-online-shopping-spikes.

49. Kari Paul and Dominic Rushe, "Tech Giants' Shares Soar As Companies Benefit from Covid-19 Pandemic," Guardian, July 30, 2020, https://www.theguardian. com/business/2020/jul/30/amazon-apple-facebook-google-profits-earnings..

50. Tyler Clifford, "Jim Cramer: The Pandemic Led to 'One of the Greatest Wealth Transfers in History,'" CNBC, June 4, 2020, https://www.cnbc.com/2020/06/04/cramer-the-pandemic-led-to-a-great-wealth-transfer.html..

51. Diarmid Campbell-Lendrum, et al., "COP24 Special Report: Health & Climate Change," World Health Organization, 2018, https://apps.who.int/iris/bitstream/ handle/10665/276405/9789241514972-eng.pdf?sequence=1&isAllowed=y..

52. Marc Morano, "Canadian PM Trudeau Confirms Great Reset: 'This Pandemic Has Provided an Opportunity for a Reset'—We Need 'to Re-Imagine Economic Systems' by 'Building Back Better,'" Climate

Depot (blog), November 16, 2020,https://www.climatedepot.
com/2020/11/16/canadian-pm-trudeau-confirmscovids-great-
reset-this-pandemic-has-provided-an-opportunity-for-a-resetwe-
need-to-re-imagine-economic-systems-by-building-back-better/.

53.   James Delingpole, "'Build Back Better'—the Latest Code Phrase for
Green Global Tyranny," Breitbart, May 31, 2020, https://www.
breitbart.com/ europe/2020/05/31/ delingpole-build-back-
better-the-latest-code-phrase-for-green-global-tyranny/.

54.   Mark Hertsgaard and Kyle Pope, "The Coronavirus Has Lessons
for Journalists Covering the Climate Crisis," The Nation, April 20,
2020, https://www. thenation.com/article/environment/
coronavirus-climate-crisis-journalism/..

55.   Klaus Schwab, "Now Is the Time for a 'Great Reset,'" World
Economic Forum, June 3, 2020, https://www.weforum.org/
agenda/2020/06/ now-is-the-time-for-a-great-reset/.

56.   Justin Haskins, "Exposing Al Gore's Deep Connection to World
Leaders' Socialist 'Great Reset' Proposal," Stopping Socialism, June
22, 2020, https:// stoppingsocialism.com/2020/06/al-gore-great-
reset-connection/.

57.   Kevin Mooney, "The Connection Between Russia and 2 Green
Groups Fighting Fracking in US," Daily Signal, April 22, 2018,
https://www.dailysignal. com/2018/04/22/ the-connection-
between-russia-and-2-green-groups-fighting-fracking-in-us/..

58.   Antony P. Mueller, "From Lockdowns to 'The Great Reset,'" Mises
Wire, August 1, 2020, https://mises.org/wire/lockdowns-great-reset.

59.   Maurice Newman, "Dangerous Elites Planning 'the Great Reset,'"
Spectator, October 10, 2020, https://spectator.com.au/2020/10/
dangerous-elites-planning-the-great-reset/.

60.   Marc Morano, "Gore's Quest to Become a Fake Meat Billionaire—
Lobbies for Climate Policies That Limit Meat While His Firm
Invests $200 Million in Meat Substitutes," Climate Depot, August
17, 2019, https://www.climatedepot.com/2019/08/17/
gores-quest-to-become-a-fake-meat-billionaire-lobbies-forclimate-
policies-that-limit-meat-while-his-firm-invests-200-million-in-
meatsubstitutes/.

61.   Richard S. Lindzen, "An Oversimplified Picture of the Climate
Behavior Based on a Single Process Can Lead to Distorted
Conclusions," European Physical Journal Plus 135, no. 6 (June
2020): 462, https://doi.org/10.1140/epjp/ s13360-020-00471-z..

62. Freeman Dyson in "The Uncertainty Has Settled (Full film)," Marijn Poels, November 7, 2018, YouTube video, 1:09:35–1:14:15, https://youtu.be/ GuoxLggqI_g.

63. David Wallace-Wells, "Time to Panic," *New York Times*, February 16, 2019, https://www.nytimes.com/2019/02/16/opinion/sunday/ fear-panic-climatechange-warming.html?..

64. "Green Groups are China's 'Useful Idiots,'" Global Warming Policy Foundation, November 12, 2020, https://www.thegwpf.org/ green-groups-are-chinas-useful-idiots/

65. Donna Laframboise, "The BBC's Naive View of the UN's Climate Machine," Big Picture News blog, September 24, 2018, https:// wp.me/pSEKJ-7VG.

66. Barbra Streisand, "Barbra on Climate Change," barbrastreisand. com, November 2, 2012, https://www.climatedepot. com/2012/12/11/the-womanun-ipcc-warmist-michael-oppenheimer- answers-to-barbra-streisand-weighs-inin-the-wake-of-hurricane- sandy-i-cant-comprehend-how-there-are-still-climate- -change- deniers-out-there/.

67. Roger Pielke, "How Billionaires Tom Steyer and Michael Bloomberg Corrupted Climate Science," *Forbes*, January 2, 2020, https://www. forbes.com/sites/rogerpielke/2020/01/02/how-billionaires-tom- steyer-and-michael-bloomberg corrupted-climate-science/#35e5a41b702c..

68. RCP8.5, "...and Then There's Physics," May 10, 2018, https:// andthentheresphysics.wordpress.com/2018/05/10/rcp8-5/..

69. Patrick Moore (@EcoSenseNow), "Oh my!...," Twitter, March 16, 2019, 10:27 a.m., https://twitter.com/EcoSenseNow/ status/1106924843189055488.

70. Patrick Moore (@EcoSenseNow), "Key point...," Twitter, March 22, 2019, 4:27 p.m., https://twitter.com/EcoSenseNow/ status/1109189779466313728.

71. Donna Laframboise, "How the Ugliest Climate Fairy Tale Won," Big Picture News, June 29, 2020, https://wp.me/pSEKJ-9MN..

72. Climate Hustle 2 (film), 2020, www.ClimateHustle2.com..

73. "Streisand Sings Praises of Clinton's Global Initiative," Newsmax, October 6, 2005, https://www.newsmax.com/pre-2008/streisand- sings-praises-clinton-s/ 2005/10/06/id/681427/.

74. Caleb Stewart Rossiter, "Does Section 230's Sweeping Immunity Enable Big Tech Bad Behavior?" U.S. Senate Committee on Commerce, Science, and Transportation, October 28, 2020, https:// co2coalition.org/2020/10/27/ statement-for-the-record-u-s-

senate-committee-on-commerce-science-andtransportation-hearing-on-examining-section-230s-usefulness-has-the-digitalage-surpassed-it-october-28-2020/.

75. James Delingpole, "Delingpole: No, Lying BBC, Britain's Weather Isn't Getting Wilder," Breitbart, December 12, 2020, https://www.breitbart.com/europe/2020/12/12/delingpole-no-lying-bbc-britains-weather-isnt-getting-wilder/.

76. Marc Morano, "Climate Skeptic Morano: 'We Accept Former Activists Apologies for the Climate Scare—But It's Time for Reparations from Al Gore & Others!,'" Climate Depot, July 1, 2020,https://www.climatedepot.com/2020/07/01/climate-skeptic-morano-we-accept-former-activists-apologies-for-the-climate-scare-but-its-time-for-reparations-from-al-gore-others/.

77. Caleb Stewart Rossiter, "Does Section 230's Sweeping Immunity Enable Big Tech Bad Behavior?" U.S. Senate Committee on Commerce, Science, and Transportation, October 28, 2020, https://co2coalition.org/2020/10/27/statement-for-the-record-u-s-senate-committee-on-commerce-science-and-transportation-hearing-on-examining-section-230s-usefulness-has-the-digital-age-surpassed-it-october-28-2020/.

78. Marc Morano, "'F*CK YOU! DROP DEAD MOTHERF*CKER!!' Morano Receives Threat after Congressional Testimony—'May You Die by [Your Children's] Hand!'—WARNING GRAPHIC LANGUAGE," Climate Depot (blog), May 24, 2019, https://www.climatedepot.com/2019/05/24/fck-you-drop-dead-motherfcker-morano-receives-threat-after-congressional-testimony-may-you-die-by-your-childrens-hand-warning-graphic-language/

79. Larry Kummer, "An Autopsy of the Climate Policy Debate's Corpse," Fabius Maximus blog, February 12, 2020, https://fabiusmaximus.com/2020/02/12/climate-policy-debate-is-dead/.

80. Michael Bastasch, "Liberal Campaigner Calls 'Green New Deal' a Plan to 'Redistribute Wealth and Power' from Rich to Poor," Daily Caller, February 5, 2019, https://dailycaller.com/2019/02/05/ocasio-cortez-green-deal-redistribute-wealth/.

81. David Montgomery, "AOC's Chief of Change," Washington Post Magazine, July 10, 2019, https://www.washingtonpost.com/news/magazine/wp/2019/07/10/feature/how-saikat-chakrabarti-became-aocs-chief-of-change/.

82. Marc Morano, "Debate No More! Jailed for Scientific Dissent?! Twenty Climate Scientists, Including Top UN Scientist, Call for RICO Investigation of Climate Skeptics in Letter to Obama," Climate Depot (blog), September 17, 2015m https://www.

climatedepot.com/2015/09/17/twenty-climate-scientists-including-top-un-scientist-call-for-rico-investigation-of-climate-skeptics-in-a-letter-to-obama-argue-skeptics-guilty-of-disinformation-like-tobacco-companies/

83. Anthony Watts, "Quote of the Week—Still 'Wirthless' after All These Years Edition," WattsUpWithThat.com, June 26, 2011, https://wattsupwiththat.com/2011/06/26/quote-of-the-week-still-wirthless-after-all-these-years-edition/.

84. Bruno Waterfield, "EU Policy on Climate Change Is Right Even If Science Was Wrong, Says Commissioner," *Telegraph*, September 16, 2013, https://www.telegraph.co.uk/news/earth/environment/climatechange/10313261/EU-policy-on-climate-change-is-right-even-if-science-was-wrong-says-commissioner.html.

85. Karl Mathiesen, "Europe's Climate Goal: Revolution," Politico, June 19, 2020, https://www.politico.eu/article/europe-climate-goal-revolution-net-zero-emissions/.

86. Kurt Zindulka, "Watch: Extinction Rebellion Cofounder Wants to 'Sabotage' Civilization," Climate Dispatch, February 5, 2020, https://climatechangedispatch.com/extinction-rebellion-sabotage-civilization/.

87. Catriona McKinnon, "Climate Crimes Must Be Brought to Justice," UNESCO Courier, July–September 2019, https://web.archive.org/web/20200215050824/https://en.unesco.org/courier/2019-3/climate-crimes-must-be-brought-justice.

88. Marc Morano, "Update: Video: Robert F. Kennedy Jr. Wants to Jail His Political Opponents—Accuses Koch Brothers of 'Treason'—'They Ought to Be Serving Time for It,'" Climate Depot, September 21, 2014, https://www.climatedepot.com/2014/09/21/robert-f-kennedy-jr-wants-to-jail-his-political-opponents-accuses-koch-brothers-of-treason-they-ought-to-be-serving-time-for-it/.

89. Marc Morano, "Bill Nye, 'The Jail-the-Skeptics Guy!': Nye Entertains Idea of Jailing Climate Skeptics for 'Affecting My Quality of Life,'" Climate Depot, April 14, 2016, https://www.climatedepot.com/2016/04/14/bill-nye-the-jail-the-skeptics-guy-nye-entertains-idea-of-jailing-climate-skeptics-for-affecting-my-quality-of-life-exclusive-video/

90. Vaclav Klaus, interview in *Climate Hustle 2* (film), 2020, www.ClimateHustle2.com.

Chapter 15: The Ultimate Achievement of the Political Left

1. Chris Mooney, "What to Know about the Big Climate Change Meeting in Katowice, Poland," *Washington Post*, December 11, 2018, https://www.washingtonpost.com/energy-environment/2018/12/10/whats-happening-poland-right-now-fix-climate-change-why-you-should-be-paying-attention/.

2. Robin McKie, "We Must Change Food Production to Save the World, Says Leaked Report," *Guardian*, August 4, 2019, https://www.theguardian.com/environment/2019/aug/03/ipcc-land-use-food-production-key-to-climate-crisis-leaked-report.

3. "Paris Climate Accord Debunked by Former IPCC Chair," Junk Science blog, https://junkscience.com/2019/11/paris-climate-accord-debunked-by-former-ipcc-chair/.

4. Contributing author, "John Kerry Admits Paris Climate Agreement Does NOTHING to Halt Temp Increase," Headline USA, December 10, 2020, https://headlineusa.com/john-kerry-admits-paris-climate-agreement-does-nothing-to-halt-temp-increase/https://headlineusa.com/john-kerry-admits-paris-climate-agreement-does-nothing-to-halt-temp-increase/

5. "New Climate Pact Will Be 'Firmer' against Defaulters: Pachauri," *Indian Express*, December 23, 2009, http://archive.indianexpress.com/news/new-climate-pact-will-be-firmer-against-defaulters-pachauri/558303/0.

6. Marc Morano, "Every UN Climate Summit Hailed As 'Last Chance' to Stop 'Global Warming' before It's Too Late," Climate Depot, November 6, 2015, https://www.climatedepot.com/2015/11/06/every-un-climate-summit-hailed-as-last-chance-to-stop-global-warming-before-its-too-late/. See Katherine Bonamici, "A Global Warming Treaty's Last Chance," Time, July 16, 2001, http://content.time.com/time/world/article/0,8599,167699,00.html, Mark Lynas, "Climate Change: It's Now or Never," *Independent*, November 28, 2005, https://www.independent.co.uk/environment/climate-change-its-now-or-never-5349187.html.

7. John Vidal et al., "World Leaders Hail Paris Climate Deal As 'Major Leap for Mankind,'" *Guardian*, December 12, 2015, https://www.theguardian.com/environment/2015/dec/13/world-leaders-hail-paris-climate-deal.

8. John Vidal, et al., "World Leaders Hail Paris Climate Deal as 'Major Leap for Mankind,'" *Guardian*, December 12, 2015, https://

www.theguardian.com/environment/2015/dec/13/world-leaders-hail-paris-climate-deal.

9. Joby Warrick and Chris Mooney, "196 Countries Approve Historic Climate Agreement," *Washington Post*, December 12, 2015, https://www.washingtonpost.com/news/energy-environment/wp/2015/12/12/proposed-historic-climate-pact-nears-final-vote/.

10. Maria Neira, "The Paris Agreement Will Save Our Lives," Newsweek, December 13, 2018, https://www.newsweek.com/climate-change-cop24-paris-agreement-pollution-health-opinion-1257587.

11. Marc Morano, "U.N. Accords Can't Control Climate: Opposing View," USA Today, November 30, 2015, https://www.usatoday.com/story/opinion/2015/11/30/united-nations-climate-marc-morano-editorials-debates/76583680/.

12. Rush LImbaugh, "Now That They Fixed Climate Change, Can We Stop Hearing About It?" The Rush Limbaugh Show, December 14, 2015, http://www.rushlimbaugh.com/daily/2015/12/14/now_that_they_fixed_climate_change_can_we_stop_hearing_about_it.

13. Aditya Ghosh, "Lured by Marriage Promises, Climate Victims Fall into Trafficking Trap," Reuters, March 8, 2015, https://in.reuters.com/article/trafficking-sundarbans-scam-idINKBN0M4067201503 08, Justin Doom; "Global Warming Sparks Fistfights and War, Researchers Say," Bloomberg, August 1, 2013, https://www.bloomberg.com/news/articles/2013-08-01/global-warming-sparks-fistfights-and-war-researchers-say; "Fasten Seat Belts: Climate Change Could Mean More Turbulence," NBC News, February 19, 2014, https://www.nbcnews.com/science/science-news/fasten-seat-belts-climate-change-could-mean-more-turbulence-n33956.

14. Chip Knappenberger, "Climate Impacts of Waxman-Markey (the IPCC-Based Arithmetic of No Gain)," Master Resource blog, May 6, 2009, https://www.masterresource.org/climate-policy/part-i-a-climate-analysis-of-the-waxmanmarkey-climate-bill-the-impacts-of-us-actions-alone/.

15. Oren Cass, "The 'Overheated' Costs of Climate Change," Manhattan Institute on YouTube, March 18, 2018, https://www.youtube.com/watch?v=AkoP6bNj-Yg.

16. Marc Morano, "Skeptical Scientists Urge World to 'Have the Courage to Do Nothing' at UN Conference," U.S. Senate Committee on Environment and Public Works press release, December 11, 2007, https://www.epw.senate.gov/public/index.cfm/press-releases-all?ID=c9554887-802a-23ad-4303-68f67ebd151c&Issue_id=.

17. Nick Sobczyk, "Romney 'Looking at' Carbon Tax Bill," E&E News, June 5, 2019, https://www.eenews.net/eenewspm/2019/06/05/stories/1060491139.

18. Jay Lehr and Tom Harris, "Conservatives Must Stand Up to Climate Change Bullying," PJ Media, May 9, 2019, https://pjmedia.com/columns/tom-harris-and-dr-jay-lehr/2019/05/09/conservatives-must-stand-up-to-climate-change-bullying-n120157.

19. Steve Milloy, "The GOP's Carbon Capture Dodge," American Greatness, February 12, 2020, https://amgreatness.com/2020/02/12/the-gops-carbon-capture-dodge/.

20. Steve Milloy, "The GOP's Carbon Capture Dodge," American Greatness, February 12, 2020, https://amgreatness.com/2020/02/12/the-gops-carbon-capture-dodge/.

21. Viv Forbes, "The Carbon Capture Con," American Thinker, March 6, 2020, https://www.americanthinker.com/blog/2020/03/the_carbon_capture_con.html.

22. Lisa Friedman, "A Trillion Trees: How One Idea Triumphed over Trump's Climate Denialism," *New York Times*, February 12, 2020, https://www.nytimes.com/2020/02/12/climate/trump-trees-climate-change.html.

23. Sophie Lewis, "Planting a Trillion Trees Could Be the 'Most Effective Solution' to Climate Change, Study Says," CBS News, July 8, 2019, https://www.cbsnews.com/news/planting-a-trillion-trees-could-be-the-most-effective-solution-to-climate-change/.

24. Michael Holtz, "Why Planting Some Trees Could Make Global Warming Worse," Christian Science Monitor, February 5, 2016, https://www.csmonitor.com/Environment/2016/0205/Why-planting-some-trees-could-make-global-warming-worse.

25. Laura Geggel, "Want to Fight Climate Change? Plant 1 Trillion Trees.," Live Science, July 5, 2019, https://www.livescience.com/65880-planting-trees-fights-climate-change.html.

26. Daniel Bastardo Blanco, "We Can't Just Plant Billions of Trees to Stop Climate Change," Discover, July 10, 2019, https://www.discovermagazine.com/planet-earth/we-cant-just-plant-billions-of-trees-to-stop-climate-change.

27. Seth Borenstein, "Best Way to Fight Climate Change? Plant a Trillion Trees," AP News, July 4, 2019, https://apnews.com/article/8ac33686b64a4fbc991997a72683b1c5.

28. Tim Radford, "Planting Trees Will Not Slow Global Warming," Climate News Network, May 26, 2017, https://climatenewsnetwork.net/planting-trees-not-slow-global-warming/.

29. Matt McGrath, "Climate Change: Planting New Forests 'Can Do More Harm Than Good,'" BBC News, June 22, 2020, https://www.bbc.com/news/science-environment-53138178.

30. Alexandria Ocasio-Cortez (@AOC), "I'm willing to hold you accountable. . .," Twitter, November 2, 2020, 11:44 a.m.,https://twitter.com/velardedaoiz2/status/1323489931227004928.

31. James Taylor, "The World Owes U.S. Climate Reparations," CFACT, January 10, 2020, https://www.cfact.org/2020/01/10/the-world-owes-u-s-climate-reparations/.

32. "EPA Administrator Scott Pruitt Resigns," CBS News, July 5, 2018, https://www.cbsnews.com/news/scott-pruitt-resigns-epa-andrew-wheeler-interim-today-2018-07-05-live-updates/.

33. Rupert Darwall, "Energy and Race: The Media's New Intersectionality," Real Clear Energy, November 3, 2020, https://www.realclearenergy.org/articles/2020/11/03/energy_and_race_the_medias_new_intersectionality_582903.html.

34. Katelyn Caralle, "'We Should Put Them in Jail!' Joe Biden Wants to Prosecute Fossil Fuel Executives for Environmental Damage—but Doesn't Mention Son Hunter Who Helped Run Ukrainian Natural Gas Giant," *Daily Mail*, December 30, 2019, https://www.dailymail.co.uk/news/article-7837265/We-jail-Biden-wants-prosecute-fossil-fuel-executives-environment-damage.html.

35. Steve Milloy, "Joe Biden's Green Dreams Are About Controlling You, Not the Climate," August 3, 2020, The Federalist, https://thefederalist.com/2020/08/03/joe-bidens-green-dreams-are-about-controlling-you-not-the-climate/#.Xyf86uRxg2s.twitter.

36. Ari Natter, "Climate Groups Prod Biden to Bolster Kerry by Declaring Crisis," Bloomberg Green, November 25, 2020, https://

www.bloomberg.com/news/articles/2020-11-25/
climate-groups-prod-biden-to-bolster-kerry-by-declaring-crisis

37. Bjørn Lomborg, "The 'No Growth' Prescription for Misery," Project
Syndicate, October 17, 2018, https://www.project-syndicate.org/
commentary/no-growth-economy-malthusian-hypocrisy-
by-bjorn-lomborg-2018-10.

Index